Intimate Relationships and How to Improve Them

Recent Titles in
Developments in Clinical Psychology
Glenn R. Caddy, Series Editor

Psychophysiology for Clinical Psychologists
Walter W. Surwillo

Strategic Health Planning: Methods and Techniques Applied to Marketing and Management
Allen D. Spiegel and Herbert H. Hyman

Behavioral Medicine: International Perspectives, Volume 1
Don G. Byrne and Glenn R. Caddy, editors

Behavioral Medicine: International Perspectives, Volume 2
Don G. Byrne and Glenn R. Caddy, editors

The MMPI: A Contemporary Normative Study of Adolescents
Robert C. Colligan and Kenneth P. Offord

Adult-Child Research and Experience: Personal and Professional Legacies of a Dysfunctional Co-Dependent Family
Robert E. Haskell

Behavioral Medicine: International Perspectives, Volume 3
Don G. Byrne and Glenn R. Caddy, editors

Reprogramming Pain: Transform Pain and Suffering into Health and Success
Barry Bittman, M.D.

Personal Construct Therapy: A Handbook
Linda L. Viney

The Natural Limitations of Youth: The Predispositions That Shape the Adolescent Character
John J. Mitchell

Distance Writing and Computer-Assisted Interventions in Psychiatry and Mental Health
Luciano L'Abate, editor

Beyond Psychotherapy: Programmed Writing and Structured Computer-Assisted Interventions
Luciano L'Abate

Intimate Relationships and How to Improve Them

Integrating Theoretical Models with Preventive and Psychotherapeutic Applications

Luciano L'Abate and
Piero De Giacomo

Developments in Clinical Psychology
Glenn R. Caddy, *Series Editor*

PRAEGER

Westport, Connecticut
London

Library of Congress Cataloging-in-Publication Data

L'Abate, Luciano, 1928–
Intimate relationships and how to improve them : integrating theoretical models with preventive and psychotherapeutic applications / Luciano L'Abate and Piero De Giacomo.
p. cm.—(Developments in clinical psychology)
Includes bibliographical references and indexes.
ISBN 1-56750-676-3 (alk. paper)
1. Psychotherapist and patient. 2. Interpersonal relations. 3. Interpersonal communication. 4. Communication—Psychological aspects. I. De Giacomo, Piero. II. Title. III. Series.
RC480.8.A236 2003
616.89'14—dc21 2002190812

British Library Cataloguing in Publication Data is available.

Library of Congress Catalog Card Number: 2002190812
ISBN: 1-56750-676-3

First published in 2003

Praeger Publishers, 88 Post Road West, Westport, CT 06881
An imprint of Greenwood Publishing Group, Inc.
www.praeger.com

Printed in the United States of America

The paper used in this book complies with the Permanent Paper Standard issued by the National Information Standards Organization (Z39.48–1984).

10 9 8 7 6 5 4 3 2 1

Copyright Acknowledgments

The editors and publisher are grateful for permission to reproduce material from the following:

L'Abate, L. (1994b). *A theory of personality development*. New York: John Wiley & Sons. Copyright © 1994 by John Wiley & Sons. Reprinted by permission of John Wiley & Sons, Inc.

L'Abate L., De Giacomo, P., McCarty, F., De Giacomo, A., & Verrastro, G. (2000). Evaluating three models of intimate relationships. *Contemporary Family Therapy: An International Journal, 22*, 103–122. Reprinted by permission.

L'Abate, L., Farrar, J. E., & Serritella, D. A. (1992). Prevention of addictive behaviors. In L. L'Abate, J. E. Farrar, & D. A. Serritella (Eds.), *Handbook of differential treatments for addictions* (pp. 308–324). Boston: Allyn and Bacon. Copyright © 1992 by Pearson Education. Reprinted by permission of the publisher.

To our friend and colleague, Florence W. Kaslow, Ph.D., past president of the International Academy of Family Psychology, who brought us together, as she has done with so many other people around the world.

Contents

Preface:
Integrating Different Theoretical Models

In effect, theory is itself a form of practice. (Gergen, 2001, p. 811)

Given a bewildering array of theoretical models about intimate relationships, which model should be chosen and why? From knowledge and comparison of many existing relationship models, to be reviewed in Chapter 1, it should be possible to integrate them into a more encompassing "super-model." This model might produce better ways of understanding functional and dysfunctional relationships, as well as new ways to intervene with them, preventively, psychotherapeutically, and rehabilitatively. By including different theoretical perspectives, there is the possibility of choosing which model is more appropriate for specificity of intervention; that is, which model and what type of intervention are more appropriate for which problem? Furthermore, by integrating different theoretical viewpoints, by respecting the integrity of each model or theory, one can arrive at a better appreciation of theory-building and theory-testing. By comparing various theories and models, it is possible to evaluate convergences and divergences that will lead to a greater appreciation of each model.

From an integration of various models it will be possible to appreciate the following possibilities:

1. As already mentioned, from comparisons of different models could emerge new and more encompassing models that would produce more effective preventive, psychotherapeutic, and rehabilitative applications.
2. From individual, dyadic, and multi-relational models we may be able to produce a more encompassing "super-model" that will stress:

a. Greater relativism
b. Multiple perspectives about the complexity and variability of interpersonal and intimate relationships
c. Differences in language and meaning about intimate relationships might turn out to be similar, as in the analogy of the elephant and six blind observers

Admittedly, the theory and model proposed (and published) by both authors are like the "new kids on the block." They have not received as yet the attention from the psychiatric and mental health communities afforded to at least three models—interpersonal, attachment, and family paradigms—as discussed in the next chapter. The latter models have received a great deal of attention as well as a great deal of research evidence not enjoyed by the theory proposed by the first author and by the model proposed by the second author. However, both the theory and model proposed here have a distinct advantage over the other three models. They have led to distinct preventive, psychotherapeutic, and rehabilitative applications that are lacking in the other, better-known models. The other three models, in spite of their research popularity in the laboratory, have failed to produce direct clinical as well as non-clinical applications, as far as these authors know. There may have been indirect extensions in the attachment model (Cassidy & Shaver, 1999). However, these extensions are not as direct as those extended from the theory and the model presented here.

In Chapter 1, a selective overview of predecessors who have substantially influenced both authors as well as five major theoretical schools of therapy provide a historical background and an introduction to the rest of the book. In Chapter 2 a developmental theory of relational competence is summarized, and it is evaluated in Chapter 3 in terms of its laboratory studies. An original model of relational styles is summarized in Chapter 4 and evaluated in Chapter 5 through laboratory studies. In Chapter 6, the theory (Chapters 2 and 3) and the model (Chapters 4 and 5) are reviewed in terms of complementarities that lead to specific and testable applications (Part II). From here on, the terms "theory" and "model" are applied, respectively, to developmental competence theory (Chapters 2 and 3) and a model of relationship styles (Chapters 4 and 5), unless otherwise specified.

Chapter 7 includes preventive, structured enrichment programs and workbooks that derive from models of the theory (Chapter 2). Chapter 8 presents (with case studies) three major psychotherapeutic interventions also derived from the theory: sharing of hurts, drawing lines, and hugging, holding, huddling, and cuddling (3HC). Chapter 9 includes various preventive methods derived from the model (Chapter 4). Chapter 10 contains various psychotherapeutic interventions that derived also from the model. Chapter 11 notes how preventive and psychotherapeutic interventions derived, respectively, from the theory and the model can be applied to structured, computer-assisted Internet applications and interventions. In Chapter 12, we integrate competing and seemingly disparate models of relationships into one "super-model" that ranges from internal states or traits to external relationships.

Therefore, the purpose of this book is to introduce a theory and a complementary model of intimate relationships (close, prolonged, and committed) in their applications in the laboratory as well as in the three aspects of primary, secondary, and tertiary prevention. This purpose means explaining what a theory, a model, and practice are, especially the practice of prevention, psychotherapy, and rehabilitation. A theory can mean different things to different people. Usually it means (1) a coherent body of generally accepted, more or less verified, established propositions or statements used as principles of explanation for a specific class of events, factors, or variables, in this case, not just relationships in general, but *intimate* relationships, that is, those characterized by committed, close, and prolonged ties or connections, or (2) a proposed explanation based on provisional and conjectural principles or hypotheses. A theory is different from a model to the extent that it includes many models. A model may be a theory in and by itself if it does include a hierarchy of statements or propositions, going from the general to the specific. For instance, going by this distinction, attachment theory is a model derived and wholly representing object relations theory. Since attachment theory does not have a hierarchical structure required of a theory, it is actually a model, no matter what its followers call it. The same distinction applies to many other relationship theories that, lacking a hierarchical structure, are, in reality, models, to the extent that there are no other models derived from the same theory. The model represents the whole theory from which it was derived. Applied to relationships—and here we mean intimate relationships, like in couples, families, and parent–child dyads—we shall see how these two definitions represent the two extremes of a continuum, along which the most influential theories and models of relationships are considered in Chapter 12.

THEORY AND PRACTICE

Practice is what a professional helper does when faced with a problematic relationship that cannot and will not change unless an external intervention takes place. This distinction is neither idle nor trivial. Dealing with problematic relationships requires a different practice than dealing with relationships with a problem, since we are dealing with different degrees of severity. How are we to help both types of relationships? What we do to help problematic relationships or relationships with problems constitutes our practice. Preventive and clinical practice with intimate relationships in trouble requires an array of specialized techniques and relevant methods that differ vastly from individual and group interventions. In dealing with individuals, a professional helper is handicapped by the one-sided view given without confrontation of views from another partner or other family members. In groups composed of individuals, the same one-sided view takes place without corroboration or confrontation from intimate others.

The main issue here lies in the connection between theory and practice. How is what we do to help families related to the theory that we are currently following or that we swore allegiance to? This is an issue of *isomorphism*—how theory and practice are related to each other. There are three possibilities. In the first, one could theorize without practice. One could then be a theorist, a researcher, or a scholar, but without practice one could not be called a professional helper of "intimate relationships." Theorizing or researching without practice is eminently possible. One could theorize about relationships, even intimate relationships, and not practice at all. For instance, researchers and theorists may be interested in experimenting with intimate relationships but may not be interested in helping individuals involved in them. In the second possibility, one could practice without theory, as some professional helpers as well as family members, friends, or neighbors do when they help each other in times of trouble. This process, although very important, does not make these people "therapists." This second possibility not only is eminently possible but takes place every day. This process, however, no matter how human, necessary, and widespread, is not a professional intervention. It would seem impossible to practice professionally with troubled relationships without some notions, no matter how vague and ill-defined, about the nature of relationships, especially intimate relationships. Thus, the second possibility has to be ruled out. In the third possibility, one could attempt to connect theory with practice. All three possibilities are logically valid, but only one, the third, is acceptable to both writers for practicing with troubled relationships. What, indeed, is the relationship between a theory and practice?

The Need for Isomorphism between Theory and Practice

Theory is how we think about how intimate relationships—connections between two or more individuals—work or fail to work, that is, how individuals connected with each other by emotional, legal, or blood ties solve problems, enjoy life, contribute to society, or depend on it, functionally or dysfunctionally. Practice is what we do to help them work better. Why do we need isomorphism? Why would we practice without it? It seems inconceivable to us that responsible practice of any kind with people who hurt could take place without a theoretical background. However, there is another problem here: what is the relevance of any theory of intimate relationships, and how verified or verifiable is that theory? There are different criteria for theories. At one extreme, one could select a very appealing, elegantly seductive theory that is not validated or verifiable. At the other extreme, one could reject a rather unappealing, even boring theory that is validated and verifiable. In real life, of course, one does not find theories in such black-and-white extremes. The issue here is one of selection. How is one to choose a theory for intervening with troubled, intimate relationships? Shall a theory be chosen on the basis of elegance, appeal, and the emotional recognition of relevance to intimate relationships, or shall one choose a theory on the basis of how empirically validated or verifiable that theory is? As we shall see, this issue is one of aesthetic versus pragmatic preferences: whether one wishes to practice as an artist or as a scientist or researcher. Is is possible to do both? We think so, and we will attempt to show how.

Two sets of value systems exist in all or most of us. On one hand, we have an exquisitely aesthetic, intuitively artistic side that relies on feelings and emotions, subjective experiences, and perceptions. We also have a calulatingly pragmatic, orderly, and coolly rational side that favors planning, predictability, and objectivity in the structure of what we do. One is the side that wants to help troubled relationships immediately. The other side wants to wait and think before helping. Can these two sides be reconciled? Again, we think so, and we will try to show how it is possible to do both.

In addition to the issue of whether or not the theory that we choose is verified or verifiable, there is an issue of consistency. Do we practice according to a theory or a combination of theories? How is what we do related to what and how we think? Can we really discriminate what we do from what we think? We need to support some degree of connection between theory and practice on the following grounds: theory and practice need to be related to each other to fulfill at least four functions, to (1) derive practice from theory; (2) use practice to evaluate, verify, and change theory; (3) use theory to change practice; and, therefore, (4) achieve a greater degree of consistency between what we feel, think, and do as professional helpers.

Can Practice Be Derived from Theory?

To answer this question affirmatively means that practice in some way or another is or should be essentially isomorphic with theory. This is an extremely difficult position to defend because as long as our practice is based on the personality of the professional helper and as long as the medium of exchange between the helper and a troubled relationship relies on the spoken word, it is virtually impossible to verify whether that relationship is indeed taking place (L'Abate, 1999b). Even though the person of the therapist and the spoken word are necessary to start and maintain therapeutic exchanges, we maintain that they are not sufficient to help problematic relationships change. Troubled relationships can be helped to change provided we use all three media of exchange: the oral, the non-verbal, and the written, as shown throughout this text. Especially if the helper operates as an artist, intuitively, immediately, and empathically, to help troubled relationships through verbal interpretations, reflections of feelings, commiserations, commentaries, interpretations, and empathic support, it will be difficult, expensive, and virtually impossible to see how the helper's actions or words are derived from any theory. Typically, one has to record or videotape what is going on between helpers and respondents. Then one has to reduce the videotape to a written transcript for analysis and coding of the content, content-free, and non-verbal behavior patterns. This very expensive process may take up to 30 hours of analysis for every hour of intervention! Only a handful of grant-supported, committed researchers can perform these operations, since the professional helper on Main Street cannot. Furthermore, what is said or done in one session with one relationship usually is not replicable with another. Consequently, we lack information, data, and materials that are repeatable from one relationship to another. Without this replicable information, we cannot really discover how the helper's words or actions are related to the theory that the helper claims or professes to follow. Is there any way out from this dilemma? We think so.

Using Practice to Verify and Change a Theory

If what we do as professional helpers is based on what we feel and think and if what we do works with troubled relationships, it might reflect on how adequate, accurate, and effective the theory is. This would be the conclusion that one would draw if the relationship between theory and practice were indeed, point by point, isomorphic. Unfortunately, human relationships, especially intimate relationships, are not that simple. Helpers have many ways of rationalizing failures to help, usually in terms of attributing negative qualities to respondents. We rationalize our failures to help because we offer a service, and like all services, one cannot expect to help everybody who wants it. Yet, we have no way of knowing beforehand which relationship will benefit from our services and which will not. Thus, we find ourselves in the position of trying to help whoever seeks our services, knowing full well, beforehand, that it is impossible to help everybody who comes into our office seeking help. At best we will help one-third of the relationships that seek our help. We may even help somewhat another third; and very likely we will fail miserably with another third. Professional interventions with intimate relationships are indeed a very chancy process!

Although some of us attempt to justify our failures to help on the basis of the negative qualities attributed to those who fail to benefit from our services, there is another view. Our failures may be due to limitations in our methods rather than in the relationships that we fail to help. A more appropriate view would be that there may be limitations in our theories, in ourselves as individual helpers and in our practices, as well as in the attitudes and behaviors of those who seek our help. We will not be able, in this text, to help change the professional helper's personality or the style used in practice, no matter how important that factor may be. We do hope, however, to improve the range of therapeutic and practical choices available to professional helpers to help relationships at risk, in need, or in crisis.

To the extent that our professional interventions derive from theory, they reflect how accurate, encompassing, and useful that theory is. If our practices do not work effectively or fail to work in some instances, we need to ask ourselves whether the theory under which we presumably operate is valid: does it reflect what is going on in a relationship, and does it explain why we were unable to help?

Using a Theory to Change Practice

If this point has not been made clear, note that as a whole, the link between theory and preventive or therapeutic practice is in some instances quite tenable, in some instances tenuous, and in some instances untenable. We do not yet know what that link is. That link is especially tenuous or untenable when the theory or the practice or both are vague, general, and unspecifiable. To the extent that a theory is clear and valid, to that extent it may generate valid methods of intervention. Consequently, there are three feasible and acceptable possibilities concerning the link between theory and practice: (1) the theory is completely independent of the practice, as when a professional helper does what needs to be done on the spur of the moment, intuitively, without any link to practice, that is, with *no isomorphism*; (2) the practice is somewhat linked to the theory, but this link is vague and ill-defined, as in most therapeutic, verbally based practices, which do possess *some isomorphism*; and (3) the practice is completely derived from the theory, with point-by-point isomorphism, as in programmed materials and as in many interventions presented in Chapters 7, 8, 9, and 10. Of course, the third possibility is ideal but difficult to achieve, given the variability of the factors involved, the theory, the practice, the professional helper, and the relationship to be helped. Knowing full well what human nature is, variable and inconsistent, we concede that the best and most realistic goal may be the second possibility, even though we attempt to be as specific as we possibly can to fulfill, at least in part, the third possibility.

Achieving Greater Consistency between Theory and Practice

How is this goal of greater isomorphism to be achieved? The answer is easy: gradually and carefully! We need to look over the available theories and see how they relate to our practices. Who is going to judge the degree of consistency (i.e., isomorphism) between theory and practice and how will that be done? As said before and as repeated often elsewhere (L'Abate, 1992, 1997a, 2002a, 2000b), as long as a therapeutic approach depends on the personality of the theorist and mainly on the spoken word used in the practice, it will be practically impossible to find out much, if anything, about this isomorphism. If we do not have a clear structure, both theoretically and practically, how are we going to obtain any clear relationship between the two processes? The clearer the two theoretical and practical structures, the clearer should be the processes deriving from them. This goal is easier said than done! The goal of professional practices is to change troubled intimate relationships for the better. What does change mean? It means leaving behind, giving up, going past self-other defeating and hurtful patterns of feelings, thinking, and behavior and replacing them with novel and more victorious patterns for everybody involved in that relationship. To obtain this change, we need to apply practices that will produce this hoped-for change. Various theories claim to produce that change. Let's look at them briefly.

WHAT THEORY SHALL WE SELECT AND ON WHAT GROUNDS?

Most theories of relationships can be broken down into the same classical viewpoints and schools that have influenced not only the field of psychotherapy and psychology but also the field of couple and family therapy (Hansen & L'Abate, 1982). We will not, of course, be able to give these theories the full coverage that they deserve because there are more treatises on theories of family therapy than there are treatises on methods of interventions (L'Abate, Ganahl, & Hansen, 1986). This book, after all, is about intervention methods derived from a particular theory and a particular model, not theories in the abstract without connection with interventions. Indeed, it is assumed that the reader has already read widely about theories of couple and family therapy, but not methods. Nonetheless, in view of what has been said earlier, we consider some basic information on these theories essential, even though we assume that the reader has attended at least an introductory course on the topic. Instead of listing these theories indiscriminately, we wish to introduce the criteria by which each theory or model can be evaluated and eventually selected.

Criteria for Evaluation

1. *Comprehensiveness and Integration*: How comprehensive is the theory, and how well does it integrate past or present theories? The range may vary from functionality to dysfunctionality and from individuals to families. It may apply to many areas of relationship functioning or to just a few. It

may include other theories or ignore them. For instance, psychodynamic theory seems very comprehensive. However, it is so at odds with other theories that it may be difficult to integrate them.

2. *Simplicity*: Relationships in general and intimate relationships in particular are not simple. Yet, can we see patterns in this complexity that allow us to use a few principles? Would these principles allow us to describe and explain a wide range of intimate relationships?

3. *Reducibility and Continuity*: How much and how well is the theory related to clinical psychology and psychiatry as sciences and as professions? Can complex intimate relationships be related to well-known and validated psychological concepts derived from monadic, individually oriented psychology?

4. *Verifiability*: How is the theory testable? In the laboratory? In the therapy office? In the statistical laboratory? Should a theory be verifiable? Some therapists consider antagonistically, even suspiciously, anything that is remotely related to empiricism and research. In fact, both *reducibility* (from family patterns to individually meaningful psychological constructs) and *verifiability* are tantamount to dirty words that go against the zeitgeist of current psychotherapy ideologies. The concept of verifiability should be differentiated from the concept of accountability. Verifiability deals with whether a theory or parts of a theory are empirically testable. Accountability deals with the kinds of outcome and results obtained from a therapy derived from a given theory (L'Abate, 1986, 2002a, 2002b).

5. *Accuracy*: How precise and accurate is a theory? Does it describe and explain accurately relationship patterns? This is a matter of face validity and recognition, not only on the part of professional helpers but also on the part of their respondents. If they recognize that what is said and done in the professional's office is relevant to their experience, then to that extent the theory may be accurate. However, relationships in crisis may be so confused that they may accept as accurate and valid whatever a professional helper says and does.

6. *Usefulness*: Kurt Lewin's often quoted dictum, "There is nothing as useful as a good theory!" applies here. We may have many theories, such as sociological theories, that describe families well. We have a host of relationship theories as well. However, can these theories be applied to intimate relationships to help them change for the better? One aspect of usefulness is *fruitfulness*. What has a theory or a model done to develop, produce, improve, and evaluate programs and plans for intimate relationships? For instance, humanistic and behavioral approaches have developed structured programs and modules to intervene preventively and therapeutically in intimate relationships. Psychodynamic theories, on the other hand, have been noticeably lacking in producing such programs (L'Abate, 1990).

CONCLUSION

We envisage that this work could be useful to (1) graduate students in clinical psychology, social work, psychiatry, counseling, and pastoral counseling because it attempts to link theory with evaluation and with definite preventive and psychotherapeutic applications and (2) mental health professionals in the various mental health disciplines, including rehabilitation. Furthermore, many researchers who have been responsible for the popularity of competing models will be challenged to come up with specific clinical applications to evaluate comparatively the validity of their models in the battlefield of clinical practice. If a theoretical model, no matter how valid it may be in the laboratory, does not lead to definite and specific preventive and psychotherapeutic applications, what is its usefulness? Both the theory and the model presented here challenge static laboratory research, including their own, isolated from practical applications. Both want to show how it is possible to link laboratory results with the school, the clinic, and even the Internet!

Part I

Two Taxonomies of Relational Styles

Chapter 1

Theories and Models of Intimate Relationships

> [A]ll of morality can be reduced to the requirement to promote happiness and reduce suffering, and . . . the relief of suffering is morally more important than the promotion of happiness. (Mayerfeld, 1999, p. 3)

THE IMPORTANCE OF RELATIONSHIPS

Human relationships, especially intimate ones that take place within the family, are important for at least two reasons: survival and enjoyment. One could survive and have no enjoyment. One cannot have enjoyment without survival. Survival can take place along a variety of dimensions: (1) physical, in terms of health, (2) financial—one needs money to survive, let alone enjoy, (3) emotional—without feelings and emotions, especially joy and pleasure, one may survive by just fulfilling the first two dimensions; however, survival under those conditions would be extremely restricted, especially without enjoyment; (4) cognitive—one needs to be able to think and think accurately, let alone feel; (5) contextual, to the extent that we recognize and are aware that the most immediate context for our personal survival and lasting enjoyment is the family.

Enjoyment comes in a variety of ways that could be classified according to (1) physical-sensory, involving exercise, movement, calisthenics, body work, sex, and sexuality; (2) experiential, to the extent that to enjoy anything, we need to see it, smell it, feel it, touch it, and hear it, (3) intellectual, involving learning, reading, discussing, sharing ideas with another person, and so on, and (4) contextual, to the extent that we are aware of what is going on inside and outside ourselves and are available emotionally to ourselves and those we love and who love us (i.e., intimates).

PHILOSOPHICAL AND HISTORICAL BACKGROUND

The history of the study of relationships can be divided into two stages: (1) early theorists; and (2) early researchers model makers: the pioneers. Current contributors will be cited throughout this work.

Early Theorists

Early theorists did not necessarily focus on relationships. However, they may have set the conceptual, philosophical (i.e., armchair) groundwork for the study of relationships. By necessity, we can only abstract and select from what amounts to an extremely large body of monumental work and thinking. We cannot do justice to all the past conceptual contributions that provided the building blocks for more recent thinking about relationships. We can only list cursorily those who have influenced our thinking the most.

Jacob R. Kantor (Kantor, 1959; Kantor & Smith, 1975; Pronko, 1980; Smith, Mountjoy, & Ruben, 1983) can be rightfully called the first "systems" thinker in psychology, a philosophical position shared also by Dewey and Bentley (1949). Before anyone else thought of it, these early thinkers stressed the interconnectedness of behavior as the outcome of relationships between human beings or between human beings and objects. Interbehavior is the outcome of an interaction as observed by others. The process of observation itself becomes part of the interaction turning it into a transaction (Spiegel, 1971). Traditionally, monadic psychology looks at only one part of the equation, whereas both components of those viewed and the viewer need to be considered. Instead of looking inside the individual's emotions, attitudes, and other internal states or traits, look instead at what one individual does and says. What Kantor called "psychological events" lie in between two or more interacting individuals. In addition, one needs to consider the whole context ("interbehavioral field" and "settings") of any interaction in order to describe and understand it. Hence, any interaction is always bi-directional. One individual changes another individual and is in turn changed by how the other individual reacts to what has been said or done. Since relationships are caused by a multitude of antecedents, one needs to observe what is happening before, during, and after the encounter of the individuals involved. Instead of laboratory research that stresses the importance of finding single "causes," naturalistic research and the narrative history of the individual give much more accurate information than any narrow and artificial laboratory experiment.

In many ways, Kantor was the precursor of behaviorism in its emphasis on observables rather than on inferred or hypothetical constructs and of the ecological school in terms of studying relationships in their natural habitat. Stress on the bi-directionality of relationships has been supported by observations of children, how they are changed by parents, and how parents are changed by their children. Narrative, post-modern psychology would find support in Kantor's stress on naturalistic, qualitative process rather than just quantitative content and on historical development rather than just cross-sections of relationships. His stress on contextual influences is revisited in Chapter 2 with the introduction of settings, contexts, and situations. His stress on observables and denial of the importance of internal states or traits find their best representation in the model propounded in Chapter 4. That model looks at the process and outcome of specifically defined relational styles rather than at internal intentions, attitudes, and even feelings and emotions or vague transactions.

Unfortunately, Kantor has not been mentioned at all in the last 20 years or so, suggesting that his ideas have been largely unnoticed by most students of relationships. However, he is remembered by both writers for his intellectual contribution to naturalistic observations.

Alfred Korzybski (1949) certainly was responsible for pointing out semantic errors in our abstract thinking and language, like thinking and acting on the basis of stereotyping, generalizing, and taking for granted erroneous ways of thinking that then lead to detrimental personal relationships. "The map is not the territory" was one of his dicta that implied how language is an imperfect approximation of the objective reality, generalizing from one part to the whole, and defining terms imprecisely and incorrectly. These semantic errors lead to faulty ways of thinking, which then lead to dysfunctionalities in relationships. These views are precursors to cognitive psychology and to rational-emotional therapies.

Ludwig von Bertalanffy (1968) and his disciples, as well as his critics (Churchman, 1979; Emery, 1969; Gray, Duhl, & Rizzo, 1969; Lilienfeld, 1988; Ruben & Kim, 1975), looked at the similarities among various levels of human functioning, biology and physics, from the molecular to the physiological, from the interpersonal to the societal, and abstracted principles of how these systems function. Among the many contributions of this way of thinking were the notion of emergent wholes, that the whole is more than its parts, and of feedback, taken from cybernetics, as a self-correcting function of most functional systems. Positive feedback keeps the systems going, while negative feedback has a destabilizing influence on the system. Permeable and impermeable boundaries allow systems to remain open or closed, respectively, to new or different information or feedback. The interconnectedness of parts, already introduced by Dewey and Bentley (1949), was another quality of systems that was present at various levels of integration.

This viewpoint, of course, was extremely influential in the rise of family therapy, which took systems thinking as a sacred dogma, never to be questioned. Again, as L'Abate and Jurkovic (1987) and L'Abate and Colondier (1987), as well as Lilienfeld (1988), pointed out, systems thinking is a "meta-theory" about how to perceive and understand the world. Like Kantor's and Korzybski's thinking, it is difficult, if not impossible, to subject to direct empirical investigation. Nonetheless, at least at the beginning of the family therapy movement, it was hailed as a breakthrough from traditionally linear ways of thinking. Its major contribution, evident in some of our work, is the importance of paradox in everyday life and in therapeutic communications (Weeks & L'Abate, 1982).

John Spiegel (1971) encapsulated Korzybski's and general systems thinking with a strong dose of anthropological knowledge to view families as fulfilling "social roles" in a "transactional field" already defined by culture. Rather than remaining at the abstract level, like predecessors reviewed above, he actually studied and observed functional and dysfunctional families, showing how they function or fail to function as systems. This transactional field is not very different from Kantor's interbehavioral field.

Gregory Bateson (1972, 1980) is responsible for variations of general systems theory. He has influenced greatly the practice of family therapy and the second author of this work. Bateson's contribution belongs to the current way of thinking that has by now become widely accepted in all fields of science, "relationism." To put it simply and very briefly, this current way of thinking tends to emphasize links, connections (connectionism), relations, interactions, rather than various elements of a system taken one by one. To understand Bateson's spirit, it will be sufficient to quote some of his examples: "Imagine a mind consisting of a man felling a tree with an axe: remove the man, or the axe, or the tree, and the mind no longer exists" (Bateson, 1972). Or, "Imagine a blind man walking along a sidewalk with his white walking stick, where does his self start? In the sidewalk? At the tip of the stick? Half way up the stick? In the man's hand?" (Bateson, 1980).

Consider the "mind" criteria according to Bateson. For something to be defined as "mind," it must meet the following six criteria: (1) it must be an aggregate of interacting parts or bodies; (2) the interaction of its multiple parts is activated by difference; (3) the mental process requires an accompanying energy; (4) the mental process requires chains of circular determinations; (5) in the mental process, the effects of differences must be viewed as transforms (i.e., coded versions of the difference that preceded them); and (6) the description and classification of these processes reveal a hierarchy of logical types that are immanent in the phenomena.

Let's examine some of these aspects. Humans, like other living beings, perceive the world through differences. All reception of information is necessarily the perception of novelty in differences (Bateson, 1980) and "no new order or pattern can be created without information" (1980, p. 50).

In the world of ideas there needs to be a relation, either between two parts or between one part at moment 1 and the same part at moment 2 in order to activate a third component, which can be called the "receiver." The receiver (e.g., an organ in the sense of a terminal) reacts to a difference or to a change. Ideas, according to Bateson (1980, p. 250), are "a difference or distinction, or news of a difference."

The fifth criterion of the mental process is that the "effects of difference are to be regarded as transformations (i.e., coded versions) of events which preceded them" (p. 102). In very simple terms this indicates that the mind works through maps ("a map is not a territory," as Korzybski said); in other words, reality can be perceived only as a derivative of the mental process ("the name is not the thing named, and the idea of pig is not the pig" [p. 210]). The mental process, in turn, originates and works according to two modes, the analogical and the digital. "As I see it, the root of the matter lies in the contrast between the digital and the analogic or, in another language, between the name and the process that is named" (p. 205). Digital communication is that of either/or relationships, entrusted with the task of drawing distinctions, of recognizing discrete elements, whereas logical communication is that of both/and relations, of discerning continuous differences (of size, frequency, distribution, etc.). Even though analogical communication is more effective in picking up nuances of meaning, it lacks the accuracy and specificity of digital communication.

Another aspect that needs highlighting is Bateson's conception of symmetric and complementary relationships. Symmetry is found in rivalrous and competitive relationships: Person A feels the drive to do something to person B because B has behaved in the same or opposite way as A, in what is called in Chapter 2 repetitive, reactive relational style. In the complementary aspect of interactions the action done by A is, in a certain sense, in agreement with that done by B, even while being essentially different from it. The category of complementary interaction includes, for example, command and submission, exhibitionism and voyeurism, aid and dependence, and so on. It is a series of models in which there is a reciprocal adaptation between the behavior of A and that of B.

Another important aspect of Bateson's discourse is what he defines as "the zig-zag ladder of dialectics between form and process" (1972, p. 215), which he compares to Mittelstaedt's (1960) concepts of calibration and feedback (Bateson, 1972, p. 216). This means both that

> the structure can determine process, and that, conversely, process may determine structure. It follows that there must be a relation between two levels of structure mediated by an intervening description of process (p. 217). . . . my procedures of inquiry were punctuated by an alternation between classification and the description of process. I had proceeded, without conscious planning, up an alternating ladder from the description to the vocabulary of typology. . . . These processes were then classified into process types and, in their turn, were named by me. The next step

Figure 1-1
Relationships between Form and Process in Bateson's Thinking

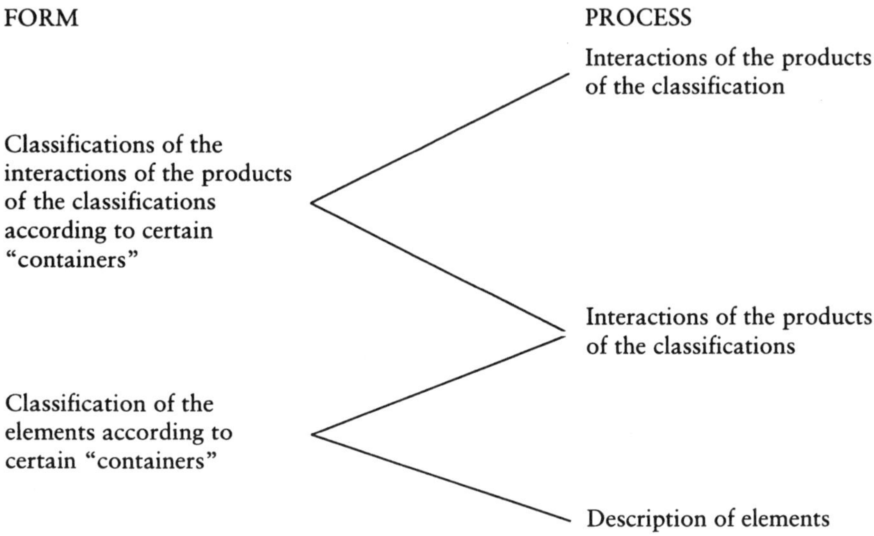

> was from the typing of process to study the interaction between the classified processes. . . . In other words, when we take the notion of logical typing out of the field of abstract logic and start to map real biological events onto the hierarchies of this paradigm, we shall immediately encounter the fact that in the world of mental and biological systems, the hierarchy is not only a list of classes, classes of classes, and classes of classes of classes but has also become a *zig-zag ladder of dialectic between form and process.* (p. 193) (See Figure 1-1)
>
> The very nature of perception follows this paradigm; that learning is to be modeled on the same sort of zig-zag paradigm; that in the social world, the relation between love and marriage or education and status necessarily follows a similar paradigm [and] can posit a mental process based only on analogical communication, or only on digital communication. Both must necessarily alternate. (Bateson, 1980, p. 195)

We should also refer to Bateson's discrimination between the mental organization of someone shooting with a rifle (*feedback*) and that of someone shooting with a shotgun (*calibration*). Let us suppose that the act is the shooting of a bird. In the first case, this is to be done with a rifle. The marksman will look along the sights of his rifle and will note an error in its aim. He will correct that error, perhaps creating a new error which again he will correct, until he is satisfied. He will then press the trigger and shoot. What is significant is that the act of self-correction occurs *within* the single act of shooting. Mittelstaedt (1960) uses the term *feedback* to characterize this whole genus of methods of perfecting an adaptive act. In contrast, consider the case of the man who is shooting a flying bird with a shotgun or who uses a revolver held under the table where he cannot correct its aim. In such cases, what must happen is that an aggregate of information is taken in through sense organs; that upon this information, computation is completed; and that upon the (approximate) result of that computation, the gun is fired. There is no possibility of error correction in the single act. To achieve any improvement, correction must be performed on a large number of actions.

The man who would acquire skill with a shotgun or in the art of shooting pistols under the table must practice his art again and again, shooting at skeet or some dummy target. By long practice, he must adjust the *setting* of his nerves and muscles so that in the critical event, he will "automatically" give an optimum performance. This genus of methods Mittelstaedt calls *calibration.* It seems that, in these cases, "calibration" is related to "feedback" as higher logical type related to lower. This relation is indicated by the fact that self-correction in the use of the shotgun is necessarily possible only from information derived from practice (i.e., from a *class* of past, completed actions) (Mittelstaedt, 1960, pp. 195, 196). It also appears that what Mittelstaedt calls *calibration* is a case of what I call *form* or *classification* and that his *feedback* is comparable to my *process* (p. 196) (see Figure 1-1). With each zig-zag of the ladder, the sphere of relevance increases. In other words, there is a change in logical typing of the information collected by the sense organ at each level (p. 198). "When we compare *learning* to shoot with a rifle with *learning* to shoot with a shotgun, another complication is introduced into the simple abstract paradigm of Russell's hierarchy of logical types" (p. 199). "From this paradigm, it appears that the idea of "logical typing," when transplanted from the abstract realms inhabited by mathematical philosophers to the hurly-burly of organisms, takes on a very different appearance. Instead of a hierarchy of classes, we face a hierarchy of *orders of recursiveness.*" (p. 217)

To make Bateson's arguments sound simpler, consider the following (1980) example: You happen to see feet as they are moving about (process); the movement of the feet follows a given order so that you realize it's a dance (form), and subsequently you realize that all the feet you see are moving according to a certain order (process) in such a way that you realize it is not just a dance but a choreography (form).

Bateson's theoretical contribution to schizophrenia allows us to adopt a different perspective. He discovered how (based on communications existing inside the system) rules of classification are defined, which allow us to distinguish, for example, what is metaphorical from what is literal. (For example, if I were to say to a person that children are like young plants that need to be watered and he were to go home, get a watering can, and water his children, evidently, he would be exhibiting a dysfunction in his system of classification.) Here is what he says (1972):

> If a sequence of events combines a random component with a selective process, so that only certain results of randomness can last, this is called a stochastic sequence. In Greek, stochazein meant "to aim at a target with a bow," i.e. to distribute the events in a partially random way, so that some of them will have a more favourable outcome than others. Then, unless there is a random element, there can be no new things. And to get the new out of random, if and when the new becomes manifest, there has to be some selective mechanism that accounts for the persistence of the new idea with time. There must be some sort of natural selection with all its self-evident tautology. To continue to exist, the "new" must be such that it will last longer than its alternatives.
>
> Mutations, so generated at random, are stored in the population heterogeneous gene pool, and natural selection acts by eliminating unfavourble alternatives from the point of view of such things as survival, thereby favouring, on the whole, harmless or beneficial alternatives. Similarly, with respect to a person, the assumption is that mental processes will generate a large number of alternatives, and that these are subject to a selection determined by something acting like a reinforcement (which could then be more properly defined as "preference").

Thus, according to Bateson, the human mind follows the same organization of nature. There is one rigid part, organized in a repetitive fashion by the world of replication. This organization is based on epigenesis, that is, progressive evolutionary embryological developments. Each developmental step is based on a previous, pre-existing step. Hence, the validity of links between each epogenetic step in development is unquestionable, as in the case of euclidean geometry. Against these worlds that are analogous to one another but derive from different realms (epigenesis from the realm of nature and tautology from that of thought), there is juxtaposed a fluid and changing part, namely, the whole realm of creativity, art, learning and evolution in which the dynamic processes of change are sustained by randomness. The essence of epigenesis lies in the replication of the predictable; the essence of learning and evolution lies in the exploration of change.

Early Researchers and Model Makers: The Pioneers

There is no way that we can cover the early contributions of pioneers in the study of human relationships in an evenhanded way in one brief chapter. Someday, someone more adept than we are will be able to review the historical roots of this field in a more thorough way than this cursory and selected coverage. It is difficult to identify early contributors and even more difficult to identify their contributions within only a generation from their work to arrive at an accurate appreciation of their contribution. Only time, after one or two generations, will tell (Harvey & Weber, 2002).

Clifford H. Swensen (1973), as far as we can tell, was one of the first to review in a complete text the field of "interpersonal relationships," up to the early 1970s, including an introduction to the eventually dominating contributions of social exchange theorists, like Thibaut and Kelley (1959), and many other prominent social psychologists (Burgess & Huston, 1979; Kelley, 1979; Kelley & Thibaut, 1978; Kelley et al., 1983), resource exchange theory (Foa & Foa, 1974), and interpersonal attraction (Bersheid & Hatfield-Walster, 1969). He was also one of the first to study a heretofore taboo topic, love (Swensen, 1985). Taking the spin from the psychiatry of interpersonal relationships, especially Harry Stack Sullivan, his benchmark text covered communication and the double bind in schizophrenic families, proxemics, kinesics, paralanguage, transactional analysis and games people play (with each other!), existential phenomenoloy and the experiencing person, the psychological measurement of interpersonal behavior, attitudes, attributions, attraction, needs and interpersonal relationships, conflict and game theory, role theory, and the rules of encounter. Within this context, one cannot forget an early contribution about the link between development and relationships (Hartup & Rubin, 1986).

Steve Duck, since his first contribution (1973), has been an extremely prolific and influential investigator in the area of "meaningful relationships" (1994). It would take all of this chapter to cover his contribution, a relevant task that must be left to someone with a different purpose from ours (Duck, 1982, 1988, 1993; Duck & Gilmour, 1981a, 1981b; Gilmour & Duck, 1986; Montgomery & Duck, 1991). Suffice to aknowledge, all too briefly, his contribution to the empirical study of this area. For an easy introduction to the field of social interaction and personal relationships, the reader is referred to Miell and Dallos (1996). For a survey of theoretical viewpoints on this area, the reader is referred to Erber and Gilmour (1994).

Robert A. Hinde (1979, 1997) can be considered the latest major theorist in this field. He defined a relationship as "a sequence of interactions, whose qualities, frequency, content, and diversity produce diverse patterns." After reviewing the controversial area of complementary and reciprocal relationships, he reviewed, as most scholars reviewed above had already frequently done, the importance of similarity in relationships, a dimension considered in greater detail in Chapter 2. He also considered topics like intimacy and commitment as well as topics already introduced above by most theorists, like symbolic interactionism, learning paradigms and processes, exchange and interdependence theories, and negative and positive feedback. He also considered the developmental aspects of relationships, which, with the exception of Hartup and Rubin (1986), were usually ignored by most other scholars in this field. Finally (1997), he highlighted the study of relationships as a science, a position supported by the first author (L'Abate, 1998,

2002a, 2002b). Even more relevantly, he differentiated between similarity as reciprocity and similarity as difference and complementarity, an issue confronted in the next chapter.

John Birtchnell (1993) developed a theory of how humans relate that in many ways overlaps with the theory summarized in the next chapter. His contribution has already been summarized in greater detail elsewhere (L'Abate, 1997b). Some of its general principles and dimensions ("axes") bear significant similarity to those found in Chapter 2.

A SYSTEMATIC SUMMARY OF CURRENT THEORIES OF RELATIONSHIPS

While the previous section reviewed contributors chronologically from a historical perspective, this section reviews theories of relationships from a systematic viewpoint, in terms of major theoretical frameworks or schools of thought that have influenced current thinking.

Most theories of relationships are also theories of how families function or fail to function. In fact, both the theory presented in the next chapter and the model summarized in Chapter 4 focus on one special type of relationship: relationships within a couple and within the family (i.e., intimate relationships). However, before we go any further, we need to define a family as a unit or set of individuals who are linked by physical (blood), legal, economic, or emotional ties. Theories may stress one or many of these qualities, yet the major interest may be the emotional bonds that link individuals together. For some others, what a family does is more important than what its members say, feel, or think.

Theories of family relationships and of family therapy have been classified in many ways, such as psychodynamic, intergenerational, contextual, experiential, structural, strategic, functional, and behavioral. Gurman, Kniskern, and Pinsof (1986) listed 15 different schools of therapy, which overlapped with and expanded on those give by Hansen and L'Abate (1982). The latter used a classic division for these theories: (1) *humanism*, (2) *psychodynamic*, (3) *behaviorism*, and (4) *systems*. One more school is added in the next chapter, a school that stresses the importance of awareness. Whether this topic is really represented by a "school" in the same sense of the term as used here is rather questionable. There may not be a school per se. However, some investigators and theorists, reviewed above, stress the importance of this area, namely Swensen (1973), Noam and Fischer (1996), and Ferrari and Sternberg (1998).

Humanism

By *humanism* is meant a school that includes other viewpoints, such as phenomenology, existentialism, and experientialism, as exemplified by, but not limited to, influential family therapists such as Whitaker (Neill & Kniskern, 1982) and Kempler (1981). This school stresses the importance of the immediate present, that is, the subjectively available, the personal experience of the individual as expressed verbally and non-verbally. In this school the emotional reactions as well as the therapist's contribution to a family are considered paramount to the process of change. This school is relevant to our awareness of *input* variables, how a family and a therapist process subjectively felt events. In fact, representatives of this school eschew the importance of theories and theorizing, stressing instead the therapist's gut feelings about a particular family.

In terms of comprehensiveness and integration, this school integrates just one part of the family's experience, its subjectivity, in some cases belittling the importance of reason and rationality while emphasizing the metaphorical, the symbolically experiential, and the role of perceptual input in family relations. It is not as much concerned with output as is, for instance, the behavioral school. Because of the stress on subjectivity and experience, it is not a simple school to understand and to master. Its reducibility and continuity can be traced to influential, individually oriented therapists such as Carl Rogers and theorists such as Abraham Maslow and Rollo May, among others (Hansen & L'Abate, 1982). Verifiability is usually a dirty word to humanistic therapists. It smacks of mechanical accounting and engineering qualities that deny and dehumanize the therapeutic process. Accuracy may be relevant to the reflection of feelings and of subjective experiences, but it remains limited when applied to behavior patterns. Its usefulness lies in furnishing a relevant way to recognize and help family members express warm, positive feelings toward each other, such as love and intimacy, as well as feelings of frustration and hurt. Using the criterion of fruitfulness, L'Abate (in press-a) has argued that this school has helped produce and shape many, if not most, of the psychoeducational marital and parenting programs in primary and secondary prevention (Chapter 11). It has been incorporated and integrated into a theory of individual and family competence that is reviewed briefly in the following pages and expanded in Chapters 2 and 3.

Psychodynamic Theory

Psychodynamic theory is by now an established school of therapy that has spawned important family therapists, such as Bowen (Bowen, 1978; Kerr & Bowen, 1988), Boszormenyi-Nagy (Boszormenyi-Nagy & Spark, 1973), and Stierlin (1974) and the object relations school. Like any school, it includes other less influential viewpoints, like orthodox psychoanalysis and combinations thereof. This theory stresses the importance of past, unconscious experiences in the family of origin, as understood, first of all, by genograms or intergenerational family history, as well as developmental traumas and experiences. Its methods stress a rational, step-by-step understanding of these past experiences. Its stress on a rational approach is shared by other subschools that are similar in giving importance to rational factors, such as rational-emotive therapy (Ellis), reality therapy (Glasser), and the so-called cognitive school of therapy, an offshoot of behaviorism (Meichenbaum).

From the criteria of comprehensiveness and integration, psychoanalytically oriented family therapies certainly can claim to cover a wide range of phenomena, both overt and covert, to deal with unconscious and conscious behaviors. They can rationalize (verbally) most, if not all, behaviors in terms of past experiences and defense mechanisms acquired during development. They stress the importance of how experience is processed rationally in individuals and families (throughput). It is not a simple, easy school and practice to learn and to master. It is, however, reducible to individual factors and is in continuity with ego psychology and object relations schools. Unfortunately, it is not an easy theory to verify, and its accuracy is questionable, since what one therapist selects as important for verbal interpretations may not be seen as important by another therapist of the same school. Thus, a great deal of variability in viewpoints and practices falls under the rubric of the psychodynamic-psychoanalytic school. On the face of it, going back to one's family of origin seems to be useful to many of us. Certainly, many families seem to benefit from going back to past individual experiences, but how far in the past does one need to go? For how long shall we deal with it? How does this rehashing of past history relate to change in the present? These questions can probably be answered by trying this approach, since all therapists need to be aware of their own past family history as they probe into another family's past. Psychoanalysis, of course, has influenced a great many individually oriented, group, and marital therapists, to the point that no therapist worthy of her or his clinical salt can readily dismiss it. The major shortcoming of this theory, however, from a criterion of usefulness and fruitfulness, has been its failure to produce psychoeducational marital and family programs that can be used in primary and secondary prevention (L'Abate, 1990). The exception to this conclusion can be found by the followers of Alfred Adler, who have been very influential in generating and producing many marital and parenting programs (Dinkmeyer, Pew, & Dinkmeyer, 1979).

Behaviorism

Behaviorism, like all the schools reviewed here, includes a variety of smaller viewpoints. Its representative and influential theorists are Jacobson (Jacobson & Margolin, 1979), Stuart (1980), and Patterson (1985), among many others. The main contribution of this school lies in its unrelenting stress on observables and measurables in terms of consequences resulting from internal drive states (e.g., anxiety) or from external reinforcers. It stresses the output side of behavior, with a parallel belittling of hypothetically inferred internal factors, such as feelings and thoughts. Its stress on empiricism may have become a psychology of rats, stats, and graphs, which was, at least in the beginning, devoid of the awareness of possibly nonmeasurable contextual factors.

From the criteria of comprehensiveness and integration, behaviorism stresses the output side at the expense of input and throughout and contextual factors. It is relatively simple to understand and implement, perhaps deceptively so. Its reducibility to frequencies and reinforcements allows it to be in continuity with accepted individually oriented behavioral principles, and it is highly verifiable but selectively accurate in its methodology and clinical applications with families. However, in its stress on immediate solutions, it has forgotten the importance of dealing with subtly critical factors, such as the style of the therapist and the importance of this style in dealing with initial crises and resistances (Patterson, 1985). It is unquestionably useful in many family situations, and it has been fruitful in producing a variety of psychoeducational marital and family programs in primary and secondary prevention (L'Abate, 1990). This school stresses the importance of skill training, especially in an area neglected by other schools, namely, problem solving and negotiation, an area that has been incorporated in a theory of individual and family competence that is reviewed below and in Chapters 2 and 3.

Systems Thinking

Systems thinking attempts to deal with the family as an irreducible whole. Individual behaviors are understood and described as mainly the result of transactions among family members. These transactions are separate from individual contributions to those transactions. This general school has been divided into subschools that have important and influential leaders, such as Minuchin (1974) for the structural approach, Haley (1976) for the strategic approach, and the so-called (now deceased) Milano group (Hansen & L'Abate, 1982). This kind of holistic thinking has pervaded and influenced almost every professional who works with families. No one can deny that families operate like systems, in which one member is related to other members. This wholeness is seen as the outcome of complexity (at the expense of reducibility) and of circularity in causality rather than a linear, step-by-step, one cause and one effect. One cause may produce many different outcomes (equipotentiality); one outcome may be the result of many different causes (equifinality). The reflexivity or feedback functions of family transactions produce circular loops that defy empirical measurement but that are visible to the naked eye of many family therapists.

The undeniable face validity of these concepts should not blind us to their inherent shortcomings. One should be able to derive the same principles from the same assumptions. This is not true of systems thinking. Various approaches claim direct derivations from systems thinking. In fact, one could maintain that systems thinking is not a theory, because it does not have the formal, hierarchical structure of a theory, in which one concept or construct is derived from another superordinate construct. It is not verifiable, as a theory should ideally be. It fits a definition of a theory as a hierarchical framework: it consists of a set of beliefs based on conjectural, provisional, and hypothetical constructs. However, its greatest shortcoming lies in its being separate and discontinuous from psychological constructs and in not being verifiable. As L'Abate and Colondier (1987) argued:

1. A great deal of what goes for family systems thinking is mostly a meta-theory that is unrelated to the field of psychology. It may be vaguely related to it, but it is not connected. *It lacks specificity.*
2. A great deal of what goes for theory in therapies is untestable or, at best, *an unrelated set of unverifiable hypotheses*, some of them without substance.
3. A great deal of what goes for theory is methodologically sterile and vacuously unproductive. In short, *it lacks empirical productivity.*

Consequently, it may work as a metaphor or as a meta-theory, but not as a theory per se. Furthermore, this way of thinking was developed from the metaphor of gun sights in cybernetics and of the thermostat in heating and air-conditioning. How are these two metaphors applicable to human behavior? Systems thinking has been very critical of past theories, proclaiming a new era, a novel ecosystemic epistemology that would replace shopworn theories as well as outdated linear practices in favor of more circular practices. As Gurman, Kniskern, and Pinsof (1986) concluded in their review:

> Unfortunately, the passion with which advocates of the "new epistemology" criticize the continuing use of family therapy research methods based on the "old" epistemology has been rarely translated into the development of experimental designs more consistent with ecosystemic views. . . . To our knowledge, there does not yet exist a single outcome study of family therapy whose design has been perceptibly influenced by such ecosystemic ideas. (p. 569)

This view sees itself as discontinuous from psychology as a science and as a profession. Thus, the attempt at comprehensiveness and integration claimed by this thinking may have been a goal achieved at the cost of giving up other goals, such as parsimony, reducibility, and continuity with psychology, and denying verifiability as an important criterion in theory-building. Accuracy, if it exists, lies in the eye of the beholder, the therapist, and no one else, since objective, external verifications are considered puerile and unnecessary. From the viewpoint of usefulness, this thinking has ben extremely useful in providing certain new paradoxical modes and strategies of interventions with families (Chapters 7, 8, 9, & 10; Weeks & L'Abate, 1982). From the same criterion of fruitfulness, however, it has failed to produce any marital or parental programs for primary and secondary prevention. On the plus side, this thinking has spawned hybrid theories and therapeutic approaches that include an eclectic mixture of systemic and humanistic, systemic and psychodynamic (Skinner, 1976; Stierlin, 1977), and systemic and behavioral schools (Alexander & Barton, 1995; Hansen & L'Abate, 1982).

Awareness Research

A missing component to the schools of thought summarized above and a trend that is not even a school, because of the limited contributions that have been made to it and the limited number of scholars who may claim to belong to it, is the field of Awareness research (Ferrari & Sternberg, 1998), conceived here as a feedback loop or change agent that is part of a theoretical model that is inclusive of all these schools, including awareness, the ERAAwC mentioned below and elaborated in Chapter 2. Of course, most of the schools summarized above would lay claim to Awareness as an essential component of their thinking. However, conceived as a feedback loop, it can have positive and negative connotations; it can be extremely restricted or so enlarged as to become all-pervasive. Either extreme, restriction or expansion, would be negative in its change functions. Only the middle ground in this continuum, linked also to the other components of the model, Emotionality, Rationality, Activity, and Context, would be positive and functional as far a change is concerned. One aspect of awareness, so dear to the psychodynamic school, would be the concept of "insight." However, insight per se, without any connections to the other components of the model, might be insufficient to produce change.

DISCUSSION

What can we learn from this extremely but necessarily brief review? All these theoretical orientations can be integrated into one processual model of negotiation—the ERAAwC model, which will be presented in Chapter 2. All these schools have contributed significantly to our understanding of behavior seen along a continuum from experiencing on the receptive, internal input end to the expressing, external output end. Humanism has contributed the importance of input factors in subjectively felt emotions (*E*). Psychoanalytic-psychodynamic schools have stressed the importance of the rational (*R*) processing of these emotional experiences (throughput). Behaviorism has stressed the importance of output, expressive activities, and their internal or external reinforcements (*A*). The Gestalt school has stressed the feedback function of Awareness as a change mechanism (*Aw*), which may or may not work with families; the family therapy field has stressed the undeniable importance of contextual (C) family factors in behavior (L'Abate, 1986). The humanistic and behavioral schools, however, have been more fruitful in their contributions to primary and secondary prevention programs than have the psychodynamic and systems schools. Consequently, even though all of these schools have been integrated into one model of the theory, ERAAwC, the humanistic and behavioral schools have been integrated into the postulates of a theory of individual and family competence presented in the next chapter.

CONTEMPORARY MODELS OF RELATIONSHIPS

Among the many models of relationships available at the present time, we have selected three that are relevant to what is presented in the rest of this work: (1) attachment, (2) circumplex, and (3) family paradigms. The reasons for selecting these three are simple: (1) these models are the ones that have influenced our thinking the most; (2) they are empirically validated to the point of almost no return; that is, their validity has been ascertained beyond any doubt; and (3) they lie along a continuum of internality to externality that is elaborated in the final chapter, which integrates the theory and the model considered in this work. However, as argued further in that chapter, all three models lack direct applications to preventive and therapeutic interventions, a quality that both the theory and model presented here do share.

Attachment

The attachment model, derived from object relations theory, has been subjected to countless research papers and secondary references in the last decade. Only a few secondary sources need citing in this regard (Bartholomew & Perlman, 1994; Cassidy & Shaver, 1999; Feeney & Noller, 1996; Sanford, 1997; Simpson & Rholes, 1998). Most research with adults tends to support the validity of four attachment patterns, a functional, secure one, and three dysfunctional, insecure patterns. The three insecure patterns most frequently mentioned, at least in adults, are Dismissing, Preoccupied, and Fearful. Dismissing is a pattern where the individual is positive about self and negative about other. Preoccupied is a pattern where the individual is negative about self and positive about other. Fearful is a pattern where the individual is negative about both self and other. Because of its extensively validated research record that supports its validity, this model was adopted as the criterion to evaluate the concurrent validities of two other models (L'Abate, De Giacomo, McCarty, De Giacomo, & Verrastro, 2000).

Circumplex

This term stands for a variety of models made up into a circle enclosing dimensions that differ from school to school and from researcher to researcher, depending on what statistical or empirical method was used to arrive at the enclosed dimensions (Kiesler, 1996). Starting with the original and pivotal contribution of Leary (1957), who considered the circumplex as composed by two orthogonal axes, affiliation and power, variations on the same theme of the two basic dimensions have proliferated.

One could legitimately ask what this model has to do with relationships. The answer lies in the fact that dimensions of affiliations and power with all their derivatives and expansions to as many as 16 enclosed dimensions, even though part of artificial and contrived paper-and-pencil, self-report questionnaires, are actually interpersonal constructs, even though they may have not been evaluated relationally. Essentially, this model, in spite of its relational importance, still belongs to an intrapsychic, monadically acontextual school of personality psychology that evaluated individuals in contrived, short-lived laboratory situations that have little to do with interpersonal relationships in real life. This issue is reopened in Chapter 12.

Relevant to the model in Chapter 3, however, many of the 16 dimensions composing this model have a great deal of overlap with the relational styles presented in Chapter 4. Their overlap with other models is discussed in Chapter 12.

Family Paradigms

In the last few years, the study of relationships has seen the development of a plethora of models about intimate relationships and their possibly intrapsychic and extrapsychic components: Schwebel's (1993) family defense mechanisms, Constantine's (1993) circumplex model of family paradigms, Olson's (1993) circumplex, McCubbin, Thompson, Pirner, and McCubbin's (1988) family types, Reiss' (1981) family paradigms, as supported by Cobb's (1996) recent research, and Fisher and Ransom's (1995) family types. Integrating these models may yield possible links between internal, individual, and external, family dimensions. Whether these hypothetical links are valid depends a great deal on future research oriented toward finding empirical links among various models. Hence, the future is open for comparative testing about the validity of theoretical models in intimate relationships. We may disagree about the validity of many models. However, we cannot disagree that models in general fulfill relevant and important functions as (1) compasses to direct research and clinical applications; (2) maps to describe the territory to be explored; (3) concrete summaries of more complex and abstract theories; (4) delineating limitations in the territories to be explored; and (5) specific representations that allow empirical testing. Each model may have its peculiar language that is specific to assumptions of that model that are not shared by any other model (Hinde, 1997).

CONCLUSION

Consequently, if models are important stepping stones toward progress in theory-construction and theory-testing, then their comparative testing becomes a crucial undertaking for family-oriented therapists and researchers. Certain models may or may not overlap, leading to restrictions and refinements of those that do not overlap and that do not show similarities. For instance, if an intrapsychic model correlates significantly with an interpersonal model, then links between these two territories, internal and external, can be made. However, if these two models do not correlate, then comparisons with other models may be necessary to discover and establish these links, as discussed in Chapter 12.

Chapter 2

A Developmental Theory of Relational Competence

> [T]he literature indicates that two fundamental dimensions exist whereby people define their relationships. These dimensions are intimacy and control. (Canary, Emmerts-Sommer, & Faulkner, 1997, p. viii)

> [T]he two robust interpersonal dimensions of dominance and nurturance hold considerable promise for integrating the literature on personality and gender differences in love. (Fehr & Broughton, 2001, p. 115)

> [T]heoretical perspectives constitute discursive resources. As such, they enrich practice—in both the profession and the society more generally. (Gergen, 2001, p. 809)

The purpose of this chapter is to summarize a developmentally contextual and relational theory of interpersonal competence and personality socialization in the family and other settings (L'Abate, 1976, 1986, 1990, 1994, 1997, 2002a, 2002b). Before the theory is introduced, two basic requirements of reducibility and verifiability are considered. The theory consists of three meta-theoretical assumptions about the horizontality and verticality of relationships and settings from which derive three models. Theory-derived assumptions cover processes in space and time, from which are derived two respective processual postulates about the ability to love and the ability to negotiate. The contents of the theory consist of three modalities about what is exchanged between and among intimates and non-intimates in different settings. From these processes and contents derive

Table 2-1
Summary of a Theory of Interpersonal Competence and Personality Socialization in the Family and Other Settings

Conceptual Requirements	Reducibility and Verifiability
Meta-theoretical Assumpions	Horizontality (ERAAwC): Model[1*]
	Verticality (Levels of Observation/Interpretation): Model[2]
Settings	Home, School/Work, Surplus Time, Transit and Transitory: Model[3]
Theoretical Assumptions	Space (distance) and Time (control) Regulation: Model[4]
Postulates (Processes)	Ability to Love (Being or Presence) and Ability to Negotiate Power: Model[5]
Modalities (Contents)	Being = Importance + Intimacy = Presence
	Doing = Services + Information = Performance
	Having = Goods + Money = Production
	Power = Doing + Having: Model[6]
Testable Models	Likeness Continuum and Differentiation: Model[7]
	Styles in Relationships: Model[8]
	Selfhood and Personality Propensities: Model[9]
	Priorities (Horizontal and Vertical): Model[10]
	Negotiation: Model[11]
	Intimacy: Model[12]
	Dysfunctionality and Drama Triangle: Model[13]
	Distance Regulation: Model[14]
Conclusion	Toward a Classification of Relationships: Model[15]
Integration of Various Models	Model[16]

*These numbers denote specific models to be evaluated in Chapter 3 and discussed in Chapters 7, 8, and 12.

additional models about a development continuum of likeness and styles in intimate relationships, selfhood and personality propensities, intimacy, dysfunctionality and the Drama Triangle, and Distance Regulation (see Table 2-1). This theory can be evaluated in the laboratory through self-report, paper-and-pencil tests (Chapter 3) and in applied and clinical settings through enrichment programs and workbooks (Chapter 7) and therapeutic tasks and prescriptions (Chapter 8). From here on in the rest of this work, past references to this theory are avoided unless absolutely necessary to guide the reader.

A primary purpose of this theory is to link and reconcile characteristics of individuals with intimate relationships and to view them as partially determined by and determinants of intimate relationships. Rather than "personal" or individual, couple, or family relationships, the term "intimate relationships" is used throughout this work to define close, committed, and prolonged relationships among people linked together by blood, financial, logistical, or emotional ties, whether individuals, couples, or families. Even individuals carry relationships within and without themselves, whether they like it or not. A secondary purpose of this chapter is to suggest how a theory of interpersonal competence and personality socialization can be reduced to psychological principles and constructs in ways that are verifiable. To fulfill this second requirement, a theory needs methods that are derived from and are isomorphic, insofar as possible, with the theory itself, through models derived from the theory. Replicable methods, not techniques, are needed to verify this or any other theory or interventions (Routh & DeRubeis, 1998). The term "techniques" applies to methods that have been used, changed, and converted idiosyncratically by professionals for their own needs in ways that make them difficult, if not impossible, to replicate and verify.

A tertiary purpose of this theoretical framework is to view intimate relationships in both their functional and dysfunctional aspects, an approach that has not been followed, generally, by the "personal relationships" literature. A quartic purpose is to bridge the inevitable gaps between (1) theory and clinical practice, as discussed in the preface, (2) theory-building with theory-testing, and (3) theory with types of interventions in prevention and psychotherapy.

To fullfill multiple purposes, this theory attempts to meet two additional, formal requirements to be considered first—reductionism and verifiability. How and how much can one reduce functionality and dysfunctionality in relationships to psychological principles and constructs? Or, as family systems thinking would like us to believe, is the family an irreducible whole that should not be considered in terms of its parts, that is, its individual members? Is the family as a whole greater than the sum of its individual members, or is it something different? Is reductionism necessary to ensure verifiability? At this time, the answer to this question seems to be in the affirmative: one cannot have one without the other.

The thesis of this theory is that at the bottom of interpersonal competence and personality socialization in intimate relationships there are underlying hurt feelings and fears of being hurt that are inevitably produced in the family of origin, in the family of procreation, and in intimate relationships. Personal competence and personality socialization, in this regard, can be viewed as a process of creating, at least metaphorically, an artichoke. Underneath its external leaves, after passing through the prickly choke of anger and even rage, at its very bottom, there are feelings of hurt and fears of being hurt. They are often, but not always, fully solved and resolved in functional relationships through reciprocal sharing with loved ones. However, they are not confronted and shared and usually not resolved in dysfunctional relationships. They linger on and influence personality socialization and levels of relational competence throughout individual and family life cycles (Bradley, 2000; Hayes, Strosahl, & Wilson, 1999; Watson, 2000). Before reaching these feelings of hurt, however, one must deal with many leaves that cover, defend, and protect them. One cannot get to these feelings, because the prickly chokes of anger and sometimes rage make it difficult and, in some cases, impossible to reach them.

A theory of intimate relationships needs to fulfill at least eight criteria. It needs to be, of course, (1) *relational*, inter-individually rather than solely intra-individually, as seen in intimate relationships rather than in hypothetical or inferred internal traits or states, or short-lived, limited, and limiting artificial and contrived laboratory situations; (2) *applied* to the whole gamut of functional and dysfunctional relationships—one cannot have a theory that applies solely to individuals and not to couples and families, since the latter two are made up by individuals, who are the products and producers of those very same relationships; (3) *contextual*, applying to intimate relationships as well as to specific settings, like school/work, banks, grocery stores, and so on, rather than in vague and general terms like "environment," "culture," or "situation"; (4) *developmental*, over the individual and family life cycles, from dependency in childhood to denial of dependency in adolescence, inter-dependence in adulthood, and return to dependency in old age, starting from couple relationships, their offspring, and ending in death; (5) *verifiable*, with results not only from the laboratory, self-report, and paper-and-pencil tests (Chapter 3), but also (6) *accountable*, in evaluating results obtained from primary and secondary prevention interventions with functional as well as with semi-functional relationships (Chapter 7), as well as (7) *applicable*, to psychotherapy with distressed relationships (tertiary prevention; Chapter 8) and (8) in some respects, *dialectical*, to the extent that more than one model of the theory still needs evaluation in its applications to intimate relationships. A summary of this theory (Table 2-1) and evidence to support it (Chapters 3, 7, & 8) should show how the theory has endeavored to fulfill, at least in part, the eight criteria listed above.

This theory is composed of two assumptions combined with three modalities, which in turn generate an even greater number of models (Table 2-1). Moving from assumptions on top to modalities below and then to models, a sequence starts with (1) levels of abstraction, beginning with seemingly very abstract terms, like space and time, to less abstract modalities and to even more concrete models; and (2) levels of generality, starting with general assumptions, like space and time, to more specific modalities and to even more specific models. While assumptions may seem too abstract and too general to appear testable, they become so when they are combined into one model of distance (space) and control (time) regulation, while modalities, as we shall see, do become somewhat more testable than assumptions, once there is a model to describe them.

Models, because of their concreteness and specificity, are even more testable. If modalities and models at the bottom of the theory (Table 2-1) are valid, then the assumptions of the theory on top may become valid as well. Models in general fulfill relevant and important functions as (1) compasses to direct research and clinical applications, (2) maps to describe the territory to be explored, (3) concrete summaries of more complex and abstract theories, (4) delineating boundaries and limitations in the territories to be explored, and (5) specific representations that allow empirical testing. Each model may have its peculiar language that is specific to the assumptions of a model that are not shared by any other model (Hinde, 1997).

Consequently, if models are important stepping-stones toward progress in theory construction and theory-testing, then their comparative testing becomes a crucial undertaking for relationship-oriented preventers, therapists, and researchers. Certain models may or may not overlap, leading to restrictions and refinements of those that do not overlap and do not show similarities. For instance, if an intrapsychic model correlates significantly with an interpersonal model, then links between these two territories, internal and external, can be made. However, if these two models do not correlate, then comparisons with other models may be necessary to discover and establish whether any links among them exist. This possibility is explored in greater depth at the end of Chapter 12.

Some models may be more valid than others. Some models are more easily testable than others. If a few models are wanting, the theory tends to wobble. If most, if not all, models are invalid, then the theory will crash of its own weight. If models are valid, the theory will be able to stand on its own. It is crucial for this theory to be evaluated in a variety of ways that are relevant in laboratory (Chapter 3), prevention (Chapter 7), and clinical (Chapter 8) settings. There are many competing theories, theorettes, and models in the marketplace of theory-construction, prevention, and therapy in psychology. If a theory wants or needs to establish its superiority over competing theories, theorettes, and models, it has to show that it is "better" than those competing for superiority. "Better" means more valid and more encompassing from one setting to another, in short, more verifiable and accountable than competing theories.

From the viewpoint of comprehensiveness and integration, this theory is quite ambitious in attempting to integrate different theories as well as to cover the full range of functionality and dysfunctionality in intimate relationships of individuals and couples and in families. It is quite simple in its structure and concrete in its stress on visible and measurable constructs and resources. Its reducibility, continuity, and verifiability with already existing psychological constructs or concepts are discussed at length in the following pages. Readers will have to decide and evaluate for themselves whether the theory is accurate and useful.

CONCEPTUAL AND PRACTICAL REQUIREMENTS

Before going into the theory proper, however, one needs to consider conceptual and practical requirements that belong to psychological theories in general and that go beyond this particular theory. Even though these requirements may stand apart from the theory, directly or indirectly, they are shared with other theories. They need highlighting in their own right, before entering meta-theoretical assumptions and the theory proper. Nonetheless, these requirements may become part of the theory, because they introduce two basic issues that apply to this as well as to other theories about relationships. All psychological theories, especially personality theories, need to consider them, no matter what their theoretical allegiance may be.

Reducibility: Links Between Individual and Multi-relational Functioning

This first requirement is attained by using psychological terms that are both interactional and relational. Love and negotiation, for instance, imply the presence of a second party (partner, offspring, parent, siblings, relatives, friends, acquaintances) to love and to negotiate with. Both sets of abilities are necessarily vital for personal, interpersonal, and intimate functioning. In fact, most dysfunctionalities in intimate relationships are the outcome of deficits or deviances in either or both of these abilities. This framework also draws from and is linked to developmental, cognitive, personality, and social psychology. It is consistent, continuous, and even reducible, if not indeed isomorphic, with monadic models of behavior by expanding them to relationships rather than keeping them, as they have been heretofore, in a vacuum, acontextual and non-relational. One can thus expand systematically from seemingly acontextual psychological constructs into intimate relationships between and among individuals in functional and dysfunctional relationships with intimates and non-intimates.

The theory seems continuous and consistent with monadic (i.e., acontexual and intra-individual rather than inter-individual) psychology through at least eight different links. The first link is found in the emphasis on constructs such as self or personality that, although derived from individual psychology, have been redefined here according to relational and inter-relational concepts (e.g., love and negotiation). A second link is found in attachment theory, which is related to the spatial assumption of approach-avoidance and the development of dependencies and interdependencies in intimate relationships. As shown in Chapter 5, there are definite correlations between instruments constructed to evaluate attachment theory and at least one model of the theory. The third link is found in the temporal dimension of discharge-delay in control functions that are basic to the development of the ability to negotiate. The fourth link is found in the emphasis on individual differences, especially gender differences, that differentiate two strategies for dealing with stress, one presence-related (to be explained below) and the other performance-related (to be explained below). The fifth link is found in reordering and applying resource exchange theory in social psychology (Foa, Converse, Tornblom, & Foa, 1993; Foa & Foa, 1974) to a selfhood model of interpersonal competence in relationships. A sixth link is found in sex and sexuality, which are, respectively, two of the biological and social bases for the formation and development of relationships. L'Abate and Hewitt (L'Abate, 1994b, 2002b) have applied a model of the theory, modalities of exchange (Table 2-1), to a classification of sex and sexuality. They argued that most sexual dysfunctions are based on the inability to be together emotionally with another human being and observed that our culture stresses sexual performance or production or both at the expense of sexual presence (Baumeister & Tice, 2001; Bullough et al., 1997; Koch & Weis, 1998; Macy, 1996). Functional and enjoyable sex and sexuality imply an ability to be available emotionally to one's partner before one can be available sexually and sensually. A seventh link is found in relating a negotiation model in its structural and processual aspects to known psychological characteristics. Finally, an eighth link is found in relating a model of functionality and dysfunctionality in selfhood to DSM-IV (*Diagnostic and Statistical Manual of Mental Disorders*, 4th ed.) characteristics, as explained below.

Verifiability: Evidence to Support a Theory of Intimate Relationships

As stated initially, a purpose of this chapter is to suggest how a theory of interpersonal competence and personality socialization can be reduced to psychological principles and constructs in ways that are verifiable. This theory and most psychological theories can be supported and validated through three different sources of evidence that is (1) inferentially and *independently* but conceptually similar to parts of the theory itself, (2) *indirectly* related to it, and (3) *directly* derived from the theory itself. Support that is inferential and independent of the theory can be found in work done by other researchers whose results and evidence are completely independent but conceptually similar to certain aspect of this theory. For instance, among many, a great deal of literature and evidence is conceptually and empirically related to the ability to love and to the ability to negotiate. In other words, inferential evidence is theoretical or empirical work that has been gathered independently, outside this theory itself. A great deal of this theory-building has been originally derived from clinical observations. On the other hand, Swensen's (1985) and Sternberg and Barnes' (1988) work on love and works on the process of family negotiation and problem solving (Vuchinich, 1999), are examples of theory-independent evidence that would inferentially influence the relevance and validity of the two basic assumptions of theory itself.

Another inferential link can be found in the work of McAdams (1988). He studied the content of the Thematic Apperception Test and life stories from many individuals, concluding that the two basic themes in the content of all these stories are intimacy and power, the very same abilities (presence and power) that are fundamental not only at intrapsychic, internal levels but at the personal, dyadic, and multi-relational, intimate levels. Furthermore, the two abilities—to love (intimacy) and to negotiate (power)—are important at all levels of functioning, both internal and external. Both humanistic and behavioral approaches can be integrated into this theory. The ability to love, stressed by the humanistic school, is related to the support received in empowerment. The importance of negotiation, stressed by the behavioral school, is related to enablement, that is, learning instrumental problem-solving skills (Dunst, Trivette, & Deal, 1988). Bakan's (1968) pioneering distinction of communal and agentic realms as well as Clark and her collaborators' (1996) distinction between communal and exchange relationships suggest the importance of two fundamental factors that may even have different hemispheric origins (L'Abate, 2001a; McMahan & L'Abate, 2001). These two dimensions, called by various names by different investigators—intimacy and control (Canary, Emmers-Sommer, & Faulkner, 1997) or nurturance and dominance (Fehr & Broughton, 2001)—represent different views of the same behaviors, which have been named presence and power in this theory (see Table 2-2) The list given in this table is by no means exhaustive. Previous publications by the first writer contain similar lists that include different theorists and researchers.

Furthermore, these two dimensions include two sets of skills necessary for successful psychological interventions: relationship and structuring skills. Relationship skills include those that denote personality, style, and presence of the professional helper and that, supposedly, lead toward a therapeutic alliance, dear to the hearts and minds of humanistically oriented helpers. Structuring skills, dear to behaviorally oriented helpers, include those that deal with treatment plans inside the professional office as well as homework assignments, tasks, and exercises to be conducted by respondents in their homes and elsewhere.

Indirectly related to this theory is the resource exchange theory of Foa and Foa (1974) and their collaborators (Foa, et al., 1993). They developed paper-and-pencil, self-report tests to measure resources exchanged. The

Table 2-2
Fundamental Dimensions of Intimate Relationships Deriving from Two Assumptions of Space and Time

Space	Sources	Time
Communal	Bakan (1968)	Agentic
Intimacy	McAdams (1988)	Power
Empowerment	Dunst et al. (1988)	Enablement
Communal	Clark et al. (1996)	Exchange
Intimacy	Canary et al. (1997)	Control and power
Nurturance	Fehr & Broughton (2001)	Dominance
Distance	L'Abate (1986)	Control
Being	L'Abate (1986)	Doing and Having
Presence	L'Abate (1986)	Power
Love	L'Abate (1986)	Negotiation

results of their work may bear on the validity and viability of at least two important models in the present theory: modalities and selfhood.

To test the theory directly, a variety of paper-and-pencil, self-report tests have been validated to verify models derived from the theory since its inception (Chapter 3). The theory can be verified processually through content analyses of audiotapes and videotapes, especially the ARC model, to be explained below, and intimate interactions derived from the very same models of the theory. More dynamically, this theory, in addition to being evaluated in the laboratory, can be evaluated according to three levels of prevention. In primary prevention, the theory can be evaluated through structured enrichment programs, some of which were also derived from models of the theory (Chapter 7). In secondary prevention, the theory can be evaluated through the use of theory-derived, self-administered, para-preventive, and paratherapeutic workbooks and materials (L'Abate, 2002a, 2002b, in press-a). In tertiary prevention, that is, psychotherapy and crisis intervention, the theory is evaluated through administration and prescription of three tasks or prescriptions: hurt-sharing, line-drawing, and being together (3HC). Evaluation, however, takes place through models, rather than through assumptions and postulates, unless the latter are reduced to models, as shown below.

THREE META-THEORETICAL ASSUMPTIONS

Three Meta-theoretical assumptions go beyond the theory and are directly or indirectly common to most theories of personality and relationships that are shared by this theory as well, namely, the experiencing-expressing continuum levels of analysis/observation/interpretation, and settings.

Horizontality: The Experiencing-Expressing Continuum: Model[1]

This assumption deals with the width of relationships along a flat, horizontal axis. It is composed of five components that must be considered before even entering the major thrust of this section. This axis describes how relationships unfold from their inception: (1) when information is received and experienced (input), (2) how this information is processed (throughput), (3) how and where it is eventually expressed (output), (4) how what is expressed feeds back to input, and (5) the context of relationships. The schools of thought or of therapy underlying each of these five components have already beeen reviewed in Chapter 1.

Emotionality (*E*)

The important role of feelings in competence and personality socialization in intimate and interpersonal relationships has been acknowledged and stressed by a variety of sources (Averill, 1997; Bonanno & Keltner, 1997; Cacioppo & Gardner, 1999; Kennedy-Moore & Watson, 1999; L'Abate, 1986, 1994b, 1997b; Mascolo & Griffin, 1998). Among these and other sources, too many to cite and list here, there is a great deal of controversy about the number and function of emotions as well as their nomological location in personality functioning. Furthermore, a major area of continuing debate in the study of emotions is the differentiation between the experiencing of emotional stimuli or events on the receptive, input side, including moods and affect, which are general, versus the expression of these stimuli or events on the output side. L'Abate (1994a, 1997b) has stressed the importance of separating clearly between emotional stimuli on the receptive side, as affect, moods, and feelings, versus the output of such feelings on the expressive side, as emotions. Between the experiencing of such feelings and their expression lies the importance of cognition or rationaliy in the reception, processing, and expressing of emotional stimuli. Originally, L'Abate (1969b, 1971) made this distinction in the evaluation of intellectual functions in kindergarten children and adolescents. However, in more recent writings, this distinction has been expanded to the difference between feelings on the receptive side and emotions on the expressive side. This distinction is supported by, among others, the work of Gross, John, and Richards (2000) and Thayer (1996).

When the experience, management, and regulation of feelings and emotions are used as a criterion of functionality-dysfunctionality, functionality is defined as the ability to experience a wide range of feelings and to express them helpfully without blaming, criticisms, put-downs, and attacks on anyone else. In functionality, rationality, in the form of appraisal, plays an important role in how feelings are expressed with reliance on a wide repertoire of expressed emotions. Dysfunctionality is defined as overreliance on the experience of one single, two, or few feelings with a subsequent expression of similarly limited emotions as well as avoiding any rational processing or appraisal, jumping immediately and impulsively into action without reflection on the possible outcome of destructive expressions of feeling, that is, emotions. Indeed, a limited repertoire of expressed, mostly negative emotions is the hallmark in the etiology of schizophrenia (Nicholson, 1998).

Once all theoretical schools are viewed as stemming from one of the various components of relationships, we can make sense of what might seem at first blush a confusing state of affairs. Humanism stresses the subjective, phenomenological perception of events, as represented by feelings, moods, and affects (input). This school includes such luminaries as Rollo May, Abraham Maslow, and Carl Rogers and is now culminating in the therapeutic school that stresses feelings and emotions (Greenberg & Paivio, 1997). This school has seen a veritable growth of treatises on feelings and emotions, most decrying the lack of attention that this component has received in the past. Now, with the advent of ways to measure "emotional intelligence" (Bar-On & Parker, 2000; Saarni, 2000), the ground is set for even more precise foundations for this basic component as well as more controversies (Scherer & Davidson, 2001).

Rationality (*R*)

If information is experienced and in some cases accepted emotionally, it is processed cognitively in terms of appraising and evaluating it, deciding what kind of information it is, and how it should be responded to. Is it dangerous? Threatening? Painful? Joyful? Pleasurable? To be acted upon immediately? To be delayed to a later date? To be kept inside and never shared with anyone? This processing requires the rational resources of the individual (*R*). Processing involves also deciding how to express or not express that information. Verbally? Non-verbally? In writing? Aggressively? Assertively? Passively? As we shall see, from *R* stems discharge-delay, that is, control tendencies that expand over time into the ability to negotiate (Table 2-1). There are feelings that cannot be processed rationally. When facing a sudden, unexpected death or loss, however, when there is not room for appraisal, grief and sadness are usually the outcome.

This quality, processing feelings and thinking (or not thinking) about how to express them outwardly, is essentially independent of intellectual functioning usually assessed as "intelligence." One can be extremely intelligent, as measured by standard tests, and at the same time retarded and limited in how to become aware of feelings and how to express them, let alone convert them into emotions.

Therefore, we are confronting at least two types of intelligence, those related to processing of feelings and their expression and those related to intellectual pursuits and problem-solving. Actually, a workbook on this topic (L'Abate, 1996, 2002a) distinguishes among 15 different abilities that, altogether, would compose a wider construct of intelligence. Even the process of negotiation, which is, or at least should be, a rational process, does have emotional foundations on how one feels about the issue to be negotiated. Unless these feelings are expressed from the very outset, the whole process of negotiation will be derailed and rendered ineffective. Here is where cognitive schools of therapy, like emotional-rational, psychodynamic, and reality therapies, have made their distinct contribution.

Activity (*A*)

The expression of emotions, therefore, takes place through some kind of activity (*A*), either internal and invisible to the naked eye or external and visible to observers. This component of the model is composed of movements and gestures, what one does, and words, what one says. There may be correspondence or discrepancies between these two channels. For instance, in one set of twins, one usually speaks out negatively but does the correct thing, indicating an extremely sensitive awareness of intimate others' feelings. His sister, however, never disagrees or says anything negative, but she "does" negatively the opposite of what is expected of her. Of course, *A* means behavior, as generally meant by most theorists. Emphasis on observable behavior only and whatever consequences or reinforcements follow was stressed by the behavioristic school, starting with Watson, followed by Kantor, and accomplished most systematically by B. F. Skinner. As is readily seen, behavior (i.e., *A*) is just one component of this model. What is more relevant here is not only what one does and says but also *how* one does and says it as well as what one feels before it is said and done as well as afterward. This point is especially relevant to the outward expression of feelings, that is, emotions, which contain both face expressions, gazes, and hand and leg movements, as well as tone and timbre of voice. Emotions, therefore, as defined here, are *A*, what one expresses outwardly in gestures, gazes, and words, disclosing or not disclosing inner feelings that may or may not be expressed outwardly. Here is where behavioral schools and the model to be reviewed in Chapter 4 have made their contribution.

Awareness (*Aw*)

A, in turn, leads to a feedback loop involving a corrective change. After expressing *A*, one needs to be aware of the impact that such an expression has had on a target. *Aw*areness implies a corrective process whereby one becomes cognizant of the outcome of what was expressed. Was it helpful? Was it hurtful? Was it pleasurable? Was it negative or positive? *Aw*, therefore, is the corrective loop that leads to change, provided one reflects on the consequences of one's actions (*A*). Without reflection, either before (*R*) or after *A*, that is, *Aw*, there is little room for change. Furthermore, *Aw*, not only involves internal reactions but involves external *Aw* of the distal and proximate context (*C*). Replies to provocations, demands, requests, criticisms, or put-downs, most of the time, require an Awareness (i.e., reflection) of one's internal reactions (*E*), how one feels, as well as awareness of contextual factors (*C*) that need to be taken into consideration before responding. Here is where Gestalt and other schools, like the Eastern philosophies, have made their conceptual and therapeutic contribution.

Context (*C*)

Historically, at least since Watson's stress on external, observable behavior and Freud's stress on intrapsychic processes, including awareness, cognitions, and feelings, one needs to consider the pioneering contribution of J. R. Kantor (Chapter 1) to stress the interbehavioral nature of events, neither external behavior nor internal processes but what happens and what is exchanged when two or more people meet or when unexpected events or impersonal objects are met. Is it the outcome of the encounter that counts, not just the nature of individuals A and B with events or objects? Hence, Kantor was one of the first to consider what he called the "interbehavioral field," what would now be called the Context of a relationship or what was later called interactions (no Context) and transactions (Context) by systems theorists (Spiegel, 1971). This naturalistic trend will be continued by the model presented in Chapter 4. Here is where the various schools of family therapy have made their contribution.

Any component part of this model can be avoided (denied, repressed, suppressed) and therefore short-circuited, leading to a lowering of functioning. For instance, if *E* is avoided (suppressed, repressed, denied), this avoidance may lead to obsessive rumination and compulsive behavior (i.e., *A*). If *R* is avoided in addition to *E*, it may lead to a magnification of *A*, as in the case of impulsivity and criminal behavior. Avoidance of *E* may lead to a restriction in *Aw* as well—the individual is unable to reflect on the consequences of his or her actions *A*, as in the case of acting-out individuals. A restriction in *Aw* may lead to a denial of *C* or, in some cases, externalization on *C*, to avoid taking personal responsibility and reflection of one's behavior by putting responsibility for its outcome on others. Too much emphasis on the importance of *C*, on the other hand (What will neighbors think?), may be present in internalization disorders, where the individual pays so much attention to *C* that the other four components

(ERAAw) are diminished. By the same token, one may be so preoccupied with *A* that the other four components of this model become restricted.

Verticality: Model[2]

The depth of behavior (i.e., verticality) can be understood in terms of levels of analysis, observation, or interpretation. That is why this model and the previous model[1] are called meta-theoretical. They go above and beyond the theory itself. Furthermore, they belong to various theories independent of this one. This model pertains to how to look at relationships and how to make sense of them on a dimension of depth. While relationships and models to be considered vary along an observable, horizontal dimension of extensionality, as in the ERAAwC model, this model is concerned with the multilayered or multilevel nature of relationships, from external to internal. It discriminates among two major levels, descriptive and explanatory. Each level is subdivided into two other levels (see Table 2-3).

Descriptive levels include (1) the presentational, external facade, how we manage to appear in public, and (2) the phenotypical, how we behave in the safety and privacy of our homes, away from external observation and possible judgment and in the heat of prolonged, close, and sometimes intense relationships. Both levels can be observed, recorded, and visible if we are allowed to observe them over time to make sense of them. Two explanatory levels are less observable and recordable. They need to be inferred rather than observed directly. The first genotypical level involves how individuals see themselves, a process that involves inferred or hypothetical constructs as self-concepts, like self-esteem, internal working models (ego, superego, etc.), ascribed needs (drives, motivations), or inferred traits (extroversion, open-mindedness, introversion, etc.). This level is not only inferred but also hypothetical, because, as far as one knows, no one has been able to photograph or videotape a person's self-esteem or similarly internal or intrapsychic constructs. These constructs are dear to theorists who stress the importance of specific traits or states inferred from self-report, paper-and-pencil instruments such as the Big Five Factors model (Costa & Widiger, 1994; McCrae & Costa, 1997). They include a variety of internally inferred conditions that supposedly "explain" the behavior of an individual at the two previous levels: "He killed his wife because he was extroverted, neurotic, possessive, insecure, etc."; "She is liberal because she is extroverted, open-minded, etc." The second explanatory level is historically chronological, generationally developmental, and situational, how an individual's events in the past family of origin and in the present family of procreation "explain" the three other supraordinant levels. Here is where past traumas, illnesses, and painful and joyful events help us to understand how one relates to intimate and non-intimate others.

Table 2-3
Levels of Observation/Interpretation: Model[2]

A. Descriptive Levels: Visible and recordable
   1. Self-presentational sublevel: How does one present himself/herself to others, in front of an audience, especially outside the home?
      a. Superficial and short-lived.
      b. Physical appearance (neat–disorderly, clean–dirty, orderly–sloppy).
      c. First impression, impression management (good–bad, remarkable–indifferent).
      d. Social facade (nice–nasty, smooth–rough).
      e. Self-handicapping versus self-enhancing strategies.
      f. Degree of emphasis on this level at the expense of the lower, phenotypical level ("Make a good impression at all costs").
   2. Phenotypical sublevel: How does the individual behave in close, prolonged, and committed (i.e., intimate) relationships or under stress?
      a. How does the individual function affectively, intellectually, and behaviorally in relation to intimates over time in the confines of home?
      b. Consistency–inconsistency, congruence–incongruence between the two descriptive sublevels.
B. Explanatory Levels: Why do individuals act the way they do? Inferential or hypothetical levels not available to the naked eye or direct observation, left strictly to interpretation of present conditions.
   1. Genotypical sublevel: Self-view or concept underlying structure of self.
      a. Strictly inside the individual, feelings, inferred traits (extroversion–introversion) or hypothetical states (ego, superego, id), self-concept and/or "self-esteem."
      b. Self-differentiation according to a likeness continuum and multiple identities (Models[7 & 8]).
      c. Attribution of importance to self and intimate others (Model[9]).
      d. Self-determination.
      e. Consistence–inconsistence, congruence–incongruence with descriptive levels.
   2. Historical or present situation (i.e., context): How do individuals develop their genotypes?
      a. Transgenerational transmission from family of origin (parental practices and influence of siblings).
      b. Chronological and developmental determinants specific to individuals.
      c. Situational determinants and events of the moment.
      d. Determinants from the family of procreation (marriage and children).
      e. Consistence–inconsistence, congruence–incongruence with other levels.

Source: L'Abate, 1994b, p. 17. Reprinted with permission.

The first descriptive level signifies what is publicly visible and immediate, to the point of being photographed, audiotaped, or videorecorded. Description can be either public, including how a relationship is presented to outside observers, the impression-making facade ("I am a nice person, with a nice marriage and nice children"), versus more private, phenotypical aspects that may be hidden from the self, intimate others, and public observation and even measurement. What really happens in the secrecy and privacy of one's own home? The publicly "nice" person may actually behave like a nasty despot, a mean partner, and an abusive parent in the home setting. The connection between presentational and phenotypical levels can be minimal and consistent between the two levels ("What you see is what you get") or can be reversed. What is presented publicly may be fairly consistent with what happens inside the home, or it could be extremely inconsistent, for instance, nice on the outside but nasty inside the home. By the same token, this connection could be conceivably reversed, that is, nasty on the outside and nice on the inside, with all possible consistencies and inconsistencies between the public and private levels of observation and interpretation.

Levels of analysis/observation/interpretation are helpful in understanding how people present themselves to therapists, either to make a necessarily poor impression ("I am really sick.") or to make a very positive impression ("I am OK; it's my partner [or our child] who is sick."). In addition, it is important to understand discrepancies among the various levels (i.e., how an addict may consider himself "good and healthy," while his co-dependent wife is "sick" because "she is depressed" while the addict denies being "depressed"). A couple may appear lovey-dovey in public but fight like cats and dogs in the privacy of their home.

No testable model has been derived from these levels of analysis/interpretation as yet, perhaps because one might not be needed. However, there is no reason that these admittedly dialectic levels should not be formalized further. At least qualitatively, this still remains a model in the way it summarizes theories that have stressed any one of the four levels. For instance, there have been theories about "impression management" in self-presentation, as well as theories about how people behave phenotypically in different settings (i.e., "cross-setting" or "cross-situational" variability). There are many theories about the nature of the genotype. Indeed, most personality theories, starting with the "bad seed" and continuing with Freud and many others, were theories about the nature of the genotype. By the same token, some theories, like psychoanalysis, included the importance of past, historical events in affecting the present nature of the genotype as well as behavior at presentational and phenotypical levels.

Verticality and Emotional Presentation

Taking off from Jones et al.'s (1984) model of emotional presentation, Clark, Pataki, and Carver (1996) presented research to show how emotional expression at the presentational level may be due to four factors originally considered by Jones et al. (1984). These authors suggested that there are definite links between how emotions of anger, sadness, happiness, and irritability may be expressed or not expressed (i.e., regulated presentationally, in different ways, for a variety of reasons or purposes): (1) ingratiation (2) supplication, (3) intimidation, and (4) self-promotion. In addition to these four, Clark et al. suggested other internal states or traits that may be responsible for how emotions are presented interpersonally: (1) nervousness, (2) threats to the self, (3) self-protection or defense, (4) intentions to live up to intimate others' expectations, and (5) to avoid social disruption (Thayer, 1996).

At the end of their outstanding chapter, Clark et al. (1996) cited studies of victims of major negative life events, such as death of a loved one or rape, showing that "feelings of distress and sadness may linger for years following such events" (p. 265), even (or especially?) if intimate others expect a speedy recovery from those feelings. As discussed in previous publications, as well as by other investigators (Bradley, 2000; Hayes, Strosahl, & Wilson, 1999; Watson, 2000), feelings of distress and sadness are close to what here and elsewhere have been called "hurts." Clark et al.'s conclusion concerning "lingering feeling of distress and sadness" tends to support the thesis that hurts are at the bottom, the genotypical level, of many feelings expressed either at the phenotypical or presentational levels or both. This conclusion is illustrated in Table 2-4. Even though Clark et al. go on to stress the importance of differentiating feelings "versus" expressing emotions, a distinction already made above, they failed in differentiating between feelings that are free from value judgments and emotions as the expression of such feelings, which, as already stated, may be positive or negative, constructive or destructive.

Furthermore, these investigators failed to differentiate between public presentation of feelings versus phenotypical expression of the same feelings, because their research was based on laboratory studies. We may differ in how we avoid presenting certain emotions in public situations, like work, from how we express them in more private (and safer?) settings, like the home. We may express feelings in the privacy of our home, that is, at the phenotypical level, that we would not dare express publicly. For instance, we may avoid public displays of irritability for any of the reasons outlined above. However, we may show it in the private confines of our homes. Some feelings, usually happiness and similar states, are expressed publicly at the presentational level. However, we may limit the expression of anger and sadness within the safe confines of our homes, at the phenotypical level. Even then, some individuals avoid expressing these feelings even in the home, keeping them to themselves and not sharing them with anyone, not

Table 2-4
Levels of Observation/Interpretation and Expression of Feelings into Emotions

A. Descriptive	**Expressed Emotions**
1. Presentational	**nice, neutral, nasty (sadness, anger, happiness, irritability, etc.)**
2. Phenotypical	**nice, neutral, nasty (sadness, anger, happiness, irritability, etc.)**
B. Explanatory	**Feelings**
1. Genotypical	**Hurts, Shame, Guilt, Likeness, and Sense of Self-Importance**
2. Historical, developmental, situational factors that are antecedents to the formation of hurt feelings, other feelings, likeness, and sense of self-importance	

even one's partner. Of course, hurt feelings are the hardest ones to express and share with loved ones, perhaps to avoid hurting loved ones' feelings, another reason to add to the nine traits listed above. Hence, what is relevant here is how genotypical feelings are expressed outwardly at the two descriptive levels and what consistencies or inconsistencies exist between these latter two levels and the explanatory, genotypical level.

Here is where the ERAAwC comes into relevance, because feelings (*E*) need to be processed through *R*, expressed as emotions in *A*, and reflected upon through *Aw* of self and of Context. Consequently, this model is useful in describing how relationships are formed, as in friendships, courtships, and marriage, to the point that short-lived and superficial relationships, as in acquaintances, occur mostly at the presentational level. As relationships become closer, eventually the presentational level decreases to make room for the phenotypical level. In even closer relationships, as in friendship, courtship, and eventual marriage (or the equivalent), the genotypical and historical levels will be shared. This sharing will take place in functional relationships, but it will be spotty, selective, and probably distorted in dysfunctional ones.

SETTINGS: WHERE DO RELATIONSHIPS TAKE PLACE? MODEL[3]

The importance of settings in determining behavior and interactions in personality socialization was stressed long ago by ecological psychologists (e.g., Barker, 1968, to cite one pioneer among many to follow). Each setting has its peculiar, explicit, or implicit rules, predictable or unpredictable regulations, consistent or inconsistent requirements, and task demands that are setting-specific and that differ from one setting to another.

The theory distinguishes among five classes of settings: (1) home, (2) school/work, and (3) surplus time divided into (4) transitory and (5) transit settings, to move from one setting to another. Surplus time is divided into survival time and leisure-time enjoyment. Transitory means settings that change over one's life cycle, such as schools, grocery stores, barbershops, beauty salons, shopping malls, restaurants, churches, and sport arenas. Transit settings are used for transportation from one setting to another, such as cars, buses, planes, trains, highways, parking lots, airports, hotels, or train stations. All settings interact and overlap with each other. In some cases, survival and enjoyment overlap. For instance, some people have fun at work and no fun at home. Some have fun at home and none at work. Some have fun in both settings. Some have no fun in either. Others work very hard at settings that are supposed to produce enjoyment, like gyms, parks, and recreation facilities. Furthermore, each setting has specific exchange functions. For instance, banks exchange money. Schools, bookstores, and libraries exchange information. Hospitals and clinics exchange services. Stores provide and exchange goods for money. The home, ideally, should provide importance and intimacy in addition to all other resources. However, not all homes provide importance and intimacy. On the contrary, they may provide some goods, services, and information but no importance or intimacy.

Competencies and abilities vary according to the task demands and requirements of each setting. The number of settings is finite and objectively defined. In order of functional importance, settings are home, school/work, surplus time (survival and enjoyment), transit, and transitory. Again, there may be overlaps among all five settings. For instance, leisure activities may take place at home or, in some instances, in work settings, as, for example, fitness rooms in workplaces. Competence in one setting does not necessarily predict and transfer to competence in another setting. One could be a terrific parent but a mediocre employee. By the same token, one could be a remarkable athlete during leisure hours but a poor provider at home.

Competence in various settings helps to define the level of functionality of an individual. For instance, superior functioning may include being a caring and effective partner and parent who excels at work, enjoying leisure-time activities after successful completion of survival tasks. By the same token, settings are necessary to discriminate among levels of functionality in personality socialization, from superior to adequate, to mediocre, to inadequate, and to failure, as discussed later in this chapter.

Home

A house is not a home. This saying attests to the difference between a physical structure, a residence, and the meaning that that structure may have for those who live in it. Is it a harbor to retreat from the stresses of daily living? Is it another battleground full of tensions and conflicts? This setting has task requirements that are related to the maintenance of a family as an emotional unit and to the home as a physical entity. Most of the responsibilities can be broken down into four specific roles: caretaker, provider, partner, and parent. Each role demands specific skills. For instance, responsibilities of the caretaking role are of two kinds. One refers to the nurturant qualities that deal with love, being present and emotionally available. The other kind refers to instrumental qualities that deal with the physical and material well-being of the home, such as cooking, cleaning, purchasing, repairing. The role of provider deals with the economic aspects of family living. Salary, income, credit rating, mortgages are aspects of this role. How much money comes into the home, and how is it spent? Both the caretaker and the provider roles depend a great deal on the kind of person one is. How well one functions as a partner depends on a variety of personality competencies that can be summarized in the models presented below. In this role, the abilities to love and to negotiate are necessary. The fourth role—parent—is probably one of the most difficult and demanding of our lives. Often, this is the role for which we have received little, if any, training except for what we learned as children by watching our parents. Most of us perpetuate their errors and forget their assets because the task requirements of today are different from those of any preceding generation. The ability to love and the ability to negotiate become crucial at this stage. Consequently, an appropriate developmental sequence requires, first of all, the development of personhood as being basic to partnership. Being able to be a partner is basic to being a parent. Unfortunately, very few of us are lucky or healthy enough to follow such an orderly sequence. One would even question whether such a sequence is possible or desirable.

School/Work

Both settings require two separate but interwined sets of skills. The first set consists of specific educational/occupational skills that are necessary to perform a job, such as, initially reading, writing, and arithmetic and then turning into filing, typing, drawing, writing, ditch digging, public speaking, delegating, and so on. The second set of skills is extra-job, consisting of interpersonal, citizenship performance skills (Borman & Penner, 2001) to get along with schoolmates, peers, coworkers, subordinates, authorities, clients, or customers. This set of skills may require interpersonal sensitivity, political gamesmanship, and contextual awareness. It may have little to do with the substantive job skills necessary for success. Yet, these skills may make the difference between promotion or stagnation on the job!

Below are the leftover settings that are neither home- nor school/work-related. Making fewer demands and having fewer requirements, these skills may be considered more discretionary than obligatory.

Surplus or Leisure Time

Leisure activity is sometimes spent at home, sometimes in other settings. It takes place in the company of others, or it can be solitary. It can be active or sedentary, indoor or outdoor, oriented toward people or toward things. Working in one's basement on a hobby, participating in the Elks Club, watching television, going to church, or running a marathon—all are examples of activities in this setting. Leisure activities are important for one's enjoyment of life and for personality development. They are an integral part of how we function as individuals. These activities specify the value that we put on friends and relationships. Leisure settings require skills that are specific to the activity being performed in a particular setting as well as skills to develop and maintain relationships that are formed within each setting.

Objective Settings versus Subjective Contexts

The ability to negotiate requires also the skill to separate Being from Doing and Having in these settings. This theory acknowledges the importance of specific developmental competencies as a function of interactions with specific settings. The acquisition of personal and interpersonal competence is a developmental process that acknowledges the importance of specificities peculiar to a given setting. This theory maintains that these personal specificities are particular to the interaction between task characteristics and demands in settings that interact with specific skills and abilities in individuals.

How settings are perceived by viewers (positively/negatively, neutrally/intensely, etc.) constitutes a context, spatially and temporally. One setting may mean more than others, and there are different interpretations given subjectively to most settings. The home may be a safe harbor or a battleground. Work may be a source of accomplishments and achievements or give a sense of failure and stagnation (Roberts & Hogan, 2001). Household chores may mean being bored because of their repetitiousness or as something that needs to be done daily to keep the household going. Hence, a context is the subjective view or interpretation of an objective setting. More about this issue will be considered in the conclusion of this chapter.

ASSUMPTIONS SPECIFIC TO THE THEORY: MODEL[4]

Personality socialization and interpersonal competence in relationships assume space and time as two basic processes that subsume, respectively, regulation of distance and regulation of controls. Previously, regulation was conceived as synonymous with control, an erroneous equation. Now the concept of regulation is applied to both space and time. Space is defined by extremes in distance regulation, that is, approach-avoidance functions among, between, and within individuals (Elliot & Church, 1997; Elliot & Covington, 2001; Sutton, 2002). For example, extremes in approach could be seen in symbiotic attachments ("I cannot live without you") that result in internal (against the self rather than against others) self-abuse, apathy, or neglect. Extremes in avoidance-withdrawal are seen in abandonments and rejections. Somewhere in the middle of this dimension lie the proper balance and regulation of distance, ultimately culminating in closeness and intimacy.

This function eventually becomes socialized into the ability to love and to be intimate, stemming from *E*. The ability to love is defined as the attribution and assertion of importance to self and intimate others (parents, partners, children, siblings, relatives, friends, and neighbors). Intimacy is defined as the sharing of joys as well as of hurts and fears of being hurt. Intimacy is frequent in functional relationships and defective, if not absent, in dysfunctional ones. Distance, physical as well as emotional, is measured by energy and time involvement, investment, and availability among intimates. It is one way to evaluate close, committed, and lasting intimate relationships.

Time subsumes a dimension of control defined by extremes in discharge or disinhibition (immediate, quick, or fast responding), on one hand, and delay or inhibition (slow or no apparent responding), on the other (Smith, 1992). Extremes in discharge are visible in externalizations, as in hyperactivity, impulsivity, and acting-out behaviors. Extremes in delay are visible in internalizations, as in compulsive thinking and ruminations, shyness, anxieties, depressions, and, ultimately, alienations and suicides. Functionality is found in a balance in the regulation of discharge-delay processes.

Developmentally, the infant is born in a world of space (distance) that with age becomes a world of time (control). Functionality is found in a regulated balance of discharge-delay tendencies. One could go as far as hypothesizing that distance is more related to right-side hemispheric functions, while control is more related to left-side hemispheric functions (L'Abate, 2001; Reid, McMahan, & L'Abate, 2001). As Muris, Merkenlbach, Schmidt, Gadet et al. (2001) found in normal adolescents, self-reported inhibition correlated with anxiety and depression, suggesting that inhibition is more present in disorders of internalization (anxiety, depression, fear) than in disorders of externalization (anger, hostility, aggression).

Both distance and control underlie the concept of interpersonal and intimate competence, implying interactions among individuals, parents, partners, relatives, and friends. This framework is consistent, continuous, and reducible to monadic models of behavior that follow acontextual and intra-individual rather than inter-individual thinking, as already discussed. Both distance and control are well-accepted constructs in the psychological literature, even though they are not used within an intimate, interdependent context as they are used here. Both assumptions underlie the concept of competence. Ever since White (1959) brought forth this concept, it has captured considerable attention in motivational and personality theories (Ford, 1985; Marlowe and Weinberg, 1985; Phillips, 1968; Wine & Smye, 1980).

The concept of competence seems more relevant, specific, and concrete than nonspecific and vague concepts of "personality" and "environment." The concept of competence implies an interaction of someone with someone else or of someone with something. One cannot talk about competence without specifying the context in which such competence is manifested. Ford (1985), for instance, in reviewing past and present definitions of competence, referred to it as (1) the ability to formulate and produce persistent, goal-directed activity, (2) one's behavioral repertoire of specified and specifiable skills and abilities, and (3) effectiveness in relevant contexts. Consequently, we need to specify the nature of the contexts in which these capabilities, effectiveness, and skills are manifested and used. Competence can be specified, even assessed in a specific setting much more easily than personality can be. Although personality seems to encompass a wide range of traits and states, most of them internal and difficult to measure, competence is limited to a definite number of settings. It may be a more restricted term than personality. However, it may also be easier to define and measure because the interaction is more specific than a "person x situation." A "competence x context" interaction may be more specific and concrete than the former.

Competencies derive from the two assumptions of space and time. Abilities underlie the two postulates of love and negotiation, and the three modalities of Being, Doing, and Having underlie six resource classes. These resources are summarized by testable models that require different sets of skills (Table 2-1). Applications of two different sets of skills pertain to the concept of setting, introduced earlier. Competencies need to be differentiated from abilities and skills, instead of being used synonymously with them. Competencies lie on the subjective, experiencing side (input); skills lie on the expressive side (output). One may feel competent but actually be incompetent when confronted with a task for which competence was claimed. Abilities lie in the middle of this continuum (throughput), implying the ability to think (*R*) and to process feelings. Assumptions, then, subsume the notion of competence to regulate distance, an internal, developmental process that is eventually transformed into the ability to love. This ability to love is expressed on the output side by very specific skills, like care and concern. The competence to modulate, regulate, and modify control over oneself is transformed developmentally into the ability to negotiate, which is also expressed through specific skills, to be detailed below.

Individual characteristics are socialized from the original family context and, in turn, affect that context as well. We are the products and the producers of past and present relationships. Two individuals start a family by conceiving children and, usually, living under the same roof. Both individuals are the products of contexts from their families of origin. Both carry these influences with them into their new family of procreation. These individual characteristics must adapt to new demands from different settings, which in turn influence the functioning of their offspring. How can one reconcile family functioning with psychological constructs? This theory straddles individual and family system perspectives by viewing competence socialization in the context of family relationships. This task requires keeping the importance of the family context primary, relating individual determinants to family functioning, and using specifically relational rather than generic and vague systems language.

If the family is a unit(y) of interacting personalities (Burgess, 1926/1972), then we need to define personality within its developmental and relational context or within various contexts or settings. Thus, this theory defines relational socialization and functioning in intimate relationships as a set of competencies in diverse settings. The most relevant setting of interest here is, of course, the family, where the foundations for socialization are set. This view of personality and competence development has been strongly influenced by Kantor's interbehaviorism, discussed in Chapter 1, and by what has been called "interactionism" (Ekehammer, 1974; Endler & Magnusson, 1976). Hence, personal and interpersonal competence and personality socialization are the product or outcome of a "competence x context" interaction, which becomes a transaction when a viewer affects it (i.e., the Heisenberg principle). Since both "personality" and "situation" are quite vague and are usually unspecified, it has been found more useful to break down the concept of personality into specific competencies. It seems more meaningful to break down "situation" into specific settings and contexts, as is done later in this chapter. This issue is reconsidered at the conclusion of this chapter.

POSTULATES ABOUT PROCESSES

Both assumptions underlie competencies that become developmentally transformed into two postulates dealing with two more specific abilities—the ability to love (distance) and the ability to negotiate (control). The notion that these two abilities are indicative of the competence level and coping strategies of families is supported by a great many theorists of different persuasions, disciplines, and interests. Regardless of the terminology used, there seems to be a consensus among theorists that most interpersonal behavior, especially in the family, can be reduced to these two abilities, even though different terminologies may be used. They are considered the two abilities most fundamental to personal and interpersonal competence and coping under stress.

The First Postulate: Ability to Love

Love is expressed through (1) attributing, asserting, and affirming the importance of self and of loved ones, as shown through care and concern for self and other, and (2) the ability to be intimate, that is, being emotionally available to oneself and intimate others through reciprocal sharing of hurts and fears of being hurt. This process means being together unconditionally, without demands for performance, perfection, production, or problem-solving. The ability to love, therefore, even though it may posses a cognitive component, is based on the ability to experience, accept, and share a wide spectrum of feelings, painful and joyful. Hence, emotionality (*E*) is at the very bottom of our intimate existence. It consists of feelings of love between partners, between parents and children, and among relatives and friends. These are the people whom we all need to share hurt feelings that unavoidably occur in everybody's life, whether we like them or not. Once these feelings are shared, joys and pleasures can be shared as well, or perhaps better.

E, therefore, is the primary component of model ERAAwC already reviewed. In *E* lie feelings of hurt and fears of being hurt that are shared reciprocally in functional relationships. They are avoided and even put down, ridiculed, suppressed, and repressed through internalizations or externalizations in dysfunctional ones. *E*, therefore, is the basic context of socialization. Infants are born in an emotional context of single or couple caretakers and their absence thereof and growing up in an emotional network of family relationships.

The Second Postulate: Ability to Negotiate Power: Model[5]

The ability to negotiate, problem-solve, brainstorm, and bargain is developed from the ability to regulate the self in relationship with intimate others (Vuchinich, 1999). Hence, the ability to negotiate is based on *R*, planning, reflecting, and considering alternative courses of action with their pros and cons. This ability is based on a balance and regulation of discharge-delay processes that are present in functional relationships but defective or even absent in dysfunctional ones. It means being able to regulate oneself through the various components of Model[1] and, in so doing, allowing others to express themselves openly, giving them the freedom of free discharge in helpfully democratic and creative ways without detours, delays, distractions, and procrastinations. If there is no balance in personal and intimate controls, then severely abusive, neglectfully and contradictorily inconsistent, and hurtful discharges would result in rebellions and retaliations, on one hand, or extremes in delays and withdrawals, on the other.

Negotiation and problem-solving take place successfully within functional, democratic relationships, where the singular importance of all participant members is not only acknowledged but valued. In dysfunctional relationships, where either immediate discharge (name-calling, blaming, put-downs, etc.) reaches abusive proportions or procrastinating delays take place, there is no possibility of reaching agreement and consensus about how to solve even the smallest, irrelevant issues (making mountains out of molehills). The next chapter discusses how both abilities have been evaluated.

The Third Postulate about Contents: Modalities of the Life Triangle: Model[6]

Assumptions and models are linked together through three intermediary modalities: (1) *Being* or *Presence*, (2) *Doing* or *Performance*, (3) *Having* or *Production*. These modalities derive from resource exchange theory (Foa & Foa, 1974), which postulates six classes of resources exchanged among people: (1) status or importance, (2) love or intimacy, (3) information relevant to educational settings, as in teaching institutions, media, and libraries, (4) services, as in welfare and professional settings, (5) possessions or goods, as in industry, agriculture, manufacturing, and (6) money, as in banks and savings institutions. Status was changed in this theory to importance, while love was changed to intimacy. Combining dialectically both classes, one obtains the modality of Being Present in emotional availability, let alone physical and logistical availability. Combining information and services, one obtains the modality of Doing or Performance. Combining money and possessions, one obtains the modality of Having or Production. Combining performance and production together defines the construct of Power. Who controls decisions about all or part of these resources has power to some degree. Performance is defined as Doing whatever has to be done to survive and to enjoy life. Having or Production is defined as the wherewithal relevant to survival and enjoyment. The combination of Doing and Having defines power and the ability to negotiate. Love and intimacy are not negotiable. They are shared with selected intimates. Doing and Having require some negotiation.

Being or Presence means being emotionally available to ourselves and intimate others through attribution of their importance and sharing of hurts and fears of being hurt, that is, intimacy. While presence is shared and is non-negotiable in functional relationships, it becomes fused, confused, and diffused with issues of power in dysfunctional relationships. In the latter, presence is not shared appropriately, while power is either not negotiated or negotiated negatively and unsuccessfully. In functional relationships issues of power are kept separate from issues of presence and are negotiated successfully (i.e., positively and effectively). In democratic relationships, power is shared and negotiated equitably, in win-win processes. In chaotic, rigid, or dysfunctional relationships, either power is in the hands of one family member who uses it despotically, or there is no power negotiated at all, because everybody defeats everybody else. No one wins. Power, therefore, is negotiated effectively and successfully in functional relationships but is not negotiated at all or is negotiated ineffectively or unsuccessfully in dysfunctional ones.

These resource classes and the three modalities make up the equilateral triangle of living, with Being at the base, Doing on the left side, and Having on the right side of the triangle. If Being is restricted or shrinks, Doing and Having will be elevated. If Being spreads out, both Doing and Having become more restricted. Once the base is limited and Being is shortened, equilaterality gives way to an obelisk, where Doing and Having are heightened. Here is a descriptive way to show functional and dysfunctional relationships. Functional ones balance these three modalities flexibly and relevantly according to the demands of life cycle stages involved. In dysfunctional relationships, Being is restricted to make room for Doing and Having. When importance and intimacy are not expressed and shared unconditionally, they become conditional on Performance or Production or both. Consequently, Doing or Having often becomes a substitute expression of Being ("If you loved me, you would do . . ."; "If you loved me, you would buy me . . .").

The higher the competence level of family members, the greater the chances of successful negotiation. Unwillingness or inadequate ability to negotiate power is the basis of conflicts and struggles. We need to negotiate about what kind of information should be allowed at home, who should provide what services within and without the home, and what should be bought with the money earned. For instance, L'Abate and Hewitt (1988) applied the distinction of Power (Performance + Production) versus Presence (Importance + Intimacy), that is, Being Present, to a classification of sex and sexuality. They argued that most sexual dysfunctions are based on the inability to Be emotionally present to self and to a partner. Perhaps our American culture stresses sexual performance and production at the expense of sexual presence, the sharing of past hurts and fears of being hurt again. That process often means being vulnerable to the partner's whim and will. Functional sex and sexuality imply the ability to be emotionally available to one's partner before becoming fully available sexually (Lutz, 1999). A couple cannot share a good orgasm unless they are able to cry together. Sexual performance or production, that is, the physical act of intercourse at the expense of emotional presence, is bound to produce deviations and disturbances that will affect subsequent developments of how sex and sexuality are going to be shared between partners. Sex and sexuality become equated with Doing, like in sport sex or one-night stands, while Having is equated with pornographic literature, sexual props, and paraphernalia.

Personal and interpersonal competence in intimate relationships, therefore, is defined by what an individual is, does, and has in different settings. Various skills and testable models can be derived from the two sets of abilities and the three modalities. Support for this seemingly abstract dichotomy of power and presence, as defined through modalities of exchange, in addition to the early work of Foa and Foa (1974) (Table 2-2), is given in L'Abate (2002c). More recently, the importance of money and possessions as sources of power has been stressed by Doyle (1999). He developed models of personality socialization and interpersonal competence very similar to those presented here and elsewhere.

HOW ARE RELATIONSHIPS EVALUATED? THROUGH TESTABLE MODELS

Models are visual summaries, simplifications, and representations of more complex concepts, derived from assumptions, postulates, and modalities of the theory. Other models derive from two assumptions of space and time. Models allow us to understand how both presence and power are related. The modalities summarized above lead to a variety of models. In addition to ERAAwC and levels of analysis/observation/interpretation, Model^1 and Model^2, already reviewed, other models were developed to account more adequately for interpersonal competence and personality socialization in the family and other settings. For instance, the two assumptions of space and time become more concrete and visible when distance and control, with their respective polarities, are visualized as two orthogonal dimensions, making them into Model^3, which determines four quadrants: (1) high approach-high discharge; (2) high approach-low discharge; (3) low approach-high discharge; and (4) low approach-low discharge. Quadrant No. 1 would be composed of relationships where there are a maximum of physical closeness and a great deal of emotional sharing. This is perhaps the most functional quadrant. Quadrant No. 2 would be composed of close relationships with a minimum of sharing. Quadrant No. 3 would be composed of relationships with little or no closeness but a great deal of expressiveness and, possibly, acting out. Quadrant No. 4 would be composed of relationships without closeness and without much sharing, a most dysfunctional possibility.

By the same token, the two abilities of love and negotiation in Model^4 can be viewed as orthogonal dimensions, producing four quadrants: quadrant 1 included high love and high negotiation, possibly the most functional possibility. Quadrant 2 includes high love and low negotiation, quadrant

3 includes low love and high negotiation, and quadrant 4 includes low love and low negotiation, the most dysfunctional possibility. The three modalities of Being, Doing, and Having can be visualized as an equilateral triangle, making them into Model[5]. Ways to evaluate these and the following models are presented in Chapter 3.

A Developmental Continuum of Likeness in Intimate Relationships: Model[7]

Likeness deals with how we learn to differentiate ourselves, our genotype, identity, or self-definition, according to developmental comparisons with significant and intimate others (caretakers, peers, mentors, partners, friends, etc.) over the life cycle. As Clark et al. (1996, p. 259) concluded, "Perhaps one of the most well established effects in social psychology is that people seek out similar others with whom to interact." However, these and many other investigators in social psychology and relationship science seem to have forgotten Thorndike's old dictum that, paraphrased, declares, "If anything exists, it exists in some amount and, therefore, it can be measured." Clark et al. (1996), for just one instance, fall into the digital differentiation that is still common in the social psychological literature, that is, to juxtapose similarity with dissimilarity and nothing else, no degrees or types of similarity. This digitality was expanded by L'Abate (1976) into a continuum of likeness that discriminates not only in degrees of similarity but also in kinds of likeness along a variety of dimensions (L'Abate, 2000b, 2002a).

Likeness is represented by a dialectical, curvilinear continuum composed of six ranges: (1) *symbiosis* ("I cannot live without you. . . . You are me and I am you. . . . We are one."), (2) *sameness* ("Do as I tell you, and you will be all right. . . . Conform blindly to what you are told. . . . Follow my instructions to the letter and you will be rewarded."), (3) *similarity* ("You can be somewhat like me but there is room for you to develop independently of me."), (4) *differentness* ("Feel free to be whatever you want to be as long as it is positive"), (5) *oppositeness* ("I am the opposite of you and will go counter to and rebel against anything you say or do."), and (6) *autism* or *alienation* ("I am not . . . I am nothing . . . I am a thing . . . not a human being . . . I am s—t.").

Years earlier, Peak, Muney, and Clay (1960, p. 1) suggested the beginning of a continuum:

> [T]he opposites pattern may emerge as a result of the differentiation of a similarity dimension and consequently may involve greater distances between parts of the structure than do less differentiated similars. . . . Similarity has usually been defined as a relationship in which events share one or more common properties. Opposed events, like similars, also have common properties, the principal difference residing

in the greater psychological distance between opposites, a distance which has become sufficiently large to produce subcategories within the common dimension.

This quote was the beginning of thinking about a continuum of likeness in self-differentiation that culminated in revisions and additions since its inception (L'Abate, 1976). This dialectical continuum follows a bell-shaped distribution where, from the viewpoint of functionality and positive change, the two center ranges, similarity and differentness, are the most functional; the two extreme ranges, symbiosis and autism/alienation, are the most dysfunctional, with the two other ranges, sameness and oppositeness, being intermediate between the two other levels in extent of functionality. These ranges are dialectical in the sense that they coexist together; one range cannot exist without its dialectical counterpart. Each range is needed to help define the corresponding range and would not have any meaning without it. Furthermore, dialectical implies also that these ranges are difficult to evaluate experimentally, unless one relies on the vast research on similarity-dissimilarity (L'Abate, 1976, pp. 69–117, 1994b, 1997b, 2002a, 2000b).

Consequently, symbiosis is coupled with autism/alienation. Sameness is coupled with oppositeness because individuals who are oppositional to their parents, to authority figures, or to accepted social norms are also very conforming to and similar with equally oppositional individuals. Similarity has no meaning without differentness. This last pair of ranges is the basis for positively creative intimate relationships, while the other two pairs do not have such a basis. The dialectical combination of symbiosis/autism describes abusive-apathetic (neglectful) styles in intimate relationships (AA). Sameness/oppositeness describes repetitively reactive styles (RR). Similarity/differentness describes creatively conductive styles (CC). Hence, the ARC model describes the functionality of behavior, ranging from most functional (CC), to semi-functional/dysfunctional (RR), to most dysfunctional (AA).

The theory has already differentiated how this continuum can be expanded and applied to a variety of areas. Most functional individuals behave in the middle in most areas of this distribution. A few functional individuals may function in the same-opposite ranges either in one or two areas. A smaller number of semi-functional individuals may function well in just a few areas but may be unable to behave in most other areas. Very dysfunctional individuals are unable to function in the middle of most areas. Hospitalized or incarcerated individuals are dysfunctional in all areas because they function in the two extremes of most areas.

This continuum of likeness has been derived in part from the social comparison (SCT) model (Suls & Wheeler, 2000), which aims at explaining much social behavior on the basis of comparative evaluations of one with others. Even though SCT is an eminently relational model, not a theory as it claims to be, and in the sense that it is used here, as a hierarchical structure, it has not been used or applied to or even hypothesized within an intimate relational context. It has found its empirical bases on contrived and artificial laboratory situations with subjects who met for one time only and never met again. This statement does not even imply to demean the model or its laboratory evaluation. On the contrary, laboratory evaluation has been one source of validation for the present theory. However, laboratory evaluation is not enough because, as long as it is limited to evaluating strictly intra-individual measures, it is still necessary to evaluate relationships, provided other sources of evaluation and validation are also used, as discussed in the next chapter.

Social comparison takes place according to various explanatory (i.e., genotypical) processes, namely (1) uncertainty, which would support an attachment model, (2) an intergenerational transmission of relationships as internalized by the genotype, (3) developmental and contextual antecedents of social comparison, and (4) according to another intrapsychic, non-relational concept, which has been criticized previously (L'Abate, 1994b, 1997b), and that is "self-esteem" (Hogg, 2000), as a purely intrapsychic, non-relational construct. In brief, relationally, we do not go to a funeral on the basis of our self-esteem or the deceased's self-esteem. We go to a funeral as well as to many other social events on the basis of how important that person or a host is to us, not on the basis of our self-esteem or the deceased's self-esteem! Furthermore, SCT has failed, thus far, to show how universal this process is. It may work in competitive cultures like the North American and European ones, but does it work in poor, Third World countries where there is little to compare except misery? It may well operate in cultures other than ours, but it needs to be demonstrated that it does.

In spite of these shortcomings, there is no question that SCT is a very powerful, descriptive, and, to a certain extent, explanatory model that does stress valid relational processes, even though it still lacks a developmental basis, which is found in the likeness continuum. From the day when infants are born they become observers of social relationships and begin with time to compare themselves with others. From relating to a caretaker, the child can begin to compare that relationship with those of other child-caretakers. Comparisons are made according to objects, clothes, toys, furniture, houses, and cars. One 15-month-old child can already identify her mother's car and differentiate it from her grandfather and grandmother's cars and those from other cars, according to a similar-different dichotomy. The process of self-differentiation, therefore, is one aspect of object and social comparison, which, until now (Suls & Wheeler, 2000) has been described dichotomously (similar-dissimilar) rather than on a continuum, as proposed here.

Conville (1991) presented a model of transitions in personal relationships that tends to support conceptually the validity of a continuum of likeness. In the first place, he stressed the importance of "difference" rather than dissimilarity in a field where similarity is still the only variable studied in the laboratory:

> Difference is both inevitable and problematic in personal relationships. Often Difference is what brings people together, as in curiosity or physical attraction. . . . Thus, Difference may prove to be a useful tool for thinking about interpersonal communication. (p. 2)

In the second place, Conville, in addition to stressing the importance of differences in relationships, used many terms that are part of this continuum of likeness, such as "sameness" (p. 119), "opposition," which is used quite often throughout the text, and finally "alienation," in ways that are conceptually similar to the same concepts used here and in previous presentations of the same continuum. In the third place, he stressed a dialectical view that is paramount to a conceptualization of a likeness continuum that is the counter-opposition of terms defining any dimension. Curiously, in spite of using so many terms that are similar to those defining this continuum, Conville failed to use, even once, the concept of "similarity," which in a dialectical way stands in counter-opposition to difference. Nonetheless, Conville's contribution is another independent source of conceptual validation for a continuum of likeness.

Instead of presenting a figure of the curvilinear model, which has been published repeatedly elsewhere (L'Abate, 1976, 1994b, 1997b, 2002a, 2002b), this time a more differentiated view of this continuum is presented in terms of degrees of sameness, similarity, differentness, and alienation (see Figure 2-1). Here, two circles represent two persons, with the overlapping space representing the degree of involvement between them. A somewhat similar representation is found in Chapter 4 in regard to a complementary model of relationships. Symbiosis between two individuals is not shown in Figure 2-1 because it would be represented by just one circle for two completely overlapping circles. Instead, various degrees of sameness, similarity, differentness, oppositeness, and alienation are represented by degrees of darkness to represent the amount of overlap between the two circles and the number of strands connecting the two circles. The greater the overlap and the number of strands connecting the two circles, the greater is the strength of the relationship, and the more difficult it is to change it.

While contents of likeness processes according to a continuum have been described elsewhere (L'Abate, 2002a, 2000b), this time, this continuum is applied to the process of identity formation, which over time becomes developmentally additive. From the child's concept of gender and age, additional identities are developmentally added about education ("I am a first grader."), sports ("I play first base in baseball."), and hobbies ("I like stamp collecting."), alongside adding an identity about where one was born or where one lived the longest. Eventually, political and job identities may

Figure 2-1
Degrees of Self-Differentiation in a Continuum

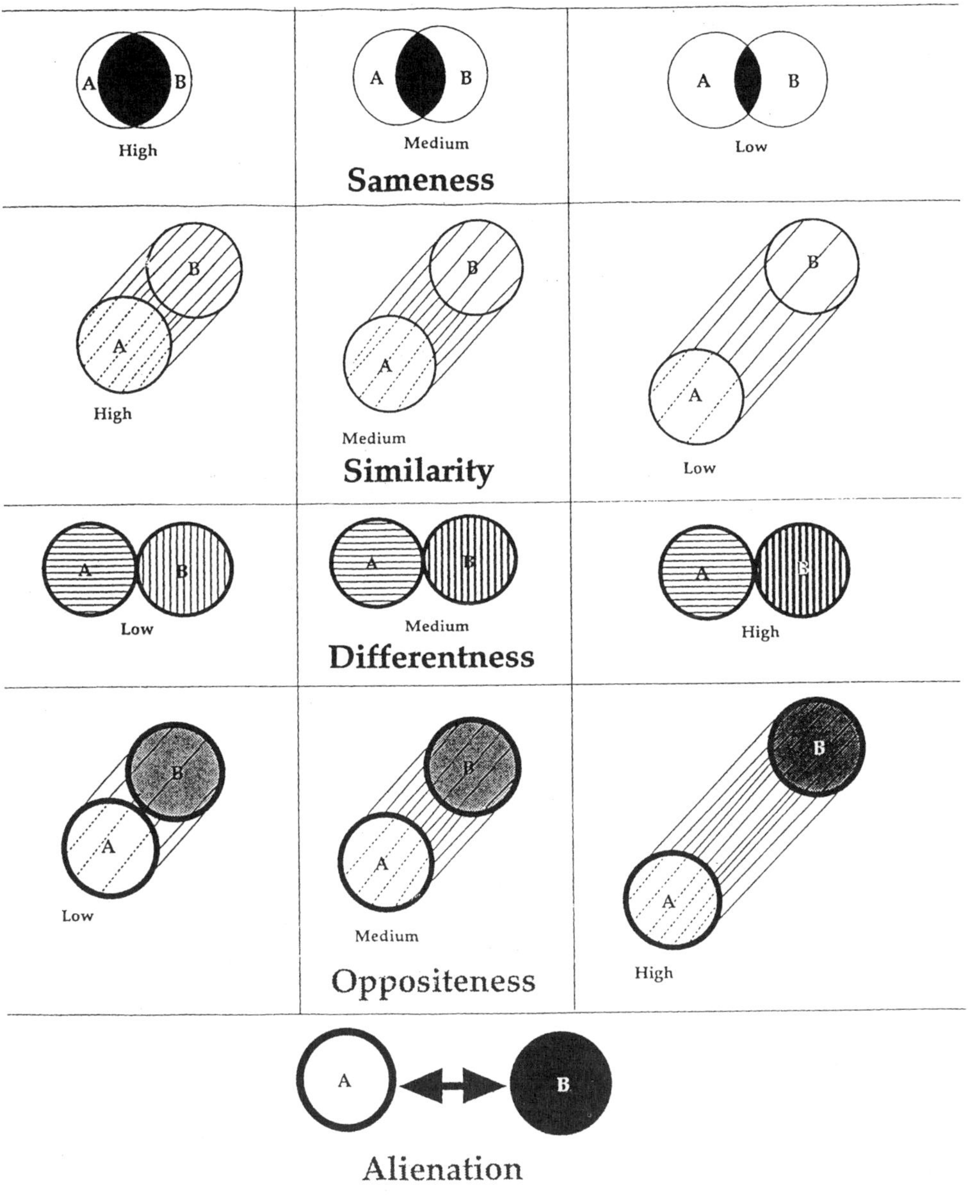

become powerful determinants of one's multiple identities and how one relates to intimates and non-intimates. A list of these identities developed over time through a process of social comparison and likeness is given below. Recently, Barnett and Hyde (2001) proposed a model (which they called "an expansionist theory"), after decrying the irrelevance of past "classical" theories because of their inadequacies in describing gender differences and work. They argued for the "beneficial effects of multiple roles" that presumably, produce multiple identities. They failed, however, to specify what these multiple identities are, a shortcoming that is satisfied below. They also indicated how many identities (i.e., roles) are related to priorities, an issue considered toward the end of this chapter (Tesser et al., 2000).

Likeness and Multiple Identities [1]

In previous publications (L'Abate, 2002a, & 2000b), a variety of relational dimensions (selfhood, parental styles, identification, reactions to authority, dependency, level of functioning, etc.) illustrated how this continuum lends itself to describe and classify a variety of interpersonal dimensions. A more recent application of this continuum relates to identities, how one defines self according to how one views oneself in comparison with intimate others. On the basis of these comparisons, we build our selves around a variety of identities (Canary et al., 1997). Our identities are indeed multiple and are the developmental outcome of additions of one identity upon another, starting with biologically constructed sex and culturally constructed gender. Some identities are individually relevant, and some are not. Which identity is more important than others is a matter of priorities and situations, as argued later in this chapter. However, it could be questioned whether one can have an identity without a role. For instance, one's place of origin may be important to someone. However, in that respect, one is not required to play nor would one want to play any role. Hence, one's identity is not always tied to the number and quality of roles that one plays.

Gender: Clearly, this is one of the first identities developed from an early age and constructs most of the following ones. On the basis of cultural stereotypes, one develops preferences in clothes, toys, mannerisms, attitudes, and expressions that, at least superficially, indicate one's gender.

Sexual Orientation/Preference: Gender, however, is not always a determinant of preferences, sexual or otherwise. Some individuals desire to have a body of the opposite sex. Some individuals prefer to dress all the time with the clothes of the opposite sex while retaining the same body. Some individuals like to dress occasionally with clothes of the opposite sex but retain their bodies and clothes match their gender (Bullough et al., 1997; Koch & Weis, 1998; Macy, 1996).

Where We Were Born: Our birthplace can be a source of identity, mixed with some pride ("I was born in an affluent neighborhood.") or, in some cases, shame ("I was born across the railroad tracks.").

Where We Lived the Longest: Where one has lived the longest may be an identity that supersedes the one developed where one was born ("I was born in Brindisi, but I am a Florentine because I lived in Florence during the formative years of my youth, and there is where my family still lives."). There are further extensions of this identity if one extrapolates from birthplace to the larger region in which the birth took place ("I was born in Brindisi, which makes me a Pugliese, which is the region surrounding Brindisi; hence, I am a 'redneck.' However, I am also a Tuscan, which is the region surrounding Florence.").

Where Our Heart Is: No matter where we were born and how long we lived in one place, there are still sentimental attachments to places that have a special meaning for us: "Even though I have lived in Atlanta the longest, making me a southern American, my heart is still in Florence."

Son/Daughter: Being the offspring can be a source of pride or of shame depending on the nature of one's parents. If one parent was an alcoholic, this origin may be a source of shame. If one parent or both were very honest, it could be a source of pride.

Brother/Sister: By the same token, depending on the character of one's siblings, this relationship could be positive, negative, or neutral. It could be a source of pride ("My sister is a college graduate.") or a source of shame ("My brother is in the penitentiary.").

Partner: The nature of one's partner could be a source of identity ("I am married to a great woman.").

Parent: Being a parent could be an identity with positive, negative, or neutral features, depending on the salient characteristics of one's offspring.

Grandparent: Being a grandparent can be an additional source of identity in one's later years. Again, this identity depends on the nature of the grandchildren ("I am the grandfather of a beautiful, smart, playful granddaughter with a great sense of humor.").

Homemaker: This role means a great deal to many individuals, mostly women, who stereotypically have been socialized in this role, taking care of the house, possessions, and intimate others. This role, however, has been taken over by some men.

Caregiver: One's role as caregiver can be a major identity in individuals who spend a great deal of time and energy taking care of housekeeping chores and responsibilities involving the welfare of intimate others.

Provider: Depending on one's success as a provider, this activity could become a source of one's identity.

Ethnic/Racial/Cultural Background: This could be a powerful source of identity, ranking perhaps next to gender in its influence on behavior, attitudes, and convictions. With the many cultural diversities present in the

United States, comparisons according to one's ethnic or racial origin may become the primary source of identity.

Religion/Spirituality: Religion, its presence as well as its absence, may rank second or third in how one defines oneself.

Education: Being a high school dropout or college graduate may make all the difference in how one views oneself.

Occupation/Work: In our culture one's work or occupation may become a primary source of identity. In cases of workaholics, it may be the major source at the expense of other identities.

Political Affiliation or Ideology: One's political ideology and affiliation are another way to define self. In some cultures, this identity, like the religious ones, may become the source of endless conflict and even warfare.

Leisure-time Activities: How one uses surplus time can become another source of identity, ranging passively from watching television to active participation in volunteer activities. These activities can be one's hobbies as well as one's sport preferences.

Hobbies: In some cases, one's avocation may overshadow one's major identity, especially if one succeeds in a hobby and is not too successful in other roles.

Sport Preference: Being actively engaged in a sport can become a strong source of identity ("I am a runner."), again overshadowing other identities.

Sport Fan: While one can be actively engaged in one sport, one can also become a passive participant in other sports. One need not be active in one sport to be fanatic about another one.

Military Identity: For many individuals, acquiring and retaining throughout their lives a military identity is a major source of self-importance.

Selfhood: Model[9]

Balance and regulation in approach-avoidance and discharge-delay functions eventually lead to a personality propensity named *Selfulness*. When approach is greater than avoidance and discharge is greater than delay, a personality propensity named *Selfishness* develops. When avoidance is greater than approach and delay is greater than discharge, a personality propensity named *Selflessness* develops. When there are extreme, inconsistent, and contradictory imbalances in both distance and control functions, a personality propensity named *No-self* develops. These personality propensities are expanded below as derivations of this model.

Here is where the meta-theoretical model about levels of observation and interpretation comes into being. People behave in different ways in different settings and at different levels of observation and interpretation. How one relates privately at home does not necessarily predict how one is going to relate in public places, school/work, or leisure-time activities. Furthermore, the resource class of importance (status) needs to be expanded into a full-fledged model concerning how the Self manifests itself. This model is needed to describe, if not explain, personality propensities that predict how individuals relate to each other in the privacy of home and not in public settings. Hence, this selfhood model assumes that attribution, ascription, and assertion of importance to self are the primary, fundamental resource exchanged among intimates as well as in non-intimates, verbally, nonverbally, and in writing.

Importance is attributed according to four personality propensities. These four propensities complete the model according to its application to intimate relationships. Selfhood in its four propensities becomes the centerpiece of exchanges between and among intimates (parents, parent–child, siblings) and non-intimates. The self is shown by how one relates to intimates in close, prolonged, and committed relationships, away from the scrutiny of occasional outsiders. The self-presentational, short-lived facade in public cannot last long and be sustained in private. Eventually, this facade will crumble to give way to who an individual really is by how he or she relates to intimate others in the privacy of one's home. It is relatively easy to make a good impression in short-lived, superficial, and even contrived relationships. It is much more difficult to behave positively, with care and concern, in the heat of prolonged closeness and familiarity.

Selfhood is evaluated in part by how close one comes toward (approach) or comes away (avoidance) from intimates and strangers (i.e., distance) and by how fast or how slow one is in discharging or delaying what needs to be said and done during such exchanges (i.e., control). As already noted, developmentally, distance turns into the ability to love, while control turns into the ability to negotiate. Functionality means a balance in distance and control functions, ability to love and to negotiate, while dysfunctionality means imbalances in both functions. Balances in distance and control functions produce a personality propensity called selfulness, leading toward personal and interpersonal functionality (Figure 2-2). In this propensity, self-importance is exchanged democratically with intimate others, where "everybody wins." When approach is greater than avoidance and discharge is greater than delay, a personality propensity called selfishness develops. In this propensity, self-importance is asserted at the expense of others ("I win, you lose."). In its extremes, this propensity leads toward externalizations and criminalities, including theft, rape, and murder. When avoidance is greater than approach and delay greater than discharge, a personality propensity called selflessness develops. In this propensity, self-importance is denied or negated, while the importance of others is asserted and affirmed ("You win, I lose."). In its extremes, it leads toward internalizations, affective disorders, and suicide. When there are extreme imbalances (inconsistencies, contradictions) in distance and control functions, a personality propensity called No-self develops. In this propensity the importance of self and other is denied and negated ("We both lose."). In its extremes, this propensity leads toward severe psychopathology. Hence, Selfulness represents the most functional level of personality socialization in relationships. No-self represents the most dysfunctional level, with Selfishness and Selflessness somewhere in between the previous two levels, intermediate as far as levels of functionality/dysfunctionality are concerned.

In this nomological network it is possible to include psychiatric, DSM-IV classification according to a theoretical framework rather than just descriptive lists of symptoms, which traditionally seemed to be put together without seeming relation among them. Instead of a categorical, descriptive classification, within this theoretical model it is possible to include symptoms that correlate with each other and that are now contiguous and continuous with each other. For instance, depression correlates higher with anxiety than with impulsivity, while impulsivity correlates higher with acting out than with measures of internalization. Instead of just a list of symptoms and syndromes, within this scheme DSM-IV becomes an aggregate of conditions that achieves meaningful continuity and contiguity with personality functioning and dysfunctioning. Instead of criminality being a separate condition from both personality and psychopathology, for instance, it is possible to see relationships among these conditions that up to the present were viewed and reviewed as separate and discontinuous from each other (L'Abate, 2002a, 2002b; L'Abate, Lambert, & Schenk, 2001).

To expand on the four propensities in their interpersonal implications, they are:

1. *Selfulness*, the positive attribution of importance to self and to intimate others, results in a positive outcome and growth in the relationship ("We both win.") because selfulness tends to balance appropriately distance and control functions and separate issues of presence from issues of power. There are at least three levels of selfulness according to how fully functioning one is in the four settings distinguished by the theory: home, school/work, and leisure-time activities. A superior personality functions fully in all three settings. An intermediate personality functions fully in two out of the three settings, while an adequate personality functions fully in one out of the three settings. Within each level, there are various degrees of functioning, varying from fully functioning to adequately functioning. Selfulness represents the positive attribution of importance to self and intimate others, resulting in positive outcomes and synergistic growth in the relationship ("We both must win together."). In Selfulness it is possible to balance appropriately distance and control, separating issues of Presence from issues of Power. Within the context of this propensity mostly functional relationships develop using a CC style.

2. *Selfishness*, the positive attribution of importance to self and the negative attribution of importance to intimate others, results in a conflictful outcome and no growth in the relationship ("I win, you lose."). Selfishness represents the positive attribution of importance to self and the negative attribution of importance to intimate others, resulting in conflictful out-

comes and no growth in the relationship ("I win, you lose."). Selfishness tends to rely more on approach than on avoidance and on discharge more than on delay at the public, presentational, and phenotypical levels. However, genotypically, avoidance is greater than approach in relation to soft, hurt feelings. Individuals characterized with this propensity tend to push limits on their partners, authorities, and anybody who lets them do that, such as seen in the pathological extremes of this propensity, like addictions and criminalities. Extremes in selfishness are therefore represented by externalizations, where the self is asserted at the expense of others, as in assaults, thefts, rapes, and murders, using an RR style, where the importance of others is denied to enhance self.

Examples of how selfish (that is, in common parlance, self-centered, egotistical, and narcissistic) individuals, usually and stereotypically men, are linked with selfless individuals (defined below), usually and stereotypically co-dependent women, are shown theoretically in Figures 2-2, 2-3, and 2-4, and clinically in Table 8-1. This match seems based on the law of "opposites attract," at public presentational and phenotypical levels of description. However, at a genotypical level, both personality propensities derive from either reactively repetitive (RR) or abusively apathetic (AA) family constellations.

Criminality is one extreme of selfishness in being characterized by its oppositeness. Maruna (2001) describes incarcerated criminals, some of them "persisters" in crime, who follow a "condemnation script" and others, "desisters," who have abandoned a criminal career through a "redemption script." The trait that was most prominent in both desisting and persisting criminals was "antiauthority" or "nonconformism" (p. 58), disliking taking orders and refusing to be obedient (p. 59), thinking of themselves as "adventurous, rebellious, and independent (p. 59). This is one of the most neglected populations by society as well as by most personality textbooks, as if personality did not also include criminality or, for that matter, psychopathology (L'Abate, 1997b). The validity of this personality propensity is supported by Baumeister, Smart, and Boden (1996), who challenged the prevailing view of "low self-esteem" in violent criminals: "Instead, violence appears to be most commonly a result of threatened egotism—that is, highly favorable views of self that are disputed by some person or circumstances" (p. 5). Egotism, of course, is another synonym for selfishness. Further evidence to support this propensity is found in the results of Arnt and Veen (2001), who reported that borderline and character disorders tended to downgrade the importance of significant others.

3. *Selflessness* represents the negative attribution of importance to self and positive attribution of importance to others, resulting in conflictful stasis in the relationship ("You win, I lose."). Sometimes this propensity is equated with altruism (Ozinga, 1999) in a non-relational context. This propensity tends to rely on avoidance more than on approach and on delay more than on discharge. Individuals characterized by this propensity are

unable to draw lines to protect themselves and their bodies ("the condom line"). This is the case of co-dependent individuals, usually spouses or partners of addicts and criminals (Jordan & L'Abate, 1995; L'Abate & Harrison, 1992). Selfless individuals tend to be gullible, loyal, and responsible, trying to make up complementarily for qualities not usually found in selfish individuals. They are nonetheless attracted to selfish individuals, just as the latter are attracted to the former, relating with each other predominantly with an RR style. In the long run, this attraction becomes antagonistic and conflictful, where either depression, suicide, hospitalization, or divorce becomes the inevitable outcome.

Another characteristic of selfless individuals is unrealistic optimism, hoping that somehow selfish partners will eventually, by some miracle, change for the better (L'Abate & Harrison, 1992). However, except for their partners, many selfless individuals are rather pessimistic about themselves, with a low sense of self-importance (Garber & Flynn, 1998). Extremes in selflessness are seen in internalizations, including anxieties, depressions, panic attacks, and affective disorders leading to suicide, either slow and prolonged as in some addictions or sudden and seemingly unexpected (Muris, Merckelbach, Schmidt, Gadet et al., 2001).

4. *No-self* represents the negative attribution of importance to self and to others, resulting in a negatively nihilistic and ultimately destructive breakdown at the personal and interpersonal level ("We are not going to win. We both must lose."). No-self results in a negative and ultimately destructive deterioration and breakdown in relationships. No-self relies on contradictory and inconsistent extremes in both distance and control functions. Extremes in no-self are represented by psychopathology, as in paranoias and schizoid and schizophrenic disorders.

This model is applicable also to a classification of personality, criminality, psychopathology, sexual deviations, and addictions, as discussed in greater detail in previous works. From the selfhood model it is possible to extrapolate to a classification of delinquency (externalizations), affective disorders (internalizations), and psychopathology (extremes in both externalizations and internalizations) (see Figure 2-2). The process of internalization for depressives and of externalization for paranoia, for example, is supported in part by the results of Kinderman and Bentall's work (1997). They found that "[d]epressed patients tended to attribute negative social events to internal (self-blaming) causes . . . paranoid individuals tended to choose external attributions that located blame in other individuals" (p. 341). Instead of categorical lists of psychiatric syndromes without any rationale, except comprehensive description and classification, this model views psychiatric categories as being integratively contiguous and continuous with each other according to a relational scheme rather than a monadic, non-relational, and categorical classification. In the past, delinquency was kept separate from psychiatric classification, while personality was

Figure 2-2
The Selfhood Model and a Classification of Personalities, Criminalities, and Psychopathologies

---

Selfulness
Superior
Creative–Conventional
Intermediate
Adequate
Impulse Anxiety
Disorders
Histrionic Dependencies
Selfishness Criminalities **Hurts** Depressions **Selflessness**
Narcissistic Personalities
Borderline Disorders
Paranoias Dissociations
Schizophrenias
No-self

---

viewed as discontinuous from either delinquency or psychopathology. Instead of personality being separate and distinct from delinquency and psychopathology, this model views these conditions according to levels of functionality versus dysfunctionality vertically and according to directionality of behavior, internal versus external horizontality (L'Abate et al., 2002a).

Intimacy, defined previously as the sharing of hurts and fears of being hurt, is possible and present in selful relationships, which are characterized by cooperative equality and helpful reciprocity. It is sporadic and present only on special occasions (funerals, baptisms, marriages) in selfish/selfless relationships. It is absent in no-self relationships. Selful relationships are characterized by successful negotiations with a minimum of acrimony and conflict and a CC style. Selfish/selfless relationships are characterized by a great deal of conflict and questionable ability to negotiate an RR style. No-self relationships are characterized by an inability to negotiate and an AA style.

This model predicts gender differences to the extent that selfulness contains equal ratios of men and women. Selfishness predicts a higher ratio (up to 5 to 1 depending on the criterion used) of men over women; more men are socialized for selfishness than women, at least in the United States. Selflessness contains a reverse ratio; more women are socialized for selflessness than men. Equal gender ratios are predicted in no-self. From these ratios the model predicts specific relationships between personality propensities and emotions, especially how to deal with hurts. For instance, in selfulness there is a preponderance of positive feelings and emotions like joy, surprise, and pleasurable intimate interactions because hurt feelings are expressed in conjunctively constructive ways. In selfishness the preponderant emotion is anger, followed by envy and hostility, usually expressed through externalizations, using others as targets and holding them responsible for the individual's behavior. In selflessness the preponderant emotions are shame, guilt, and sadness, downgrading the self as an intrapunitive target and excusing and exonerating others from responsibility. In no-self the preponderant emotions are fear, disgust, and withdrawal, with extremes between externalizations and internalizations. Hence, this model allows us to see emotions according to a theoretical model that raises questions about list theories of emotions without an underlying framework to classify them.

When this four-partite model is applied to couple relationships, at least three research studies, in addition to evidence summarized elsewhere (L'Abate, 1994b, 1997b, 2002a, 2000b), support a classification of couples according to how importance is attributed and asserted, even though different constructs and measures were used. Theoretically, a model developed by Rusbult and her associates (Bissonnette, Rusbult, & Kilpatrick, 1997) fits well into a typology of couples derived from the selfhood model. According to Rusbult's model, two major orthogonal axes of constructive-destructive behaviors and activity-passivity produce four different interpersonal outcomes: (1) *exit*, the quadrant between destructive and passive behaviors, involves separating from the partner, threatening to end the relationship, or reacting abusively, (2) *voice*, the quadrant between active and constructive behaviors, involves talking things over, suggesting solutions to problems, or asking for advice, feedback, and assistance, (3) *loyalty*, between passive and constructive behaviors, involves optimism, hoping that things will improve and that the relationship, no matter how destructive, will change, making excuses, and defending the partner in face of criticism, and (4) *neglect*, in the quadrant between destructive and passive behaviors, involves refusing to discuss matters, avoiding interaction with the partner, or criticizing the partner for unrelated matters.

By comparing this model with the selfhood model, selfulness implies constructive behaviors, as in *voice*. Selfishness implies destructive behaviors, as in *exit*. No-self implies *neglect* of the intimate other as well as self, while selflessness implies *loyalty* to the other, no matter how destructive the behavior may be. Hence, the similarities between the propensities of the selfhood and Rusbult's model seem (at least to this writer!) impressive. Two more studies tend to support generalizing from selfhood to couples. Gray-Little, Baucom, and Hamby (1996) used an independent measure of how power was shared to classify distressed couples. They found couples (1) whose power was shared in an egalitarian fashion, (2) couples where husband or (3) wife was dominant (more power to one and less to the other), and (4) couples who did not share power, producing anarchic relationships. From a selfhood model one would predict that egalitarian couples would be better adjusted than the other three types, especially couples with an anarchic pattern. A measure of adjustment (Gray-Little, Baucom, & Hamby, 1996) showed better outcome after couple therapy for egalitarian couples and worse outcome for anarchic couples, with intermediate outcomes for spouse-led or spouse-dominant couples. The same outcomes would be predicted by the selfhood model. Hence, it seems as if egalitarian couples might have been composed of selful partners. Couples where either partner was dominant would fall into the selfish/selfless propensities, semi-functional axis. Couples who did not share power would tend to fall within the no-self personality propensity.

Harter, Waters, Pettitt, Whitesell, Kofkin, and Jordan (1997) used a sample of adults between 18 and 70 years of age who responded to a newspaper survey to describe their own and their partners' styles. Each style was defined by dimensions of dominance-submissiveness, sensitivity to partner's feelings, clarity of feelings, separateness versus intimacy, and concern for the relationship. Three styles were identified: (1) self-focused autonomy, (2) other-focused connection, and (3) mutuality. Other-focused women most often reported self-focused male partners, while self-focused men most often identified their female partners as other-focused. Mutuality was characterized by similarity in style between partners, who reported highest levels of perceived validation and authentic self-behavior. Other-focused women paired with self-focused men reported lowest levels of validation and authentic self-behavior. Self-focused autonomous men paired with other-focused women fell somewhere in between the other two styles regarding validation and authentic self-behavior. The two most extreme styles, self-focused autonomy and other-focused connection, showed more liabilities than mutual couples. This typology also seems to fit well with the selfhood model, even though no fourth group was found, perhaps because there were no index of adjustment and no direct observation of behavior. Mutuality fits with selfulness, self-focused autonomy fits with selfishness, and other-focused connection fits with selflessness. A no-self group could not be found, given the nature of the methodology used in this study, which screened out possible extremes in dysfunctionality.

Settings and Selfhood

It follows from this model that settings are linked to attribution, assertion, and expression of importance toward self and others. Some individuals receive a sense of self-importance by being homemakers. Some receive their sense of self-importance from where they work and their job or occupation. Some receive their sense of self-importance from their leisure-time pursuits. According to their level of selfhood and importance (Figure 2-2), there are "superior" individuals who are exceptional in all five settings. Some individuals may be exceptional in one and mediocre in the others, creative in one pursuit but conventional anywhere else. Some, at an intermediate level, are average in all settings. Then, some are inadequate in one or more settings because of character or personality disorders. Instead of attempting to define level of personality competence through self-report, paper-and-pencil tests, it is much more accurate to evaluate individuals according to their functioning in all five settings, including how many tickets or accidents one receives on roads and highways.

Likeness Continuum and Selfhood

Relationships between the likeness continuum and the selfhood model are summarized in Table 2-5.

Selfhood Model and List Theories of Emotions

The marketplace of emotion theories is composed by what have been called "list" theories (L'Abate, 1997b) of emotions. These theories consist essentially of various lists of emotions, anywhere from 8 to 15. One reason that these lists cannot be tested comparatively is due to their very nature. Lists cannot be evaluated because there is no criterion available to evaluate them. These theories—and this is said with a great deal of respect and admiration for all of their authors—are not theories in the sense of what is understood as theory (i.e., a list does not a theory make). If a theory consists of a hierarchical structure made up by assumptions, postulates, models, and ways to evaluate the models, then these lists do not qualify as theories. They qualify eminently for what they are: lists but not theories. This is one of the reasons that these lists cannot find a criterion that allows their comparable evaluation among themselves.

Whether they claim 8 or 15 emotions, the issue is not how many emotions there are but how these theories can be evaluated, especially when the commonalities among them are greater then their discrepancies. It is not the number of emotions that counts but how these emotions are located in a nomological network. What is meant by a nomological network? This term means a model that will allow us to locate emotions in some kind of order or classification. The selfhood model allows us to place and locate emotions according to some semblance of order and classification. What does this classification of functionality/dysfunctionality have to do with emotions and their classification (rather than their simple listing)? It has everything to do with them, because in Selfulness one is most likely to find happiness/joy, surprise, interest, and desire. In Selfishness, one is most likely to find anger, disgust, hate, and contempt. In Selflessness, one is most

Table 2-5
Continuum of Likeness (Model[7]), Styles in Intimate Relationships (Model[8]), and the Selfhood Model[9]

Likeness Ranges	Styles in Intimate Relationships	Selfhood Personality Propensities	Qualities of Relationships	Interpersonal Outcomes
Similarity/Differentness	Conductive/Creative	Selfulness	Equal/cooperative Reciprocal/fulfilled Stable/growing	Affirmation Intimacy Synergism Flexibility Functionality
Sameness/Oppositeness	Reactive/Repetitive	Selfishness/Selflessness	Unequal/unhappy Sad/angry Impulsive/passive Unstable/polarized	Conflictful Semi-functional Divorce
Symbiosis/Alienation	Abusive/Apathetic	No-self	Extremely chaotic/rigid/ unstable inconsistent/ contradictory	Chronic dysfunctionality Psychosis, murder/suicide Extreme dependence

Source: L'Abate, 1994b, p. 126. Reprinted with permission.

Figure 2-3
Hurt Feelings, Distance Regulation, and the Selfhood Model

S		SELFUL		S
E		**Positive and balanced approach—Avoidance to Hurts and Self**		E
L	**Positive Approach to Self**		**Negative Approach to Self**	L
F	**Negative Avoidance of Hurts**	**Hurts**	**Collection of Hurts**	F
I	**Negative Avoidance of Others**		**Positive Approach to Others**	L
S		**Extreme, Negative, and Contradictory**		E
H		**Approach—Avoidance to Self and Others**		S
		NO-SELF		S

Figure 2-4
Selfhood Model, Expression, and Control Regulation of Hurt Feelings

S		SELFUL		S
E		Positive and Balanced Discharge—Delay of Hurts		E
L	Self-indulgence		Indulging Others	L
F	Negative Discharge	**Hurts**	Negative Discharge	F
I	against Others		against Self	L
S	Little if any delay against Others		Positive Discharge toward Others	E
H		Extreme, Negative, and Contradictory		S
		Approach—Delay toward Self and Others		S
		NO-SELF		

likely to find anxiety, sadness, and grief. In No-self, one is most likely to find distress and fear. When most lists of emotions are compared with each other according to this model, very few discrepancies among them appear, as shown in Figure 2-3 for feelings as determinants of distance regulation and in Figure 2-4 for emotions as determinants of control functions.

This model allows a classification of emotions that permits greater ease of evaluation than just a list about how many emotions we should have. Now it is possible to evaluate different list theories of emotions comparatively according to where emotions are likely to be found. For instance, using a self-report, paper-and-pencil test used to measure the four personality propensities listed above (L'Abate, 1997b), it is possible to use any measure of emotionality developed from each theory to evaluate whether this model is indeed valid or not (Thayer, 1996).

Additionally, list theories of emotions seem to miss the fact that at the bottom of all our feelings and emotions lie feelings of hurt, as discussed earlier. We all, in one way or another and to some degree or another, are hurt human beings. If we are not hurt or if we deny our ultimate vulnerability to being hurt, we are bound to hurt those who love us. How we deal with our hurt feelings, called by many authors "distress," has a great deal to do with how we relate to intimate others. We can suppress, repress, avoid, deny, and hide those feelings, clutching them inside very carefully, or we can express them verbally, non-verbally, or in writing. Their expression can occur in thoughtlessly impulsive and very likely destructive ways. It can occur caringly and positively, or it can occur much later or not at all. We may not have choices on how we are hurt by others, but we do have choices on how we are going to deal with these hurt feelings and how we are going to express them to those whom we love and who love us.

Priorities: Model[10]

All the previous models are developmental predecessors of those that follow. One model is the basis for the next one; one cannot understand this model unless he or she understands the previous ones. To understand how we allocate space, time, and energy within each setting and from one setting to another, we need to invoke the concept of priorities. This concept is motivational in nature and is similar to "goals" in the work of other theorists (Carver & Scheier, 1999; Vorauer & Ross, 1996; Zirkel, 2000). Priorities pertain to definite choices that we make about who and what are important to us in our lives to survive and to enjoy. How important is a person, an object, or an activity? How important is one's self in relation to other selves? How successful one is in any setting depends a great deal on the priorities of the individual. If one defines oneself primarily in occupational terms ("I am an engineer.") rather than domestically ("I am a husband and a father."), it follows that that person may be more successful at work than at home. By the same token, avocational pursuits may overshadow domestic and occupational roles. Most of us need to balance modalities and settings so that no one modality or setting is stressed at the expense of the others. Hence, this model of priorities is linked to the list of multiple identities given earlier, a list that finds support in the arguments of Barnett and Hyde (2001) about the beneficial effects of multiple identities, provided, however, that, according to the selfhood model, these identities do not deny the importance of identities and roles in intimate others.

In a way, the selfhood model is another way of looking at priorities. However, this model goes beyond selfhood. It includes settings and contexts within each setting. One setting can be enhanced or reduced in importance by increasing or decreasing the importance of other settings. For example, activities in the leisure arena may become antidotes for the negative effects of stresses at work or at home. How one juggles and counterbalances demands and difficulties to maintain balance in one's life reflects one's priorities. Priorities motivate people to move toward or away from other people or to negotiate or avoid negotiation with significant others over important issues in their lives. Love is not enough, just as negotiation is not enough. A person needs both to survive and to enjoy life, the two major priorities from which all the other priorities derive.

From the resource of importance, it is possible to differentiate what modalities, individuals, and settings are important to one. For instance, one individual may stress presence at the expense of performance and production, as in the case of very altruistic individuals. Another may stress performance and production at the expense of presence, as in the case of workaholics. Functional priorities stress an appropriate balance between all three modalities. Dysfunction results from stressing one modality at the expense of either of the other two or both. As far as individuals are concerned, when the self is subordinated to others (partner, parents, offspring, friends) a dysfunctionality is bound to occur. Developmentally as well as pragmatically, the importance of the self needs assertion throughout the life cycle, provided that the assertion is not obtained at anyone else's expense. If school/work is stressed at the expense of home life and its demands, either or both settings will suffer. If leisure in surplus time, after home and school/work, is valued over either setting, eventually a dysfunction will take place either in the individual, in surrounding relationships, or in both. If one spends too much time traveling from work to home (transit settings), either home or school/work is bound to suffer. If one spends too much time and energy in a transitory setting like a bar, less time is available for either home or work settings, producing conflicts at home or at work. If a student spends more time on the football field than in academics, grades might be lower.

Hence, priorities represent a motivational concept that is necessary to evaluate the ability and willingness to negotiate. This ability is a multiplicative function of (1) *skills*, represented by all five components of the ERAAwC Model and, as stressed by Vorauer and Ross (1996), the information that we need to gather about intimate others and information about how they view us; (2) *ills*, or levels of functioning of those involved in the negotiation, as represented by the ARC Model[8]; and (3) *wills*, or motivation to negotiate and priorities: what is important to those involved in the process of negotiation. Does one want to reach a successful outcome, or will one sabotage the process of negotiation because of a hidden agenda or mixed-up priorities? Does one want to negotiate with others, or does one want to pursue one's priorities regardless of and even against the opinions of intimates?

By the same token, priorities can be applied also to the ERAAwC Model. For instance, one can choose *E* at the expense of *R* and derail the whole process of development or choose *R* at the expense of *E* and again derail the same process. One needs to balance *E* with *R* and with the other components of the model. Without this balance, it will be difficult to fully use one's available assets.

Priorities become involved in the next model, where one needs to choose whether *E* is more important than *R* or other components of the ERAAwC Model and whether relying on *E* is made at the expense of the other components of the model.

Priorities can be measured easily by time analysis. How much time does one spend in each of the settings? What modality of expression for Being, Doing, or Having is being used in a primary, secondary, and tertiary manner (Juster & Stafford, 1985)? Of course, Being is much more relevant to the home setting than are the modalities of Doing and Having. They are more relevant and primary at work and in leisure settings.

Negotiation: Model[11]

Negotiation is composed of two parts, structural characteristics that determine the process of negotiation and the process of negotiation proper. Structural characteristics, ignored by a recent treatise on problem solving in families (Vuchinich, 1999), consist of (1) *authority* (who makes the decisions) versus *responsibility* (who carries out those decisions); (2) nature of the *decisions*, which can be classified according to orchestrational ones, concerning major critical choices about changing jobs, buying a house or car, versus instrumental ones about everyday routine tasks; and (3) *content* of decisions, where the three modalities of presence, performance, and production play a part. Who should carry out the garbage? What program should be watched on television? How should moneys earned be allocated? What should be bought for the holidays?

The process of negotiation involves the five components of the ERAAwC Model, either in sequence or in some kind of order, as discussed by Vuchinich (1999). In functional relationships there are usually a balance and sharing in who has the authority to make decisions and who carries them out, who makes orchestrational decisions, and who makes instrumental ones. Decision making is kept separate from being close together, and there is a fairly orderly, formal/informal, casual/planned sequence on how to express feelings (*E*), brainstorming and coming out with possible solutions and their pros and cons (*R*), how to carry out the decision that seems best for a certain period of time (*A*), with continuous feedback whether that course of action is working or not (*Aw*), and awareness of how participants reflect on how they feel about the process and contents as well as about the context (*C*), whether the process itself is taking place successfully or not. A great deal of this feedback may even be indirect or not expressly discussed, but it's there nevertheless (Vuchinich, 1999).

Intimacy as the Sharing of Joys, Hurts, and Fears of Being Hurt: Model[12]

The foregoing definition of intimacy leads to several implications and derivations in clinical practice. We cannot share joys unless we share hurts and fears of being hurt with our loved ones. This statement derives from three seemingly paradoxical conclusions:

1. We hurt those whom we love the most because they are more vulnerable to what we say and what we do than strangers. A stranger can physically hurt us, but if someone we do not know is rude or discourteous to us, we eventually forget it. We do not forget when a loved one is rude to us. Loving someone means giving that person (more often than not our partner) the power to hurt. By the same token, our partners are vulnerable to whatever we do that may be hurtful to them. This is why loving and hurting are intrinsically intertwined. There is really nothing paradoxical about this conclusion, if we conceive of the child who is spanked or punished for a misdeed and who needs to seek comfort from the very parent who punished him or her. We may forgive or be forgiven for an error. However, the painfulness of that error may still be remembered, especially if the same error is repeated.

2. We need to be separate as individuals in order to be close and together as a couple. Being separate as an individual means (1) being in charge and in control of oneself, (2) avoiding reactions to provocations or distractions from loved ones, (3) keeping focused on substantive issues rather than on tangential ones, (4) being able to empathize about a loved one's plight, and (5) being emotionally available when the partner hurts. It is important for this process of being and keeping separate to take place because it provides reciprocity. When we hurt, we want that very same intimate to be emotionally available to us. Whenever there is a loss of a family member, for instance, death of the parent of one partner, grieving that loss may be much more intense for the partner who is the child of that parent. Hence, the partner who might not be as affected by the loss as the other needs to be available to the one who is grieving more. One day in the future, the same loss of a parent may occur to the partner who is grieving less now but who will grieve more later.

3. Support, comfort, and forgiveness need to be present in ourselves as well as in those whom we have hurt or who have hurt us. This presence is the outcome of a process whereby trust and reciprocity are paramount. We need support and forgiveness from the very one whom we have hurt. The ultimate act of intimacy is demonstrated in crying together. Inflicted hurts need to be shared and forgiven and then used to improve and deepen the relationship to avoid further and future hurts.

These three conclusions also suggest that the ultimate nature of our existence is composed of:

1. Our *fallibility* in hurting those we love, in spite of our best intentions not to hurt them. Whether intentionally or unintentionally, there is always room for error even in the very best relationships: a stupid forgetting of an important anniversary; a thoughtless remark, meant as a compliment, that turns sour, as in a criticism; an unintended word that sounds offensive, and so on. We may mean well, but what ultimately counts is how what we say or do is received by our partner. Even the best intentions may not be enough, as demonstrated by the proverb "The road to hell is paved by good intentions."

2. Our *vulnerability* in being hurt by the very one(s) whom we love. We are not hurt (at least emotionally) by mere strangers, who mean nothing to us. We are much more vulnerable to the words and deeds of those whom we love because they are the most important persons to us above anyone else. They are important for our survival and for our enjoyment of life (L'Abate, 1997b). Therefore, whatever loved ones say or do becomes important. How else will they know that we love them? Once a sense of importance is attributed and imparted to the partner, anything that is said and done that detracts from that sense of importance will become hurtful. For instance, a man could tell his partner that he loves her immensely. However, if he comes home late at night drunk, this behavior would indicate that alcohol is more important to him than his partner, especially if this behavior repeats itself.

3. Our *neediness* in wanting and in giving, exchanging love from the very people whom we might have hurt or who might have hurt us. We need to love and to be loved. Very few of us deny the need to be dependent on someone who is reciprocally needy of us. Once dependence is accepted as a necessary and indispensable ingredient of intimate relationships, there are at least three possibilities: (1) both partners are extremely needy of each other but are unable to express and exchange their needs, and—contradictorily and inconsistently—deny their needs for dependency, (2) one partner is extremely needy, while the other partner denies any dependency, and (3) both partners acknowledge, accept, and express congruently their reciprocal need for dependency. This need also leaves room, however, for personal autonomy, producing, therefore, autonomous inter-dependence. The first possibility is extremely dysfunctional. The second possibility is semi-functional. The third possibility is functional.

By this process of reciprocal admission of our frailties, "faults," foibles, and failures, that is, the full admission of our humanness rather than its denial, we obtain autonomous inter-dependence, that is, reciprocal and mutual understanding that we and our partner acknowledge and admit to being as fallible, needy, and vulnerable as we are. Unless we are able to admit reciprocally to being fallible, vulnerable, and needy, it is difficult to become intimate with another human being. It takes a great deal of strength to admit being "weak." Only "strong" people can admit to being "weak."

"Weak" people find it very difficult to admit to any shortcomings lest someone take advantage of them or crucify them for their perceived or admitted inadequacies. Adequate people have no trouble admitting to inadequacies. It is much more difficult for inadequate people to admit any inadequacy.

Hence, intimacy, thus defined, because of its complexity and its paradoxical nature, can be found in well-functioning couples because they are able to express, acknowledge, and share their vulnerability, fallibility, and neediness while still loving each other unconditionally. The expression of intimacy is sporadic and occasional in semi-functional or semi-dysfunctional couples because one partner is either too dependent, on one hand, or too adamant in denying dependency, on the other. Intimacy is absent in very dysfunctional couples, who are not able to admit to any inadequacy lest these inadequacies be used against them. These couples cannot tolerate stresses of any kind, especially the admission of possible inadequacies in either partner. The denial of dependency and its extremes is found in everyday news media. Stereotypically, many men ignore and neglect their partners emotionally. Neglect is the other side of the coin of emotional abuse. This is another way to deny their own dependency on their partners. Dependency is a dirty word for many men. However, when women want to leave or do leave them, indicating in their own way that they no longer want to be dependent on their men, men typically push the limits, from harassing, to stalking, and to killing these women because "they cannot live without them any longer." Hence, under these conditions, dependency and denial of dependency become confused. Extremes are found in the murder-suicide of couples where one partner, usually the woman, cannot put up with the emotional abuse and neglect from the man any longer. These couples cannot be emotionally available to each other.

Being emotionally available means sharing both hurts and joys. The sine qua non of intimacy is reciprocity in sharing feelings, especially hurt ones. It is relatively easy to share superficial victories and triumphs. Any bar will do if you are willing to celebrate a victory in that kind of setting. It is much more difficult to share deep and lasting hurts with a loved one because this process makes us more vulnerable to the whims and will of the other. This inequality upsets the balance of power established in the couple, including the possibility of losing the partner. Admitting to hurts may be tantamount to being perceived as weak, wanting, inadequate, and incomplete. This is why many men may have greater difficulty in crying and admitting to their hurts than women. Many men are still raised in the steps of John Wayne: strong, silent, and surly, the stereotype of the macho man, that is, selfishness. We can celebrate victories in a bar, but we cannot share our defeats with our partners because, in doing so, we may feel diminished and "less than a man."

Consequently, joys cannot be shared fully unless hurts are also shared just as fully, as in crying congruently together. Unfortunately, many men see their partner's tears as manipulation. Hence, they prefer to withdraw and leave rather than feel manipulated. Without reciprocity in sharing feelings, however, there cannot be intimacy, because a one-way street in sharing feelings cannot work. Reciprocity in functional couples assumes such a sharing. In semi-functional couples, where reactivity rather than reciprocity is the norm, it is much more difficult to achieve such a sharing. It is virtually impossible to achieve it in dysfunctional couples, where abuse and neglect are the norm. Most of us want to be close. On the other hand, many of us are scared of being close, especially if we have never experienced intimacy growing up in our families of origin. Most clinical couples, for instance, do not remember seeing their parents crying together. If one parent did cry, usually the mother, the other parent, usually the father, would get mad or drunk or leave the house. An early version of this model defined intimacy as the sharing of joys, hurts, and fears of hurts, including also caring, seeing the good, and forgiveness (L'Abate, 1986).

A more elaborate version of this model includes the following dimensions (Cusinato & L'Abate, 1995; L'Abate, 2002b): (1) communicating values, (2) respecting feelings, (3) accepting limitations, (4) affirming possibilities, (5) sharing hurts, and (6) forgiving errors.

Origins of Dysfunctionality and the Drama Triangle: Model[13]

The inability to experience and express hurt feelings and fears of being hurt leads to three dysfunctional roles in intimate relationships, namely, Rescuer, Persecutor, and Victim, forming what has been called the Drama Triangle (L'Abate, 1986, 2002a). Given that triangle, there are four possible roles on how to deal with hurt feelings:

1. The Rescuer, Savior, or Saint role, trying to make things better for those who are hurting, often at one's own expense, by not valuing one's own feelings and valuing others' feelings more than one's own, leading to the personality propensity of Selflessness, already discussed.
2. The Persecutor role means inflicting hurts on others, whether intimates or non-intimates, leading to Selfishness.
3. The Martyr or Victim role, keeping hurt feelings inside without ever expressing them or, at the other extreme, exploding in a destructive manner, assuming all three roles at the same time, that is, stoic Victim, hateful Persecutor, or noble, compassionate Savior, leading to No-self.

These three roles are played out in dysfunctional relationships, with each individual switching from one role to another. A fourth alternative is played out in functional relationships:

4. The normalizing role of sharing hurt feelings with those whom we love and who love us through crying together, being together physically and emotionally, lead-

ing to Selfulness. Sharing hurts means not playing the three destructive roles and becoming sane and intimate.

Distance Regulation: Model[14]

This model is a variation on one part of Model[4] about distance rather than control regulation. In this model, there are three roles played: (1) Pursuer, who wants physical, sexual, or emotional closeness, that is, approach; (2) Distancer, who does not want some or all forms of closeness, that is, avoidance, and (3) Regulator, who is conflictful and contradictory about wanting or not wanting, needing or not needing closeness ("Come here, go away"), asking for help but finding something wrong or not helpful when help is given. This third role is usually found in depressed individuals.

Toward a Classification of Relationships: Model[15]

Riva (2001) introduced a seminal classification of relationships that was the stimulus for the one in Table 2-6. Even though he considered his framework as a method for Internet research, this framework seems valid for a classification of relationships that is complementary to the one shown in Table 2-6. He distinguished among three levels of analysis: (1) context, with frames from institutions, objects like shared history and social rules to be studied quantitatively through survey questionnaires and qualitatively through social network analysis; (2) situation, with frames from microgroups, including the social and physical environment, with their norms, roles, environmental constraints, and practices, to be studied quantitatively with survey questionnaires and qualitatively with social network analysis, interviews, and focus groups; and (3) interaction with frames from relations, actors, and artifacts, consisting of goals that include competencies, affordances, and behaviors, including also communicative ones to be studied quantitatively with individual questionnaires, quantitative interaction analyses of duration and structure, computer monitoring, eye tracking, and so on and qualitatively through speech acts, discourse and conversation analyses, participant observations, interviews, and diaries.

Relationships are a function of priorities, settings, contexts, situations, and interactions. A summary of a classification based on these variables is shown in Table 2-6. Riva (2001) has developed a similar classification for different purposes. He did not consider settings but did discriminate among contexts, situations, and interactions in a completely different fashion. Nonetheless, his classification is worthy of note and further study because he suggested how to study different interactions, a suggestion that cannot be made at this time here.

Table 2-6
Toward a Classification of Relationships: Model[15]

Priorities	Settings	Contexts	Resources	Situations	Interactions
Survival	Home	Communal versus Agentic	Importance and Intimacy versus Information Services	Intense–relaxed	Parent–child
Enjoyment	School/Work	Personal versus Impersonal	Money	Involved–uninvolved	Partner–partner
	Leisure Time	Egalitarian versus Dominant/submissive	Goods	Superficial–profound	Sibling–sibling
	Transit	Causal versus Formal		Short-lived–prolonged	Extended family
	Transitory	Intimate versus Non-intimate		Relevant–irrelevant	Friends
		Cooperative versus Competitive		Friendly–hostile	Neighbors
					Acquaintances
					Employer–employee
					Employee–employee
					Stranger–stranger

SUMMARY AND CONCLUSIONS

A theory of developmental competence derived from assumptions of space and time postulates two sets of abilities that are necessary and sufficient for functional family living: the ability to love and the ability to negotiate. The sets of skills derived from both abilities interact with five different settings: home, work, leisure, transit, and transitory ones, according to one's developmental and structural priorities. Personal competence can be understood if one looks at the setting in which it takes place and the priorities that one assigns to different modalities of expression in daily life. Love, intimacy, and the ability to negotiate with others are essential for living. They lead to different modalities of presence and power (performance and production). From these it is possible to derive testable models that seem continuous and consistent with developmental, individually oriented, monadic psychology, especially with a social psychological theory of resource exchange. These models are reducible to psychological constructs and can be verified directly and indirectly at various levels of prevention. Of course, this theory needs further theoretical and empirical refinements. Thus far, it seems (to its author) to work as a link between individual and family psychology. Others will have to judge how well it does link. Hence, there are many different ways to evaluate this theory, especially in applied and clinical practice. We define what practice means in Chapters 7 and 8.

According to this theory, interpersonal competence and personality socialization are manifested in relationships, especially intimate ones. There is a variety of models rather than one model. This is, indeed, the major difference between this theory and the model summarized in Chapter 4. While the other model may seem to lack a background theory—one model essentially summarizes the theory and is isomorphic with the theory that it represents—the models of this theory are quite a few. Both this theory and its models lead to preventive (Chapter 7) and therapeutic (Chapter 8) interventions.

NOTE

1. An introductory assignment to a workbook based on these identities is presented in Chapter 7.

Chapter 3

Evaluating the Theory

> The question is not whether hypotheses are true or false in any ultimate sense but whether the particular predictions have any utility outside the local game of truth. . . . An effective empiricism requires a posture of culturally, ethically, and politically informed pragmatism. (Gergen, 2001, p. 808)

To explain the title of this chapter, instead of indulging in theoretical musings, it is necessary instead to insert a historical introduction that will, in part, explain how relationships can be improved in respondents at a distance from, and without direct contact with, a mental health professional. Improvement at a distance from respondents can take place provided one uses standard operating procedures in evaluation and in writing in the hands of subprofessional and paraprofessional personnel with the support and supervision of a professional. Initially, practice rather than theory was the basis for evaluating this theory. Eventually, however, theory grew from practice and evolved over time (L'Abate, 1976, 1986, 1990, 1994b, 1997b, 2002a, 2000b).

The theory is composed of both demonstrable and dialectical models, some probably non-testable, some testable and, in some cases, tested. Evaluation of these models has taken place in the laboratory through self-report, paper-and-pencil tests measuring the ERAAwC, Likeness, Relationship Styles, Selfhood, Priorities, Intimacy, and Drama Triangle models (see Table 3-1). In primary prevention, the abilities to love and to negotiate have been evaluated through enrichment programs administered to functional and semi-functional couples and families (Chapter 7). In sec-

Table 3-1
Validation of a Contextual and Developmental Theory of Relational Competence in the Family and Other Settings

Models	Tests (Chapter 3)	Enrichment (Chapter 7)	Workbooks (Chapter 7)	Tasks (Chapter 8)
Meta-theoretical Assumptions				
Horizontality				
ERAAwC Model[1]	Relational Answers Questionnaire (RAQ)	Negotiation Potential	Negotiation	
Verticality				
Levels of Observation/Interpretation: Model[2]	to be evaluated			
Theoretical Assumptions				
Space (distance) & Time (control) regulation: Model[3]	WATMTIAW?			
Ability to Love		Helpfulness and intimacy	Intimacy	
Ability to Negotiate Power[4]				
Modalities[5]			Assignment in Negotiation	
Settings[6]	Time estimates			
Theoretical Models				
Likeness Continuum & Self-differentiation[7]	Likeness Scale Likeness Grid WATMTIAW?		Who Am I?	
ARC: Styles in Relationships[8]	PIRS	Negotiation Potential	Negotiation Assignment	f2f interviews
Selfhood & Personality Propensities[9]	SOPC, PIRS, DRT		Self-Other Co-dependency	Drawing lines
Priorities[10]	Grid, Inventory	Negotiation Potential	Negotiation Assignment	
Negotiation[11]			Negotiation	
Intimacy[12]	SOHS	Helpfulness	Intimacy	Sharing hurts, 3HC
Drama Triangle[13]			Depression Assignment	
Distance Regulation[14]			Depression Assignment	
Classification of Relationships: Model[15]		to be evaluated		
Integration of Models: Model[16]		partially evaluated (Ch. 5)		

WATMTIAW = "What Applies to Me That I Agree With?" (Appendix B); PIRS = Problems in Relationship Scale; SOPC = Self-Other Profile Chart; DRT = Dyadic Relationships Test; SOHS = Sharing of Hurts Scale.

ondary prevention, assumptions and models have been evaluated through mental health workbooks (L'Abate, 2002a, 2000b, in press-b). In tertiary prevention or psychotherapy, three tasks have been used to evaluate this theory clinically, in face-to-face (f2f) verbal contact rather than empirically: (1) sharing of hurt feelings in couples, (2) drawing lines in co-dependent individuals, and (3) hugging, holding, huddling, and cuddling in couples and families (Chapter 8).

As already argued in the previous chapter, theories can be evaluated in three ways: (1) comparing them with conceptually similar theories and models that are, however, independent of a theory itself, as already done in the previous chapter; (2) indirectly, using the evidence for theories and models that furnished the background for some models of the theory; and (3) directly, evaluating the validity of the models derived from the theory. For instance, many constructs indigenous to the theory, like love, negotiation, selfhood, priorities, and intimacy, can be found easily in the extant literature. However, in this regard, the only criterion of face validity is the conceptual similarity of theory-related constructs with concepts found in other theories or models that are independent of this theory. These comparisons have been made in previous publications already cited.

Hence, the theory can be evaluated statically and statistically in the laboratory through test instruments, as well as dynamically through applications in primary, secondary (Chapter 7), and tertiary prevention (Chapter 8) approaches.

THE LABORATORY METHOD IN CLINICAL PSYCHOLOGY

Over the last third of the past century, the first author was involved in an enterprise called the Laboratory Method in Clinical Psychology (L'Abate, 1964, 1968a, 1968b, 1969a, 1973), which served as the basis for subsequent, preventive and therapeutic work to improve intimate relationships. This method was set up as an attempt to (1) lower costs of mental health practices, (2) find more cost-effective ways of service delivery, (3) link clinical practice with research, and (4) develop theory on the basis of practice. Part of the motivation for the creation of this method was strictly practical. How can a professional help as many people as possible per unit of time at the lowest possible cost without sacrificing standards and criteria of responsible practice? Consequently, the first writer became convinced, initially, that the best way to help people at risk for personal, marital, or family breakdown and in need of help was to work at a distance from them through intermediaries (L'Abate, 2002c).

This hierarchical approach is no different from other existing structures in human enterprises, be they businesses, medicine, construction, or even war. The reason for these structures is efficiency. Architects and engineers cannot build skyscrapers with their bare hands. After designing the blueprints of a skyscraper, a host of specialized personnel with different skills is necessary to carry out the actual work. There is no way we are going to help all the relationships at risk or in need through face-to-face contact with individual professionals (Chapter 11). There are too many intimate relationships at risk and in need to think that this goal can be achieved only by qualified professionals. Forthofer et al. (1996), for instance, estimated that "work loss associated with marital problems translates into a loss of approximately $6.8 billion a year" (p. 597). If one extrapolates this figure to individuals and families, the loss may be 10 times as much.

Consequently, we need to rely either on subprofessional and paraprofessional personnel or on even more efficient ways to reach troubled intimate relationships than through the therapeutic format of one-respondent/one-therapist, be that respondent an individual, a couple, or a family. This format may be necessary with relationships in crisis. However, for every relationship in crisis there are at least four or five other relationships at risk or in need that need some kind of preventive intervention (L'Abate, 1990; L'Abate, Farrar, & Serritella, 1992; L'Abate & Thaxton, 1981). There are not enough professionals trained or interested in preventive work to deal with so many troubled relationships. Hence, different and cost-effective approaches are needed to reach and help them. In addition to intermediaries, distance writing and computer-assisted training, among other approaches (L'Abate, in press-a, in press-b; L'Abate & Odell, 1995), will allow us to get the job done (Chapter 11).

Evaluation as the Cornerstone of the Laboratory Method

Evaluation has always been one of the two tracks of theory-building (L'Abate, 1983, 1985a, 2002a, 200b). One track did not go ahead of the other, but *pari passu*, both at the same time. Actually, evaluation as a standard operating procedure preceded theory-building, as discussed below. This method started in St. Louis Children's Hospital by creating a psychodiagnostic laboratory that included three levels of expertise: (1) the director, a doctorate-level licensed, board-certified clinical psychologist, responsible for running the laboratory, training and supervising para- or subprofessional personnel, writing psychodiagnostic reports, and consulting with medical and professional staff (mostly pediatricians and neurologists), (2) a graduate student responsible for administering standard intelligence tests (Wechsler Intelligence Scale for Children [WISC], Stanford-Binet) and the Rorschach and other projective techniques; and (3) a group of part-time volunteer paraprofessionals trained to administer and score the Draw a Person (DAP), the Peabody Picture Test, the Columbia Intelligence Test, the Benton Figure Retention Test, and Sentence Completion, while taking careful notes of a child's responses to each test. Different test batteries were created to take into account age differences (approximately 3 to 5, 6 to 12, and 13 to 16 years of age). These volunteers were eventually supplanted by full-time diagnostic technicians.

From a small number of children during the first year of operation (circa 1960), over the next 20 years, this laboratory was able to evaluate thousands of children. From an estimated cost of $120.00 (in 1963 dollar value) for each psychological evaluation, the cost was brought down to $34.00. Each test battery was administered fully with no shortcuts or short forms in the administration of each test.

After the first writer moved to Atlanta, he was able to set up three psychodiagnostic laboratories, in the Psychology Department at Georgia State University, in the Pediatrics Department of Emory Medical School at Grady Hospital, and at Aidmore Children's Hospital. Using this method, he was able to evaluate about 10 children per week in about one day of his time. This experience has been described elsewhere (L'Abate, 1990). This method was not set up on a theoretical basis but strictly on practical grounds. This practice, however, did yield a theoretical input-output diagnostic model (L'Abate, 1969b, 1971, 2002a) that convinced this writer about the importance of the receptively experiencing-outwardly expressing continuum not only in intelligence (L'Abate & Wildman, 1979) but also in emotionality and personality socialization and interpersonal competence, as already highlighted in the previous chapter.

Evaluation of individual children, couples, and families (L'Abate, 1969a, 1994a; L'Abate, et al., 1975), therefore, became the cornerstone of the laboratory method. However, evaluation without re-evaluation may become futile unless one is responsible for the whole process of evaluation-intervention-re-evaluation, and follow-up. Evaluation for evaluation's sake may be needed when responsibility for intervention is in the hands of another professional, who might not be interested in evaluating the final outcome of the intervention. As a clinical psychologist, however, it mattered to the first writer to find out the final outcome of any intervention for which he was responsible, even and especially at a distance from respondents. Consequently, the laboratory process was then applied to play therapy, an intervention that was then (L'Abate, 1973, 1979) and is still in dire need of research approaches.

The Concept of Structure: Standard Operating Procedures

The concept of structure as well as the laboratory method are basic for an understanding of preventive programs to improve intimate relationships. Not much has been written on this concept since Baer (1982), as far as this writer knows. Rather than structure in responses, however, the concept of structure applies to what stimuli are imposed and offered to whoever wants and needs psychological services. We cannot control the responses of other people. However, we can control what stimuli we administer to them, as we do in testing. Why should we not do the same in our interventions? Briefly, a structure of standard operating procedures is needed in providing cost-effective, preventive, psychotherapeutic, and rehabilitative psychological services to evaluate their outcome. Hence, standard operating procedures need to be followed not only in evaluation but also in interventions, with post-intervention evaluation as part of this structure and process. To obtain such a structure, one needs to distinguish clearly between technical, paraprofessional, and professional skills and responsibilities. Administering an intelligence test, for instance, may take one hour and a knowledge of its manual to administer it, a technical skill. However, evaluating the results of this test takes a great deal of knowledge about the statistical properties of the test and its relationship to organic and psychological conditions, a professional skill.

The values of structure were discussed more than a quarter of a century ago (L'Abate, 1976, pp. 206–207) in terms of their advantages, not only in evaluation but also in interventions:

1. Structured methods of intervention can be used with larger numbers of individuals, couples, and families than with unstructured techniques or approaches.
2. Structured methods can be used preventively.
3. Structured methods can be used propaedeutically.
4. Structured methods can be administered by subprofessional intermediaries.
5. Structured methods are cheaper than unstructured methods because of (a) a wider range of applications to large numbers of respondents and (b) handling by subprofessionals whose time and availability are greater than those of professionals.
6. Structured methods belong to the demonstrative realm, allowing replication and more control and, therefore, direct testing of theoretical expectations.
7. Unstructured techniques or approaches, on the other hand, belong to the dialectical realm, making them more difficult to replicate and to evaluate.

Differentiating between Technical and Professional Skills

In evaluation, technical skills consist of the administration and scoring of test instruments, while professional skills consist of the interpretation of test battery results, reporting psychodiagnostic results, and recommendations to clients and referring professionals. This conclusion is based on two axes of time and knowledge. Technical skills, like the administration of an intelligence test, take more time but less knowledge than the knowledge necessary to interpret that test. Professional skills, like the interpretation of results from an intelligence test, take less time but much more knowledge about the empirical background of the test, its statistical properties, its research results, and so on. Paraprofessional skills may be limited to advanced graduate students supervising beginning graduate students in the administration of standard enrichment programs with the support and supervision of the professional (Jessee & L'Abate, 1981). DeLuca (1989; DeLuca & Putman, 1993) has advocated the use of technicians in neuropsychology, following L'Abate's (1964) original suggestion.

Once this differentiation is applied to preventive interventions, technical skills consist of the administration of structured interventions found in enrichment programs and programmed materials, involving keeping in touch with respondents and reporting to a supervising professional (Chapter 7). These technicians need to have people skills to establish and maintain rapport with respondents as well as responsibly administering materials with complete notes for the supervisor's consumption. Professional skills consist of abilities in (1) crisis intervention and symptom reduction, (2) decision making about different interventional approaches, and (3) training, support, and supervision of technical personnel.

Hence, to test the theory directly (Table 3-1), a variety of paper-and-pencil, self-report tests have been validated to verify some of the models derived from the theory (L'Abate, 1976, 1994b, 1997b, 2002a, 2002b; L'Abate & Wagner, 1985, 1988).

EVALUATION OF MODELS

As models of the theory evolved over time, various instruments and even test batteries were developed to evaluate them. Results from previous research have been reported in past publications cited above. Hence, this chapter is devoted to more recent results from ongoing research, most of it directed by Mario Cusinato with his collaborators and students at the University of Padua and performed also by Eleonora Maino and her coworkers at the Nostra Famiglia Center in Bosisio Parini, Italy.

In addition to descriptive functions, summarizing complex and elaborated patterns, as already discussed in Chapter 2 and in previous publications, models fulfill at least two other important functions: (1) diagnostic, that is, putting a label that classifies, synthesizes, and specifies the nature of a condition, and (2) in this way matching interventions with specific diagnoses. As shown in the rest of this chapter, each model in its own right points specifically to whatever is functional and dysfunctional in relationships. Even if results apply to responses of single respondents, rather than couples or families, as in most studies reported here, extrapolations to intimate relationships are possible once the instrument representing a model produces clear differences between functional and dysfunctional respondents. Therefore, if results are diagnostically valid, they should serve as blueprints for direct preventive and psychotherapeutic interventions, as elaborated in Chapters 7 and 8.

ERAAwC: Model[1]

Cusinato (personal communication, August 15, 2001) and his students in research in progress have developed a visual "Good Star" model with an instrument called Relational Answers Questionnaire (RAQ) consisting of 10 items for each of the five spokes of the model (L'Abate, 2002a, p. 196). The final, seventh version of this test uses the most reliable items culled from about 300 items administered to thousands of respondents. Respondents answer each item formulated as an assertion on a five-point Likert scale (5 = always, 1 = never) on how one sees things and not how one would want them to be. Raw scores are calculated for each subscale and transformed into standard scores using conversion tables established on the basis of past pilot studies. Cronbach's alpha coefficients to assess the reliability of the five scales, based on 515 respondents of both sexes (Corsi & Colombi, 2002), were, respectively: $E = .81$; $R = .85$; $A = .74$; $Aw = .63$; $C = .74$.

Cusinato is involved in replicating these results with his students. To evaluate the construct validity of each component of the model, items defining each component are paired with scales developed by other investigators that measure the same component. For instance, the scale for Emotionality is paired and administered with other measures of emotionality. Items for Rationality are paired and administered with scales measuring cognitive functioning and rational problem-solving. Items measuring Awareness are paired and administered with other measures of Awareness, like other tests, developed by North American investigators and translated into Italian.

Historically, of course, these instruments represent the five major theoretical schools reviewed in the Preface and Chapters 1 and 2, where ERAAwC encapsulates what have been and still are considered major aspects of behavior seen horizontally, on a flat surface, so to speak. The guiding hypothesis for the development of this instrument (L'Abate, 1994b, 1997b, 2002a, 2002b), in addition to answering the question about the intra-psychically internal bases for relating with intimate others, including self, lies in predicting that functional respondents would use all five variables (components, dimensions, resources) of the model, while dysfunctional respondents would stress one or more variables at the expense of the other variables. Put another way, functionality represents evenhanded reliance on all five variables, representing a varied and flexible repertoire of internal resources. Dysfunctionality, on the other hand, is represented by a more limited and lopsided repertoire that relies more rigidly on fewer internal resources while other resources are avoided, either ignored or unused, repressed, or suppressed.

Functional Respondents

In a preliminary report with 124 university students (Cusinato, personal communication, November 3, 2001), age and sex were significantly different in four scales except *R*. On *E*, women achieved significantly greater scores than men ($F = 41.65$, $p < .001$). On *A* and *Aw*, men achieved significantly greater scores than women ($F = 6.25$, $p < .01$ and $F = 4.73$, $p < .03$, respectively). On *C*, women achieved significantly greater scores than men ($F = 5.74$, $p < .02$). Significant ($p < .05$ or better) correlations among the first four variables were found in a pilot study (Mario Cusinato, personal communication, February 19, 2002) that analyzed results separately for men and women. A significantly ($p < .01$) negative correlation was consistently found between *Aw* and *C*, suggesting that the more restricted the *Aw* the greater is the stress on *C* (i.e., the environment). This finding could support a hypothesis that externalizing individuals, who might be more restricted in their awareness, may be more alert to external, environmental cues, especially those with threatening qualities. By the same token, individuals who are high on *Aw* may concentrate on themselves and internal cues, thus avoiding looking at the environment for cues. In 245 men, *E*, *R*, and *A* correlated significantly with each other, while *E* correlated significantly with *R*, *A*, and *C*. *A* correlated significantly with *Aw*. In 260 women, *E* correlated significantly with *C*. *R*, *A*, and *Aw*, while *A* correlated ($p < .5$) negatively with *C*.

These differences would stereotypically support stress on communal (i.e., emotional) factors in women and agentic factors in men. However, as discussed in Chapter 12, sex and gender similarities and differences need to be considered within the context of the selfhood model and levels of functionality-dysfunctionality.

Colombi (2002) administered the RAQ to 515 non-clinical respondents, 207 males and 308 females in four different age groups (14–19, 20–30, 31–40, and 41–60), to evaluate the internal consistency of this instrument and to establish whether it would distinguish among developmental patterns. An analysis of variance (ANOVA) found significant interactions between age and *E* [$F(3) = 24.79$; $p < .001$], *R* [$F(3) = 22.35$; $p < .001$] and *A* [$F(3) = 20.59$; $p < .001$], but no interactions with *Aw* or C. When sex was introduced in ANOVA as a main effect, it demonstrated significant interactions with *E* [$F(1) = 168.65$; $p < .001$], with *Aw* [$F(1) = 7.14$; $p < .01$] and C [$F(1) = 8.47$; $p < .01$]. When age and sex were introduced together, R showed a significant interaction with *E* [$F(3) = 6.57$; $p < .001$] and smaller interactions with *R* [$F(3) = 2.83$; $p < .05$] and *Aw* [$F(3) = 2.81$; $p < .05$]. All five variables correlated positively with each other ($p < .001$) except negatively for *A* with C ($p < .05$) and C with *Aw* ($p < .001$). In males, a significantly positive ($p < .01$) correlation was found between *E* and *R*, which was not present in the whole sample, with *C* continuing to show a significantly negative correlation ($p < .001$) with *Aw*. In females, *E* was correlated positively ($p < .01$) with *Aw*, which in turn correlated negatively ($p < .001$) with *C*. Hence, one could conclude that *E* is more relevant to females than to men, who, relatively speaking, tend to stress *A* more than *E*. When correlation analysis was applied to age groups, some interesting age differences were found that suggest more confused and less self-regulated views in teenagers and young adults, while clearer and more balanced patterns among the five variables appeared in the two older groups.

Corsi and Scilletta (2002) replicated the study summarized above by administering both the RAQ and the Self-Other Profile Chart (SOPC) to 435 respondents stratified according to ages 14–19, 20–30, 31–40, 41–60 and divided into 184 men and 251 women. Overall correlations for the whole sample were positive and significant ($p < .01$ or better) for *E* with *A*, *C*, and Others. *R* correlated positively ($p < .01$ or better) with *A*, *Aw*, *C*, and Self. *A* correlated negatively with *C*, while *C* correlated positively with Others and negatively with Self. As usual, *Aw* correlated negatively with *C*.

In males, *E* was correlated positively with *A* and *C*, while *R* correlated positively with *A*, *C*, *Aw*, and Self. *C*, of course, correlated negatively with *Aw*. There were no correlations between any of the five variables with Others.

Women showed a different correlation matrix. *E* correlated positively with *A* and *C*. *R* correlated positively with *A*, *Aw*, and *C*. *A* correlated negatively with *C*, which in turn correlated negatively with *Aw*, by now an established outcome. *C* correlated positively with Others and negatively with Self, a result that would support the possibility that women are more concerned with relationships, while men are more concerned with themselves. In their extremes, both tendencies would explain greater selfishness for men and greater selflessness for women. There were also interesting differences among the age groups that support the importance of age as an independent variable in relationships. What is more relevant is the relationship between the RAQ and the selfhood model, as shown by Corsi's separating respondents into the four personality propensities and correlating them to the five variables of the RAQ. In this ANOVA analysis, *E* was found as a main effect [$F(312) = 3.90$, $p < .01$] for Selfishness and No-Self personality propensities, while *R* produced main effects [$F(412) = 2.37$, $p < .05$] for Selfullness and Selflessness. A Scheffe multiple comparison test showed that differences among mean scores were marginally significant ($p < .05$), with Selfishness > No-self, and Selfulness > Selflessness.

An ANOVA between the RAQ and the two measures by the Self-Other-Profile-Chart (SOPC), Self and Others (an instrument to be described below), produced significant main effects between Self and *E* ($F = 2.72$, $p <$

.06), *R* ($F = 6.58$, $p < .002$), *A* ($F = 5.71$, $p < .004$) and *Aw* ($F = 3.56$, $p < .03$). Others was related only to *E* ($F = 3.40$, $p < .03$) and minimally with *C* ($F = 2.56$, $p < .09$). Implications of the results from these studies for competence socialization in age, gender, and other independent variables (education and socio-economic levels) await further empirical evidence before arriving at definite conclusions.

If valid, these results would suggest that men tend to attribute importance to Self through rational processes, while women tend to attribute more importance to Others within the confines of *C*, which also would suggest an external rather than internal orientation. These differences are in line with the prediction of the selfhood model that men might be more Self-oriented than women, producing Selfishness in extreme cases, while women, if indeed they are more Others-oriented, may tend toward Selflessness in extreme cases.

Additional information about results from the RAQ was obtained by Nardin, Gallo, Carubolo, Fabrizio, and Aquario (2002) in a preventive program designed to evaluate the outcome of emotional coaching with 46 couples. A Parenting Styles Questionnaire comprising 20 items measuring the three major parental roles of (1) Emotional Coach, (2) Judge, and (3) Dismissing Parent was administered with the RAQ. Both tests were administered before and after administration of an enrichment program focusing on the three parental styles (L'Abate & Weinstein, 1987).

On pre-test, *A* correlated ($p < .01$) with *R*, which correlated ($p < .05$) with *Aw*. The latter correlated ($p < .001$) negatively with *C*, indicating that this is a consistently stable and significant pattern, already found in the two previous studies reported above. The only possible relationship between the RAQ and Parental Styles was a suggestively negative but small correlation between *R* and the Judge role. On retest, *E* and *A* did not correlate with any other variable, while *C* continued to correlate ($p < .001$) negatively with *Aw*, which in turn correlated ($p < .05$) with *R*. This time, *Aw* was highly correlated negatively ($p < .001$) with the Coaching role, which in turn correlated ($p < .01$) negatively with the Dismissing role. These results suggested that there were changes in the constellation of variables due to training in the emotional Coaching role.

Dysfunctional Respondents

Further evidence for the validity of the RAQ was reported by Franzoso and Modica (2002) using a sample of 55 male and 5 female drug addicts between the ages of 14 and 60 matched with normal (non-clinical) controls on gender, age, education, and civil status (married vs. non-married). In the experimental group of drug abusers both *E* and *R* were not at all correlated with the other three components of the model, indicating that these respondents cannot or are unable to rely on either *E* or *R* as resources in their lives. *R* was correlated ($p < .05$) with *Aw* and with significant Others, as measured by the SOPC. *C* correlated significantly but negatively ($p < .001$) with *Aw*, replicating the negative correlations found in previous studies, while ratings of Self-importance from the SOPC correlated ($p < .05$) with Others.

A different constellation of correlations was found by Franzoso and Modica in their control, non-clinical respondents. *E* correlated significantly ($p < .001$) with *A*, which in turn correlated ($p < .05$) with *R*. *R* correlated significantly ($p < .001$) with *Aw*, which in turn correlated negatively ($p < .001$) with *C*. The only connection between the RAQ and the SOPC was found between *E* ($p < .05$) and Others. The latter correlated significantly ($p < .001$) with ratings of Self-importance. Hence, these results, thus far, would suggest that drug addicts are unable to use their internal resources, especially *E* and *R*, while functional respondents tend to use a web of relations among all the components of the model.

Salvo and Radoni (2002) studied self-importance and relationship competence in eating disorders, taking off from predictions from the selfhood model that in psychosomatic disorders, delay is greater than discharge, and avoidance is greater than approach. Hence, they represent one extreme of internalization. This study aimed at investigating further and discussing this perspective using data obtained from 32 respondents with eating disorders (specifically, anorexia and bulimia) who were referred to the Eating Disorders Centre of Portogruaro Civic Hospital (Venice, Italy) and who were motivated to start a therapeutic intervention. They were administered the SOPC and the RAQ. Their mean scores on both tests were compared with those from the same number of non-clinical respondents matched for sex, age, educational level, and marital status. It is relevant that in the experimental sample there were 31 women and one man, reversing the ratio found by Franzoso and Modica with drug addicts, where men outnumbered women by a ratio of 10 to 1. This reversal is in line with the prediction from the selfhood model that acting-out externalizations would include more selfish men than women with an overall ratio of 5 to 1, depending, of course, on what criterion is used. This ratio would be reversed in eating disorders composed mainly of selfless women, as in this case.

Salvo and Radoni (2002) found that in experimental respondents *E* was not correlated with any other variable, while *R* was correlated ($p < .01$) with *A* and no other variable. *A* was correlated negatively ($p < .01$) with *Aw*, which in turn, predictably, was correlated negatively ($p < .001$) with *C*. There was a slight trend for *R* to correlate with Others. Non-clinical respondents showed a completely different matrix of correlations. *E* correlated positively ($p < .01$) with *A*, *Aw*, and *C*. *R* correlated ($p < .01$) positively with *C*, which, in turn, no longer surprisingly, correlated ($p < .001$) negatively with *Aw*. There were no correlations between the ERAAwC variables and the two aspects of the SOPC, Self and Others, an interesting outcome that needs further replication and explanation.

Verzolato, Cristante, and Salvo (2002) studied self-importance levels and relationship competence in females suffering from affective disorders. Their decision to study people suffering from affective disorders sprang from suggestions offered by L'Abate (1997b), who made this specific statement:

> Disorders of internalization, including depressions, fears, phobias, obsessions, and anxieties, can be accounted for by the developmental competence theory. Internalization refers to any disorder in which the individual keeps inside whatever is hurting, without acting out or expressing any hurt outwardly and directly acting in, so to speak. Internalizing individuals are unable to speak about whatever past hurts may have undermined their sense of self-importance. The prototypical condition for internalization is chronic, refractory depression characterized by powerlessness and . . . by demoralization, hopelessness, suicidal ideation, impairments in social adjustment . . . a self-medicating pattern of substance abuse, and suicide. (p. 236)

This study involved 40 clinical females (mastectomized, affected by anxiety, climacteric women asking for psychological support) and the same number of non-clinical females (matched by age and socio-cultural status). The clinical subgroup was recruited in the psychological service of Portogruaro Civic Hospital (Venice, Italy). Respondents were administered the SOPC, the RAQ, and the Minnesota Multiphasic Personality Inventory (MMPI). Results from correlations among these instruments will be reported in future publications and discussed to highlight theoretical implications and the clinical pictures corresponding to subgroups with different functionality levels, so that this information can be useful in giving therapeutic support and bring about a more satisfactory relational climate within the family.

Implications of Results

As indicated at the outset of this section, the results from the studies summarized above support the three major functions of models as (1) summaries of more complex patterns, (2) diagnostic in clearly differentiating between functional and dysfunctional respondents, and (3) blueprints for preventive and psychotherapeutic interventions. These results support construct and concurrent validities of the RAQ and of the model underlying its construction. Functional respondents, indeed, tend to use all five components of the model without preference for one component at the expense of the others. Dysfunctional respondents, on the other hand, clearly show deficiencies in how to avoid *E* and sometimes *R* in dealing with relationships.

Levels of Observation/Interpretation: Model[2]

This model has not been evaluated directly because no instrument or method has as yet been devised to evaluate it, except for social psychological research on impression formation and management at the presentational level. It should be compared empirically with evidence from studies on impression formation and maintenance at the presentational level with measures of repression and avoidance of hurt feelings at the genotypical level.

McMahan and L'Abate (research in progress) are analyzing results from a quantifiable, structured Social Information Form with items concerning family background, personality characteristics, and marital adjustment in 45 seminarian couples. This study would add information to the relationship between historical explanatory background factors and specific genotypical personality factors, as measured by various instruments. Most evidence about linking presentational with genotypical levels comes from impressionistic, clinical accounts suggesting the possibility of such a link. Most reports about shame (Gilbert & Andrews, 1998), for instance, also indicate how shame can take place at various levels of awareness, some of them unacknowledged and some completely outside the awareness of shamed individuals. Relationships between these levels and the other models will give ample room for future investigations.

Settings: Model[3]

This is still a dialectical model based on indirect evidence derived from time studies of how people spend their time. This evidence is reviewed in greater detail below in regard to evaluating the Priorities Model[10].

Assumptions of Distance and Control Regulation: Model[4]

The most important function of this model, in addition to description, diagnosis, and intervention, lies in its linking the whole theory to psychoneurological functions, hemispheric dominance, and the nervous system in general (L'Abate, 1997b, 2001a). This and most models of the theory can be evaluated now with the multi-modeled "What Does Apply to Me That I Agree With?" questionnaire, which is contained in Appendix B. This questionnaire, however, has not yet been subjected to empirical verification. It is appended here to facilitate its use for anyone willing to apply it for research only and not yet for clinical purposes.

Ability to Be Together: Model[5] and Ability to Negotiate Power: Model[6]

These models were evaluated through assignments in a workbook, as described in Chapter 7.

Likeness: Model[7]

The continuum of likeness had been evaluated in the past with two global instruments, the Likeness Scale and the Likeness Grid (L'Abate & Wagner, 1985). Another, more specific instrument, "What Applies to Me That I Agree With?" contained in Appendix B, has been designed to evaluate it with a paper-and-pencil self-report. From this continuum can be derived another Model[8], the ARC that stands for two dysfunctional styles, Abusive-Apathetic (AA) from the two extremes of the likeness continuum, and the Reactive-Repetitive (RR). A functional style Conductive-Creative (CC) derives from the combination of Similarity with Differentness. These three styles are observable from any face-to-face (f2f) interview with clinical and non-clinical respondents.

Likeness and Selfhood

Cusinato, Ambrosini, and Pastore (2002), on the basis of a factor analysis of the SOPC, which found two factors for Self and two factors for Others, as described below, combined the six steps of the likeness continuum with the items in Self and Others. Qualities that were thought to be important to the self (horizontal axis) were combined with individuals (vertical axis) who were considered as contributing to the sense of Self-importance according to a range of six levels of similarity, ranging from symbiosis ("Exactly like me"), sameness ("Very much like me"), similarity ("Somewhat like me"), differentness ("Different from me"), oppositeness ("The opposite of me"), and alienation ("Like no one else"). After some trials with paper and pencil, this combination was computerized online and administered to hundreds of respondents, as described in greater detail below.

Selfhood: Model[9]

The selfhood model has been subjected to many forms of validation over the years (L'Abate, 1994b, 1997b, 1998b, 2002a, 2002b) and produced at least three different tests: (1) the Problems in Relationships Scale (PIRS, L'Abate, 1992; McMahan & L'Abate, 2001); (2) the Self-Other Profile Chart (SOPC, L'Abate, 1997b); and (3) the Dyadic Relationships Test developed by Cusinato and his students (1997). The latter is summarized below. A more detailed paper about the latter has been submitted for publication (Cusinato & L'Abate, 2002).

Conceptually, this model finds a great deal of similarity with Aron and Aron's (1996) self-expansion model. They substantiated five hypotheses about relationships between the self and intimate others that expands on the selfhood model in its four propensities:

Hypothesis 1. Cognition about self versus other is on a continuum from self through close others to non-close others.

Hypothesis 2. This continuum is produced by the extent to which close others are "included in the self."

Hypothesis 3. Developing a relationship expands the self by including other in the self.

Hypothesis 4. People are motivated to enter a relationship by the perceived opportunity to expand the self.

Hypothesis 5. Changes in relationship satisfaction over time are linked to changes in experiences of, and perceived opportunities for, self-expansion in the context of the relationship.

Unfortunately, the self-expansion model has not been expanded as yet (no pun intended!), as far as the first author knows, to include extreme or clinical cases, a possibility that would severely limit the scope of the model. This shortcoming is not present in the selfhood model to the extent that it does cover functional, semi-functional, and dysfunctional relationships.

Self-Other Profile Chart (SOPC)

An independent finding that is relevant to the expansion of the selfhood model to the DSM-IV classification of psychopathology was reported by Johns and van Os (2001). They reviewed evidence for the continuity of psychotic symptoms with normal experiences, focusing especially on symptoms of hallucinations and delusions. Their conclusion supports the selfhood model's dimensional continuity and contiguity of psychopathological experiences rather than being composed of discretely separate entities discontinuous from normal experiences:

> Several sources of evidence indicate that psychosis exists as a continuum of experiences with a distribution in the general population. The implications of this evidence suggest that it may be rewarding to further incorporate the notion of a psychosis continuum in scientific research and clinical practice. (p. 1137)

This conclusion supports an expansion of the selfhood model to include all of the diagnoses included in the DSM-IV (L'Abate, 2002a; L'Abate et al., 2001) into one integrated whole that views functionalities and dysfunctionalities as continuous and contiguous extensions of the four personality propensities, Selfulness, Selfishness, Selflessness, and No-self.

The Self-Other Profile Chart (SOPC, L'Abate, 1992, 1997a) was designed to test directly the selfhood model by rating personal qualities, to be listed below, on a five-point Likert scale that contributed to a sense of self-importance in the present, past, and future. Significant others, to be listed below, are also rated on a five-point scale for how much they contributed to a sense of self-importance in the present, past, and future. This test takes a few minutes to administer and to score. Its construct and concurrent validities have been reported elsewhere (L'Abate, 2002a) and in

Chapter 5. To test the four personality propensities derived from the selfhood model, scores are cut at the median of Self and Others distributions (high-low). In this way, it is possible to obtain High Self/High Others = Selfulness, High Self/Low Others = Selfishness, Low Self/High Others = Selflessness, and Low Self/Low Others = No-self.

In a first factor analysis of the taxonomic structure of the SOPC, Pastore and Bertuola (1999), with 198 advanced psychology students (184 women and 14 men), found two factors for Self and two factors for Others. The first Self factor was loaded with school achievement, work, physical appearance, sport activities, intelligence, and creativity. The second factor was loaded on sense of humor, morals, and self-esteem. The first Others factor was loaded on partners, mother, father, siblings, and children, representing the family. The second Others factor was composed of friends, buddies, coworkers, and acquaintances.

Cusinato and Pastore (2001) administered an Italian revised version of the SOPC adapted for most ages to 1,166 respondents between the ages of 14 and 41+. A factor analysis of the data produced two factors for Self and two factors for Others, replicating only in part Pastore and Bertuola's results. The first factor for Importance to Self was composed of academic success, work performance, intelligence, creativity, morality, and self-esteem. The second factor was composed of physical appearance, sport activities, and sense of humor.

They distinguished these two factors by linking them to levels of interpretation ($Model^2$), with the second factor relating to the self-presentation and the first factor relating to the genotypical level. Others were separated into one factor composed of partner, mother, father, siblings/cousins, children, and friends. The second factor was composed of schoolmates, coworkers, and other acquaintances.

Maino (personal communication, February 14, 2001) replicated the same study by administering it to 824 respondents of all ages from a control rather than an experimental group. She used the oblimin method, hypothesizing a correlation between Self and Other. She then switched to the varimax orthogonal rotation method. In both methods, she found a variance of 29.2% for both Self and Other. Since saturation did not seem clear, she attempted to extract factors using the screen test of Cattell. At an eigen value > 2, she obtained five factors that are responsible for 46.2% of the variance. She used both oblimin and varimax methods. In both analyses, factorial saturations were well defined and high for almost all the items of both Self and Other dimensions.

According to the oblimin method, the five factors were as follows:

Factor 1 was composed of intelligence, creativity, sense of humor, morality, and, partially, self-esteem, aspects that compose the genotypical level of the individual.

Factor 2 related to partner, children, and, in part, work performance, aspects that include the individual's priorities, where the family is primary and work is secondary.

Factor 3 was composed of mother, father, and siblings in the family of origin.

Factor 4 was composed of friends, schoolmates, coworkers, and other intimates that compose the individual's social network.

Factor 5 related to physical appearance, sport activities, and, in part, work performance and self-esteem, aspects that speak to the public level of self-presentation.

Using the varimax method, Maino found essentially the same factors, with the same saturations but in a somewhat different order: (1) social network, (2) family of origin, (3) genotypical aspects, (4) family of procreation, and (5) phenotypical aspects. It should be mentioned that her respondents were all married adults with children, and not college undergraduates.

Selfhood and Likeness

Cusinato and Ambrosini (2002) made the relationship between Likeness and Selfhood even tighter. Instead of using the RAQ as in the previous research, they combined the Self and Other scales together by asking respondents to rate how Others were similar to the various attributes of the Self according to the six points representing the six ranges of the Likeness Continuum, described above. They administered the computerized version of the SOPC, Self and Others to 236 adolescents and to 168 psychology major undergraduates. They divided the sample into three groups: Group 1, respondents from 15 to 17 years of age, Group 2, respondents from 18 to 20 years of age, and Group 3, respondents from 21 to 27 years of age.

Scilletta (Claudia Scilletta, personal communication, May 4, 2002) was responsible for the administration of the SOPC according to the likeness continuum to the adolescents, while she, Ambrosini, and Cusinato were responsible for administration of the two tests to the fourth-year undergraduates attending a course in psychology of the family. Initially, the sample was composed of 168 students, decreasing to 104 on retest. Scilletta divided her sample into three age groups (15 to 17; 18 to 20; and 21 to 27). Respondents in Groups 1 and 2 were administered the computerized forms connecting Likeness and Selfhood according to how similar Others were to self-attributes on a pre-post basis without intervention. Both forms were administered to undergraduate respondents before and after group discussions and workbook completion or after workbook completion alone.

Undergraduates agreeing to participate in a study for class credit were divided into three groups. Group 1 was composed of discussion groups of 10 to 12 members led by a student chosen as leader by the group but supervised by Cusinato, who was teaching the course. They had to attend class. These groups met for eight sessions of one and one-half hours and had to keep notes about their experiences during group meetings. These notes were given to a class secretary, who then transferred them to each group leader, who then summarized these notes into one final report.

Group 2 was administered a workbook relating to family psychology and attending class. The workbook consisted of eight weekly assignments designed to foster reflection about qualities and persons who were important in one's life with concrete illustrations of these relational experiences. Each assignment was to be answered in writing at a stated time, lasting for about one hour each week. Completed assignments were given to the teacher, who read them to determine class credit and final grade, but were given back to respondents to safeguard privacy and confidentiality.

Group 3 attended class and was not asked to either answer test forms or any of the other tasks required of the other two groups.

To evaluate the outcome of workbook and discussion interventions, only those students who were retested, 104, were included in the final analysis of the results.

Scilletta (2002) found statistically different mean Self scores between groups 1 and 3 but not for groups 1 and 2. She did not find any differences among the three groups in mean Other scores, not even when she analyzed her data from one year to the next. These results suggest that there are developmental changes in the sense of self-importance with no changes in how adolescents and young adults perceive intimates who, according to them, contributed to the development of a sense of self-importance. Once that sense is given and received from Others, it seems to remain the same over time without any change with age.

Test-retest scores for the two experimental groups are shown in Figures 3-1 through 3-4, showing the evident reliability for individual scores, most if not all of them centered around the Selful propensity. The results shown in these figures are relevant on two counts. In the first place, they show the reliability of individual scores from test to retest and from one group to another. In the second place, they all center around the Selfulness quadrant, which is to be expected in a relatively well functioning population. These scores are in contrast to those obtained from clinical samples, as shown in Chapter 5.

The Others items were compared statistically with Self qualities according to a non-parametric, contrast analysis (Keppel, 1991) that has allowed finding whether there were significant relationships between similarity and oppositeness (the three scores on similarity, symbiosis, sameness, and similarity were collapsed into one similarity score, while the three scores on differentness, opposition, and alienation were collapsed into one oppositeness score). Significant values were found between attractiveness, athletic ability, and morality with relevant Others, usually Mother and Father. Results from the post-test showed a significant decrease in the level of simi-

Figure 3-1
SOPC Results for 55 Undergraduate Students

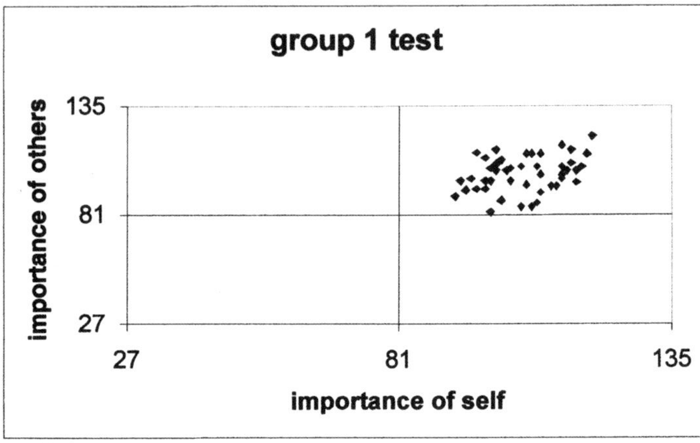

Figure 3-2
SOPC Results for 48 Undergraduate Students

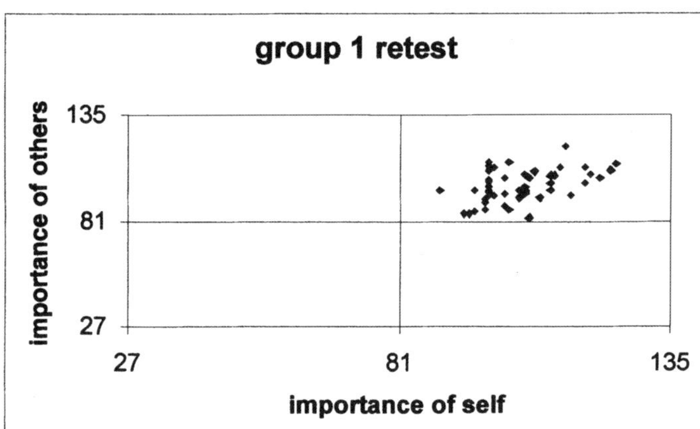

larity or opposition. These trends would suggest a greater degree of differentiation as a result of either group discussion or workbook completion. This important study combines primary prevention (group discussion) and secondary prevention (workbook) with undergraduates that is worthy of replication.

It is important to underscore (Claudia Scilletta, personal communication, April 30, 2002) that in comparing the three age groups, Self-differentiation grows as a function of age, when affirmation of Self-importance seems increasingly necessary. This finding seems especially relevant in primary

Figure 3-3
SOPC Results for 42 Undergraduate Students

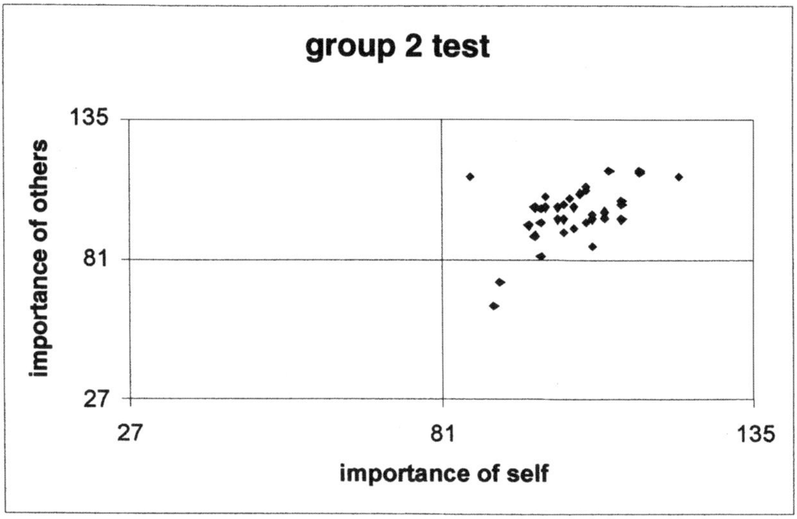

Figure 3-4
SOPC Results for 40 Undergraduate Students

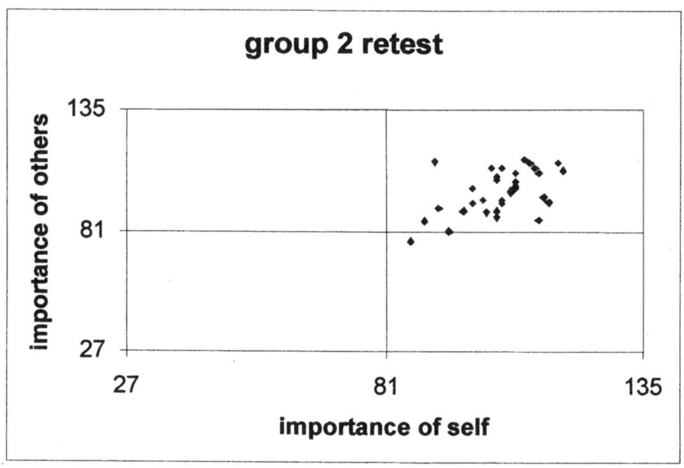

prevention to help struggling adolescents become more aware of possible deficiencies in their sense of Self-importance. Especially when there is too much stress on Self-importance at the expense of Others, as in Selfishness, or too little sense of Self-importance, as in Selflessness, let alone No-self extremes, early identification of extremes might allow targeted interventions that may prevent these extremes to reach dysfunctional proportions in adulthood.

> Significant values were found between attractiveness, athletic ability, and morality with relevant Others, usually Mother and Father. Results from the post-test showed a significant decrease in the level of similarity or oppositeness, which decreased at a statistically significant level ($p < .01$) in "physical attractiveness" and "athletic ability."

This outcome would suggest that the workbook and group discussions favored a lowering in tendencies toward oppositeness in external qualities. Another interesting aspect of this research lies in the decrease in likeness in internal qualities, as in the case of intelligence and sense of humor in regard to likeness with Father and schoolmates, in creativity in regard to schoolmates, and in morality in regard to the major part of significant Others.

These results also suggest that through targeted interventions, like workbooks, it would be possible to lower levels of oppositeness as well as of dependency from significant Others. When high levels of likeness reach symbiotic proportions, the possibility of future dysfunctionalities could remain high unless preventive interventions take place as soon as identification takes place, especially with adolescents. Given the crucial importance of this research and its results, its replication would appear not only necessary but imperative.

Dyadic Relations Test: A Decade of Research

During the last decade, Cusinato and his students and collaborators have been involved in evaluating models from L'Abate's contextual, developmental, and interpersonal theory of intimate relationships. One model that seems pivotal to the whole theory is Selfhood, already summarized in Chapter 2. To evaluate the validity of this model, relying in part on the notion that a picture is worth 1,000 words, as well as experiences of solely visual tests developed originally by L'Abate and his collaborators (L'Abate & Wagner, 1985), Cusinato developed the Dyadic Relations Test (DRT). This instrument was created to evaluate couple relationships in their functional and dysfunctional aspects (1) by relying on both visual and verbal vignettes, (2) by being seemingly well accepted by respondents, (3) by being easy to administer and score, and (4) by research on its psychometric properties (validaties and reliabilities) that were found to be within acceptable statistical parameters. Results give information and interpretation not only for couples together but also for individual determinants of the relationship functionality or dysfunctionality.

Construction of the Instrument

An early edition of this instrument consisted of 10 stimulus situations for pre-marital couples. Each situation included (1) two introductory lines of the relational situation, (2) a picture of partners in the foreground talking with each other, (3) representative elements of the situation in the background, (4) a few words, as in comic strips, from one partner who represents the presenting issue requiring a response from the other partner, and (5) close to the vignette, four possible answers that correspond to the four personality propensities of the model. Later on, an analogous form for married couples was developed. The first trial of this instrument with married, non-clinical couples showed that the test is not only well accepted but also felt as being non-intrusive, allowing a certain degree of identification with the two figures depicted in the vignettes. The test can be administered in about 15 minutes. The final edition of this test contains one vignette with the introductory question and four possible answers.

A third version of the same test was developed for couples with a child in school that evolved eventually to six different forms of the same test to cover all the six stages of the family life cycle, empty nest, old age, and so on. Each form has 12 vignettes for each particular stage.

Psychometric Properties of the Instrument

Thus far, there have been approximately 20 research studies about the psychometric properties of this instrument. Recent factor, discriminant, correlational, and item analyses, using data from all 720 respondents from previous studies, reproduced the presence of a major, common factor, attribution of importance with four propensities predicted by the model. However, the data in regard to some propensities required further investigation. There are negative correlations between Selfulness and Selfishness and positive correlations between Selfulness and Selflessness. Test-retest reliabilities for all propensities were all highly significant ($p < .001$).

Concurrent Validities

We were struck by the similarities between the selfhood model and the four attachment styles predicted by the model developed by Bowlby and researchers around the world (L'Abate, 1994b, 1997b). This model has been evaluated in thousands of studies, proposing four styles with intrapsychic rather than relational characteristics: (1) secure, (2) avoiding, (3) preoccupied, and (4) fearful. These characteristics seem similar to the four personality propensities, respectively, Selfulness, Selfishness, Selflessness, and No-self. They could be conceived as the internal, therefore inferred representations of external and visible relationships.

In parallel with the development of the DRT, Cusinato and his students have developed a paper-and-pencil, self-report test containing items translated and adapted for Italian respondents from English-language attachment questionnaires. This test has been used in various studies that showed interesting correlations between the four attachment styles and the four personality propensities. The scale measuring a secure style correlated positively with Selfulness and negatively with an avoiding style, and Selflessness correlated positively with a preoccupied style, while Selfishness correlated also with an avoidance and fearful style.

These results suggested a link between the two theoretical models that specific internal models correspond to specific personality propensities. Whether these propensities predict specific relational styles remains to be seen. Other studies focused on the following topics, using the DRT in conjunction with other instruments: (1) conjugal and parental styles; (2) discriminant and concurrent validity in specific relational contents, such as resources in fathers and mothers; (3) resources of temporary families prior to adoption; (4) emotions and relational life in retired couples; (5) intimacy and communication in married couples; and (6) the usefulness of the DRT in evaluating psychoeducational interventions.

On the basis of these studies and results obtained from them, the DRT seems useful in understanding and following the evolution of couple relationships, also lending validity to the selfhood model and, more distantly, to the theory on which this model is based.

Intimacy: Model[12]

Cusinato (1998) revised the Sharing of Hurts Scale, developed by Stevens and L'Abate (1989), to expand it to the hypothetical factors formulated by Cusinato and L'Abate (1995). They conceptualized couple intimacy beyond self presentation in terms of a seven-factor, circularly spiral model containing (A) relational realism, which deals with how real both partners are in presenting themselves, (B) communication of personal values, (C) respect for personal feelings, (D) acceptance of personal limitations, (E) promotion of potentialities, (F) sharing of hurts, and (G) forgiveness of errors, then going back to a revised communication of personal values.

A pilot study with 82 couples produced the following test-retest correlations: A = .63**; B = .51**; C = .33*; D = .42**; E = .50**; F = .76**; and G = .66** (* $p < .01$; ** $p < .001$).

Cronbach's alphas of internal consistency for the same factors were A = .74*; B = .36; C = 40; D = .25; E = .22; F = .57*, and G = .34. Only the values for A and G were acceptable. Consequently, split-half correlations provided more satisfactory results: A = .63**; B = .29*; C = .42**; D and E did not reach significance, while F = .43**, and G = .36 (* $p < .01$; ** $p < .001$).

A factor analysis of the data yielded five recognizable factors, while a regression analysis showed a circular spiral for factors A, D, and E.

A second study with 41 married couples and with their undergraduate children replicated the findings of the first study, yielding all highly significant ($p < .001$) test-retest correlations for both parents but not very high alphas for internal consistency and highly significant ($p < .001$) split-half correlations. Regression analysis showed significant gender differences. A factor analysis replicated the five factors found in the first study.

A third study based on a revision of items to improve internal consistency with 60 couples yielded the following Cronbach's alphas: A = .62*; B = .45; C = 68*; D = .52; E = .70*; F = .62*; and G = .58. Split-half correlations were all highly significant ($p < .001$) except for B ($r = .23$, $p < .01$) (* $p < .01$; ** $p < .001$).

A fourth study, with 166 couples, again yielded highly significant alphas and split-half correlations.

On the basis of these results, Cusinato constructed a couples workbook based on the seven factors of the hypothetical model validated by the four studies.

Multiple Validation of Various Models of the Theory

Maino (2002) conducted one of the first studies where multiple models of the theory were evaluated concurrently. The objectives of this research with families with a handicapped child were to (1) study the impact of genetic diagnosis on parents as partners and family relationships, (2) identify if there are specificities in the reactions of parents and family relations in families with a malformed child in comparison to families with a child not affected by a genetic disability; (3) identify if there are specificities in the reactions of parents and in the reorganization of family relations connected to the type of transmission of the syndrome in the child (neomutation versus recessive or dominant transmission); (4) locate effects on individual parents and on family relations with particular attention to the couple relationship in the communication of the diagnosis of a genetic type; and (5) intervene with a small group of parents with the malformation syndrome using a structured workbook approach focused on the couple relationship.

To reach those objectives and evaluate the impact of the diagnostic information given, the following self-report instruments were administered relevant to the individual personality of partners: the SOPC, the RAQ, Couple Commitment, Optimistic Attitudes, Couple Social Desirability, the Conjugal Intimacy Scale, and the Family Environment Scale.

To achieve the objectives of this research, data from the following samples of respondents were obtained: (1) an experimental group of 40 couples with a child between 1 and 16 years of age with a a diagnosis of malformation syndrome coupled with mental retardation; (2) an experimental group of 15 couples with a child between 1 and 16 years of age with a non-genetic disability with mental retardation, as in infantile cerebral palsy; (3) a control group of 247 couples with healthy children with at least one child between 1 and 16 years of age.

These three groups were paired according to most demographic variables except presence/absence of disability and genetic versus non-genetic type of disability.

Data analyzed with ANOVA and multiple step-wise regression showed statistically significant differences among the three groups, not only as far as personality propensities were concerned but also for relational variables. In greater detail, as far as personality was concerned, ANOVA showed how couples with a malformation syndrome tend to respond to events with a modality of answers centered on Rationality more than couples in the control group ($p = .03$), at the time adopting answers centered on Emotionality more than couples with a cerebral palsy child ($p < .04$).

This result was confirmed by multiple regression analysis. In the control group the important feedback role of awareness around all the variables considered in the evaluation battery was upheld. In couples with a malformation syndrome child the fundamental role of Rationality affected all the other personality variables as well as the presence of less regulated Emotionality than in couples with a child with infantile cerebral palsy.

As far as relational aspects centered on couple relationships are concerned, ANOVA evidenced a greater capacity to express to the partner one's feelings ($p < .03$), greater capacity to share hurts ($p < .0001$), and a tendency toward major capacity to forgive reciprocal errors ($p < .041$), from couples with a malformation syndrome child in comparison to control couples. Furthermore, this analysis indicated greater effort from parents with a malformation syndrome child to accept the partner's limitations ($p < .05$) and to value potentialities ($p < .034$) in comparison with couples with a cerebral palsy child. Nonetheless, on this matter, multiple regression analysis evidenced the important positive influence on the stability of the relationship in couples with a malformation syndrome child and the value of reciprocal valuing. Perhaps this finding is a way of contrasting the fact that partners with a malformation syndrome child are somewhat more implicated than couples with cerebral palsy children.

This last variable seems to indicate greater fear in regard to deeper intimacy on the part of respondents in the control group in comparison to the two experimental groups. Finally, there emerged the presence of a less conflictual climate ($p < .03$) in the couples with a genetic disability child in comparison to control couples. Additionally, this climate appears closer ($p < .05$) and less conflictual in couples with a malformation syndrome child on the basis of genetic tests rather than on the basis of clinical evidence.

It is relevant to note (Maino, 2002) that the two models ERAAwC and Intimacy seem to work with each other synergistically, as shown in families with a cerebral palsy child, where *E* is more open in comparison to the other groups and where sharing of hurts seems more frequent, rendering the couple relationship much more stable. In the families with a malformation syndrome child, on the other hand, *R* is stronger and seems to serve as mediator with *E*, where one finds greater valuing of the partner, a pattern requiring notable rational effort.

CONCLUSION

The results presented above tend to support the validity of test instruments derived from some models of the theory. These results, added to those presented in previous publications (L'Abate, 1994b, 1997b, 2002a, 2002b), tend to support the validity of these models and, consequently, of the theory behind them. Nonetheless, these results confirm the theory's validity only in the laboratory and by investigators involved with the first author. It is a question whether these models can be evaluated by uninvolved researchers in their applications with non-clinical relationships. This question is answered in part in Chapters 7 and 8.

Chapter 4

A Model of Relational Styles

The Elementary Pragmatic Model (EPM) was first proposed in the English language by De Giacomo (1993, 1995). A review (L'Abate, 1994a) commended its author for a specificity previously not achieved by existing and traditional systems theory. The latter has been criticized for its vagueness and generality, failing to specify what kind of interactions take place in families as well as outside families (L'Abate & Colondier, 1987; L'Abate & Jurkovic, 1987). Moyer (1994) is just one of the many critics who leveled these charges over the last decade. Additional references critical of systems theory can be found in L'Abate's review (1994a).

The EPM was created to expand cognitive functioning and awareness through 16 interactive styles. It owes its existence to two schools of thought, "relationism" and general systems theories. Consequently, it belongs to what is now called "systems optic." It is also, to some extent, related to "connectionism," from which it naturally flows into the neural networks concept. It does differ from that concept owing to the greater complexity of its basic elements, namely, its 16 functions or 16 interactive styles. Its basic features are similar to those of general systems theory. It was first utilized as a clinical tool in the areas of interactive therapy and psychiatry. However, at present it can be usefully employed also to develop and expand creativity.

In this chapter, the model's 16 interactive styles have been translated into 16 possible mental states, corresponding to 16 different angles, points of view (angulations, constructions, formulations, translations, representations, configurations) by which the mind can think and can solve problems skipping from one angle to another. Of these 16 "functions" (i.e., mental states and interactive characteristics), 8 belong to convergent thinking (logical, consequential, orthodox) and 8 to divergent thinking (unconsequential, amplifying, paradoxical). The latter are more suitable to develop creative thinking.

This interactively relational model was designated as elementary pragmatic because it deals with elementary interactions in which separate bits of communication are exchanged. More precisely, these are Shannon's (Shannon & Weaver, 1964) original triads: (1) first subject's proposal, (2) second subject's proposal, and (3) result of the interaction. The model refers to behavioral aspects of communication that reflect behavioral changes, hence, the "pragmatics" of communication.

The EPM came into being to develop relational concepts in a coherent manner. In particular, it starts from the assumption that the mind is not in the objects—in our case, inside people's heads—but in relations, contacts, and communications. Incidentally, the equivalent for relationism inside people's heads (e.g., in the brain) is so-called connectionism, upon which neural networks are based.

Basically, the purpose of this model is to provide a key for understanding and classifying aspects of the social world, other than the ones that our mind uses every day, more or less consciously. However, as Korzybski (Chapter 1) would say, this map is rather a short, basic introduction to a poor version of reality. Models, by the same token, could impoverish reality. However, it is equally plausible to argue that they also enrich it. It is the spirit of this model to allow those who use it to recognize occasionally certain aspects of this reality that would otherwise be left without understanding or explanation. Obviously, that does not mean that the model claims to replace in any way all that is natural and traditional in the process of comprehending the world. To observe relationships around us in a different manner means to be able to act upon them in a different manner. Indeed, the main purpose for creating the EPM was to help during preventive and psychotherapeutic interventions. As time went by, the model could also be usefully applied for reading much more general social phenomena and as a tool for predicting how events could develop in theory, quite apart from the work of a mental health professional.

In spite of the second author's insistence in calling the EPM a "model," the first author, acting in an editorial prerogative, maintains that it is in reality a theory to the extent that it does have four levels of construction, in the same way as the theory reviewed in the previous chapter: (1) two assumptions, (2) two postulates, (3) 16 models, and (4) 256 interactions.

ASSUMPTIONS OF THE EPM

Shannon's triad (see Figure 4-1) provides the starting point for this way of reading: first subject's statement, second subject's statement, and result

Figure 4-1
The Triads of the Elementary Pragmatic Model

[1]Obviously, during the interaction there is a perfect correspondence with the other subject. However, in order to evaluate how the latter changes, his or her functions must be read horizontally, not vertically.

of the interaction. Necessarily and inevitably, this triad leads to the definition of four interactive modalities presented in Figure 4-2.

Postulates of the EPM

The EPM is based on the four possible modalities that derive, for instance, from A's (husband) and B's (wife) interaction. This interaction is made up of elements that form the content of the shared (common) worldview of participants in an interaction: (1) internal-external to one's world, (2) internal-external to the other's world, (3) what is not common to either one, and (4) whatever is common between the two (see Figure 4-3).

Thus, in addition to the four assumed dimensions, the two other major dimensions of this model are internality versus externality and common versus uncommon ($4 \times 2 \times 2 = 16$). The process of changing as the result of mutually coming together forms four coordinates of the model:

Coordinate No. 1. Something that did not exist in the husband's world but existed in the wife's world is accepted in the interaction. For instance, when the husband says, "I don't want to watch TV," the wife replies, "Come on, in a little while a great program will be on." As a result, the husband acquiesces to his wife's proposal, and he watches television.

Coordinate No. 2. Maintenance of one's own world, occurring when something that existed in the husband's world but did not exist in the wife's world is accepted. For instance, when the husband suggests, "I want to watch TV," and the wife instead replies, "I want to go out," but she nevertheless acquiesces and watches television.

Coordinate No. 3. Sharing of one's world with another when something existing in both the wife and husband's world is accepted. For instance, the husband says, "Tonight I want to watch TV," and the wife replies, "Me too, dear" and they both watch television.

Figure 4-2
Shannon's Triad

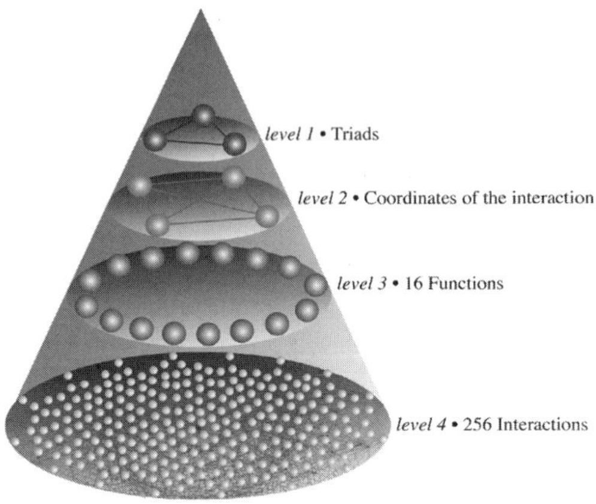

Shannon's triad: How much and how do we change?

Shannon's triad characterizes, both qualitatively and quantitatively, a subject's response as he/she impinges upon another. Such a response can be defined as

1. something that did not exist in the world of the subject, or of a given set, and that is accepted in the interaction with the other.
   (0 1 → 1 = acceptance);
2. something that existed in the subject's but not in the other's world and that is maintained in the interaction
   (1 0 → 1 = maintenance);
3. something that existed both in the subject's and in the other's worlds and that is accepted in the interaction
   (1 1 → 1 = sharing);
4. lastly, there is the paradoxical possibility that something that did not exist in either's world is accepted
   (0 0 → 1 = antifunction)

—world of art, of folly, creativity, humor, etc.

SISCI 1 is a good example of how Shannon's triad can be used in a test: a person is shown Holtzman's 90 inkblot figures (Rorschach type) and is then asked to choose which of the 90 figures he/she prefers. The slides are then administered again in an interactive fashion and the first person is shown which of the 90 figures were chosen by most subjects (or by the spouse, or by another significant person). Subsequently, in a further presentation, the first person is asked to reselect which of the same 90 figures he/she likes best.

A comparison between the final choice (after interacting with the other) and the first choice (before the interaction) shows the percentages of:

- acceptance (0 1 → 1),
- maintenance (1 0 → 1),
- sharing (1 1 → 1), and
- antifunctions (0 0 → 1)

that are specific in a given relation.

Figure 4-3 shows the modalities of possible interactions according to the typology considered in our model. The area between heads represents the "synapse" between two subjects (or between two sets).

Figure 4-3
Communication Coordinates

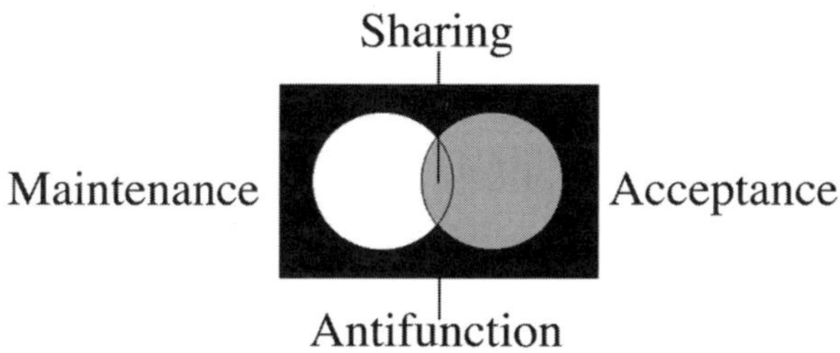

011 Acceptance
101 Maintenance
111 Sharing
001 Antifunction

Communication Coordinates

This figure shows the four basic modalities of communication:

- acceptance, which occurs when something is accepted in the interaction that did not exist in the subject's world (or in that of a set, broadly speaking), but existed in the other's world (0 1 → 1);
- maintenance, which occurs when something is accepted in the interaction that existed in the subject's world (or in that of a set, broadly speaking), but not in the other's world (1 0 → 1);
- sharing, which occurs when what exists in one's own or in the other's world is accepted (1 1 → 1);
- antifunction, which occurs when what does not exist either in one's own or in the other's world is accepted (0 0 → 1).

In the upper part of the figure the same four possibilities are represented according to the Venn diagrams:

—the left circle represents the first subject's world;

—the right circle represents the second subject's world;

—the intermediate part represents the intersection (the area that is common to both circles);

—the area outside the circles represents what does not exist in the two subjects' worlds.

Coordinate No. 4. Antifunction, which represents acceptance of a proposal that is neither in one's nor in the other's world. For instance, when the husband says, "I do not want to watch TV," the wife replies, "Neither do I," but they both nevertheless end up watching television.

These four modalities (acceptance, maintenance, sharing, antifunction) are the components of 16 interactive styles (i.e., of 16 functions). These 16 functions are a logical classification of possible human interactions. Each function derives from the composition of the four triads that correspond to the four basic coordinates. In order to offer a more convenient description, each function is translated into a Venn diagram (see Figure 4-4).

This model, therefore, addresses not only individual interactions but also groups of individuals, such as a family, who have certain characteristics in common. The model can also be extrapolated to social aggregates and institutions.

The representation in the form of two-variable Venn diagrams must be read as the second subject's world; the dark portion shows how the first subject's world has changed as a result of the interaction. The four coordinates are represented by the four spaces in a Venn diagram: the left circle represents the party's space and the right circle that of the second subject, the intersection represents the common space, and the outside rectangle represents all that does not exist in the worlds of the two parties. The shaded space or spaces represent the change undergone by one party in the interaction with the "other." That means that the filling of one of the four areas in the diagram indicates the interactive style shown by the first party as he or she interacts with another party. The text that follows will help the reader to acquire the full understanding of what is meant. The meaning of all 16 functions in terms of common, everyday language is explained later on.

These four modalities (acceptance, maintenance, sharing, antifunction) are the components of 16 interactive styles (i.e., of 16 functions). The 16 functions provide a logical classification of possible human interactions, as well as of 16 mental states viewed as being the product of interactions. In other words, each function derives from the composition of the four triads that correspond to the four basic coordinates. For the sake of simplicity, each function is described as corresponding to one of the Venn diagrams. The representation of the 16 functions as two-variable Venn diagrams must be read as follows: the left-hand circle represents the first party's world, the right-hand circle represents the second subject's world, and the shaded portion shows how the first subject's world has changed as a result of the interaction. The four coordinates are represented by the four spaces in a Venn diagram: the left-hand circle represents the space of the first subjects and the right-hand circle that of the second subject, the intersection represents their common space, and the area of the rectangle outside the circles

Figure 4-4
Sixteen Interactive Styles

Sixteen Interactive Styles

In the sequence on the right side of this page, it is shown that the interaction between the two subjects (or between two sets) can be further analyzed with respect to the four possibilities listed in Figure 4-3 (acceptance, maintenance, sharing, and antifunction). In addition, the way in which the first step occurs in the definition of the language of the Elementary Pragmatic Model is described. As a matter of fact, by composing the four initial possibilities, one obtains the 16 functions (i.e., the 16 "interactive styles").

Each style is to be interpreted as follows: the left circle represents the first subject's world, the right circle the world of the other, and the stained part shows how the world of the first subject has changed as a result of the interaction.

For example, the second diagram from the top means that, following the interaction, the subject has occupied the space in the intersection. Hence, this is a person who, in the interaction, accepts only the intersection namely, only the shared elements.

In the next diagram the subject, after the interaction, has taken up only the space corresponding to his/her world, so the meaning is that this individuals withdraws into his/her own world during the interaction. The first diagram at the top of the page means that, as a result of the interaction, the subject goes blank, becomes void, etc.

Thus, the model's language originates from the meanings of the diagrams' formalis.

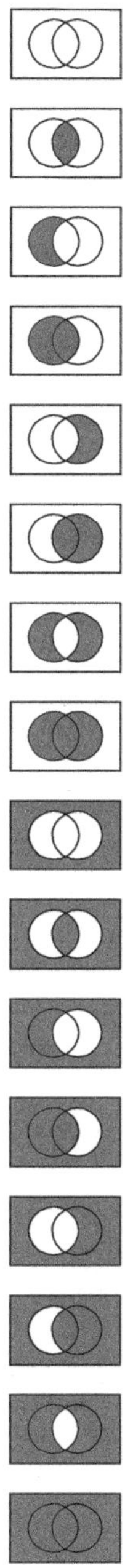

F0: The subject who obliterates him/herself in the relation

F1: The sharer

F2: The acceptor of one's own world only

F3: The maintainer of one's own world

F4: The acceptor of the other's world without sharing

F5: The acceptor of the other's world

F6: The acceptor of one's own and of the other's world, without sharing

F7: The acceptor of one's own and of the other's world

F8: The acceptor of what only exists neither in one's own nor the other's world

F9: The acceptor of what only exists, or does not exist, in one's own and in the other's world

F10: The anti-other or "Mary, Mary quite contrary"

F11: The complete maintainer of one's own world, with tendencies to expand

F12: One who, while accepting the other's world without sharing, and while accepting what exists neither in one's own nor in the other's world, behaves like a maintainer of one's own world

F13: The exaggerated acceptor who refuses solely what exists in one's own world

F14: The total acceptor who is nevertheless unable to share

F15: The total acceptor

represents what does not exist in the two subjects' worlds. The shaded space or spaces represent the change undergone by the subject as a result of interacting with the other, which is like saying that the filling of one of the four spaces in the diagram indicates the interactive style taken up by the first subject in his or her interaction with the other. From all this one can derive the meaning of each diagram, that is, each function.

The interaction between two parties (or between two sets) can be further analyzed with respect to the four possibilities listed in Figure 4-3 (acceptance, maintenance, sharing, antifunction). Also, the way in which the first step occurs in the definition of the language of the EPM is described. By composing the four initial possibilities, one obtains the 16 functions (i.e., the 16 "interactive styles").

Each style is to be interpreted as follows: the left circle represents the first party's world and the right circle the world of the other, and the stained part shows how the world of the first subject has changed as a result of the interaction. For example, the second diagram from the top means that, following the interaction, the subject has occupied the space in the intersection; hence, this is a person who, in the interaction, accepts only the intersection, namely, only the shared elements.

In the next diagram the subject, after the interaction, has taken up only the space corresponding to his or her world, so the meaning is that this individual withdraws into his or her own world during the interaction. The first diagram at the top of the page means that, as a result of the interaction, the subject goes blank, becomes void, and so on.

If we have four coordinates:

antifunction	0 0 ' 0
acceptance	0 1 ' 0
maintenance	1 0 ' 0
sharing	1 1 ' 0

(i.e., if the value of each coordinate is 0) the following Venn diagram will result:

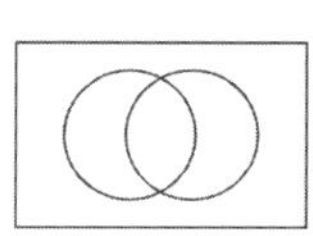

F0

This function is defined as F0. In terms of human relations this "interactive style" means that, in the interaction, one party goes blank, as it were; it will be "an individual that obliterates himself in the interaction."

If we then have the following values for the four coordinates:

antifunction	0 0 ' 0
acceptance	0 1 ' 0
maintenance	1 0 ' 0
sharing	1 1 ' 1

(i.e., if the only positive value is given by accepting only what is common to the two interacting subjects) the following Venn diagram will result:

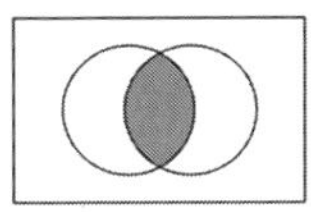

F 1

This function is defined as F1. In terms of human relations this "interactive style" means that, in the interaction, one party accepts only the things that he or she has in common with the other and will thus be a "sharer."

If we then have the following values for the four coordinates:

antifunction	0 0 ' 0
acceptance	0 1 ' 0
maintenance	1 0 ' 1
sharing	1 1 ' 0

(i.e., if the single positive value describes only acceptance of what exists in one's own world), the following Venn diagram will result:

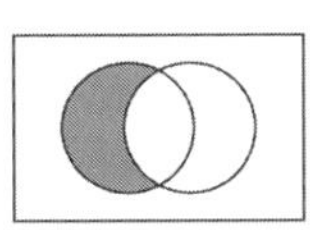

F 2

This function is defined as F2. In terms of human relations this "interactive style" means that, in the interaction, one party accepts only what exists in his or her own world and will thus be an "acceptor of one's own world only."

If we then have the following values for the four coordinates:

antifunction	0 0 ' 0
acceptance	0 1 ' 0

maintenance	1 0 ' 1
sharing	1 1 ' 1

(i.e., if the positive value means accepting what exists in one's own world and what is shared with the other), the following Venn diagram will result:

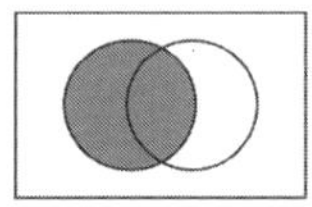

F 3

This function is defined as F3. In terms of human relations this interactive style means that, in the interaction, one will accept all that exists in one's own world including what was shared (or what was held in common) with the other; this individual will then be a "maintainer" of one's own world.

If we then have the following values for the four coordinates:

antifunction	0 0 ' 0
acceptance	0 1 ' 1
maintenance	1 0 ' 0
sharing	1 1 ' 0

(i.e., if the only positive value means that only what exists in the other's world is accepted), the following Venn diagram will result:

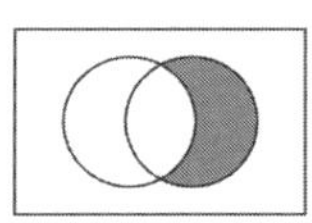

F 4

This function is defined as F4. In terms of human relations this "interactive style" means that, in the interaction, one will accept only what exists in the other's world; one party will be "one who gives in to the other's world" (or else, an acceptor of the other's world without sharing—"without sharing" means that common things are not accepted, and the intersection space stays empty).

If we then have the following values for the four coordinates:

antifunction	0 0 ' 0
acceptance	0 1 ' 1

maintenance	1 0 ' 0
sharing	1 1 ' 1

(i.e., if the acceptance and the sharing coordinates are both positive), the following Venn diagram will result:

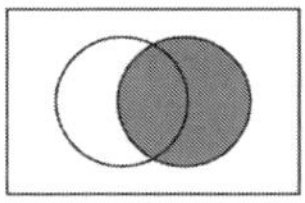

F 5

This function is defined as F5. In terms of human relations this "interactive style" means that, in the interaction, one will accept what exists in the other's world, including the common elements, and will thus be an "acceptor of the other's world."

If we then have the following values for the four coordinates:

antifunction	0 0 ' 0
acceptance	0 1 ' 1
maintenance	1 0 ' 1
sharing	1 1 ' 0

(i.e., if the values of the acceptance and the maintenance coordinates are positive), the following Venn diagram will result:

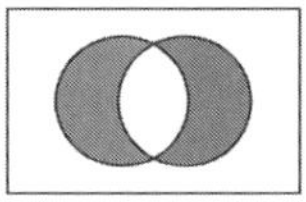

F 6

This function is defined as F6. In terms of human relations this "interactive style" means that, in the interaction, one will accept what exists in one's own and in the other's world but nothing that is common to the two worlds and nothing outside the two worlds; this individual will be an "acceptor of one's own and of the other's world, without sharing."

If we then have the following values for the four coordinates:

antifunction coordinate	0 0 ' 0
acceptance coordinate	0 1 ' 1
maintenance coordinate	1 0 ' 1
sharing coordinate	1 1 ' 1

(i.e., if the third and the fourth coordinates are both positive), the following Venn diagram will result:

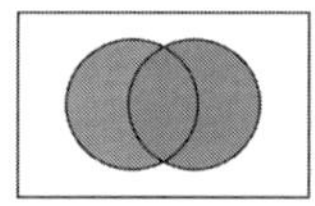

F 7

This function is defined as F7. In terms of human relations this "interactive style" means that, in the interaction, one will accept both what belongs to one's own and what belongs to the other's world, including what is shared, and will thus be an "acceptor of one's own and of the other's world."

If we then have the following values for the four coordinates:

antifunction coordinate	0 0 ' 1
acceptance coordinate	0 1 ' 0
maintenance coordinate	1 0 ' 0
sharing coordinate	1 1 ' 0

(i.e., if the only positive value is expressed by accepting what does not exist either in one's own or in the other's world, the following Venn diagram will result:

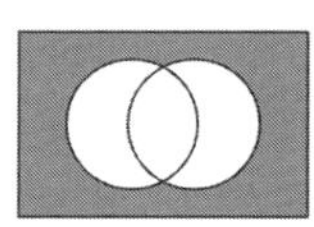

F 8

This function is defined as F8. In terms of human relations this "interactive style" means that, in the interaction, one accepts only those things that do not exist in the worlds of the interacting parties and will thus be "an acceptor of only what does not exist either in one's or in the other's world."

If we then have the following values for the four coordinates:

antifunction coordinate	0 0 ' 1
acceptance coordinate	0 1 ' 0
maintenance coordinate	1 0 ' 0
sharing coordinate	0 0 ' 1

(i.e., if the positive values describe only the acceptance of what does not exist both in one's and the other's world and what is shared between one's own and the other's world, the following Venn diagram will result:

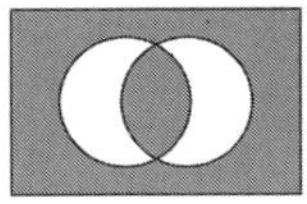

F 9

This function is defined as F9. In terms of human relations this "interactive style" means that, in the interaction, one will accept only what does not exist in both worlds, in one's own and in the other's, or else what exists in both worlds (both in one's own and in the other's): "the acceptor of only what exists, or does not exist, in one's own and in the other's world."

If we then have the following values for the four coordinates:

antifunction coordinate	0 0 ' 1
acceptance coordinate	0 1 ' 0
maintenance coordinate	1 0 ' 1
sharing coordinate	1 1 ' 0

(i.e., if the acceptance coordinate of what does not exist in one's own and in the other's world and the maintenance coordinate of what exists in one's own world are both positive), the following Venn diagram will result:

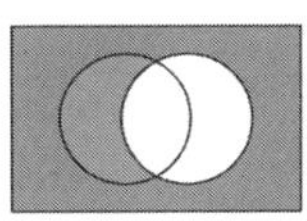

F10

This function is defined as F10. In terms of human relations, this "interactive style" means that, in the interaction, one will accept only what exists in one's own world and also what is foreign to one's own and to the other's world and will neglect what belongs to the other's world and the things that are shared; thus, this subject will be "an antiother" or, as we are going to see later on, a "Mary, Mary, quite contrary" or, to make this less sexist, "Jerry, Jerry, quite contrary"!

If we then have the following values for the four coordinates:

antifunction coordinate	0 0 ' 1
acceptance coordinate	0 1 ' 0
maintenance coordinate	1 0 ' 1
sharing coordinate	1 1 ' 1

(i.e., if only the things that in fact belong to the other's world are excluded), the following Venn diagram will result:

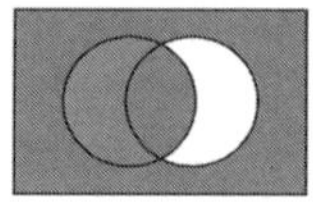

F11

This function is defined as F11. In terms of human relations, this "interactive style" means that, in the interaction, the first party is one who accepts one's own world including that part that is shared with the other and also all that is foreign to one's and to the other's world; this subject will be "a complete maintainer of one's own world, with tendencies to expand."

If we then have the following values for the four coordinates:

antifunction coordinate	0 0 ' 1
acceptance coordinate	0 1 ' 1
maintenance coordinate	1 0 ' 0
sharing coordinate	1 1 ' 0

(i.e., if the positive values mean accepting what does not exist in the worlds of the interacting subjects and only what exists in the other's world), the following Venn diagram will result:

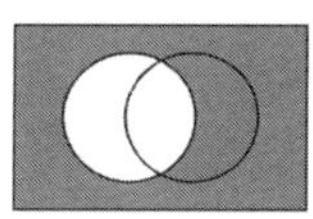

F12

This function is defined as F12. In terms of human relations, this interactive style means that, in the interaction, one accepts only those things that exist in the other's world, though without sharing, and will also accept what does not exist in one's own and not even in the other's world. As we are going to see, with reference to the "table of interactions," whichever function is confronted, this particular function will always give a uniform response (i.e., it will always change into F3).

Because it does not accept what exists in its own world, while accepting what does not exist in its own and in the other's world, F12 will necessarily delete the outside space precisely because it belongs to its own way of being (i.e., to one's own world in the sense of a mechanism), the right-hand moon crescent (the other's world) will always be eliminated because it exists in the other's world, and, as already mentioned, only things that do not exist either in one's or in the other's world are accepted. Instead, the left moon crescent and the intersection will always be filled, either because they do not belong to one's own and to the other's worlds or because they belong to the other's world (this explanation will be clearer later on). The meaning of this style, based on its own interactive mechanism, is that of an F3, namely, the maintenance of one's world without sharing. A subject of this kind can be defined as "one who, while accepting the other's world without sharing, and while accepting what exists neither in one's own nor in the other's world, behaves like a maintainer of one's own world" (a sort of person that will impose one's own "altruism" and that is thereby "selfish," a kind of "pseudo-altruistic egotist").

If we then have the following values for the four coordinates:

antifunction coordinate	0 0 ' 1
acceptance coordinate	0 1 ' 1
maintenance coordinate	1 0 ' 0
sharing coordinate	1 1 ' 1

(i.e., if the only negative value refers to the acceptance of one's own world), the following Venn diagram will result:

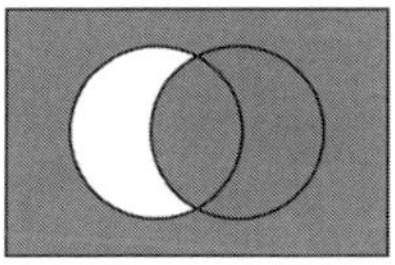

F13

This function is defined as F13. In terms of human relations, this interactive style means that, in the interaction, one will accept the other's world and all that is shared and what does not exist either in one's own or in the other's world and will thus be "the exaggerated acceptor who refuses what exists solely in one's own world."

If we then have the following values for the four coordinates:

antifunction coordinate	0 0 ' 1
acceptance coordinate	0 1 ' 1
maintenance coordinate	1 0 ' 1
sharing coordinate	1 1 ' 0

(i.e., if the only negative value refers to the coordinate of sharing elements with the other's world), the following Venn diagram will result:

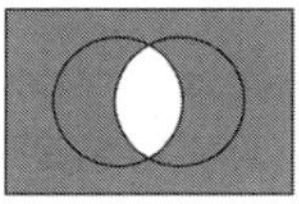

F14

This function is defined as F14. In terms of human relations, this "interactive style" means that, in the interaction, one will accept what belongs to one's own world as well as what belongs to the other's world and also what doesn't belong to either's world but will not accept anything that is shared; this subject will thus be a "total acceptor who is nevertheless unable to share."

Lastly, if we have the following values for the four coordinates:

antifunction coordinate	0 0 ' 1
acceptance coordinate	0 1 ' 1
maintenance coordinate	1 0 ' 1
sharing coordinate	1 1 ' 1

(i.e., if all of the four coordinates show positive values), the following Venn diagram will result:

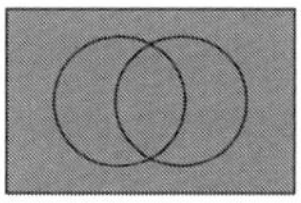

F15

This function is defined as F15. In terms of human relations, this "interactive style" means that, in the interaction, all that belongs to one's own world and to the other's world, the things that are shared, and those that do not exist either in one's own or in the other's world are accepted. (First author's note: each function could be conceived as a model in its own right if one accepts that the assumptions and postulates of the EPM really represent a theory in its own right.

Table 4-1 is a summary of the 16 interactive styles.

A Theoretical Prediction of How Interactions Evolve: The Logic of Human Interactions and of Their Changes According to the EPM

Another point of interest is that the typology just described produces a system by which one can predict theoretically how interactions among the 16 types are going to evolve. This possibility is summed up in the so-called table of paradoxes (or of interactions) (see Figure 4-5).

From this figure, one can then transfer to Figure 4-6 according to the possible combinations and permutations of the 16 functions in diagrams.

To expand on the 16 functions and make sure that they are understood, following are further descriptions of them.

Table 4-1
Summary of Interactive Styles

F0.	The subject who obliterates him/herself in the relation
F1.	The sharer
F2.	The acceptor of one's own world only
F3.	The maintainer of one's own world
F4.	The acceptor of the other's world without sharing
F5.	The acceptor of the other's world
F6.	The acceptor of one's own and of the other's world, without sharing
F7.	The acceptor of one's own and of the other's world
F8.	The acceptor of only what exists neither in one's own nor the other's world
F9.	The acceptor of only what exists, or does not exist, in one's own and in the other's world
F10.	The anti-other or "Mary, Mary quite contrary"
F11.	The complete maintainer of one's own world, with tendencies to expand
F12.	One who, while accepting the other's world without sharing and while accepting what exists neither in one's own nor in the other's world, behaves like a maintainer of one's own world
F13.	The exaggerated acceptor who refuses solely what exists in one's own world
F14.	The total acceptor who is nevertheless unable to share
F15.	The total acceptor

F0. Emptiness of mind, when nothing is accepted and there is no acceptance of one's world, the world of the other, or of external elements, as in a comatose person or in an individual who, during an interaction, loses contact with the other by going blank. Figure 4.5 shows that, in the interaction with the other, this interactive style always amounts to 0. It cannot be otherwise, because its processing mechanism does not consider taking up elements from the other's world or common elements or foreign elements.

F1. Sharing part of one's world with another, when only what is common to both worlds is accepted, as two coworkers who work on something that they have to do at work but who then go their separate ways or two sex addicts who have a one-night stand without even knowing anything about each other and do not plan to meet again. It can stay only F1, and this can happen only with those styles that have an intersection (with styles without an intersection, the outcome is always 0). Indeed, there can be only a very limited response because, by its own nature, F1 can consider accepting only elements that are shared with the other but not elements from the other's

Figure 4-5
Table of Paradoxes

f_I \ f_I	0	1	2	3	4	5	6	7	8	9	10	11	12	13	14	15
0	0	0	2	3	0	0	6	7	7	6	15	15	3	2	15	15
1	0	1	2	3	1	1	7	7	6	7	14	15	3	3	15	15
2	0	0	0	3	2	2	4	7	5	4	13	15	3	2	13	15
3	0	1	0	3	3	3	5	7	4	5	12	15	3	3	13	15
4	0	0	2	3	0	4	2	7	3	2	11	11	3	6	11	15
5	0	1	2	3	1	5	3	7	2	3	10	11	3	7	11	15
6	0	0	0	3	2	6	0	7	1	0	9	11	3	6	9	15
7	0	1	0	3	3	7	1	7	0	1	8	11	3	7	9	15
8	0	0	2	3	8	8	14	15	7	14	7	15	3	10	7	15
9	0	1	2	3	9	9	15	15	6	15	6	15	3	11	7	15
10	0	0	0	3	10	10	12	15	5	12	5	15	3	10	5	15
11	0	1	0	3	11	11	13	15	4	13	4	15	3	11	5	15
12	0	0	2	3	8	12	10	15	3	10	3	11	3	14	3	15
13	0	1	2	3	9	13	11	15	2	11	2	11	3	15	3	15
14	0	0	0	3	10	14	8	15	1	8	1	11	3	14	1	15
15	0	1	0	3	11	15	9	15	0	9	0	11	3	15	1	15

world or from what exists outside the worlds of the two subjects, nor can it maintain its own world.

F2. Exclusive acceptance of one's world but not of the other or whatever the two may have in common; for instance, a self-centered individual who ignores, dismisses, and discounts the proposal of the other and whatever they may have in common in the relationship. For instance, in spite of a partner's lack of interest in a computer, one is given as a gift by the other partner, ignoring the partner's lack of interest but following exclusively, instead, his or her own interest in maintaining his or her world but refusing everything else, including things that are shared. The resulting response is maintenance of one's own world and a refusal of everything else. Like with all the functions that are characterized by a shaded left crescent (i.e., with the functions in which one's world is maintained, either alone or in association with other characteristic features, since F2 does not accept anything that is shared, it changes coherently into F0. No relation is possible with persons who have a tendency to stick to their own point of view; what is obtained is only the annihilation of the subject's ability to interact.

F3. Maintenance of one's world through the acceptance not only of one's own world but also acceptance of whatever is common with the world of the other, as seen in extremely selfish, rigidly unbending individuals who take from the other what is already in his or her world, for instance, the individual who does whatever he or she wants, regardless of the desires of

Figure 4-6
Table of Paradoxes in Diagram Form

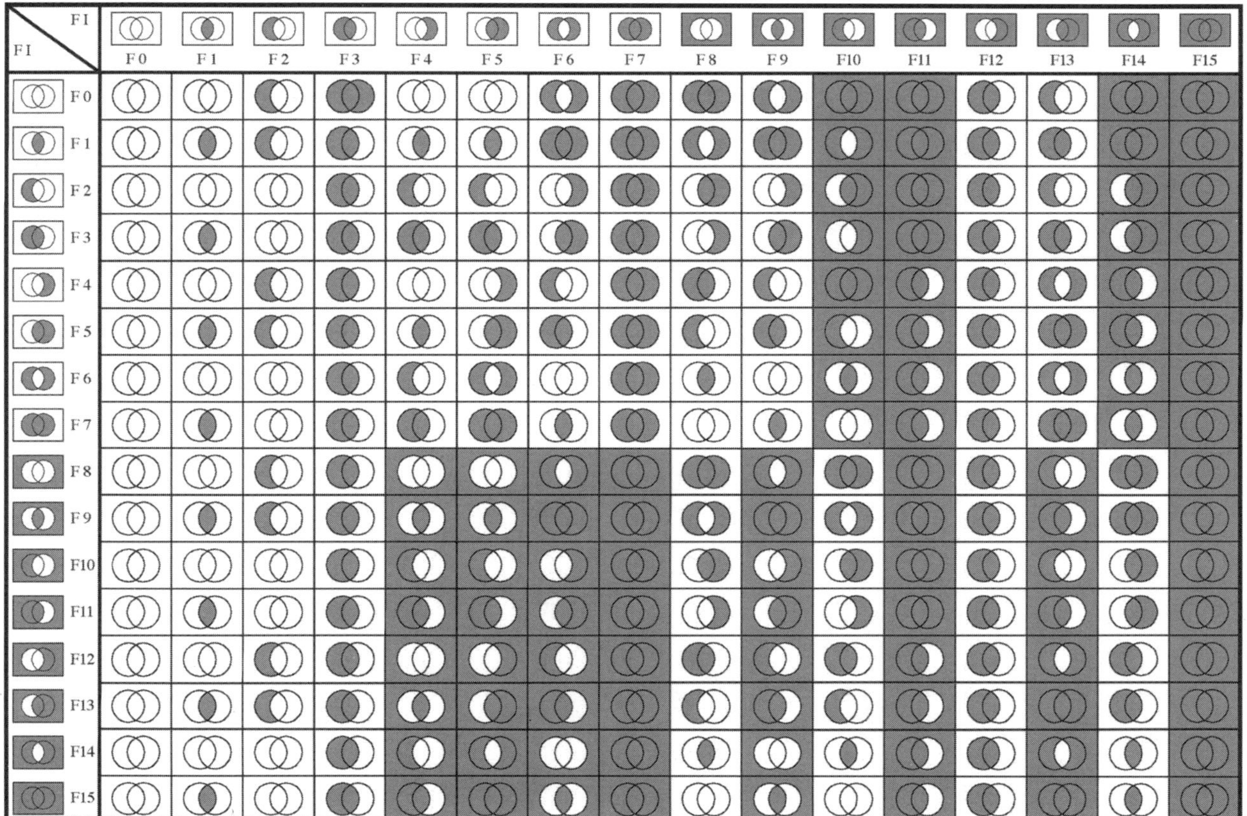

others. Since only the possibility of maintaining one's own world is admitted, there can be only a single stereotype response: staying F3.

F4. Accepting the world of another without sharing it, for instance, in the passive individual who yields uncritically and flexibly to the other's world, surrendering his or her world to the world of the other, as in the case of a partner who is willing to accede to the other partner's sexual wishes or practices, no matter how extreme these wishes or practices may be. Because only the possibility of accepting the other's world is admitted, but not the things that are common to both, the following are some of the possible solutions: F4 with F0 becomes F0; F4 with F1 becomes F1; F4 with F3 becomes F3; but F4 with F4 becomes F0 (the result of someone's being changed into F0 is due to the fact that one cannot accept one's own world). F4 with F5 become only F1 because its own left crescent cannot be accepted since it is common to the other's world as well. Similarly, F4 with F6 becomes F2, with F7 it becomes F3, with F8 it becomes F8, with F9 it changes to F9, with F10 it becomes F10, with F11 it becomes F11, but with F12 it becomes F8 because it cannot accept sharing the crescent, and so on.

F5. Accepting only the other's world and what is common to both worlds, for instance, individuals who altruistically and actively accept proposals of the other, as in cases of extreme identification, where individuals are transformed by taking on the characteristics of the partner. It is not at all difficult to understand; in fact, since its characteristic is that it conforms to the other's world, it will thereby acquire the characteristics of that world.

F6. Accepting of one's and the other's world, without sharing it, as in so-called selfish altruists, who ambivalently hesitate in sharing either world, oscillating between accepting and refusing his or her own world or the world of the other, without connecting with either world, or the individual who cannot make up his or her mind one way or another, because there is an underlying agenda that has not been faced by either partner. For instance, in the case of a girl who as been raped but whose family knows about it and does not talk about it, producing a great deal of oscillation that may show itself in conflicts over decisions; or in the case of a couple where one partner has had an affair, of which both partners are aware but about which they do not talk, producing a distortion in the relationship. Due to the fact that an F6 accepts one's own world and the other's world but not what is common to both (the intersection), the responses are quite varied. For instance, F6 with F0 becomes F6. Why is that so? Owing to the fact that the subject's own world and also that of the other, which is, however, defined as not existing, are both accepted, the only possible outcome is the replication of one's own world. With F1, the subject's response can be only F7; in fact, in addition to the two moon crescents corresponding to the first subject's own structure, the intersection represents the characteristic of the other's world. With F2, the outcome will be F4 because, by its own nature, F6 must exclude what is shared, hence the left crescent, which is shared. With F6, the result of the interaction will be F0 because, since what is in common is not accepted, then the two crescents are deleted. Again for the same reason, with antifunctions it may be, for instance, that F6 with F8 becomes F14; in fact, to the subject's own world consisting of the two moon crescents, there is added the outside space, which belongs to the other.

F7. Accepting one's own and the other's world and harmoniously mediating both worlds without getting lost in the other's world, as in the case of a very close couple, where each partner is available to the other in any possible way, without losing his or her world. This function is not difficult to explain. Since both the other's and one's own worlds are accepted and also what is common to both, only two outcomes are possible: with functions, F7, and with antifunctions, F15.

F8. Acceptance only of what does not exist in one's own and in the other's world but acceptance also of external elements of the outside world, which were not previously present in the interaction and which were not common to both worlds. For instance, words or acts that are irrelevant or outside the context of what is going on in an interaction, such as asking about the price of eggs in China during sexual intercourse, represent the basic antifunction style, which means that what does not exist in one's own world and/or does not exist in the other's world is accepted. As a result, whichever the style with which it interacts, F8 will always result in a "function-style" because the outside space, typical of F8's world, cannot be accepted. Of the remaining three areas, only those that are not filled by the other will be accepted. With F0, F8 becomes F7; as we just mentioned, the outside space is not accepted, and the three remaining areas are not filled by the other. Conversely, with F7, F8 becomes F0; the outside space is not accepted, and the three remaining areas are filled by the other.

F9. Accepting only what exists and what does not exist in one's own and the other's world, such as unquestioning and uncritical sharing of what one has in common in the internal and external worlds, as seen in an extremely symbiotic couple, where one partner cannot accept that the other partner has a separate world from his or her own and cannot accept his or her own world, behaving very much like F6, but this is so because of a different interactive organization. Here the intersection is accepted and so is what was not present in either of the two interacting subjects. A possible outcome may be, for example, that F9 with F0 becomes F6. Why is that so? Answer: the outside area is not accepted because it is present in the first but not in the second subject's world, and the intersection area becomes void because it is not present in the other's world; hence only the two crescents (left and right) are common to both and are therefore filled. By the same principle, as it interacts with F1, F9 becomes F7, and then again F9 with F2 becomes F4, and F9 with F3 becomes F5. With F4 it becomes F2, with F6 it becomes F0, and with F7 it becomes F1. F9 with F8 becomes F14. As mentioned earlier, in the interaction F9 takes up what is common to both and also what is absent in both. Thus, as F9 interacts with F8, the outside space is common to both whereas the two crescents are absent in both parties' worlds and so F14. F9 with F9 becomes F15, F9 with F10 becomes F12, F9 with F11 becomes F13 (remember that the intersection is admitted since it exists in both worlds), F9 with F12 becomes F10. With F13 it becomes F11, with F14 it becomes F8, and with F15 it becomes F9.

F10. Accepting only either what exists in one's internal world as well as the external world but not what exists in the other's world or whatever is shared, as in "Mary, Mary, quite contrary," that is, in the active, systematic opposer and spiteful negativist and obstructionist, as seen in individuals who do exactly the opposite of what is proposed by others. This function is simple to explain; since its actions are dictated by an "antiother" mechanism, it will always act exactly to the contrary.

F11. Accepting one's own world, including whatever is shared with the other's world, as well as whatever is foreign to one's own and the other's world, as seen in the exaggeration of sticking to one's own world while attempting to expand toward the world of others. If there is opposition, however, these individuals become confused, as seen in bullies, dictators, and arrogant egotists when they are faced by strong opposition that they cannot control or dominate. It is also easy to explain because this function accepts one's own world (left crescent), all that is shared (the intersection area), and what does not exist either in one's own or in the other's world (the outside space) but does not accept what belongs only to the other's world (right crescent). This can be summed up as follows: F11 accepts everything (and thus has a tendency to change to F15) except what belongs solely to the other's world. Therefore, it changes to F15 if the subject fills only those areas that are also filled by F11; this equally applies in the interaction with F0, F1, F2, F3, F8, F9, F10, and F11; instead, F11 will not change as it interacts with subjects who have something that is solely their own (those who fill the right crescent, in particular, F4, F5, F6, F7, F12, F13, F14, F15).

F12. Accepting only what is in the other's world without sharing it but accepting whatever does not exist in one's own world or in the other's world, as in pseudoaltruists who appear to accept the other's world but in reality maintain their own world, as seen in martyrs who make sacrifices for their own sake and not for the sake of others or in those who receive pleasure vicariously after giving pleasure to others. This function has a univocal response; it always changes to F3. The reason is that F12 typically accepts the other's world, never its own. Now, since this style's own world is represented by the right crescent and by the outside space—which cannot be accepted by definition, being its own world—the only possible response is to accept what does not belong to its own world (i.e., the left crescent and the intersection space).

F13. Acceptance of the other's world and whatever there is in common that does not exist in one's own and the other's world but not of what is part of one's own world, as seen in the amplification of the world of the other while refusing to accept one's own world, refusing only what exists exclusively in one's own world. For example, if one likes pets, the partner who hates pets gives the other an elephant as a gift. Basically, this function accepts the other's world and also the outside space, leading to a multifaceted response. We may say that the interaction modality of F13 is symmetrical to that of the F11 that we have already discussed; indeed, F13 accepts everything except what belongs solely to its own world. Or, to put it the other way round, it accepts only all that does not belong solely to its own world. At first, its world—the right moon crescent—is empty; hence, no matter with whom it interacts, the outcome will always be the acceptance of the right-hand crescent (basically, it is an F12), plus all that is shared with the other. With F0 and F2 it has nothing in common, so it becomes only F2; with F1 and F3 it has the intersection in common, so it becomes F3; with F4 and F6 it has the right moon crescent in common, so it becomes F6; with F5 and F7 it has the right circle in common, so it becomes F14.

F14. Total acceptance of one's own, the other's, and the external world of both without accepting shared elements, as seen in individuals who cannot focus directly or who cannot complete interactions successfully, as in premature ejaculation or individuals who cannot address issues directly and speak in metaphors, as seen in the language of mobsters. Its main characteristic is the acceptance of everything with the exception of all that is shared (the intersection). Consequently, with F0 it becomes F15 because, since it has nothing to share, it accepts everything; same thing with F1 (as a matter of fact since it has nothing to share, F1 is the negative of F14). With F2, F14 becomes F13 (all that is held in common is discarded, i.e., the right crescent).

With F3 it becomes F13 because the left crescent has been discarded due to the fact that it is a common element. With F4 it becomes F11 because the left crescent has been discarded as it was the common element. With F5, the outcome will be F11 because the left crescent (the common element) has been discarded but not so the intersection area, which is not a shared element. With F6, it becomes F9 because both the left and the right crescents are discarded. With F7, it becomes F9 again since both crescents are discarded, as mentioned above, but not the intersection, which is present (like in the previous case) only in the other's world. With F8, the outcome will be F7. With F9 it will be F7. With F10 it will be F5 because the shared crescent is discarded. Same thing with F11. With F12 it becomes F3. With F13, it becomes F3. With F14 it becomes F1. With F15, it becomes F1.

F15. Total acceptance of whatever exists in one's own and the other's world internally and externally, as seen in individuals who unselectively and inconclusively accept whatever exists and who accept both extremes of any situation without boundaries. Since this function is characterized by the acceptance of its own world, of the other's world, and of the intersection, the outcome will always be F15. By this analysis of the table of interactions we have succeeded in giving the reader an idea of how the logic of change in human interactions works according to the Elementary Pragmatic Model, and we also hope we have been able to offer hints for reflection.

EPM AND LANGUAGE: HOW TO PASS FROM FORMAL TO COMMON LANGUAGE

An element of interest in the EPM classification system lies in its identifying precise categories to describe and classify relations among individuals that are not found in everyday language. Words and phrases like the "sharer," one who "gives in to the other's world," the "maintainer of one's own world," the "total acceptor" have no equivalent in common vocabulary. That is so because the terminology required to define the various aspects of people's interactions has not been adequately developed in everyday language.

The theory behind the EPM and the resulting need to discuss its formal aspects allow us to broaden the terminology of that part of our language that describes human interactions. How do formal language (mathematical and symbolic—the Venn diagrams), the meaning we have attached to such language (see the preceding pages), and common language relate to one another? If, for example, one reads the words contained in a dictionary of the official language or in a slang vocabulary or also in the dictionary of synonyms and antonyms, one will find a certain number of words (truly, quite few) that show some connection with the language of the EPM. These connections may range from almost complete to minimal overlap. The relation existing between the two languages is similar to Escher's figures when this painter represents geometric figures, such as rhombuses, depicting flying birds. This concept will be explained with a few examples.

Between the "sharer" and the "concordant" (a word that can be found in any dictionary), there is some overlap but only a partial one; as a matter of fact, the word "sharer" in our model means someone who accepts only what is common to his or her and to the other's world, while the word "concordant" in the dictionary means someone who agrees, thinks along the same lines, consents, is unanimous. Hence, the two words are somewhat akin, though only in part. It seems obvious that the word defining the Model's F1 is much more precise and gives a much clearer definition.

Another example: how are the expressions "maintainer of one's own world" (F3) and "Selfishness" mutually related? Certainly there is some connection between the two. Being a "maintainer of one's own world" means that only what already existed in one's own world is accepted, whereas "selfish" describes someone who thinks only in terms of self and of what may prove useful. According to the F3 connotation, it may happen that the subject's world admits being generous toward the other; maintaining this position of generosity is something quite different from being selfish according to the meaning given in a dictionary of everyday language.

We are not going to discuss at length all possible instances so that this chapter will not be too cumbersome. We have summed up in a schema the definitions that, in our opinion, best depict each of the 16 functions. Consider the funnels in Figure 4-6. The lower end of the funnel can be used to represent the mathematical expressions, then, further up, the Venn diagrams. Immediately above this, the figure shows the word or words best describing the diagram; then as one gradually proceeds toward the top of the funnel, one will find terms that are more loosely connected. As one moves from the bottom upward, one passes from the most formal to the less formal language.

To fully appreciate the terminology we have been using to give a strict definition of what the function and the Venn diagrams really mean, the reader should be aware that we have also taken into account the table of interactions published above. One may in fact encounter situations that are quite complex and pose more problems of subdividing even within the model's formal meaning. To quote one example, F5 has been defined as accepting the other's world and conforming to it. In formal language, this function means accepting only what exists in the other's world and what is shared between one's own and the other's world; apparently, this definition sounds adequate. However, if we consider all the interactions that can develop with all of the 16 functions, as shown in the table of interactions, we realize that it is not only a matter of accepting the other's world; one can even change into the other's world. Indeed, each function represents not only the world but also the "mechanism" that goes with that function. With F5, the mechanism consists in accepting the other's world also in terms of the other's mechanism; hence, function F5 changes into the other's function. If, for example, F5 interacts with F3, it changes into F3; if it interacts with F7, it changes into F7; if it interacts with F10, it changes into F10. Briefly, what we have here is a sort of Zelig in Woody Allen's movie.

To give a full definition of F5, it is not enough to say "acceptor of the other's world"; we must also add "and conforming to it." Once F5 has been so defined, it becomes clear that this function has very little to do with the "altruist" in the dictionary. The altruist in the dictionary is defined as one who loves one's neighbor, does not act for one's own benefit, and is thoughtful of the other's good. The difference between the two terms is considerable, although one can recognize some common elements.

There is another possibility, that the theoretical rule may not be acceptable to the human mind, as when the EPM shows that moving toward the other by amplifying (F13) can never turn into moving toward a goal by amplifying (F9). In that case the spontaneous mind will reject the theoretical rule spontaneously. A numerical table of interactions, the diagrammatic table of interactions, and a reference chart help understand how a relationship is established between the table of interactions and a spontaneous reading of the interactions by the human mind. Theoretical predictions of how interactions evolve are then possible.

THE LOGIC OF HUMAN INTERACTIONS AND OF THEIR CHANGES ACCORDING TO THE EPM

Another point of interest is that the typology just described produces a system by which one can predict theoretically how interactions among the 16 types are going to evolve. This possibility is summed up in the so-called table of paradoxes (or of interactions).

To conclude this chapter, Figure 4-7 sums up the essential features of the EPM; the upper part of the figure on the left reproduces a portion of a painting by Escher. Noteworthy, as he proceeds from the bottom of the picture to the top, the painter passes from squared formal figures (the cubes) to free images of flying birds. The lozenge contains the 16 funnels. Just how each funnel should be read was described earlier. One proceeds from bottom to top, like in Escher's figures, passing from the more formal to the less formal expression. The hypercube on the right-side page, top, is a four-dimension space that, in our case, represents the space taken by all possible interactions. The persons belonging to any one system should be seen as moving inside that space, along tracks that may or may not be redundant, like in a sort of dance. The 16 funnels in the lozenge are arranged according to the numbers (from 0 to 15) written at the vertices of the hypercube. At the bottom of the page (right and left) there are two tables of interactions. The one on the right side is described earlier in this book; the one on the left side represents a table of predictions (not to be discussed here) in which the therapist (namely, the person who elicits changes) sticks permanently to his or her own value, without ever changing his or her interacting modality.

AN INTERACTIVE APPROACH

To make more concrete what at first blush seem rather abstract concepts, the rest of this chapter is dedicated to a more interactively concrete ap-

Figure 4-7
The Essential Features of the EPM

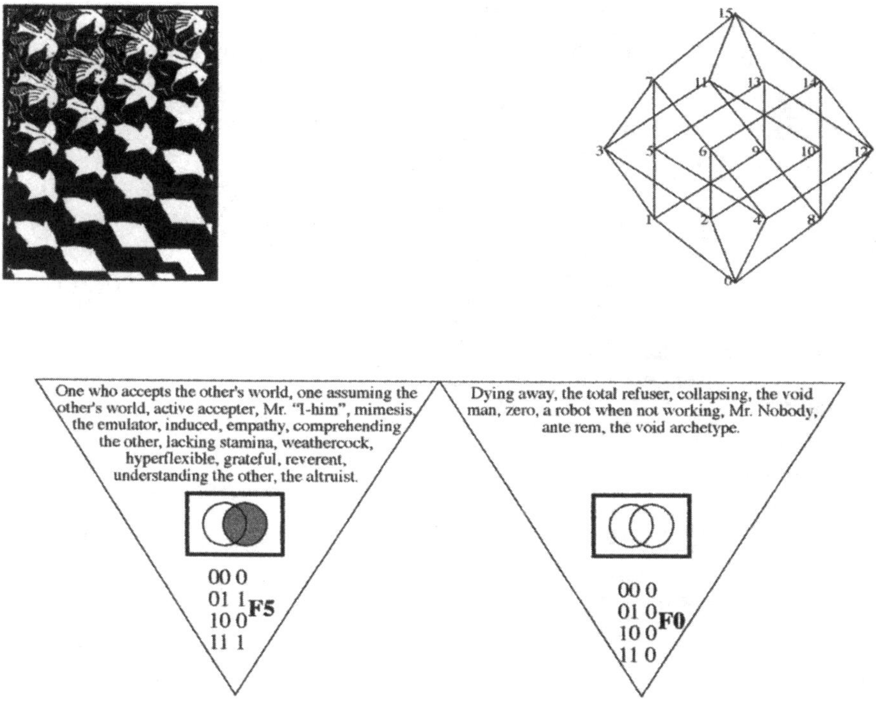

proach to help the reader understand the meaning of the 16 functions that compose the EPM.

F0: Absence (Being Absent)

We all know that every human being has a beginning and an end. We are born, we live, and we die; every 24 hours, every day, we awake, and we fall asleep. All other living beings, of whatever kind, have their own vital cycles, but not just the living beings; the whole universe started with a bang—the Big Bang—and is evolving toward its end—the Big Crunch.

So then, to explain how the mind is structured, we must start off with a box set aside for "absence." Things exist as potentialities, like a container without a content, an archetype, a thing without a thing, as in the package of a thing with no thing inside.

Is that so difficult? I shouldn't think so. If we say, "Uncle John was born in 1896 and died in 1996," we are obviously placing him in an initial, empty box that we have filled with his birth, but then we move him to a final, empty box where he no longer exists. When Peter wakes up in the morning, he will fill an empty box (i.e., something that existed before Peter was awake). If I expect a present from my wife, and the present does not turn up, there still is an empty box called "the present." If a person does not say dirty words, there still is a box for dirty words that is not filled. There are times when the human mind goes blank, is devoid of ideas, of whatever mental content can be perceived by the individual, and this "blank" can be recognized by an external observer who sees that the person before him is "absent."

Having said this, we feel authorized to identify a "zero" mental state, a blank mind state. Thus, in this program, you are requested, as a first step, to create a blank in your mind. This "emptying one's mind" can be interpreted as punctuating a sequence of mental states, just as you would punctuate a speech or when you are concluding a sentence before you start another one.

Is it difficult to empty one's mind? At first sight it would appear that it is, and then you realize that it is rather easy. As a matter of fact, we have realized that everyone is capable of making one's mind go blank, at least for a few seconds. The second author was told by some people that, to be able to empty their mind, they must think of a white wall. Of course, whatever modality you choose is all right provided that you attain your goal.

Let us now consider relations between people, for example, between the two members of a couple. Clearly, this kind of relation can be marked only by annulment, by the impossibility of a relationship, by parting, by a non-relation; nothing is exchanged between the two except for a void presence.

F1: Sharing

Consider two people who have never met before; neither of them knows anything about the other's world (how he or she sees actual reality, constructs with his or her thoughts, usually acts), and both may even be considerably limited in the knowledge of their own personal world, yet each may still share something with the other, have certain elements in common, have an "intersection" between one's own and the other's worlds. For instance, both carry out some sort of activity; both catch a bus, attend a football match, listen to music, or maybe play tennis together.

Although carrying out a common activity is an important part of sharing, sharing itself is not just that. You may share something immaterial, as you do when you have a certain target in mind as to how you would like social justice to be accomplished, or you may share some other ideal or the love for art or science.

You will not find it difficult to grasp this concept of sharing in the sense that we have described. Certainly, those who love absolute truths could advance some exception; as a matter of fact, concepts of any kind contain a clear central core, which then fades out into less well defined and more vague surroundings. We are quite aware of that; nevertheless, the notion that we have been describing holds good and is useful. Luckily, nowadays, the so-called fuzzy logic allows us to add to concepts a certain amount of flexibility that proves to be much more realistic than the "all or nothing" concept of the science of yesteryear, which used to substitute reality for artificial theoretical constructions.

However, the concept that we are talking about can be expanded in a way that might appear to be arbitrary at first sight, when we come to the concept of focalization. Here, the quality of interacting with the other one or sharing is lost, and the concept acquires a meaning of its own if attention is shifted toward a single person. Indeed, limiting the point of contract to a single element (i.e., to a single external object or even to just one part of it) implies excluding all that exists in one's own world, on the one hand, and all that forms the external world, on the other hand, except for a single selected element. In other words, if we consider a subject by himself or herself, a subject taken separately and thus unrelated to other men or women but generally related to the whole world, we can say that a point of intersection with this subject is established; between the external world and the subject there is a common point, a point of contact.

To sum up the concept, inasmuch as you get in touch with an object, a zone of intersection is established between yourself and the object. This explains why the following prescriptions are proposed for your mental attitudes:

1. If you are by yourself, concentrate strongly on an object near you (e.g., the pen on your desk).
2. If you adopt an interactive attitude, think of something that is common to you and to your partner (partner here means your spouse or someone you think is your main counterpart in the relation you care to consider).
3. Concerning the solution to a problem, how would you solve your problem should you decide about the solution together with your partner?

F2: Withdrawal

A third interactive modality or mental state is withdrawal. All of us can experience this state both in a positive and in a negative sense. There are thoughts that convey all our energies; for example, our mind can concentrate on something either pleasant or unpleasant that occurred to us the day before or maybe a dream, our very secret thoughts, our hidden reveries, or our own private mental constructions. There is, in each one of us, a private world that belongs solely to ourselves, to our very personal sphere; there are memories of the past that we don't want anybody to find out, there are certain behaviors of ours that we are not prepared to share with anyone, and there are ideas that exist only in our own world. Anyone can draw from his or her own experiences and realize that there are times in our lives when we withdraw into our own world; the world of the others does not exist, we are concentrated exclusively on ourselves, and we refuse even those elements that we share with our partner.

Not only are there recollections, ideas, and behaviors that we will not share, but there are entire constructions that belong solely to ourselves. If, for example, I have been working for years on a specific area of science that nobody else but me has been studying, that gives me unique and unshared knowledge, at least until I decide to share it and find others who are prepared to accept and assimilate it. Do you know that the Australian Aborigines used to paint pictures in utter solitude and would then leave them behind in the forest? They went as far as thinking that it was quite inappropriate for other people to have an opportunity to see their paintings.

Physical sensations perceived by our body that we alone can feel with our interior senses can again be ascribed to the sphere of privacy.

To conclude this explanation, we have mental contents and mental constructions, as well as physical sensations, that belong only to ourselves.

This is what this program has in store for you:

1. Concentrate on a part or a function of your own body that you alone may know about.
2. Think of something that exists solely in your mental world.
3. How would you solve your problem should you decide about the solution with your very personal mental organization?
4. Practice visualizing this figure and this image at hand.

F3: Maintaining One's World

There is a difference between withdrawing into one's own world and maintaining one's world. Withdrawing means shrinking away from any contact with somebody else's world, getting into one's own shell, and being quite unwilling to share anything whatsoever. In what we define as "maintaining one's own world," one can accept sharing some things with the other one provided that one does not have to recede in any way from one's established position.

Let us assume that I am a committed supporter of the importance of having some regular exercise in the morning; now, if my closest friend also enjoys having some exercise, this does not change my belief at all. Nor does it happen that because my friend performs physical exercise, I give up practicing because I can't stand sharing anything with another person. If then my friend hates training altogether, this fact does not modify my belief in the least. I am, so to speak, impervious to the other's attitude, and my own world stays intact.

That is exactly what the "maintaining" style means; I maintain my world (I stick to my ideas, my behaviors, my sensations) in whatever relation I have. One might say that I am very stable or not flexible at all, that my responses are predictable, as I will always give the same answer.

This concept leads to the following steps:

1. Concentrate on a part or a function of your body that is also accessible to the experience of others.
2. Think of something that belongs to your own world (even though it also belongs to your partner's mental world).
3. How would you solve your problem should you decide about the solution with your own personal organization?

F4: Passive Acceptance

In an earlier paragraph we described a condition of withdrawal into one's own world. We are now going to deal with an antithetical condition, a condition that corresponds to a sort of withdrawal into the other's world. In this interactive modality or, if you like, in this mental state, one accepts solely what exists in the other's world, to a point that the refusal of one's own world also includes those things that are shared; in terms of the relevant diagram, this is the refusal of the intersection. What does this mean? It means that we take into consideration and we accept only those mental contents, constructions, programs, and proposals that exist solely in the world of the other. As we are going to see in the next paragraph, because it does not include shared common elements, this kind of acceptance represents a sort of passive acceptance, a condition of acceptance to one's discharge, so to speak. By way of example, say that I don't like soccer, but my friend wishes to see a match of soccer, and I accept, although I don't like the game; I accept passively, without sharing. Or if my wife is fond of ficus plants, and I am not, still, I buy one on her request, quite passively, as if I were saying, You want this lousy plant; well, here it is, so enjoy it!

The following three items translate this concept in this program:

1. Concentrate on an object that does not belong to you and surely never will.
2. Think of something that belongs solely to your partner's mental world.
3. How would your partner solve the problem by using solely his or her own very personal mental organization? Type out that solution.

F5: Entering into the Other's World

Entering into the other's world means accepting the world of the other, including the shared elements. Therefore, unlike in the previous paragraph, common elements are also accepted, which implies not passive acceptance but acceptance with participation. By way of an extreme example, this means identifying oneself with the other, taking up his or her characteristics, becoming the other one, not passive acceptance but full acceptance.

A wife loves Bach, but her husband doesn't like music at all, yet he presents her, with participation and to his own personal pleasure, with a compact disc (CD) with Bach's music performed by the greatest orchestra in the world. So he identifies himself fully with his wife in her way of perceiving things. Remember Woody Allen's film *Zelig*? He would change into the person with whom he happened to be in contact; if it was a dictator, he would turn into a dictator, in the presence of a musician he would become a musician, and so on. Haven't you often seen a pupil taking up some characteristic attitudes of his teacher or noticed a child who has the same way of moving as his father? There is, in this style, a tendency to try to learn about the other's world and, having done that, to take up his or her characteristics until one changes into the other.

This way of interacting, this mental state, is translated into the following three items in the program:

1. Concentrate on an object that belongs to someone else.
2. Think of elements that exist in your partner's mental world.
3. How would you solve your problem if you identified yourself with your partner?

F6: Swinging

In swinging between one's own world and that of the other one, there is the impossibility of accepting common and shared elements, the pseudosecrets. There exist an interactive modality and a rather complex mental state, the recognition of which, however, opens up new horizons for recognizing the characteristics of the mind; for example, the Italian mafia and Di Pietro. Before Di Pietro and his "Clean Hands" anticorruption squad started their investigations, everyone in Italy knew that a system of bribery existed in the country, but no one ever spoke about it; it was a sort of open secret, a pseudosecret. The negative effects of the system on the economy were self-evident, but what needs to be highlighted is the ambiguity of the times, a climate in which some things were said and others were not, and certain things were said rather than others. When Di Pietro filled in the empty space of what was not said (the "empty intersection"), the country changed deeply.

In our family life, too, in our working life, and among our friends, we come across things that we are all aware of but that nobody talks about, as if there were a secret accord that some things must never be spoken clearly. A wife has an affair with another man, and her husband knows, but nobody says a word about it, to the point that the husband seems able to hide even to himself, at least in part, that he knows his wife is unfaithful to him. A girl has been raped, and the family knows but will not mention it, pretending that nothing happened.

Suppressing these elements that are shared yet untold or kept secret is obviously not without consequences. One of the consequences is the swinging between two different positions without ever finding a point of contact between the two. We all know what happens occasionally when we interact with another person. We have a certain idea, a point of view, a solution, and the other person has a different idea, a different point of view, a different solution. At this point one could choose one's own solution and withdraw completely into one's own world (see function F2) or simply decide to maintain one's own world (function F3), or even choose the other's solution and accept it either passively (function F4) or actively (function F5). One could also choose the solution of accepting only the common elements (function F1), or else choose a compromise solution. What happens instead? We swing; we do not know whether we should accept our own or the other's point of view, our own or the other's solution, and we hesitate.

Given that this falls within the field of creativity, I would like to tell you the plot of a comedy that may plausibly be written. There are a number of characters interacting in the plot. They speak about many things but never mention other things that they all know about. The conversations occasionally come to a standstill because the unsayable things cross the characters' minds, and this steers what they say along other lines, so that what emerges is a disharmonious and rambling discourse. To represent the interactive style about which we are talking, I would have another character doing the asides so that the words that he speaks are not heard by the group of friends on the stage. This character says what they do not and expresses whatever crops up in the group's conversation but remains unsaid. In the second act of the play this character finally speaks to the group directly and overtly talks about everything that has not been mentioned. At this point the group changes and becomes harmonious.

Giving presents may be another example. I know that Mary's husband, Frank, likes castles, so I give her a book on castles for her birthday. The hidden agenda here is that the present is actually for Frank. I know that, and Mary knows that, but neither of the two may say so, and we normally pretend that my present was for her, while she pretends that she is thanking me. Everyone knows, but the intersection is not filled in.

The film *Whatever Happened to Baby Jane?* may be yet another example of the style we are dealing with. This is a film directed by Robert Aldrich with Bette Davis and Joan Crawford. The plot is that apparently Baby Jane (Bette Davis) runs over her sister, a famous actress (Joan Crawford), out of envy and causes her to be crippled for life. The truth is exactly the opposite; actually, Joan wanted to run over Baby Jane, who had mockingly imitated her and teased her all evening and is eventually left paralyzed in the accident. Baby Jane is blamed for it because she was too drunk and confused to remember anything. The viewers get to know the truth only at the end of the film. Both characters in the film, however, seemingly knew what had happened; even Baby Jane did, though only partially (and this now fits into our style). The apparent benevolence of Baby Jane's sister and Baby Jane's madness were there to cover up a secret or, better, a pseudo-secret.

How should all that be translated in our program? We are proposing the following items:

1. What comes to your mind if you avoid thinking of that thing that is dominant on your mind right now?
2. Think of elements that exist in your world and in your partner's world but that nobody talks about.
3. Think of how you would not solve your problem by placing yourself alternately from your exclusive point of view and from that of your partner without finding any point of accord.
4. Or rather, think of two types of antithetical solutions and balance them so that you will not obtain any concrete solution.

F7: Mediation

What "mediation" means can be easily understood both with respect to the relationship and with respect to the mental state. More precisely, we may say that mediating between oneself and the other one means taking into account one's own point of view, one's own proposals, ideas, and mental constructions—briefly, one's own world—and also taking into account the world of the other one and recognizing the points that the two worlds have in common. It is the search for a solution that will include one's own standpoint and that of the other as well as the points in common between the two standpoints.

Incidentally, we must say that this is regarded as a level-headed attitude, and so it is actually; in a more stringent logic, however, it entails a risk, namely, that when such people, who are naturally inclined to mediating, come across someone who is insane, they tend to turn insane, too, precisely because of their propensity to mediate. This happens just because they also take the other one into account, and if the other one is a lunatic, they, too, may turn lunatic. In the social area we have often had an opportunity to realize that mediation could lead to social folly. Just think of the intemperances of 1968 and the subsequent outcomes, the massacres, the red brigades. But also in today's politics, after the Di Pietro aftermath and after the collapse of the old party system, attempts to mediate have resulted in the present chaos.

Here are the items in the program for this function:

1. Concentrate on two objects and connect them to each other; find common points and differences.
2. Think of specific elements from your world and of specific elements from your partner's world and connect them; find common points and differences.
3. Find a solution that will include both your own and your partner's world.

F8: The Absurd, the Paradoxical, the Lunatic

These are the ideas, mental constructions, actions, proposals, and so on that belong neither to one's own nor to somebody else's world, hence, all that is foreign, abstract, unbelievable, paradoxical, far from our sound common sense. In other words, this interactive style and this mental state correspond to getting away from predictable, logical lines. Suppose, for example, that I am talking with my wife about our plans for the evening, and suppose that I ask her, "Should we go to the movies?" and she answers, "The moon is checkered." Clearly, she has gotten out of that kind of unconscious contract that binds our conversations; she has moved away from the lines of predictable sequences, out of the repertory of a probable sequence of messages.

The following is a less colorful though more formal example. Suppose I believe that my 12-year-old daughter should not be given the house keys, and so does my wife, and yet we do give her the keys after all; here again there is something inconsequent and unpredictable.

It is important to realize that, from now on, the paradoxical feature just described will be present in all of the remaining six interactive styles that we will be describing in the next paragraphs, though—as you are going to realize—the nature of such paradoxicality will be different. To make this point clearer, let us take an example from art. If you think of Botticelli, you will realize that the figures in his paintings are extremely beautiful, although they correspond largely to reality. If you think of van Gogh's paintings, you will realize that the figures are readily recognized but that the painter is more detached from reality. Then think of a painting by Pollock (e.g., *Enchanted Forest*); you will realize immediately that here contact with reality is altogether absent. The style that we are discussing in this paragraph corresponds exactly to the style in Pollock's art.

It is obvious that this aspect of relations and of mental life is extremely important with respect to creativity, because creativity comes precisely from this universe that is external to the lines of logic, of the predictable, of common sense; therefore, this is a fundamental aspect in a program that is aimed at developing divergent thinking. That is why we insist on this aspect in our program when we ask you to repeat each item 5 or 10 times.

This is how you proceed:

1. Let your mind go blank; then cite the first thought that comes to your mind (repeat this drill 5 times);
2. Let your mind go blank; then type the first thought that comes to the mind (yours or your partner's, alternately);
3. Let your mind go blank; then think of the first solution that comes to your mind, no matter how absurd (repeat this drill 10 times).

F9: From Sharing to Creativity

Let us go back to our example of art and of the different art styles about which we were talking in the previous paragraph. Art may be a representation of reality that can be very close to a true photographic picture. Think, for example, of the illustrations of operas by Simbonetta, published in the illustrated supplement to the Italian daily *La Tribuna* by the end of the nineteenth century. There is also another kind of art, like that of Pollock, in which contact with reality seems to have been lost completely, and there is art in which reality can be recognized but has been modified. I mentioned van Gogh, but we could add a host of other artists: Modigliani, Matisse, Dalí, Picasso at a certain time in his life, and so on. In their art, reality is recognizable, but it has undergone a deformation; there may be a deformation of forms that depart more or less from real ones, there may be a distortion of colors, or it may be the position of the various parts with respect to space that has been distorted or the way in which the parts relate to one another or, again, the relation between form, color, shape, and so on.

These are all examples of convergence upon certain aspects that we all recognize as a shared object; however, this object undergoes deformation in one or more of its parts. In other words, these are interactive styles and mental states in which there is a center—a shared focus—that is modified by the introduction of unpredictable, strange, paradoxical, odd, crazy aspects that are marked by creativity.

Now we add something that makes our analysis of this interactive style and of this state of the mind so far a bit more complicated. This complication comes from the fact that logic does have certain requirements of its own. I must add, in fact, that for the two interacting subjects, according to this style, joining is twofold; on the one hand, they share common aspects, and, on the other hand, they share aspects that are not common (paradoxical aspects). What we have here is a sort of "supersolidarity" because the two subjects (partners?) accept what is common to both of them and also accept something that is not common to both; in conclusion, they are a kind of "supersharers."

How does the program solve the interactive aspects and the mental states that are exemplified by a particular kind of art?

1. Place a thought right at the center of your mind (your dominant thought at this very moment or just any thought, a thought that you have drawn from the style described in F8) and modify it paradoxically (by deforming, distorting, or expanding enormously just one part of it, etc.).
2. Think of something (a thought, an object, a behavior) that is common to yourself and to your partner and modify it paradoxically (by deforming, distorting, or expanding enormously just one part of it, etc.).
3. Imagine one possible solution that you share with your partner and exaggerate it paradoxically (by deforming, distorting, or expanding enormously just one part of it, etc.).

F10: Antithesis

Did you ever happen to be in the presence of someone who says and does exactly the opposite of what you would like him or her to say or to do, for example, someone who says "black" when you say "white," who will stay at home when you want to go out, who gets away if you come closer and comes closer when you get away, or who will defend the thesis Z if you defend thesis A? A person of this kind can be defined a "Mary, Mary, quite contrary" or an "anti-other."

So, clearly, there exist an interactive style and a state of the mind with which you are all familiar, which therefore I am not going to discuss at length here, and which is characterized by "doing the opposite."

As in physics, we talk about anti-matter, there is in the human mind the possibility of constructing and using contrasting items. Identifying the antithesis of something helps us, on the one hand, to define the thing itself better and, on the other hand, to work out ideas and solutions that would not emerge had we not taken that course.

In this program we have identified and defined this style and its mental state along the following three lines:

1. Think of the way in which you perceive the world right now. Build your own thought of how you perceive the world and act on it by doing something about it. Then turn everything upside down, in reverse; think of the contrary, the opposite.
2. Think of your partner's world, then turn it upside down while you think of its reverse.
3. Think of a possible solution, and then think of its reverse (think of the "anti-solution").

F11: Dictatorship

We all know what a dictator is, like Hitler; dictators are people who stick to their ideas in a rigid manner and who are also crazy, in the sense that a sort of exasperation of their rigidity makes them lose contact with reality, ending up in unlimited fanaticism. These characteristics alone tell us how the Holocaust was possible, how endless wars were started, or how cruel and despotic regimes, where all sense of humanity was lost, were established. In all cases one can realize that the dictator's mind is dominated by wrong and incorrigible ideas. No matter how much we dislike dictators, we must admit that humankind produces them at absolutely regular intervals and that, consequently, dictatorship is an interactive style of humans and a way of constructing our mind.

The following three items translate this way of being and of interacting:

1. Think of something in your world, so important to you that you would be prepared to give your life for it;
2. Think of what you would do if you had absolute, dictatorial power over your partner. What would you do?
3. If you had absolute power for solving the problem, how would you proceed?

F12: Pseudoaltruism

What is meant by pseudoaltruism? We mean those situations, easily recognizable, where apparently you move toward the other's world, though, actually, you retain your own world. Suppose St. Francis renounced all his possessions in favor of the poor, though not because of thinking of the poor but merely for his own satisfaction; we would then have an example of this particular interactive style. If I do my best to have my partner experience orgasm not because I want to make her happy but because it pleases me to see her enjoy it, this is another example of this style. Speaking of presents, here is an example: a simple girl, who always lived in poverty, meets a young man, and he presents her with a beautiful gold jewel, but he does so because he enjoys seeing the girl's reaction, a mixture of pleasure and embarrassment. This is another example of a pseudoaltruistic style. You can clearly see for yourself that this is something entirely different from entering the other's world and from the situation that we described under F5.

Many people do not consider this selfish (egotistic?) generosity with which we often happen to operate and to think, but we have been able to highlight it through our analysis, and we must keep that in mind as we work on our program. Where our relation with an object is concerned, we cannot, of course, speak in terms of pseudoaltruism. As we are going to see in the first items of the program, we can think only of an object that does not belong to us and never will, though we concentrate on it by deforming it paradoxically.

In the program, the style and the mental state corresponding to this approach have been organized as follows:

1. Concentrate on an object that does not belong to you and never will and modify it paradoxically (by exaggerating, deforming, distorting, or expanding enormously just one part of it, etc.).
2. Think of a situation where apparently you have been acting for your partner, though in actual reality you've been acting for yourself (pseudoaltruism).
3. Think of a situation that apparently favors the other one but actually favors you.

F13: Accepting the Other One by Expanding

Accepting the other one by expanding does not mean just accepting the other's world (i.e., the other's ideas, proposals, mental constructions, actions or, generally speaking, the other's contents, in other words his or her way of perceiving, constructing mentally, and acting). Rather, it means introducing, by our acceptance, something that is external to his or her world, introducing characteristics of paradoxicality, unpredictability, oddity, folly. If, for example, my wife likes animals, and I present her with an elephant, this is precisely the kind of interactive style we are talking about!

How can this interactive style, or rather this mental state, be translated?

1. Think of an object that belongs to someone else and transform it paradoxically (by exaggerating, distorting, expanding enormously just one part of it, etc.).
2. Think of something that belongs to your partner's world and modify it paradoxically (by exaggerating, distorting, expanding enormously just one part of it, etc.).
3. Think of the solution that your partner would adopt and change it paradoxically (by exaggerating, distorting, expanding enormously just one part of it, etc.).

F14: Inability to Hit the Mark

We are here in the presence of an interactive style that is characterized by accepting one's own world and that of the other one, plus what exists neither in one's own nor in the other's world but without being able to accept sharing. I have known a girl for years who must be around 30 now. She has always declared that her primary goal in life, in addition to her job, where she is doing well, is to get married and form a family, yet she does not succeed in doing so, although she is beautiful, intelligent, and honest. Still, her behavior lends itself to a perfectly clear explanation. She has been engaged for years to a clever, though sexually cold, young man, she has an affair with another chap who is instead handsome and warm, and, on the top of all that, she has sexual intercourse with a drug trafficker, even though she is a very honest girl who abides by the law. This whole story can be interpreted as follows: she wants to comply with the requirements of the orthodox world around her through her official relationship with her fiancé, she wants to stick to her own world by her affair with the passionate young man, and then she wants to add something queer like keeping her relation with the drug trafficker. By accepting three alternatives at one time, however, she cannot reach her goal, namely, her wish to have a single, stable, and final relation.

This way of interacting finds its counterpart in the way in which some people organize their speech. They never seem to hit the target, they seem unable to state explicitly, clearly, and simply the gist of their argument, they seem to be roaming around aimlessly. Every now and then they get closer to your world but then off they go into their own world, and then they say things that get nowhere; they seem to be thoughtless, abstract, absent-minded. Occasionally, however, if you listen to them carefully, you realize that they proceed along the characteristic lines of a metaphor; that is, they express themselves indirectly by uttering words and phrases that actually mean other words and phrases. Their way of speaking is somewhat reminiscent of that of the Mafia, using a language that is never explicit, that never comes to the point, a language with circumlocutions in which the gist of the argument must be understood, even though it has not been uttered.

How can this interactive style and this state of the mind be translated in this program?

1. Think of such phrases as realistic reverie, controlled delusion, controlled slipping, reasonable folly, oriented disinhibition. Try to form some such phrase yourself.
2. Think of a situation concerning your partner and yourself and change it into a metaphor (e.g., a wife had several love affairs with other men, so she told her husband that she was like a butterfly from one flower to another).
3. Transform the problem into the problem's metaphor.

F15: Total Acceptance

Total acceptance means accepting one's own world and the world of the other one, the common aspects and those that belong neither to one's own nor to the other's world. This interactive style and this way of constructing with the mind may be regarded as non-selectivity, on the one hand, hence as confusion, total paralysis, impossibility to communicate, but, on the other hand, it can be viewed as the mother of all other possibilities and also as total freedom. No indication is given in connection with F15, the last passage in the program, except that the absence of any indication is not a mistake in the program. Now that the reader has just gone interactively through the 16 interactive styles and the 16 mental states, there is the possibility that one may have learned how to utilize one's mind. To acquire more flexibility, the reader will have to practice passing from one state to another and to solve the problems, one after another, until one gets to a point where one no longer needs any help either in writing or by a computer program. The reader needs to practice until the mind has finally acquired the mental tool provided by the program submitted to you. So, this is our suggestion: once you are able to master the 16 mental states completely, pass from one state to another freely, trying all possible combinations. [1]

CONCLUSION

This brief introduction to the EPM should serve to enlarge the self-awareness of the reader. If that is the case, then the reader, on the basis of this self-expansion, may be able to expand the self-awareness of others. Evidence to support some aspects of this model are presented in Chapter 5. In addition to this expansion, additional methods for even further expansion are suggested in Chapter 9 and 10. [2]

NOTES

1. Consumer satisfaction of this method in a student population was reported by De Giacomo and De Nigris (2001).
2. Additional references about the EPM, beyond those found in this text, are available in Appendix D.

Chapter 5

Evaluating the Model

SISCI-1 is a good example of how Shannon's triad can be used in a test. A respondent is shown in slide format Holtzman's 90 inkblots and is then asked to choose which of the 90 inkblots he or she prefers. The slides are then administered again in an interactive fashion. Respondents are shown them again, with the information about which inkblots were most commonly chosen by most people. Subsequently, in a third presentation, respondents are asked to reselect which of the same 90 inkblots he or she liked best.

A comparison between the final choice (after interacting with the other) and the first choice (before the interaction) shows the percentages of the four coordinates of the EPM as well as responses relating to the 16 functions that are specific to a particular respondent and no one else:

- acceptance (0 1 ' 1)
- maintenance (1 0 ' 1)
- sharing (1 1 ' 1), and
- antifunctions (0 0 ' 1).

ATTEMPTS TO DEVISE TESTS BASED ON THE EPM

The research activities developed to provide an experimental evaluation of the EPM were started by a group of clinicians (De Giacomo, Pierri, Corfiati) and a group of computer scientists, mathematicians, and physicists (Silvestri, Lefons, Pazienza, Tangorra, Mich), all from Bari University. They were dealing with the problem related to the way in which the world of an individual changes as a result of the "perturbation" caused by an external event, called the "other person's world." The idea dominating the group was that human interactions had to be studied as one type of spectral analysis. Therefore, a procedure had to be found with which, in the first phase, the world of the subject to be tested was determined and, in a second phase, the change of this world after interaction with something that can be defined as "the other person's world" was introduced. The second subject's world ("the other's world"), interacting with the subject being tested, had to be a standard world that was the same for everybody (even though experiments were also conducted by using the spouse's actual world or the world of one or more relatives). We thought of using a series of 40 pictures randomly selected among the 90 Holtzman (1961) pictures. Consequently, the procedure had to be based on a first phase, in which the subject was allowed to freely select those pictures that he or she liked or in which he or she was interested or by which he or she was struck, out of the 90 Holzman inkblots. This administration represented the world of the subject being evaluated. In a second phase, the subject was exposed to the second subject, according to a standard presentation of slides, made up of 40 randomly selected Holtzman inkblots. Finally, in the third phase, the subject was once again asked to select inkblots out of the 90 initial ones. In this way, it was possible to see how initial choices had changed or had remained unaltered as a result of the interaction with "the other subject."

SISCI-1 was a result of this need and of this context. [1] This group, therefore, developed a relational test, derived, of course, from the EPM (Chapter 4), based on a method of observation suited for giving objective data on the relational behavior of interacting respondents. The kind of test proposed should account also for measuring changes that derive after interacting with the world of another respondent. This second interactant/respondent is represented either by a randomized world (i.e., inkblots presented in the second administration were selected randomly) or were given by the world of a partner, parent, or made-up others.

SISCI stands for Synthesis/Scission—the basic mental process of joining and separating between individuals and their environment (i.e., "world" or context, the reality as viewed by the respondent). This process was a starting point for the creation of the EPM, switching from the model's theoretical aspects to its experimental application. Indeed, as already mentioned in Chapter 4, the MPE is arranged at four levels. The triad stands at the first level: (1) the world of the first interacting subject, (2) the world of the second interacting subject, and (3) transformation of the first subject's world subsequent to the interaction. This starting point then leads to the four coordinates (acceptance of the other person's world, maintenance of one's own world, sharing, and acceptance of what does not exist in the interacting subject's world). Combinations and permutations of these four coordinates lead to the 16 functions or relational styles described in the previous chapter. These 16 relational styles then lead to 256 interaction rules (deriving from the interaction between 16 relational styles and the 16 relational styles themselves), shown in Chapter 4.

Application of this general principle actually occurs according to the following procedure.

SISCI-1 TEST

Normal and pathological respondents, couples, and families have been tested individually and in groups. The test is administered in three successive stages. The initial phase is the same for everybody. After the subject has been given an answer sheet, he or she is shown a series of 90 slides, with an average of 20 seconds per slide to "make a good choice." At the end of this stage, the answer sheet is handed back to the experimenter. *This represents the "world" of the subject before interaction.* After a few minutes the subject is shown 40 of the 90 slides, chosen at random, defined as "the pictures that most persons choose." The experimenter makes comments on each slide, describing what most people see in it. *This choice represents the world of the other subject.* After this second phase, the subject is shown the 90 slides over again at a faster rate and is again asked to make a choice; this time the subject's choices are written down on a second answer sheet. *This choice defines the world of the subject after interaction with someone's world.*

Data are processed by a computer. They are saved on a diskette, and the results of this processing show graphically relational patterns of single individuals that can be used to simulate interactions and give suggestions for relational interventions.

Instructions for Administration for SISCI-1 Test

The administration procedure for the SISCI-1 test is based on the initial preparation of the individual subject or of groups of subjects to be examined. Instructions are given in detail and very calmly, to establish a calming set in the administration. For smaller children, especially those in lower elementary classes, further advice and explanations are given, which help establish a playlike relationship with the examiner and increase their attention, so that their choices are really motivated. At the same time, each subject is given the first answer sheet, where the first choice of the inkblots is indicated.

First Stage

After the first answer sheet has been given out, the following instructions are given, which are usually standard:

The test which we are going to administer today will give us useful information on how you relate to other people. During the test you will see some pictures. After you've seen them, you must indicate which you like because of their color or their shape or because they remind you of something or for any other reason. To make what I've said clearer, for example, imagine you are in an art gallery, with a lot of pictures, and you've got to buy a few. Look at them, judge them, and decide, "I like this one, so I'll take it" or "I don't like this one, so I won't have it."

Let's look, in particular, at how to do this test. Each of you has been given a piece of paper, where there are two columns of numbers; the first goes from 1 to 45, and the second from 46 to 90. Each number corresponds to one of the pictures you will see, one after the other, on the screen.

What do you have to do? You just have to look at the pictures and make a good selection. As I said before, "good" means that you mustn't choose just a few pictures or a lot or all of them but a few good ones, those that appeal to you. This is very important for our test.

As you see each picture, put a cross with your pen next to the number that corresponds to that picture, if you choose it. If you don't like it, don't put anything. You will have time to choose each picture, and the corresponding number will be called out to help you. Next to the column of numbers you can see another column, with "Contents" written above it.

What does this mean? When we show you the pictures, perhaps you will see their contents as animals, people, objects or scenes, etc. If you see something and you have time, in the few seconds given between each picture, write it down in this column. For example, if someone sees a butterfly in picture 5, he or she writes down this content—whether he or she has chosen this picture or not. However, this point is less important to us.

We repeat: for this test, the most important thing is the choice of the pictures shown. If you manage to write the contents as well, that's fine, but that is not important for the evaluation of the test. It should be clear enough now how to do this test. We stress again that the most important thing is to choose the pictures and, above all, a good number of them.

One last point: everyone must work in silence and do his or her own work, without distracting others by asking advice or exchanging views.

Second Stage

The first answer sheet is taken in, and, after a few minutes, subjects are asked to pay close attention:

Just like you, other people have done this test before and have indicated their choices of pictures. Now we will show you which pictures have been chosen most often by the majority of people. We shall also tell you, for each picture, what the majority said they saw in it, that is, what pictures mean without choosing anything. Perhaps some of you won't agree about what you thought they could make out in the picture. You must look at these inkblots according to what others saw—it doesn't matter. You can see what you like. There is no correct answer.

Forty slides, taken at random, are then shown, and their contents are explained, which are statistically the most "popular" or commonly chosen, that is, the contents as seen by the majority of respondents.

Third Stage

Subjects are supplied with a second answer sheet, and final instructions are given:

> Now I am going to show you all the 90 pictures more quickly. You must look at them and make another good selection of the pictures you like. As you see each picture again, put a cross with your pen by the number which corresponds to the picture, if you choose it. Don't put anything if you don't. This time, you mustn't write down the contents; it's enough just to put down your choice. It doesn't matter if the figures you choose are the same as those you chose the first time.

After this phase has been completed, the second answer sheet is taken in. On the basis of this administration over the last 20 years, the following research studies have been completed and published in professional journals.

RESEARCH FROM CHILDHOOD TO ADULTHOOD

The first developmental research (Silvestri et al, 1980; Silvestri, Lefons, Corfiati, & De Giacomo, 1988) was conducted with 2,053 subjects (age range 6–18), in Italian schools from the first year of primary school to the last year of high school. A sample of adults was added later. Moreover, a comparison was made with pathological subjects. In particular, the sample was composed of 108 subjects from the first year of primary school (average age 6.5), 139 subjects from the second year of primary school (average age 7.5), 143 subjects from the third year of primary school (average age 8.5), 126 subjects from the fourth year of primary school (average age 9.5), 115 subjects from the fifth year of primary school (average age 10.5), 141 subjects from the first year of junior high school (average age 11.5), 220 subjects from the second year of junior high school (average age 12.5), 163 subjects from the third year of junior high school (average age 13.5), 149 subjects from the first year of high school (average age 14.5), 144 subjects from the second year of high school (average age 15.5), 121 subjects from the third year of high school (average age 16.5), 133 subjects from the fourth year of high school (average age 17.5), 66 subjects from the fifth year of high school (average age 18.5). The adult group included 285 subjects aged between 30 and 35. Comparisons were also made with subjects drawn from other research studies (see below).

This research aimed at determining changes in the subjects' interaction pattern in the course of the years (i.e., throughout the development of subjects from childhood to adulthood, as measured with SISCI-1). This research was also meant to compare hypothesized patterns emerging from this experimentation with results predicted from the theoretical EPM. The four coordinates of the EPM were taken into account: (1) the antifunction coordinate (acceptance of what does not exist in the interacting subjects' world, i.e., the abstract universe; (2) the acceptance coordinate of what exists in the other's world; (3) the maintenance coordinate about what exists in one's own world, and (4) the sharing coordinate, which implies acceptance of what exists in common in one's own world and in the other's world. The reason that the four coordinates, rather than the 16 functions or relational styles, were considered can be ascribed to the fact that the coordinates' calculations, starting from the triple one (choice of the first subject and choice of the second subject and result of the interaction), are mathematically possible, whereas the functions' calculation, derived from the coordinates through an algebraic formula, is not as possible. Indeed, the formula of transformation from coordinates' values to functions' values was one of the major pitfalls of SISCI-1.

Results of this research showed that with age, the first coordinate quickly decreased. The second one had the same tendency to decrease. The third one (the maintaining coordinate) remained constant and was significantly independent of age. The fourth coordinate (sharing) also showed a tendency to remain fairly constant over time. Pathological subjects did not follow the same developmental progression.

The conclusion reached by this research was that as one grows older, the ability to accept new elements in a coherent or not coherent manner decreases. It was felt that the results experimentally obtained were consistent with those predicted from the EPM hypotheses.

RESEARCH ON PSYCHOPATHOLOGY

The two major areas of psychopathology that have been investigated with SISCI-1 are depression and schizophrenia.

Depression

The first research conducted on pathological subjects (Lefons et al., 1979) concerned the diagnosis of depression based on the Italian translation of the Minnesota Multiphasic Personality Inventory (MMPI). This study involved two groups. One was composed of 146 cases with code D ≤ 29. The other comparison group included 31 subjects with code D > 29. All subjects were also administered the SISCI-1. Results showed that some values significantly differed in the two groups. In particular, those values related to the likelihood that F0 and F1 increased in depressed subjects, whereas F7 and F15 decreased. This means that the more depressed one is, the more likely he or she is to use mechanisms F0 and F1 in the interaction with another subject and the less likely he or she is to use functions F7 and F15.

According to the EPM, these functions represent the subject's relational status; a high F0 value corresponds to a situation in which the subject mainly does not give positive responses to any proposal. This behavior is typical of those functions located in the lower part of the hypercube, which accounts for the relational universe under EPM.

F1 corresponds to a tendency to a downward shift (i.e., toward F0). Therefore, F0 and F1 correspond to a status of low positive reaction index and a tendency to even lower values, respectively. F15 and F7, instead, mean the opposite. In short, this research supported the continued use of EPM in clinical practice for various mental disorders and mood disturbances. In particular, these results are consistent with the hypothesis that, in the case of depression, the tendency is toward 0 ("mental emptiness"). On the other hand, in the case of mania, which is the opposite of depression, there should be a tendency toward F15 (this function corresponds to the inability to select, which generates mental confusion). It should be noticed that, in Figure 5-1, F0 and F15 represent situations of rigidity. On the other hand, the area related to freedom of movement is shown in the middle section of Figure 5-1.

Schizophrenia

As far as schizophrenia is concerned, in the first 30 cases and then in the many other subsequent cases, the SISCI-1 showed a consistent pattern that was clearly different from that of normal subjects, as shown in Figure 5-2

By comparing the percentage of the 16 functions developed from the four coordinates through an algebraic formula, the schizophrenic pattern as a whole looks much flatter than the profile of normal subjects. What is more striking is that the percentage of the function for maintaining one's own world (F3) is much lower than the 30% representing the average for normal subjects. This finding led us to assume that schizophrenia represents the inability to maintain one's own world in a relationship. All the symptoms of schizophrenia (such as influential delusions, disorganized thought, loss of boundaries with the external world) could be ascribed to the "melting" of the schizophrenic patient in the world, due to his or her inability to have the strength and steadiness to live with and within one's own world.

Another research study was conducted by De Giacomo, Pierri, et al. (1997) with 38 schizophrenic patients randomly divided into two groups. The first group was treated with psychoactive medications, whereas the second group, in addition to the administration of psychoactive medications, followed a course of 10 one-hour sessions of family therapy, also

Figure 5-1
View of the Hypercube Developed from the EPM

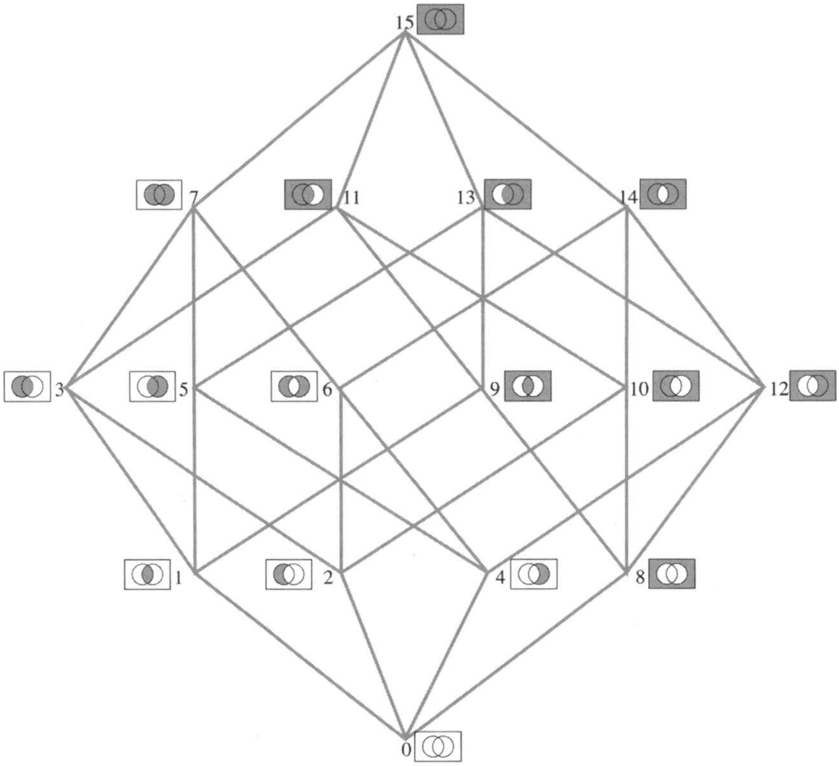

inspired by the EPM (see Chapter 10). The outcomes of these two interventions were measured with the Brief Psychiatric Scale, the Strauss Carpenter Outcome Scale (Strauss & Carpenter, 1972), the Five Minute Speech Sample (for Emotional Expression) (Magnana et al., 1986, the Active Check List (to evaluate feelings and behavior) (Gough & Heilbrun, 1972), and the SISCI-1 (for the relational aspects). The second group showed significant improvement in comparison to the first one, in terms of both clinical improvement and the number of dropouts. As far as the SISCI-1 was concerned, the most meaningful result was achieved with the antifunction or relational style F8. This function involves a tendency to choose elements that belong neither to the patient's own world nor to that of the other. Clinically, a reduction in F8 means that the patient will become more involved in interaction with other subjects and will show a more adequate pattern of relating with others.

The primary aim of another study (De Giacomo et al., 1986) was to verify whether the SISCI-1 was sufficiently sensitive to show any change in

Figure 5-2
Results from the Administration of the SISCI-1 Test to Normal and Schizophrenic Respondents

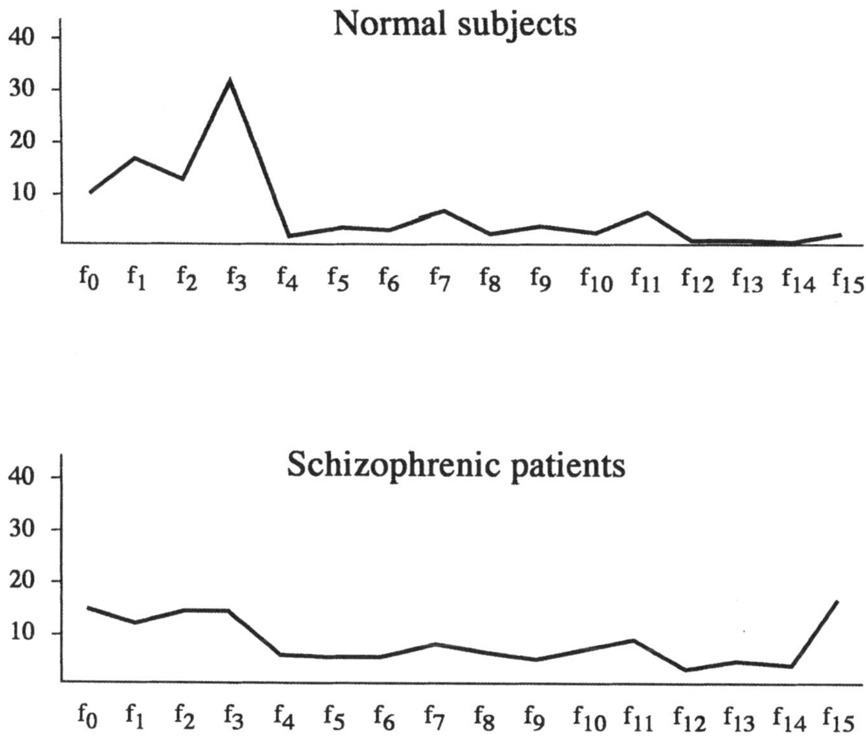

relational behavior due to the administration of psychoactive medications. This study included 32 subjects suffering from schizophrenic disorders (treated with haloperidol), 8 subjects with major depressive episodes, and 8 with manic episodes (who were treated with lithium).

The experimental procedure was as follows: (1) The SISCI-1 test was administered to all subjects before and after the administration of psychoactive medication. Considering the mean score values for pathological subjects, before and after the therapy with haloperidol and lithium, we concluded that the values of the four coordinates were significantly different from the corresponding values before the administration of medication and that the mean scores after therapy were significantly closer to those of normal subjects, as shown in Figure 5-3.

Simulation Procedures

The EPM allows the development of a series of simulations in which the patterns of the four coordinates and the 16 functions can be modified sub-

Figure 5-3
Results in Coordinate Values before and after Therapy

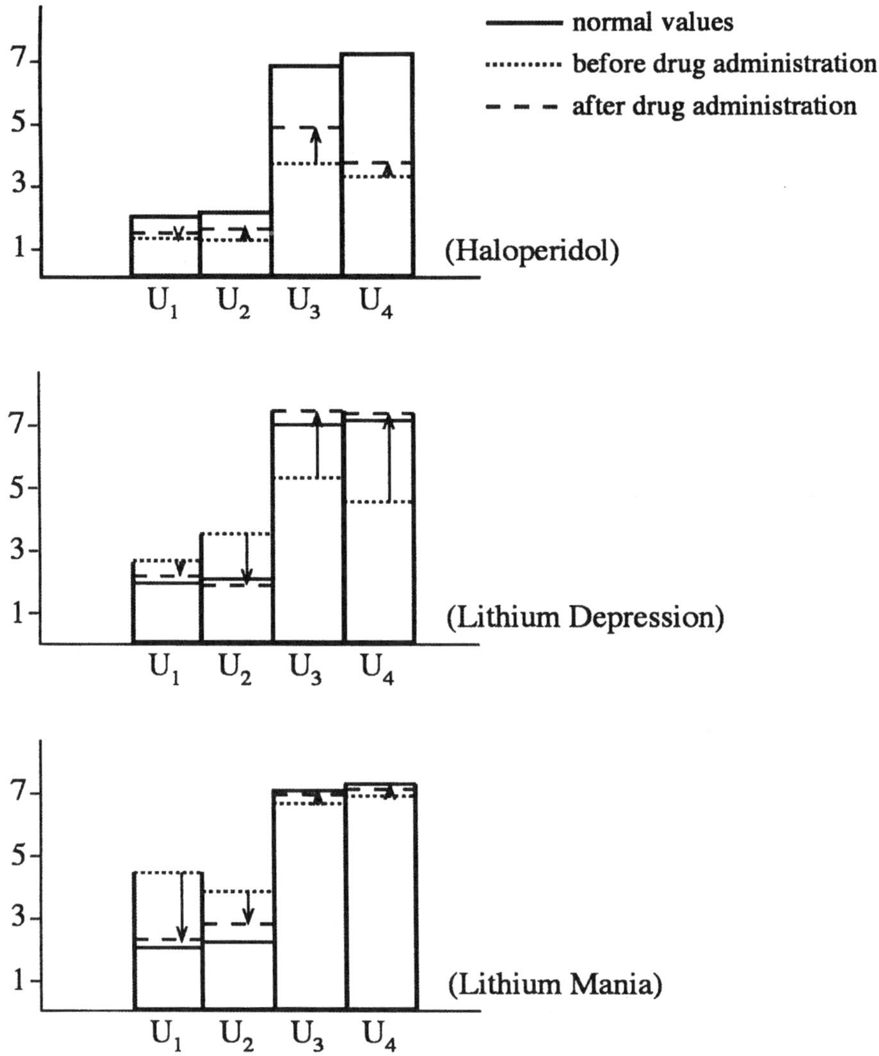

sequently to the interaction with single functions (relational styles) or patterns of two or more functions. Simulation refers to instructions given to normal subjects to switch from a normal to a schizophrenic one and then switch back to a normal pattern (De Giacomo, Pierri, Lefons, & Mich, 1990). We started from the average pattern of a normal subject, resulting from previous research works (see above), and made it interact with the 16 MPE functions (one at a time). This showed which functions cause this pattern to look similar to the one already known in schizophrenic subjects (see above). A mathematical procedure devised in previous research was applied (Silvestri, Pereira, & Ferreira, 1987). Those functions without interaction (i.e., those without shared elements) lead to the schizophrenic pattern. Among these, the F10 (the Mary, Mary, quite contrary, oppositional individuals) is the fastest to reach this outcome. You cannot fail to notice the analogy of this function with what was reported with regard to research works on hypercriticism or expressed emotions in families with a schizophrenic member, that have produced negative outcomes. The opposite simulation, which starts from a schizophrenic pattern to reach a normal pattern, shows how the most effective function is F5, equal to entering the other's world. This outcome corresponds to the way in which we intervene in cases of persecutory delusions. For example, we enter the world of deluded patients by asking them to tell all the details of the plot perpetrated against them: who is the leader in the plot, who are the people or political groups who may affect their personality, and so on. This point is expanded in Chapter 10.

SISCI-1 and Kaltest

The Kaltest was created as an alternative to the SISCI-1 (Pereira & Ferreira, 1985) and involves the display of kaleidoscopic configurations on a computer screen. It was devised with the intention of providing a tool that was (1) more alluring, by showing stimuli on the computer screen rather than using slides like in SISCI-1; (2) more dynamic and interactive (the subject uses the computer keyboard to answer) by simulating the interaction between two subjects in real time; (3) faster to administer in about 30 minutes for each individual application (like for SISCI-1, group applications are available); (4) free from memory effects, given the extreme variability of the rectangular configurations presented; and (5) meant for research purposes because all four coordinates can be calculated immediately.

For all the other characteristics, the Kaltest and SISCI-1 are similar: same number of stimuli (90), same instructions, identical number of phases, same way of calculating results. The Kaltest configurations are of rectangular shape, have the same size, with four median axes, made up of 16×18 elements with rectangular and monochromatic images, generated in color and projected in black and white in six tones of gray corresponding to blue, crimson, green, light blue, and yellow.

Once the Kaltest had been devised, it was very relevant to compare the results achieved with the SISCI-1. A total of 148 university students, male and female, aged between 17 and 59, were evaluated with both instruments. Results turned out to be concordant with each other, as shown in Figure 5-4.

Figure 5-4
Comparison Profiles between Kaltest and the SISCI-1 Test

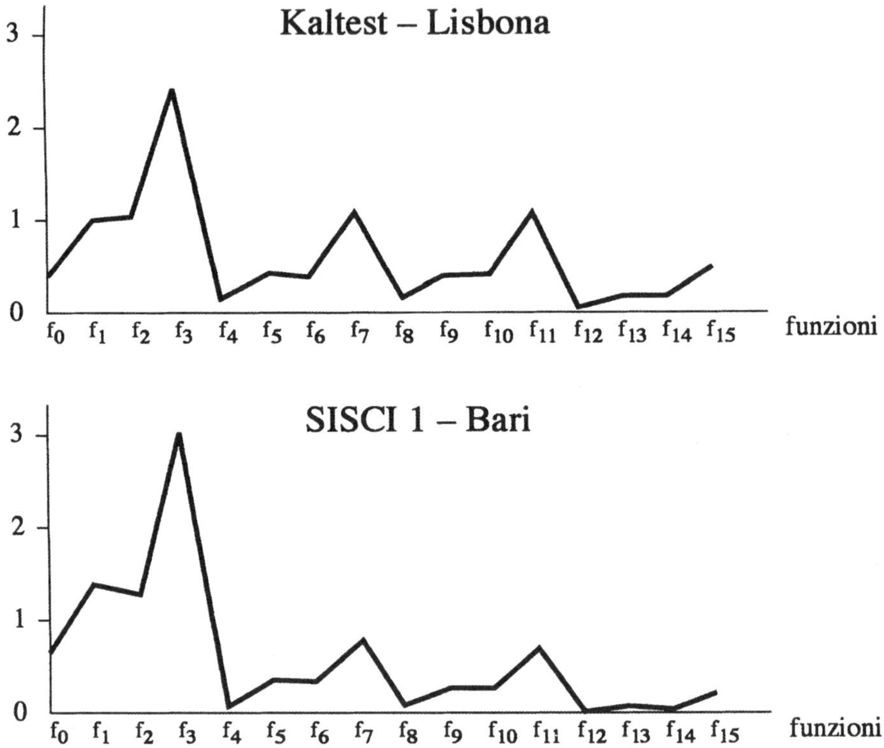

It was concluded that both the SISCI-1 and the Kaltest tests measured similar characteristic and fundamental aspects of interactive behaviors (Pereira & Ferreira, 1985, p. 174).

SISCI-3

The SISCI-1 posed three main disadvantages: (1) with regard to the statistical aspect, an accurate evaluation should be carried out on groups of subjects rather than single individuals; (2) the evaluation can refer only to the specific situation proposed by the test; (3) the evaluation does not refer to the 16 functions but to the four coordinates from which the 16 functions stem. An attempt was made, therefore, to find a test able to directly measure the functions and their changes. SISCI-3 was created to solve this problem (see De Giacomo et al., 1989 in Appendix D). The presentation of this test marked the last step in the development of this type of instrument because the group behind this effort subsequently dissolved, partly due to the transfer of some members of the group to other areas, partly because of Silvestri's death, and partly because of the increased interest by De Giacomo in the field of clinical activities based on the EPM and reported in this book (De Giacomo, 1993).

Procedure for SISCI-3

Eighty slides, each consisting of four Holtzman inkblots, are shown one at time, through a computerized administration. Five phases are foreseen in this test for each slide:

- In the first phase, after showing the slide, subjects are requested to make a choice of two among the four pictures shown.
- In the second phase, the experimenter points at three of the four pictures (one equal and the others different from those chosen by the subject), saying that they have been chosen by most of the people taking the test.
- During the third phase, subjects are invited to make a new choice, still among the four pictures, but this time they are allowed to point at none or all four pictures.
- In the fourth phase, the experimenter, on the basis of a relational style that he or she chooses for interacting with the subject, points at two pictures chosen by the most people.
- In the fifth phase, subjects are requested to make a further free choice (none or all of the shown pictures).

In addition to the relational pattern of the subject, obtained in real time, it is possible to have suggestions for prescriptions for changing the relational system of the subject.

The idea underlying this test was for the first phase to determine the subject's own world, for the second phase to create a nonspecific perturbation by exposing the subject to a standard world, for the third phase (in which the subject was given free choice, to determine the subject's world directly in terms of one of the 16 functions, for the fourth phase to determine a programmed interaction with a certain function chosen by the experimenter, and for the fifth phase to record how the subject changed as a result of the impact with the function selected by the experimenter.

In its practical application to subjects, however, SISCI-3 did not seem to be as valid and incisive as SISCI-1. For this reason, investigators in charge of developing this test opted to stay with SISCI-1.

THE SELF-VIEW QUESTIONNAIRE

A derivative of SISCI-1, called the Self-View Questionnaire (Appendix C) was created by De Giacomo and L'Abate. It was used in research on the evaluation of three different relational models (L'Abate et al., 2000). This test was developed because a more practical, group-oriented, self-evaluation test than the SISCI-1 was needed. Consequently, the 16 EPM functions were transformed/translated into 16 adjective couples, through a process whereby judges [2] completely knowledgeable of the EPM and of the SISCI-1 reached agreements about the face validity of adjectives needed to describe the 16 functions. Moreover, this instrument includes an intensity dimension with regard to people (with all the people, with most people, with some people, with none) and with regard to frequency (most of the time, sometimes, never). Three forms were provided referring to the present, the past, and the future.

Obviously, some differences must be expected between a test measuring an interactive process in a neutral manner, like SISCI-1, and a self-evaluation test, in which self-presentation, social facade, and response sets for some adjectives evaluating one's own way of being cannot help but play a role. This hypothesis is confirmed by some preliminary research studies in which we compared the percentage of each function recorded with SISC-1 in normal subjects (as described in the previously mentioned research) with the percentage of each function recorded in a population of 153 students with the Self-View Questionnaire. According to preliminary results (data not published yet), the prevailing function is not F3 (maintaining one's own world, corresponding to "tenacious-egocentric," like in the SISCI) but F5 (acceptance of the other's world, corresponding to "altruist-involved"). On the other hand, as far as the second and third functions are concerned, SISCI-1 and the Self-View Questionnaire are consistent with each other because F1 (sharing, corresponding to "participant-sharer") and F7 (acceptance of the other's world, of one's own world, and of sharing, corresponding to "collaborative-mediator") are well represented in both tests. The problem is that, when self-evaluation tests are adopted, a sort of social conformity emerges, and it is not easy to describe oneself self-servingly as "tenacious-egocentric" rather than "altruist-involved," at least in cultural contexts like the Italian!

L'Abate et al. (2000)

The purpose of this study was to evaluate convergences and divergences among three completely different models of intimate (prolonged, close, and committed) relationships: (1) attachment, (2) elementary pragmatic, and (3) selfhood. All three models, even though they derive from different theoretical sources, predict seemingly similar patterns of relationships between partners or among intimates. Each model has its own peculiar terminology that has meaning only within the parameters set by the model itself. Possible convergences and divergences among these three models have already been discussed conceptually elsewhere but only at the hypothetical level (De Giacomo, L'Abate, & De Giacomo, 1997; L'Abate, 1997b). These convergences and divergences need reviewing after the main characteristics of each model are summarized and then evaluated empirically.

The attachment model, derived from object relations theory, has been subjected to countless research papers in the last decade. Only a few secondary sources need citing in this regard (Bartholomew & Perlman, 1994; Cassidy & Shaver, 1999; Feeney & Noller, 1996; Sanford, 1997; Simpson & Rholes, 1998). Most research with adults tends to support the validity of four attachment patterns, a secure pattern and three insecure ones. The three insecure patterns, at least in adults, are Dismissing, Preoccupied, and Fearful. Dismissing is a pattern in which the individual is positive about self and negative about other. Preoccupied is a pattern in which the individual is negative about self and positive about other. Fearful is a pattern in which the individual is negative about self and other. Because of its extensively validated research record, which supports its overall validity, this model will be adopted as the criterion to evaluate the concurrent validities of the other two models.

In spite of their different theoretical origins, object relations for the attachment model, general systems for the EPM, and resource exchange for the selfhood model, it would be relevant to find out empirically whether certain convergences as well as divergences among these three models exist. While convergences between attachment and selfhood models are easier to predict (Salvo & Minervini, n.d.), it is more problematic to do so with the elementary pragmatic model because of its focus on processes rather than on contents and on attachment's "internal working models" of relationships. For instance, Secure and Selfulness may represent the highest levels of functionality, while Fearfulness and No-self may represent the lowest levels of dysfunctionality. Dismissing and Selfishness may represent an intermediate level of functionality between the two previous levels, a level occupied by both Preoccupied and Selflessness. Similar predictions cannot be made for the four coordinates of the elementary pragmatic model because it aims to classify and change dyadic interactions rather than pigeonholing individuals. Indeed, it is a classification of relationship processes rather than of individuals. Both attachment and selfhood models in one way or another manage to classify individuals rather than relationships, even though certain types of individuals do show predictable patterns of relating with others.

There are also convergences among at least two of the four characteristics of both attachment and selfhood models in terms of the externality-internality direction. For instance, Dismissing and Selfishness may tend toward externalization, while Preoccupied and Selfless may tend toward internalization. The attachment model is still "intrapsychic" to the extent that it emphasizes internal working models. The selfhood model straddles the intrapsychic and relational aspects. The EPM sticks solely to observable interaction processes, making no assumptions about specific mental contents or internal traits or states. The major difference between the selfhood model and the EPM lies in the latter's focusing only on interactive processes, while the former focuses mainly on the content rather than the process of relationships. From this difference, it follows that the two models may be complementary to each other.

Since possible convergences and divergences among the three models have been thus far strictly hypothetical (see Chapter 8; L'Abate, 1997b), they need empirical validation that would assess the relevance of each model in its own right along a continuum of inferred-observable. For instance, the attachment model stresses the function of internal and therefore inferred working models in producing different types of intimate relationships in children as well as in adults. The selfhood model stresses observably relational personality propensities that determine what kind of intimate relationships will be developed and maintained by individuals. The elementary pragmatic model stresses instead the observation of processes in mostly dyadic intimate relationships in much more specific fashion than would be possible with the other two models. The specific 16 interaction styles cannot be predicted from either attachment or selfhood models. With these styles derived it is possible to make more specific predictions than with the other two models.

Therefore, from a continuum of inferred (i.e., internal) to observable (i.e., external) directions, attachment might be the most inferred, and selfhood seems intermediate between the two other models, with the EPM referring to the most external and observable intimate situations. By the same token, while the attachment model has been evaluated extensively around the globe, the other two models are "new kids on the block" and are in need of extensive evaluation from those who are extraneous to their creation and validation. Both the attachment model and the EPM represent the theory, in the sense that theory and model are both isomorphic with and indistinguishable from each other. The attachment model summarizes and sustains by itself the whole object relations theory. The same is the case in the EPM. The model is the theory. The selfhood model, on the other hand, is but one of several models sustaining the theory, even though, admittedly, it is the major model on which a great deal of the theory stands or falls (L'Abate, 1997b).

If convergences and divergences among these three models are established empirically, then the two new kids on the block may achieve greater validity by being evaluated concurrently with a relatively established "old-timer" like attachment. In this way, a significant step forward in theory-building and theory-testing for intimate relationship models might be achieved. Perhaps, from these three and other circumplex models, it might be possible to advance to a "supertheory" that would encompass all previous models. If instruments representing the three models can discriminate along a continuum of functionality-dysfunctionality, in addition to possible correlations among the three instruments, the validity of each instrument would be upheld. If each instrument can discriminate among groups varying in functionality, then it would be important to find out how it correlates with the other two instruments. Since each instrument is derived from the model, the validity and reliability of the instrument attest to the robustness of the model underlying it (Loevinger, 1957).

A beginning toward comparative testing of three different models has been accomplished by Lindaver (1998). He evaluated correspondences among Olson's circumplex (1993), Bartholomew's version of attachment (Bartholomew, 1990; Bartholomew & Horowitz, 1991; Bartholomew & Perlman, 1994), and Selfhood (L'Abate, 1997b). He administered the Adult Attachment Questionnaire (AAQ), Olson's FACES-III, and L'Abate's SOPC-RAF (to be described below) to 261 freshman undergraduate psychology majors (148 males and 113 females). He used the four personality propensities of the selfhood model as the independent variable to evaluate scores obtained on Cohesion and Adaptability Scales of the FACES-III and the four styles of the AAQ as dependent variables. On the SOPC, 44 respondents were classified as falling into Selfulness, 13 into Selfishness, 29 into Selflessness, and 56 into No-self. Their scores on Cohesion were the highest for Selfulness, lowest for No-self, and intermediate for Selfishness and Selflessness, as predicted by the selfhood model ($F(3, 129) = 17.26$, $p < .001$). On Adaptability, Selfishness exhibited the highest score, with No-self the lowest, with Selfulness and Selflessness exhibiting intermediate scores ($F(3, 129) = 9.28$, $p < .0001$). On styles measured by the AAQ, Secure attachment scores were equal and high for Selfulness, Selfishness, and Selflessness, with No-self showing the lowest score ($F(3, 129) = 10.73$, $p < .001$). On Dismissing, scores for Selfulness were the lowest, followed by Selfishness, Selflessness, and No-self with the highest scores ($F(3, 129) = 7.17$, $p < .001$). On Fearfulness, Selfishness showed the lowest mean score (23.45), No-self the highest (31.46), with Selfulness and Selflessness in the middle (26.75 and 27.00 respectively; $F(3, 129) = 4.16$, $p < .001$). Selfhood scores for Preoccupied were very similar and did not reach a statistical level of significance. The latter was the only pattern of six that did not conform to the predictions made from the selfhood model for the other two models.

Lindaver's study suggests that there may be similarities among different models of intimate relationships and that the empirical pursuit of similarities among different theoretical models may be worthwhile.

METHOD

Instruments

Only the attachment and selfhood models rely on self-report, paper-and-pencil instruments to evaluate them with adults. Attachment, of course, has relied mainly on the Strange Situation to evaluate infants and on structured and semistructured interviews and rating scales to evaluate adults. The attachment model was evaluated with the Italian Adult Attachment Questionnaire (AAQ), developed by Salvo and her coworkers (Salvo, in press; Salvo, Cusinato, & Rossetti, 1996; Salvo & Minervini, n.d.) from existing instruments available in the English-speaking literature. This questionnaire consists of 56 items (14 for each pattern) along a five-point Likert scale, yielding four different scores, one for each pattern; the higher the score the greater the preponderance of one pattern over the other three. Internal consistency for the four attachment styles was evaluated with Cronbach's alpha as well as with the Rasch probability model on data collected from 100 parents of elementary school children. With respect to these two methods, the Secure style reached values of .38 and .39 ($p < .05$), Preoccupied .74 and .54 ($p < .05$), Dismissing .65 and .73 ($p < .05$), and Fearful .71 and .74 ($p <. 05$). Except for the Secure pattern, the other values seem acceptable.

The EPM has been evaluated repeatedly through a detailed and model-derived administration of the Holtzman inkblots (Holtzman, Thorpe, Swartz, & Herron, 1961) that parallels the four coordinates of the model. Results from these administrations discriminate reliably among schizophrenic patients, their families, and normal subjects (De Giacomo, 1993; De Giacomo, Pierri, et al., 1997). Unfortunately, concurrent validation of this test with other known and well-validated instruments has been limited to two instances. One, with the Minnesota Multiphasic Personality Inventory (MMPI) (Lefons et al., 1979), and the other, with Cattell's 16PF (Pereira & Ferreira, 1985), yielded suggestive but not sufficiently significant results.

With some misgivings about its correspondence with the process orientation of its original EPM, a new instrument was created to make group administration more feasible; the Self-View Questionnaire (SVQ) was constructed with adjectives [3] that describe the 16 interpersonal styles listed earlier along two dimensions: (1) a relational one (with everybody, with the majority of people, with some people, and with no one) and (2) the other according to frequency, that is, how often each particular adjective describes that individual's behavior (most of the time, sometimes, and never). The same list of adjectives is answered three times, in the present, in the past, and in the future. [4] According to a functionality-dysfunctionality dimension, the lower the score, the greater the degree of dysfunction. Both relational and frequency scores were added together with past, present, and future scores to obtain one single score for each pair of adjectives. Resulting scores were subjected to a principal components analysis that yielded four factors, as indicated in note 5 on page 173. These four factors were correlated with the four dimensions measured by the AAQ and SOPC.

The selfhood model was evaluated with the Self-Other Profile Chart-

Revised Adult Form (SOPC-RAF). Respondents rate how Self-importance is obtained from personal attributes and from intimate Others on a five-point Likert scale. Personal attributes are rated according to how much they have contributed to a sense of Self-importance along a temporal perspective (present, past, and future), namely, school achievement, professional success, physical attractiveness, sports and other athletic activities, intelligence, creativity, sense of humor, morality, and self-esteem. Intimate others are rated according to how much they have contributed to a sense of self-importance: close friends, partners, school buddies, coworkers, parents, siblings, relatives, children, teachers/mentors, and others to be specified.

To evaluate the four personality propensities, the higher the scores, the better the relationship potential. In group data, scores on Self-Other are dichotomized at the median to obtain four different scores for the four personality propensities of the model: Self/High(SH)-Other/High(OH) = Selfulness, Self/High(SH)-Other/Low (OL) = Selfishness, Self/Low (SL)-Other/High(OH) = Selflesseness, and Self/Low (SL)-Other/Low(OL) = No-self.

In previous studies (L'Abate, 1997b), this instrument was found to correlate significantly with much lengthier self-concept tests, like the Tennessee Self-Concept. Its internal consistency was .78 for Self and .76 for Others. In a sample of 430 Italian high school students, Cusinato (personal communication, June 16, 1997) found an alpha of .83 for Self ($p < .001$), and an alpha of .88 for Others ($p < .001$). In a sample of 100 parents of elementary school children (Salvo & Menervini, n.d.), Selflessness correlated .12 ($p < .05$) with Dismissing style on the AAQ. Selfish propensity correlated significantly ($p < .01$) with all four attachment styles, −.19 with Secure, .15 with Preoccupied ($p < .05$), .27 with Dismissing, and .18 for Fearful. No-self also showed significant correlations ($p < .001$) with the four attachment styles: −.23 with Secure, .27 with Preoccupied, .25 with Dismissing, and .29 with Fearful. Selfulness correlated negatively with Selflessness ($r = -.29$, $p < .001$) but not with the other two propensities. Selflessness correlated positively with Selfishness ($r = .12$, $p < .05$) and with No-self ($r = .29$, $p < .001$). Selfishness and No-self correlated with each other ($r = .39$, $p < .01$). In addition, a previous version of the SOPC was administered to a group of primarily female (81.5%) adults ($n = 153$) with a mean age of 23. A Cronbach's alpha of .82 was found for Self and one of .83 for Other. In the same sample, significant correlations with the Beck Depression Inventory (BDI) and with the Center for Epidemiological Studies Depression Scale (CES-D) were found. Self ratings correlated negatively with both the BDI ($r = -.57$, $p < .001$) and with the CES-D (−.55, $p < .001$). Others ratings also correlated significantly with both the BDI ($r = -.57$, $p < .001$) and with the CES-D (−.49, $p < .001$). In addition, test-retest reliability coefficients were obtained for Self and Others. Test-retest coefficients for Self were .62 and .64 for Others. Data were collected for a group of undergraduates ($n = 80$), a group of singles ($n = 32$), and a group of nursing students ($n = 45$). Alpha coefficients for Self were .83, .84, and .84, respectively. Alpha coefficients for Others were .82, .90, and .88, respectively. For undergraduates, Others was significantly and negatively correlated with the Fear of Intimacy Scale ($r = -.29$, $p < .01$).

As Salvo and Minervini concluded, it is evident that a substantial gap may exist between mental representations and behavioral outcomes; for example, a person may have a negative model of self but may behave in such a way as to disconfirm a negative mental model. Similarly, a person may hold a very high sense of self-importance while behaving in a very submissive or passive way with his or her partner.

Consequently, one cannot expect a great many convergences among measures of internal working models and measures of how one behaves in intimate relationships to assert self-importance. By the same token, how one views self according to internal working models and how important one may feel may not always predict how one behaves in close, prolonged, and committed relationships.

Respondents

All respondents who participated in this study were residing in and around the capital of a southern Italian region. They were chosen to represent varying degrees of functionality; Group 1 consisted of 61 individuals who were either on the staff, students, or friends affiliated with a psychiatric facility and a private post-graduate specialization course in family therapy. They served as a "normal" comparison rather than as a control group, because they did not share completely the same demographic characteristics of the other three clinical groups. Group 2 consisted of 43 outpatients in a private psychiatric service. Group 3 consisted of 20 outpatients in a family therapy facility. Group 4 consisted of 20 inpatients in a university-affiliated state psychiatric clinic who were tested twice. There were 93 females and 51 males in the entire sample of 144 respondents.

Procedure

All respondents were asked to answer all questionnaires as part of a research project that would allow a better understanding of their condition. Respondents in Group 1 were asked to participate to obtain a greater understanding of three important, relationship-oriented, theory-derived models.

Table 5-1
Characteristics of the Four Groups

Groups	Gender	n	Age Mean	Age SD
1	Females	50	30.62	4.91
	Males	11	38.55	6.94
	Total	61	32.08	6.17
2	Females	20	38.06	13.24
	Males	23	39.43	16.28
	Total	43	38.82	14.76
3	Females	11	37.06	12.01
	Males	9	43.17	12.25
	Total	20	39.83	12.24
4	Females	12	36.06	10.07
	Males	8	37.36	16.29
	Total	20	36.55	12.49

RESULTS

The characteristics of the four groups are contained in Table 5-1. Scores on all three tests used in this study were subjected to a variety of analyses to evaluate their statistical validities and reliabilities as well as their intercorrelations. Even though level of education was not measured, the convenience group was not only younger than the three experimental groups but very likely more educated.

Reliabilities for the three instruments were established with Cronbach's alpha. The alpha coefficient for the AAQ (see Table 5-2) overall was .82, a score similar to the reliability of the SVQ, alpha for Secure items was .60, for Preoccupied items .75, for Dismissing items .74, and for Fearful items .83. This coefficient for the AAQ was .82, for the SVQ was .89, and for the SOPC-RAF was .82. The same coefficient for the SVQ was .81 for the relational dimension and .78 for frequency dimension, acceptable levels of reliability for a new instrument. Alpha coefficients for the SOPC-RAF Self ratings were .74 and for Others were .70. These values suggested that the reliability of this instrument is not as high as the reliabilities of the AAQ and SVQ (see Table 5-3).

Further analyses were conducted to examine group differences for the three instruments. A Multivariate Analysis of Variance with two between factors, group and gender, was used to analyze each instrument. The results of this analysis showed that for all three instruments there was no gender effect or group $\times$ gender interaction. There was, however, a significant

Table 5-2
Alpha Coefficients for the AAQ by Groups

Groups	Total	Secure	Preoccupied	Dimissing	Fearful
1	.77	.51	.72	.74	.84
2	.76	.51	.73	.70	.76
3	.74	.74	.68	.67	.86
4	.88	.52	.79	.77	.83

Table 5-3
Alpha Coefficients for the SVQ and SOPC

	Self-View Questionnaire				Coordinates			Self-Other Profile Chart		
Groups	Total	Rel.	Freq.	1	2	3	4	Total	Self	Other
1	.74	.61	.65	.72	.47	.78	.04	.66	.59	.62
2	.95	.89	.89	.91	.71	.94	.71	.90	.86	.85
3	.94	.85	.91	.83	.78	.73	.42	.54	.74	.74
4	.84	.77	.70	.65	.75	.69	.36	.82	.85	.58

group effect for all three instruments. The multivariate levels of significance for group effects for each of the instruments were as follows: AAQ ($F = 3.78$, $p < .001$), SVQ ($F = 2.69$, $p < .05$), and SOPC-RAF ($F = 4.69$, $p < .001$). Based on these analyses, further univariate analyses were conducted using a one-way ANOVA verifying only group effects (see Tables 5-4 and 5-5).

On the AAQ (Table 5-4), Secure scores discriminated significantly among the four groups ($F(3, 136) = 5.61$, $p < .001$), with Group 4 showing the highest mean score, Group 2 the lowest mean score, and Groups 1 and 3 similar mean scores. The Preoccupied score also discriminated significantly among the four groups ($F(3, 135) = 5.11$, $p < .002$), with Group 1 showing the lowest mean score of the four groups, while Group 4 showed the highest mean score, with Groups 2 and 3 scoring between Groups 1 and 4. The Dismissing score also discriminated significantly among the four groups ($F(3, 136) = 4.53$, $p < .004$), with Group 1 showing the lowest mean score, while the other three groups showed increasing mean scores. The Fearful scores did not discriminate among the four groups at a very high level of significance ($F(3, 135) = 2.78$, $p < .04$), with Group 1 showing the lowest mean score, Group 4 the highest, and Groups 2 and 3 between the two. A post hoc analysis using Scheffe's test indicated that there were indeed no significant differences among the groups on Fearful scores.

Table 5-4
Means and Standard Deviations for the AAQ

Groups	Secure	Preoccupied	Dismissing	Fearful
1. (n = 61)				
Mean	35.79	29.47	34.38	31.00
SD	7.69	12.77	10.21	10.36
2. (n = 43)				
Mean	31.74	34.46	37.26	32.92
SD	7.54	9.82	9.56	9.59
3. (n = 20)				
Mean	36.20	35.35	40.60	36.25
SD	9.36	8.68	9.98	12.24
4. (n = 20)				
Mean	40.65	40.40	43.30	38.45
SD	8.80	12.83	12.52	14.42

Values for the SVQ means of the four groups (Table 5-5) decreased as the severity of functioning increased for the personal dimension. The ability of the SVQ to discriminate among the four groups on the basis of the number of interpersonal contacts was significant ($F(3, 140) = 3.57$, $p < .05$). Scheffe's post hoc test indicated that there were no pairwise differences. It should be noted that the results of this particular analysis could have been affected by unequal variances. In addition, this instrument was unable to discriminate among the four groups on the basis of frequency of contacts ($F(3, 140) = .54$, n.s.).

On the SOPC-RAF (Table 5-5), the Self ratings discriminated significantly among the means of the four groups ($F(3, 137) = 9.53$, $p < .001$), with the two groups of private psychiatric outpatients and inpatients (Groups 2 and 4) showing the lowest scores over the means of the control group (1) and the family therapy group (3). Others ratings also discriminated among the four groups almost as significantly as Self ratings ($F(3, 136) = 7.57$, $p < .001$). Group 4 had the lowest mean score followed by Group 2, with Groups 1 and 3 having similar means. A post hoc analysis using Scheffe's test indicated that the mean for Group 1 (normals) was significantly higher than the means for both groups 2 and 4.

Pearson correlations among the eight scores obtained from the three instruments were computed (see Table 5-6). On the AAQ, Secure attachment correlated negatively and significantly with the three insecure patterns, indicating a consistent difference between security and insecurity in attachment. On the SVQ measures of relational and frequency, not included in Table 5-6, correlated very highly with each other ($p < .001$). The relational dimension correlated significantly and negatively ($p < .01$) with the three

Table 5-5
Means and Standard Deviations for the SVQ and SOPC-RAF

			SVQ				SOPC-RAF	
			Coordinates					
Groups	**Relat.**	**Freq.**	**1**	**2**	**3**	**4**	**Self**	**Other**
1. (n = 61)								
Mean	143.97	99.34	100.75	58.67	35.70	47.11	109.46	95.87
SD	9.76	9.46	11.81	7.11	5.10	4.62	12.40	16.38
2. (n = 43)								
Mean	136.84	96.49	97.02	60.23	32.77	43.30	93.30	83.58
SD	21.73	15.73	20.01	11.64	7.87	10.13	19.36	21.64
3. (n = 20)								
Mean	136.35	98.80	100.25	53.70	34.75	46.45	104.60	93.10
SD	14.44	12.85	16.21	11.97	5.09	6.56	11.91	16.42
4. (n = 2)								
Mean	132.55	99.50	96.25	55.40	33.20	47.20	101.90	77.25
SD	16.88	9.01	14.69	13.85	7.50	7.25	14.59	13.66

measures of insecure attachment but not with secure attachment. Frequency correlated negatively but not very highly ($p < .05$) with Dismissing and Fearful but not with Secure and Preoccupied. Hence, only the four factors obtained from the principal component factor analysis were included in this correlation matrix. Factor 1 correlated negatively and significantly ($p < .01$) with Dismissing and Fearful patterns on the AAQ.

Factor 2 correlated negatively with the Secure pattern ($p < .01$) and positively with the Fearful pattern ($p < .05$). Factor 3 correlated positively with Secure and negatively with the other three insecure patterns. Factor 4 correlated positively with the Secure pattern and negatively with the Fearful pattern. Factors 1 and 2 did not correlate with each other at all, while Factor 3 correlated positively ($p < .01$) with Factor 1 only. Factor 4 correlated positively ($p < .01$) with Factors 1 and 3. [5]

On the SOPC, Self and Others ratings correlated with each other ($p < .01$), while Self ratings correlated positively with Secure ($p < .01$), negatively with Preoccupied ($p < .05$), negatively with Fearful ($p < .05$) but not significantly with Dismissing. Others ratings correlated somewhat ($p < .05$) positively with Secure and negatively with Preoccupied ($p < .05$), Dismissing, and Fearful ($p < .01$). With the SVQ, Self correlated negatively ($p < .01$) with Factor 2 and positively ($p < .01$) with Factor 2. Others correlated positively with Secure and negatively with all three Insecure patterns of the AAQ. With the SVQ, Self scores correlated negatively ($p < .01$) with Factor 2 and positively ($p < .01$) with Factor 3 only. Others scores correlated positively with the AAQ Secure pattern and negatively with the

Table 5-6
Correlation Matrix for the AAQ, SVQ, and SOPC-RAF

	AAQ				SVQ Factors				SOPC-RAF	
	Secure	Preocc.	Dismissing	Fearful	1	2	3	4	Self	Other
AAQ										
Secure	1.00									
Precoccupied	-.23**	1.00								
Dimissing	-.13	.41**	1.00							
Fearful	-.45**	.60**	.59**	1.00						
SVQ Factors										
1.	.15	-.15	-.34**	-.28**	1.00					
2	-.27**	.08	.09	.21*	.07	1.00				
3	.30	-.35**	-.18*	-.40**	.44**	-.10	1.00			
4	.25	-.16	-.13	-.26	.43**	.08	.34**	1.00		
SOPC-RAF										
Self	.22**	-.20	-.11	-.18*	.04	.27**	.26**	.16	1.00	
Other	.18	.19*	-.29**	-.26**	.14	-.28**	.22	.16	.42**	1.00

*$p < .05$; **$p < .01$.

three Insecure patterns. With the SVQ. Others scores correlated positively only with Factors 2 and 3 and not the other two factors. Given the disproportionate number of items (six items for Factor 1, five items for Factor 2, two items for Factor 3, and three items for Factor 4) for each factor and the uncertain nature of each factor, as surmised from these correlations, it is clear that this instrument requires further refinements in item analysis before we can draw a clear interpretation about the nature of these four factors.

DISCUSSION

The implications of these results seem relevant to the evaluation of models of intimate relationships. All three instruments, derived from three different models and theories, correlated significantly with each other with a much higher frequency of significant correlations than would be expected by chance. Furthermore, all three instruments differentiated among different degrees of functionality/dysfunctionality. Hence, all three instruments are valid in their concurrent and construct validities. On the basis of these results, one is led to believe that all three instruments were looking at somewhat different yet similar aspects of the same behavior (i.e., intimate relationships). Of course, more research will be necessary to support this conclusion.

In terms of the internal-external, inferred-observable continua, the hypothesized order among the three models seems to prevail. The AAQ seems to provide internal, inferred patterns. The SOPC-RAF seems to provide an intermediate nexus with both internal patterns and with external, observable processes, as measured by the SVQ. Apparently, the two new kids on the block seem to fare relatively well with the old-timer.

The major difference among the three models relates to their therapeutic and preventive applications. Thus far, the attachment model, being the oldest of the three, has already influenced a great many clinical applications, too many to cite here. These applications, however, were interpretations of the model rather than being directly derived from the model. The other two models, elementary pragmatic and selfhood, on the other hand, have directly produced clinical and preventive applications, not only through the use of therapeutic tasks but also in prevention through the use of computer programs and workbooks directly derived from the original models (De Giacomo, 1993; De Giacomo & De Nigris, 2001; L'Abate, 1999a). [6]

Admittedly, a major shortcoming of this study relates to its having been conducted with individuals rather than couples or families. If this shortcoming is valid, then a great deal of the evidence gathered from the attachment theory literature would suffer from the same defect. Furthermore, the three evaluative instruments are "relational" in the sense that all three include qualities with an interpersonal impact on intimate relationships. Of the three instruments, however, only the SOPC-RAF contained an explicit "Others" component that is not contained in the other two instruments. Clearly, this shortcoming indicates that further research with these three instruments should be conducted with couples or, even better, families.

CONCLUSION

Intercorrelations among measures of three theoretical models about attachment, elementary pragmatic, and selfhood indicate that there are empirical convergences among them. These convergences suggest that the three theories underlying these measures may be more similar than different, dealing with similar constructs measured, like the elephant and the blind persons, with different instruments. If this conclusion is valid, then such constructs would be observable and measurable regardless of how they are conceptualized or measured. One way to evaluate these similarities could take place through workbooks derived directly from the models rather than just from sterile and static paper-and-pencil, self-report tests. Both the elementary pragmatic and the selfhood model (as found in Chapters 7 and 9, respectively), have produced isomorphic workbooks that can be used preventively and paratherapeutically. If a workbook derived from attachment theory were to be developed, it would allow comparative evaluation of the three models through direct applications rather than only through test instruments.

NOTES

1. A Portuguese clinical psychologist specializing in test design subsequently joined the group and carried out a study correlating the SISCI-1 with Cattel's 16-PF test (Pereira & Ferreira, 1985).
2. The Self-View Questionnaire (SVQ) was developed with the help of P. Basile, G. Blasi, A. Blattman, B. Centrelli, D. De Orsi, P. Fischetto, U. Incampo, V. Logito, A. Mollica, C. Renna, B. Saccia, C. Salerno, L. Zanoianni, G. Pierri, C. Corfiati, S. De Nigris, and A. Sperideo.
3. See note 1 above.
4. See note 2 above.
5. Factor loadings for the SVQ are indicated by numbers 1 through 4; FO, empty/absent, 4; F1, participant/sharing, 2; F2, solitary/reserved, 4; F3, tenacious/egocentric, 1; F4 docile/surrendering, 4; F5, altruist/involved, 2; F6, mysterious/ambiguous, 1; F7, collaborative/mediator, 2; F8, abstract/unpredictable, 1; F9, sharing/innovative, 2; F10, rebel/antagonist, 1; F11, dominant/dictatorial, 1; F12, double-faced/false-altruist, 1; F13, unpredictable/altruist, 2; F14, inconclusive/disorganized, 3; F15, confused/chaotic, 3.
6. Additional references about the EPM are found in Appendix D.

Chapter 6

Integrating the Theory with the Model

The purpose of this chapter is to integrate the theory (Chapters 2 and 3) and the model (Chapters 4 and 5). The theory is composed of many models. Consequently, one model represents only parts of a theory. The whole theory does not stand or fall solely on one model, even though the validity or invalidity of one model may strengthen or weaken the theory. The EPM, as discussed in Chapter 4, represents a whole theory. Consequently, the whole theory is summarized in one model, as is the case of the circumplex, attachment, and family paradigms models. If the model is valid, so is the theory behind it. If the model is invalid, so is the theory behind it. Hence, we are no longer concerned about whether all these theories and models are valid or invalid. All of them, in one way or another, have shown some acceptable degree of validity. What is more relevant, however, is to find the limits of a theory or a model. For instance, both theory and the EPM presented here aim to show that they are valid in the laboratory and in primary, secondary, and tertiary prevention settings. This claim cannot be made by either the attachment, circumplex, or family paradigms models. In this regard, therefore, both the theory and the EPM have a much larger width of applications that determines their validity and applicability over other theories or models.

ACHIEVEMENT OF INTEGRATION

There are at least four ways to integrate the theory with the EPM. In the first place, the theory and the model are complementary with each other. Each, separately, helps the other achieve the goal of describing, illustrating, classifying, and, hopefully, improving intimate relationships. As the results of the study presented in Chapter 5 suggest, both the theory and the EPM look at different parts of the same domain (i.e., intimate relationships with different lenses, different assumptions, and different methods). For instance, the theory stresses internal, intrapsychic conditions like feelings (*E*), awareness (*Aw*), and cognitions (*R*), in addition to externally observable *A*ctions and Context (*AC*), while the EPM stresses specifically identifiable relationship styles in a much more particularistic way than any models of the theory itself. The EPM makes no assumptions about internal or intrapsychic states or traits. However, as shown in Chapter 5, there are relationships between the selfhood model and the EPM that were made hypothetically (De Giacomo et al., 1997; L'Abate, 1997b) and validated empirically (L'Abate et al., 2000).

In the second place, the complementarity of both theory and model lies in their increasing degrees of specificity. While the theory has developed various models that look at intimate relationships from different vantage points (i.e., models), developmentally, structurally, contextually, and even dialectically, the EPM increases the level of specificity moving from simple triads (world of first party, world of second party, and their transformation after the interaction) to the organization of the triads in four coordinates, which then compose themselves in 16 relational styles. Permutations from these 16 styles give rise to 256 (16 × 16) logically possible interactions. How more specific can one get?

A third aspect of this complementarity lies in the process versus content distinction. While the EPM is completely content-free and completely process-oriented, and there are no assumptions as to the kind of communication and what is communicated between two or more parties, the theory does include both processes (approach-avoidance and discharge-delay) and contents (Being, Doing, and Having) about what is exchanged in intimate relationships. In addition, the theory distinguishes among settings and contexts, an aspect not contained in the EPM.

A fourth and perhaps more important aspect of complementarity lies in how interventions at both preventive and psychotherapeutic levels dovetail with each other with practically no overlap, as shown in the next section.

SIMILARITIES BETWEEN THE THEORY AND THE MODEL

There are quite a few similarities between the theory and model in at least eight ways. Both theory and model:

1. search for a language about intimate relationships in which we look at a basic core, an essence, a central aspect making up an operative construction and a different language from the one commonly used. Each search, therefore, creates an original version of relationships for those who try to evaluate them or for those who receive help from either the theory or the model.

2. are deductive, going from the generally abstract to the specifically concrete, going from assumptions and postulates to models or from assumptions and postulates to relationship styles which, in some ways, represent models in and by themselves, because there are at least 16 possible ways in which each style can permutate with the other styles.
3. stress observable and measurable variables, using test instruments that derive directly from models in the theory (Chapter 3) or from the EPM (Chapter 5) itself.
4. are applied; that is, both use interventions, programs, assignments, tasks, or workbooks derived from the theory or model with non-clinical populations (primary prevention) (Chapters 7 and 9) and clinical ones (tertiary prevention) in psychotherapy and rehabilitation (Chapters 8 and 10) where face-to-face (f2f), talk-based interaction between a professional helper and a respondent (individuals, couples, and families) is necessary.
5. distinguish between one overall functional personality propensity (Selfulness) and various positive coordinate relational styles centered on Sharing as represented in a certain number of positive functions, respectively, in contrast to three dysfunctional personality propensities (Selfishness, Selflessness, and No-self) or three relational coordinate styles with different functional and dysfunctional properties (Maintaining, Accepting, and Antifunction), respectively;
6. rely on visually represented models to summarize complex concepts or constructs, as shown by the various figures illustrating models.
7. use computer-assisted, structured interventions (Chapter 11) as well as arithmetical and mathematical operations. For instance, an arithmetical model for relationships was presented in L'Abate (1976, 1997b). When two people relate with each other positively (i.e., selfully) a multiplicative growth outcome will occur, the CC style. When two people differ in how they relate with each other, one positively and the other negatively, the outcome will result in 0, producing a repetitively reactive outcome (i.e., the RR style). When two people relate with each other negatively, a negative split (division) either in the individual or in the relationship will take place (i.e., the AA style).
8. agree that reality is created in our minds, and, therefore, it can be reached only by means and theories representing reality. The theory and the EPM are creations that attempt to approximate reality, but they are not the reality itself.

DIFFERENCES BETWEEN THEORY AND EPM

Differences between the theory and the EPM speak to their complementarity in more specific ways than done earlier in this chapter. There are at least three different ways in which the theory and the EPM part company.

1. The theory (Chapters 2 and 3) encompasses both internal and external processes, contents, and relationships. The EPM (Chapters 4 and 5), on the other hand, focuses strictly on observable relationships and avoids making inferences or hypotheses about internal states or processes (feelings, emotions, thoughts, traits, motivations, or intentions).

2. The theory accounts for developmental socialization of styles in intimate relationships through the likeness continuum, model[7]; the EPM, thus far, does not. Consequently, the EPM expands on just one model of the theory, the selfhood model, and in so doing both theory and model become complementary. They deal with different aspects of intimate relationships, where the EPM expands on the four personality propensities of the selfhood model[8].

3. Differences in value judgments. The EPM views relationships as being value-neutral, that is, leaving apart considerations of social value for some kinds of relationships or diagnostic labels. EPM is characterized by a more particularistic definition of relational aspects, by means of percentages taken from each one of the 16 functions, as measured by the SISCI and the Self View Questionnaire (Chapter 5). Moreover, it spares negative definitions and remains neutral for terms such as "Apathy," "Rejection," "Abuse," or other terms used by the theory that have or imply judgmental valences. These judgments are absent in the EPM.

This is a useful complementary element in comparing the theory with the EPM when the professional helper needs to distance himself or herself from judgments inevitably related to words or gestures that he or she may use. These are connections that the theory strives to achieve by considering the whole gamut of supporting, independent, but conceptually similar theories or models, as well as theories and models that indirectly but empirically support the theory, like the Foa and Foa (1974) resource exchange theory and evidence directly supporting it (Chapter 3). The theory, therefore, strives to relate its constructs, models, and concepts to existing theories or models that, although independent of the theory, show some conceptual similarity to it. In relating to other theories and models, the theory compares itself with theories and models from which the theory was in part derived. The EPM, on the other hand, is so original that it has been difficult up to the present time to relate it to existing theories and models, except, perhaps, to Kantor's interbehaviorism, in its naturalistic bent. As we saw in Chapter 5, however, both theory and model are related to the attachment model.

From these general differences and similarities, there are more specific connections between the models of the theory and the EPM.

ERAAwC: Model[1] and EPM

When compared to the first component of the ERAAwC, *E*motionality, for those who follow the EPM, derives from a relational situation and is joined together with the relational style characterizing the relationship. If the interaction moves toward 0 (i.e., annulment), it probably generates pain, whereas if the interaction tends to fill one's own world, maybe beyond expectations, it should produce a sense of well-being. If the interaction moves toward a relational style characterized by oscillation (i.e., doubt), it presumably generates some sufferings to be related to the uncertainty. In other words, in its practical application, the model does not disregard emotions but, on the other hand, considers them as part of the "world" of the interacting subjects. Indeed, in the EPM, the word "world" means any content of all the possible contents, therefore including also something that we can call emotions. As far as the second component, *R*ationality, goes, no problem arises with EPM. The model is actually meant to be an example of the use of rationality. Being a logical model, it is suitable to provide a tool that may improve the rationality in human behavior. With regard to the third component, *A*ctivity, according to the EPM, it should be seen as an interaction, on one hand, and as a preamble to the actual actions, on the other hand. In order to "move toward the other person's world," one must carry out actions that go in that direction. As far as the fourth component is concerned, *Aw*areness, EPM offers the best awareness tool for the human mind and, therefore, the best insight of what happens inside and outside us, always, though, in terms of interaction and change. With regard to the fifth component, *C*ontext, the EPM starts and works only with interactions and, therefore, the context is a fundamental element for the existence of the model itself. Various contexts mentioned by the theory must always be looked at as something comprehensive to be defined as "the other person's world." Each context, therefore, includes people who are part of it, but it must be seen as specific worlds.

Levels of Analysis/Observation/Interpretation: Model[2] and EPM

Behaving differently in different contexts (e.g., at home or in the workplace) depends on the interaction with different worlds. At work one interacts with the office manager whereas at home one interacts with wives or husbands. Resorting to explanations to give a reason for the phenomena occurring in relational life is related to the tendency in our mind to find intersections among patterns of thought. Among the 16 functions, EPM includes a function characterized by the intersection (F1) according to certain logic. In relational terms, finding a convincing reason for a phenomenon means moving toward the world of the person who is looking for this reason (F5) to the other 15 relational styles.

Settings: Model[3] and EPM

As already said with regard to ERAAwC, speaking about the context, each setting makes up part of the interacting respondent's world and, therefore, is an element interacting with the model's usual rules and the variable percentage of the 16 functions corresponding to each setting. There are some differences between the world of a person at home, at the workplace, and so on; receiving a lover's call at the workplace during a difficult staff meeting differs from receiving it in the evening, relaxed at home. All is relative for EPM. The importance here is given by the percentage of time that one spends in each setting relative to the other settings.

Assumption of Space and Time: Model[4] and EPM

EPM's 16 relational styles define the various situations outlined by Model[3] according to the model's viewpoint. Indeed, the symbiotic attachment (i.e., extreme closeness) could correspond to the function "enter the other person's world" (F5), with a very high percentage, compared to the other 15 functions such as self-destruction, a trend toward a high percentage of the annulment function (F0); retreat, as a high percentage of the function "retreat in one's own world" (F2); and distance balancing, as a high percentage of the function related to the mediation between one's own world and the other person's world, and so on.

With regard to time, the presence of interactive units following one another in the time unit assumes the 0 percentage found in the sequence would determine the slowness or the speed of the exchanges among interactants. If, for example, the second author finds himself in the presence of a patient who speaks very slowly and continuously pauses, this behavior might be interpreted as a strong presence of F0 in the sequence of this individual's mental structure.

Postulates of Love and Negotiation: Model[5] and EPM

As already said with regard to ERAAwC, the EPM proposes itself in terms of "the world of interacting subjects." If love, as an obvious state of being, is a fundamental aim to be pursued in a creative manner (F9), the achievement of this goal makes us much stronger (EPM formula: F9 × F5 = F3). However, other aims that we creatively pursue (like the ability to negotiate and find solutions) may imply a reaction of moving toward our world, therefore making us stronger. There is a difference in the content of one's world and someone else's world between love and other important things in other fields. Love has a very high position in the scale of priorities.

The EPM and the ability to negotiate find a precise exemplification in relational style F7. Actually, this stage envisages that a respondent accepts his or her own world, as well as the other's world, and all the elements shared by his or her own world and the world of the other.

However, the model indicates that another two relational styles may fall within the notion of negotiation if, say, by the above notion we also mean the capacity of solving problems. A relational style does exist (F9) that refers to sharing something and drawing on a world that is external to what is shared, say, on the world of the abstract (without drawing on any kind of creativity that would even be possible). This style is linked to the notion of pursuing a goal creatively.

Finally, EPM foresees a minimal element, a minimum indispensable basis for a negotiation to develop. This basis is accounted for by having something in common with the other that corresponds to the pure sharing relational style F1. Hence, a combination of styles F1, F7, and F9 would be required for successful negotiation to take place. This connection illustrates the point made originally (L'Abate, 1986) that it takes two rather well functioning individuals to carry on and terminate successfully the process of negotiation.

Modalities: Model[6] and EPM

EPM concerns itself with processes rather than with contents. If we work on processes, for some people whatever moves toward their world is their "Being," for some other people it is "Doing," and for some other people it is "Having." There may be a mixture, including Being at 40%, Doing at 30%, and Having at 30%, as a total of three percentages and of what moves toward one's world. Given its neutrality and lack of judgment, EPM accepts and records anything (i.e., any type of world).

Likeness Continuum: Model[7] and EPM

The only comment that can be made here relates to certain commonalities among the EPM's relational styles. For interactions among relational styles to be seen as a continuum, one should think either in terms of traditional statistics, in the sense of thinking of larger or smaller percentages of each relational style, or in terms of fuzzy logic that refuses to conceptualize reality in terms of all-or-nothing thinking. Here is where the theory and model reach their greatest level of complementarity; that is, the theory is able to furnish the EPM with a developmental perspective that the EPM is missing except in case of theoretical simulations and step-by-step testing.

The notion of distance is implicit in the six ranges of Symbiosis, Sameness, Similarity, Differentness, Oppositeness, and Alienation. EPM forces the mind to a much higher level of precision. In fact, if pushed to the extreme, the notion of Symbiosis could mean that two interactants actually share only one world. Sameness, instead, implies the notion that two interactants are distinct and adopt the same interactive modality (the same relational style). Similarity means that the two interacting subjects have a mostly similar relational style that differs only in a few small aspects. Differentness means that the two interactants have different relational styles, whatever they may be. Oppositeness means that the two interactants have relational styles that are opposite of each other. For instance, in the style

F10 ("Mary, Mary, quite contrary") a respondent does exactly the contrary of what the other does.

According to EPM, alienation could mean two worlds that never encounter each other, or, alternatively, that the worlds of two interactants are characterized by what they draw from a world, where neither one's own world nor the world of the other nor the elements in common between the two worlds are present, as if they were extremely abstract and distracted. For instance, what happens in the interaction between two respondents (e.g., Similarity and Differentness) is defined, at a theoretical level, within the 256 interaction rules represented in the so-called interaction table (Chapter 4) that corresponds to the fourth level of EPM. On the basis of what has been said, EPM can be linked to notions of Likeness expressed by the model, but it pushes to greater precision and complexity and does not need the use of value judgments like "Abusive-Apathetic," "Reactive-Repetitive," or "Creative-Conductive," Model[8].

Selfhood: Model[9] and EPM

In the EPM there is no such thing as a value judgment, but the four positions of the model may be translated very well in terms of EPM. In addition to the results of the study reported in Chapter 5 concerning correlations among selfhood, attachment, and the EPM, we are attempting to replicate the same study with a normative sample of medical students and correlating the SISCI with the Self View Questionnaire (Appendix C). Moreover, in Selfulness, the pattern of 16 functions may show a good maintenance of one's own word, a certain percentage of accepting the world of the other, and a certain percentage of sharing and mediating functions and low null functions and low antifunctions. This is the average pattern with SISCI-1 (Chapter 5). In No-self, if we think of schizophrenic patterns, we see a rather flat distribution among the 16 functions with more antifunction than in normality (in fact, following SISCI-1, schizophrenia is characterized by a loss of capacity to maintain one's own world [low F3]). No-self would be characterized by a high F0 function, the function of nullification. We have no data on Selfishness, but it could be represented by a high percentage of maintaining one's world, F3, plus discounting of the other's world.

More specifically, possible relationships between the four personality propensities and the 16 relationship functions are possible, once a propensity is defined as a probabilitistic possibility about the likelihood of how an individual will behave in a given situation according to parameters defining relationships given in Table 2-6, Model[15]. Hence, depending on priorities, context, situation, and nature of the relationship and of the other interactant, as well as the strength of their own propensities in a particular setting, a selful individual will have a greater probability of relating in a selful, conductively creative way ("I win, you win, we both must win.") than a selfish, selfless, or no-self individual. By the same token, a no-self individual will tend to respond to a higher probability in an abusively apathetic manner ("I lose, you lose, we both must lose.") than a selful individual. Given these provisos, there are possible links between personality propensities and relational functions given by the EPM:

F0 could contain parts of selflessness and no-self propensities.

F1 could relate well to selfulness.

F2 could refer to selfishness.

F3 could contain aspects of both selfishness and selfulness.

F4 could refer to selflessness.

F5 could refer to selflessness and selfulness.

F6 could refer to some aspects of selflessness.

F7 could refer also to some aspects of selfulness.

F8 could refer to some aspects of no-self.

F9 could refer to some aspects of selfulness.

F10 could refer to some aspects of selfishness.

F11 could refer to some aspects of selfishness.

F12 could refer to some aspects of selfishness.

F13 could refer to some aspects of selfulness and selflessness.

F14 and F15 could refer to no-self or even fall outside the possibilities suggested by the selfhood model, indicating how important it is to see both selfhood and EPM as complementary.

Even more specifically, if one were to permutate all four personality propensities and likelihoods of responding according to those propensities between two partners in a transaction with each other, the way the EPM does, 16 possible transactions will take place (see Table 6-1). Possible outcomes, which, according to the selfhood model, can be only positive, questionable, or negative, can be further specified once the EPM is hypothetically correlated with possible outcomes predicted from the selfhood model. If these hypothesized correlations were valid, a distinct advance could be made in predicting what kind of parent–parent interactions will produce what kind of offspring with specific personality propensities and, even more specifically, what kind of relational styles will take place between partners.

The issue here is to find which style or outcome is similar to the 16 functions of the EPM. It will take a great deal of thinking and evidence to reconcile possible outcomes from combinations and permutations of personality propensities with possible relational functions derived from the EPM.

Table 6-1
Hypothetical Relationships between Personality Propensities and Relational Styles

Partner A Statement	**Partner B Response**	**Style**	**Resulting Outcome**	Possible interactions between personality propensities and relational styles (for complete view see Figure 4-5). Change means how Partner A behaves after interaction with Partner B; × sign means interaction.
Selful	Selful	CC	Positive	Examples: a. (F7) × (F7) = (F7) b. (F5) × (F3) = (F3) c. (F5) × (F7) = (F7)
Selful	Selfish	RR	Questionable*	Examples: a. (F7) × (F2) = (F7) b. (F5) × (F2) = (F2) c. (F7) × (F10) = (F15)
Selful	Selfless	RR	Questionable	Examples: a. (F5) × (F4) = (F4) b. (F3) × (F4) = (F3) c. (F7) × (F4) = (F7)
Selful	No-self	AA or RR	Negative	Examples: a. (F5) × (F0) = (F0) b. (F3) × (F0) = (F3) c. (F7) × (F8) = (F15)
Selfish	Selful	RR	Questionable	Examples: a. (F2) × (F1) = (F2) b. (F2) × (F7) = (F0) c. (F11) × (F7) = (F11)
Selfish	Selfish	RR or CC	Questionable	Examples: a. (F2) × (F2) = (F0) b. (F11) × (F2) = (F11) c. (F11) × (F11) = F15)
Selfish	Selfless	RR	Questionable	Examples: a. (F12) × (F4) = (F3) b. (F11) × (F4) = (F11) c. (F2) × (F4) = (F2)
Selfish	No-self	AA	Negative	Examples: a. F12) × (F0) = (F3) b. (F2) × (F0) = (F2) c. (F11) × (F0) = (F15)

Table 6-1 (continued)

Partner A Statement	Partner B Response	Style	Resulting Outcome	Possible interactions between personality propensities and relational styles (for complete view see Figure 4-5). Change means how Partner A behaves after interaction with Partner B; × sign means interaction.
Selfless	Selfless	RR or CC	Questionable	Examples: a. (F4) × (F4) = (F0) b. (F6) × (F4) = (F2) c. (F6) × (F6) = (F0)
Selfless	Selfish	RR	Questionable	Examples: a. (F4) × (F2) = (F2) b. (F4) × (F12) = (F12) c. (F4) × (F11) = (F11)
Selfless	Selful	RR or CC	Questionable	Examples: a. (F4) × (F7) = (F3) b. (F4) × (F3) = (F3) c. (F4) × (F5) = (F1)
Selfless	No-self	RR or AA	Negative	Examples: a. (F4) × (F0) = (F0) b. (F6) × (F0) = (F6) c. (F6) × (F15) = (F9)
No-self	Selful	RR or AA	Negative	Examples: a. (F0) × (F7) = (F0) b. (F0) × (F3) = (F0) c. (F0) × (F9) = (F0)
No-self	Selfish	RR or AA	Negative	Examples: a. (F0) × (F2) = (F0) b. (F0) × (F12) = (F0) c. (F15) × (F2) = (F15)
No-self	Selfless	RR or AA	Negative	Examples: a. (F0) × (F4) = (F0) b. (F0) × (F6) = (F0) d. (F15) × (F4) = (F15)
No-self	No-self	AA	Negative	Examples: a. (F15) × (F0) = (F15) b. (F0) × (F15) = (F0) c. (F15) × (F15) = (F15)

Note:*Questionable means that the outcome depends on factors outlined in Table 2-6, ranging from positive to negative.

Priorities: Model[10] and EPM

A working hypothesis is that all living beings pursue an aim in a creative manner, or, better said, they creatively pursue some aims (F9); if a positive result is achieved (i.e. toward one's own world), this hypothesis makes us stronger (formula F9 × F5 = F3). If, on the other hand, a negative reaction occurs, something that could be called "anguish" or doubt is generated (formula F9 × F0 = F6). This outcome sometimes may lead to nullifications (formula F6 × F6 = F0).

When this mechanism is automatically triggered in animals and in human beings (primary priority), it cannot be modified. On the other hand, in the secondary and tertiary priority, the mind can be guided by using the tools at our disposal. We can try to generate a reaction in the world that may work in our favor (formula F9 (F3 × F9 = F5) × F5 = F3) In this case, priority to some choices may be given according to considerations about what kind of relationships in the world could give us a positive response. We need to bear in mind that a certain number of positive answers are needed for us to survive. If, for example, a girl is predisposed to fall in love, and she goes to a ball, she might approach a less handsome guy rather than a more handsome one because the less handsome guy is more likely to give her a positive response than the more handsome guy, who is, presumably, courted more. According to this hypothesis, priorities are determined by the need to survive by strengthening ourselves.

Negotiation: Model[11] and EPM

See comments made above about the ability to love and to negotiate.

Intimacy: Model[12] and EPM

As we have already seen for other models, EPM tends to support the idea that a certain amount or number of positive responses from the world are necessary for us to survive. Responses related to intimacy are to be included in the biological stratum of the primary priorities of air, food, and shelter. It is not difficult for the EPM to accept that the same interaction rules that apply at the conscious level also apply at a biological level. The first relational action made by a newborn child is to suck his or her mother's nipple, and if a positive reply is received from that world (i.e., mother gives milk), the child strengthens his or her biological and mental world (formula F9 × F5 = F3).

Drama Triangle: Model[13] and EPM

The model would tend to specify relational styles in neutral rather than judgmental terms (please refer to what was said above on the importance of some psychotherapeutic situations in which it is necessary to distance oneself from the judgments of values with regard to both the patient and oneself to follow the mental order implied by the EPM); as a result, the judge could become the person who enforces the rules, and the persecutor could become the savior. The therapist could become a mediator. The father could be someone who enforces the rules but also moves toward the other person's world, the defendant could be the one who moves toward the other person's world (maybe excessively), a saint could be someone who apparently moves toward the other person's world but who, in reality, maintains his or her own world, and so on.

Distance Regulation: Model[14] and EPM

See comments about the assumption in space and time, Model[3].

Classification of Relationships: Model[15] and EPM

See comments about Context in Model[1].

CONCLUSION

This chapter attempted to integrate both theory and EPM through their differences and similarities. Differences speak to the level of complementarity between them. One complements the other in theory and, as shown in Part II, in practice. Similarities do not in any way decrease the complementarity of the theory and of the model. These similarities speak to the commonalities of style, goals, and intent that exist between theory and EPM. They both seem abstract, but they both strive for empirical verification. Both have developed tools and means to evaluate the validity of their statements in the laboratory and in clinical and non-clinical settings.

Part II

Applications of the Theory and the Model to Intimate Relationships

Chapter 7

Theory-Derived Preventive Interventions for Non-clinical Relationships

By preventive and non-clinical interventions is meant targeted, issue-specific ways of improving functional and semi-functional relationships. By now the reader should be able to distinguish functional and semi-functional from dysfunctional and clinical interventions. Using the ERAAwC definition of functionality, functionality would mean the appropriate use of all five Model^1 components. Using Model^2, functionality would mean sharing genotypical hurts in a consistent fashion with an intimate with a minimum of discrepancy among the four levels of observation/interpretation. Using Model^3, it means adequate to superior functioning in all settings. Using Model^4, it means appropriate balance and regulation of distance and control functions. Using Model^5, it would mean full, positive use of the abilities to love and to negotiate. Using Model^6, it would mean the appropriate balance of the three modalities of Being, Doing, and Having according to the various stages of the family-life cycle, without overdoing Having at the expense of Being. Using Model^7, it means being able to integrate one's similarities and differences with those of intimate others, with a wide range of positive identities and roles. According to Model^8 definitions, functional refers to maintaining creatively conductive (CC) relationships, while by semi-functional is meant reactively repetitive (RR) intimate relationships. Dysfunctional means any relationship where at least one partner or family member can be characterized as abusive and apathetic (AA), in extremely contradictory and inconsistent fashion, defeating whomever he or she comes in contact with, including the self. According to Model^9, functionality is characterized by selfulness, while semi-functionality is characterized by selfishness or selflessless. Dysfunctionality, of course, is characterized by no-self in at least one member of a couple or a family, where others have no choice but to be reactive. According to Model[10], functionality means priorities that recognize the long-term importance of self and intimate others over other short-term priorities.

Using Model[11] means being able to negotiate important life issues as well as everyday, routine issues in ways that recognize the importance of whoever is involved in the process of negotiation. According to Model[12], functionality means being emotionally available to loved ones, especially when they hurt. According to Model[13], functionality means not playing any of the three destructive roles of Persecutor, Victim, and Savior and playing constructive roles instead. According to Model[14], functionality means balancing approach-avoidance tendencies without using excessively any of the three dysfunctional distancing roles, Distancer, Pursuer, and Regulator.

Prevention means to improve functional and semi-functional relationships for the better. Non-clinical means relationships where one of the parties involved is not diagnosable using DSM-IV definitions of psychiatric conditions. To intervene with these relationships, either at risk or in need of help (L'Abate, 1990, 1994b, 2002a, 2002b), two structural, cost-effective, mass-oriented approaches were developed: (1) structured enrichment programs (SEP) for couples and families and (2) workbooks for individuals, couples, and families. Before addressing these two approaches, an introduction to the background responsible for both is necessary. The laboratory method in evaluation was already considered in Chapter 3. Chapter 8 considers interventions for clinical (i.e., diagnosable) relationships. That method provides the context for using large-scale, cost-effective interventions through the use of intermediaries.

CHANGING BEHAVIOR THROUGH INTERMEDIARIES

A variety of considerations prompted the change from monitored play therapy (L'Abate, 1979) with children, which was part of the laboratory method described in Chapter 3, to the creation of structured enrichment programs (SEPs) for couples and families: (1) the advent of family therapy and the need to develop structured methods of training students to work with multirelational systems (i.e., couples and families), (2) the relative ineffectiveness of play therapy without involvement of parents and siblings, who saw the identified patient as being the one in need of help, exempting them from taking responsibility for changes in the family, and, therefore, (3) the need to avoid making the referred child the "patient" and accepting implicitly a definition given by the family by evaluating the child alone and treating him or her without intervening with the family as a unit. Once this approach was undertaken, the number of referrals for child evaluation dropped dramatically.

These considerations prompted the establishment of new ways of intervening in intimate relationships, using graduate students as intermediaries, dismantling the two monitored play therapy rooms, and changing them into two family intervention rooms, with one-way mirrors. Many graduate students had never interviewed a family, or, if they had received any psychotherapy experience, it was strictly of an individual rather than of a multirelational nature.

Thus, with the help of these students and to train them, the first author started to create SEPs for couples and families that involved evaluating couples and families before and after intervention. Instead of real, live intermediaries, the advent of the computer and the Internet created mechanical intermediaries that supplanted human beings. They may be more reliable and certainly cheaper, as shown in the rest of this chapter (L'Abate, 1992, 2001a, 2002a, 2002b). Nonetheless, whether intermediaries are human or mechanical, to reach a wider number of respondents without sacrificing standards of quality, especially in prevention, it will be necessary for professionals to learn to intervene with respondents at a distance, without f2f, talk-based contact with them. This change, of course, will not take place without resistance (L'Abate, 1997a), but it will occur whether said professionals like it or not, especially if the mental health community wants to improve the immense number of relationship problems present in our nation and other nations (see Chapter 11).

STRUCTURED ENRICHMENT PROGRAMS FOR COUPLES AND FAMILIES

This approach consists of written exercises (Weintraub, 1981) to be administered by semi-professional trainers under the supervision of a professional. These exercises were administered verbatim from the text to respondents, couples, and families (L'Abate, 1990, 1999a, 1999b, 2002a, 2002b; L'Abate & Weinstein, 1987; L'Abate & Young, 1987). The first author is in the process of transforming these exercises for computer administration at a distance from respondents (individuals, couples, and families).

These programs were developed as a didactic way of teaching graduate students to work with couples and families under structured conditions, to minimize anxiety, and to teach them to start working with "functional" and "semi-functional" couples before working with dysfunctional ones. This practicum experience brought about the creation of a graduate course in preventive approaches, where students would enrich couples and families and produce also an enrichment program of their choice. Selection of the best programs produced a library of 50 programs (L'Abate & Weinstein, 1987) and accompanying case studies (L'Abate & Stevens, 1986; L'Abate & Young, 1987).

Theoretical Assumptions. No theoretical assumptions were made at the time (L'Abate, 1985). The most immediate goal was simply to give a structure for students to work with respondents under controlled conditions that would minimize anxiety and maximize learning (Jessee & L'Abate, 1981). Programs were developed eclectically from different theoretical and atheoretical sources. As this approach grew, programs were developed from a variety of theory-related and theory-independent sources. Three doctoral dissertations, to be summarized below, and a consumer satisfaction survey (L'Abate & Rupp, 1981) evaluated the short-term outcome of these programs, with positive outcomes in comparison to contrast groups. Only a handful of over 300 couples and families ever dropped out.

Ultimate Outcomes Expected and Intermediate Client Objectives. In addition to the primary goal of training students, a second goal became one of enriching (i.e., making things better for) already relatively functioning couples and families. We found that clinical families could not be enriched at the outset (L'Abate & Weeks, 1976). However, they could be enriched after the initial crisis that brought them into therapy, that is, after they had been "normalized" through therapy (Kochalka et al., 1987). By providing a structure for couples and family members to come together and talk with each other, to answer questions that had never been asked before, they may learn to love and negotiate better than if they had never had this experience. Therapy, apparently, did not provide a comparable experience.

Targeted Populations. The 50 programs are divided into lessons (three or more) with five to six or more exercises per lesson, for a total of more than 1,000 exercises coded for nine dimensions of family interaction (Kochalka & L'Abate, 1997; L'Abate, 2002b). The section of these programs relevant to prevention with couples deals with developmental stages in the family life cycle, starting with premarital and marital issues and sexuality (6 programs), man–woman relationships (7 programs), parenting (6 programs), and late stages of the family life cycle (4 programs). A second section deals with couples/families structurally, according to their level of emotional/educational/intellectual development, from introductory (3 programs), to intermediate (4 programs), affective (4 programs), cognitive (4 programs), and relational skill building (4 programs). A third section contains programs for non-traditional couples/families (divorce, single-parent, adoption, blended, and dual-employment). A fourth section contains programs for dysfunctional couples/families (general, physically handicapped, mentally handicapped, alcoholics, drugs, and depression).

Format. Each couple or family (usually obtained from the student body of a large urban university as an experiment for which they received class credit) was interviewed and evaluated on a before-after enrichment basis with a battery of marital, paper-and-pencil, self-report tests. On the basis of the (1) enricher(s)' impressions, (2) couple's stated needs and wants, and (3) objective test results, the couple was offered a choice among three enrichment programs that seemed to fit their needs, as perceived by them as well as by enrichers and supervisor (L'Abate & Young, 1987).

After a program was chosen, each couple or family was usually seen for six sessions, after which they were re-evaluated with the same test battery, receiving feedback in a debriefing session afterward. Couples and families were enriched alone with one or two enrichers. Respondents were sometimes enriched in their homes or sometimes in the Family Study Center, according to their schedules, schedules of enrichers, and the logistics of being seen either in their homes or in the Family Study Center.

Lesson Content. Each program is divided into lessons (three to six) about topics listed above. Within each topic (i.e., program) are lessons relating to it. For instance, if the marital relationship was relevant, then programs relevant to the issue at hand were presented for consideration (negotiation, assertiveness, intimacy, etc.). If the major issue requested by a couple was parenting, this program started with a lesson about deciding to have a baby, expecting a baby, parental assertiveness, parental effectiveness, parents and teenagers, and separating teenagers from their parents.

Training Methods. Because programs are written down verbatim, they can be administered with a minimum of training. Practice took place through role-playing, with "mock" families made up by trainees themselves, taking turns at being "enrichers" and family members. After becoming acquainted with evaluation and the process of structured enrichment, trainees started to work with a volunteer functional couple, being supervised in group about the process from their notes and/or videotapes. They learned by doing. This approach led to the conclusion that, given a specific and clear structure, paraprofessionals with personal but no professional qualifications can be taught to successfully enrich couples and families. Even though graduate students may not be thought of as paraprofessionals, many of them, especially those with a baccalaureate degree and no clinical experience, had not received any substantive training to qualify as yet as professionals. Paraprofessional intermediaries have now been supplanted by the computer and the Internet.

Research. Most of the research concerning the outcome of SEPs is unpublished. Quite a few case studies have been published (L'Abate & Stevens, 1986; L'Abate & Young, 1987). Coleman (1986) attempted to apply Structured Enrichment (SE) to low-income, black, single-parent families with predictably questionable results. Three (in-house) doctoral dissertations, however, were successful in demonstrating positive outcomes on termination of SE. Another doctoral dissertation (Yarbrough, 1983) was completed outside the Family Study Center.

Wildman (1976) compared the effectiveness of structured (i.e., enrichment) versus unstructured (i.e., therapy) interventions with couples using both clinical and non-clinical couples as subjects. Clinical meant that the couple requested professional help for their marriage, while non-clinical meant a couple in which neither partner asked for professional help, but they were asked to participate in the study. Up to the time of this study, clinical couples received therapy, while non-clinical couples received enrichment. The purpose of this study was to find out whether structured enrichment, instead of therapy, would help clinical couples. Fifty-eight couples were divided into two groups of 19 clinical and 39 non-clinical couples. Before treatment they were administered a 70-item battery of self-rating scales (two Marital Happiness Scales, a Marital Progress Sheet, and a Communication Reaction Form). Eight clinical couples received six weekly sessions of enrichment, while eleven couples received six sessions of psychotherapy. Twenty-five non-clinical couples received six sessions of enrichment, while 14 couples served in a seven-week no-treatment control group. The same test battery administered before treatment was administered at termination of treatment. At both pre- and post-test the scores of husbands and wives correlated significantly, while all three groups receiving enrichment and psychotherapy increased their overall total battery scores from pre- to post-test. The no-treatment control group registered a small decline. The greatest mean increase from pre- to post-test was found in the clinical group receiving enrichment, even though these gains were not significantly greater than those of the clinical therapy group. Wildman interpreted these results to support the application of structured enrichment programs for couples seeking professional help. Thus, structured enrichment programs, administered by subprofessional personnel, can be viewed as a preventive intervention in their own right as well as an adjunct to face-to-face therapeutic interventions by professionals.

Ganahl (1981) followed up Wildman's results by evaluating 126 married couples (and one cohabiting couple) who were either clients of the Family Study Center or who volunteered for research credit as part of introductory psychology classes. Couples were in their late 20s, college-educated, of diverse occupational backgrounds, and married for an average of five years, with an average of one child. This sample was composed predominantly of Caucasian couples, with either Protestant or no religious preference.

The non-clinical enrichment group results were compared to a no-treatment control group, another group that received enrichment with homework assignments, a group that received homework alone without enrichment, and a clinical enrichment group composed of couples who asked for professional help with their marriages. Using one-factor ANOVA and ANCOVA (Analysis of Covariance), improvement was measured by a battery of tests (Locke-Wallace Short Marital Adjustment Test [MAT]), the Primary Communication Inventory (PSI), the Marital Happiness Scale (MHS), and a composite test battery made up of questions concerning marital satisfaction in a variety of areas of functioning. These tests were administered on a pre-post intervention basis, with a six- to seven-week interval between pre- and post-tests. The only exception was the clinical groups, which were not evaluated on the MAT or PCI. These groups were administered the other tests listed above.

Results indicated that SEPs were effective in producing improved marital satisfaction and adjustment. The enrichment group produced positive changes on the MAT, battery, and communication items of the MHS. The enrichment plus homework assignments group produced significantly positive results on the battery, PCI, with a positive trend ($p < .06$) on the MAT. The homework group produced positive results on the battery score alone. No significant differences were noted between the raw gain scores of these groups on any measure. The clinical enrichment group showed significant improvement on the MHS only, while the clinical therapy group showed significant improvement on the battery, MHS, and the communication items of the MHS. Following ANCOVA, no significant differences between clinical and non-clinical groups were found. The clinical enrichment group was found to be inferior to the therapy group on the battery and communication items of the MHS. No sex differences were found in response to treatment, program type, or therapist sex or number (some couples were treated by a single therapist and others were treated by two therapists working together).

Sloan (1983) compared the effectiveness of two six-hour SEP workshop formats in facilitating intimacy and marital adjustment in 24 volunteer Jewish couples who were randomly assigned to two treatment conditions. Both experimental and control formats featured exercises on selfhood and differentiation, as well as on communication and negotiation skills. The exercises used in this study, in addition to being available in the original dissertation, can be found in L'Abate and Weinstein (1987). The experimental group also received a sharing-of-hurt exercise prior to negotiating. Sharing of hurt (L'Abate, 1994b, 1997b) was hypothesized as being the essential feature of the deepest level of self-disclosure. Sloan assessed all couples before and after the workshops with the following measures: Interpersonal Relationship Scale (IRS), Sharing of Hurts Scale (SOH), Feelings Questionnaire (FQ), Handling Problems Change Scale (HPCS), the Component Analysis Questionnaire (CAQ), and Feelings Expression Inventory (FEI).

No significant differences were found between the two groups on any of the self-report measures of intimacy and marital adjustment before and after the workshop. Although a relationship between pretreatment levels of intimacy and marital adjustment was found, change in marital intimacy was not accompanied by a concurrent change in marital adjustment. Significant pre-post differences were found within the experimental group for intimacy and perceived ability to deal with relationship problems but not for marital adjustment. Only the pre-post difference in perceived ability to deal with relationship problems reached statistical significance in the control group. These results suggested a trend toward an egalitarian model of emotional sharing among middle-class, college-educated couples. Although it had been hypothesized initially that hurt feelings were synonymous with the deepest level of emotional sharing, contents of this process of sharing may vary from person to person and may shift as couples progress across the marital life cycle.

Yarbrough (1983) investigated the effects of an SE negotiation program on an individual's dyadic adjustment, satisfaction, and intimacy in a group format, assessing also the durability of these effects as well as gender differences in undergraduate couples. These couples (n = 48) expressed interest in a marital enrichment program offered through the University Counseling and Testing Center and a local church. A control group consisted of couples who completed the testing but chose not to follow through on receiving this program. All couples were interviewed first to screen out couples who were in crisis or who were currently receiving marital therapy. The initial screening and assessment battery consisted of instruments designed to assess dyadic adjustment, satisfaction, and intimacy: (1) Spanier's Dyadic Adjustment Inventory, as a measure of adjustment and negotiation; (2) Barrett-Lennard Relationship Inventory, as a measure of conjugal satisfaction; and (3) Interpersonal Relationship Scale, as a measure of intimacy. Couples were randomly assigned to two treatment groups: (1) facilitation and intervention and (2) instructions given by a leader without group interaction but with dyadic interaction. All couples received six weeks of training in the SE negotiation program in six two-hour sessions with homework assignments between sessions. On termination, all couples were retested and received a closing interview to answer any questions and, when needed, offered marital therapy. They were also informed that in six weeks a questionnaire would be mailed to them for a follow-up. All these questionnaires were returned, while the couples in the control group did not receive them.

Results comparing pre- with post-intervention scores on the three measures showed that there were significant differences between couples who committed themselves to work on their relationship and those who did not. Scores of the control group remained unchanged, while those of the experimental group decreased at a statistical level of significance. These effects of negotiation training appeared not only durable but cumulative after a six- to eight-week follow-up. Subjectively, most couples in the experimental group considered the program to be effective in improving levels of communication skills, satisfaction with the relationship, improving negotiation skills, and developing greater trust and intimacy.

EVALUATING MODELS THROUGH STRUCTURED ENRICHMENT PROGRAMS

Most models listed below are matched by SEP or lessons from programs that lend themselves to controlled evaluation. Of course, they need to be evaluated by investigators independently of the theory and methods of evaluation.

Model[1]: *ERAAwC.* A whole section based on this model is contained in the Negotiation Potential program (L'Abate & Weinstein, 1987, pp. 376–383), including lessons on Emotionality and how to deal with anger in self and others, including Rationality, Activity, Awareness, and Contextual responses.

Model[5]: *Ability to Love and Negotiate.* Exercises about love and appreciation (pp. 335–337) are found in an Affective Program that includes also many exercises about feelings (pp. 331–334), as well as forgiving mistakes (pp. 280–281) in an introductory program.

Model[6]: *Modalities.* Exercises about resources exchanged, Being, Doing, and Having, are found in the Negotiation Potential program (pp. 387–388).

Model[8]: *Styles in Relationships.* The ARC model is part of the Negotiation Potential program (L'Abate & Weinstein, 1987, pp. 373–376), including lessons on Apathetic, Reactive, and Conductive response styles.

Model[9]: *Selfhood.* Generic exercises about the self in the family, social roles, role inductions, and role reversals are part of a Transactional Program (pp. 359–367) patterned after Spiegel's (1971) contribution mentioned in Chapter 1. Thus, these exercises are indirectly related to the model. However, theory-derived exercises about selfhood are part of the Negotiation Potential program (pp. 385–387).

Model[10]: *Priorities.* This model is part of the Negotiation Potential program (pp. 371–388), including lessons on intra- and extra-familial priorities, selfhood, and resources exchanged, that is, modalities (Model[5]).

Model[11]: *Negotiation.* This program, as indicated above, was administered most often and validated more than once, but it is not based on the original negotiation model itself. Instead, it consists of six lessons dealing with (1) marriage myths, (2) focus on the relationship, (3) communication in marriage, (4) communication and hurts, (5) trust, and (6) quid pro quo.

Case studies using the whole or parts of this program are found in L'Abate and Young (1987) on a dating couple (pp. 7–14), a democratic couple (pp. 17–26), a couple under stress (pp. 60–71), an "uproar" couple (pp. 195–210), alcohol in the marriage (pp. 211–229), a blended couple (pp. 230–244), and a failure to enrich (pp. 339–343).

The Negotiation Potential program (pp. 371–388) includes various exercises that are isomorphic with Models[1], [8], and [10], reviewed here.

Model[12]: *Intimacy.* An early version of an Intimacy Enrichment program was published verbatim (L'Abate & McHenry, 1983, pp. 357–362). One exercise in L'Abate and Weinstein (1987) addresses avoidance of intimacy (p. 162). A complete program (No. 29) on helpfulness (pp. 300–309) contains lessons on (1) establishing levels of caring, hurts, and strengths, (2) seeing the good, (3) caring, (4) sharing of hurt feelings, (5) forgiveness, (6) protectiveness, (7) responsibility, and (8) enjoyment. Two case studies (L'Abate & Young, 1987), illustrating specific applications of this program to issues of parentification (pp. 134–153) and to a psychosomatic family (pp. 163–179), describe how this program was applied with pre- and post-enrichment test batteries.

EXAMPLE OF AN INTRODUCTORY STRUCTURED ENRICHMENT PROGRAM

One example of a program that can be administered to practically anyone is given below (L'Abate & Weinstein, 1987, pp. 55–59). It has been revised from being administered through a trainer to be administered at a distance, through a computer. This program can be used by itself or can be used as an introductory, structured interview in conjunction with other types of interventions. Note that SEPs denote a series of "lessons" focused on a specific topic. Later on, this chapter gives examples of workbooks that contain series of "assignments" rather than "lessons." However, now that SEPs are being revised to fit into a distance format, just like the one below, the distinction between programs and workbooks is no longer tenable. Any program that can be administered at a distance to respondents from a professional as written homework assignments becomes a workbook.

CONFRONTING CHANGE

The purpose of this program is to help you think about changing relationships that have not paid off for you or that have been hurtful to you and to those who love you.

Lesson 1. Beginning to Think about Change

The purpose of this lesson is to help you think about change in your relationships, whether you want to keep them as they are or whether you want to change them for the better.

1. Meaning of Change
    a. What does change mean to you?
    b. Is the devil you have better than the devil you don't have?
    c. Why do you want to change?
    d. Things can stay as they are, or they can get worse. We want to help make them better. Which of these choices do you want?
2. Why Change?
    a. How do you think change will take place in your family?
    b. Who is going to be responsible for change in this family?
    c. If any of you expect change to take place outside yourself, how is this stance going to help your family?
    d. If any of you do not really want to change and want to live with defeat, let's find out who that one is.

e. If one partner or family member is especially resistant, the next question should be asked of him or her.

3. Power to Defeat

a. Apparently you have taken on, or the family has given you, the power to defeat and to keep things as they are rather than to win and change things for the better for you and your family. If you want to keep things as they are and you don't want things to change for the better, there must be a payoff for you. What is it? Do you get a kick out of or enjoy defeating others or yourself?

b. If you defeat others, how can you not defeat yourself?

4. Investing in Sameness

a. Each of us can choose to stay the same and thus defeat others and ourselves, or we can choose to change ourselves. Which of these choices do you want?

b. Does anyone in this family have an investment in keeping things as they are?

c. By keeping things as they are now, no one has to change. Is that what you want?

d. If you really want to change, how does each of you want to change?

5. For Whose Sake?

a. Why should any of you want to change anyway? [Pause] For whose sake should any of you change?

b. If anyone wants to change for somebody else's sake, I doubt very seriously that change can occur.

c. If anyone wants to know why nobody should not change for someone else, it means you already know what he or she wants from you—you have read that person's mind. It means pleasing that person rather than yourself. Under these conditions, it is impossible to win. What do you think?

6. Change for One's Own Sake

1. If change is to take place, it must be to satisfy ourselves. Why?

2. How can we satisfy ourselves and others in the family without defeating or hurting anybody in the family?

Homework: During the coming week, think whether you really want to change and whether or not you want to change for the better. List reasons why each of you should or should not change and have a family conference on your own before your next lesson.

Enrichment Lesson 2, entitled "How to Live," asked respondents whether they wanted to stay the same or get worse or change for the better, asking for a commitment to change and assuming personal responsibility for change. Lesson 3 dealt with priorities (Model[10]) for change: individual, couple, family, distinguishing between immediate versus long-range priorities.

PRIORITIES MODEL[10]: EXAMPLE OF AN ENRICHMENT PROGRAM FOR COUPLES THINKING ABOUT HAVING A BABY

Lesson 1. Who Am I? Who Are We?

This program is designed for couples who are thinking about whether or not to have a child. These lessons will, we hope, help you clarify issues involved in making this important decision. The purpose of this lesson is to help you explore yourselves and your priorities, that is, what is important to you as an individual, as a partner, and as a couple.

A. Who Am I?

1. The decision to have or not to have a child may be a difficult one. Right now, both of you close your eyes and relax. Take a few deep breaths and think about yourself as you are now. Let your thoughts float freely. Think of yourself in as many ways as you can. When you are ready, open your eyes and introduce yourself to your partner. Let your partner know who you are in as many ways as you think of yourself. State at least five self-definitions, that is, how you think about yourself.
2. Were you surprised at anything your partner just said?

B. Personal Priorities

1. Now, think about yourself in the future. What priorities, that is, what is important to you, do you have for yourself as an individual, say, five years from now?
2. How about 10 years from now?

C. Who Are We?

1. In this exercise, you will be thinking about who you are as a couple right now. Take a piece of paper and a pencil and draw a coat of arms for you as a couple. Include anything you consider important to who you are as a couple. You may draw some pictures or write several of your marriage's mottoes on the crest.
2. Now, describe your crests and explain to each other why you included each part of your design. [Pause] How are your designs similar? How are they different?

D. Marriage Priorities

1. Now that you have an idea of your similarities and differences as a couple in the present, think about your future priorities as a couple. Think of several priorities for you two as a couple and write them down on the other side of the papers on which you drew your coats of arms. Your priorities may relate to many different areas of your marriage—financial, recreational, sexual, emotional.
2. Now, we would like each of you to read your list. What similarities do you see in your two lists? What differences are there?

E. Priorities as a Couple

1. Each of you has heard and thought about priorities you and your spouse have for your life together. Rank these priorities according to their importance to you as a couple. Share your lists and work together.
2. On a sheet of paper for each of you draw a circle and write the priority most important to you as a couple in the circle; draw another circle enclosing the first one and write the priority that is next in importance. Draw a circle for each of the goals on your list.
3. When you have finished, explain to each other what your priorities are. Take turns in explaining each priority. After one has explained his or her priority, let the other partner explain his or hers.
4. How did it feel to negotiate your priorities for the future?

F. Babies and Change

1. Now that you have thought about yourselves and your individual priorities, your priorities as a couple, and the priorities of your marriage, imagine that the wife is pregnant. What changes do you think the baby's arrival will cause in your priorities?
2. What changes will take place to your priorities as an individual?
3. What changes will take place to your priorities as a couple?

INTIMACY MODEL[12]: EXAMPLE OF A THEORY-DERIVED, STRUCTURED INTERVIEW WITH FAMILIES—ESTABLISHING THE LEVEL OF HURT

A. *Introduction*

1. Because you care for each other, the issue that brought you to seek help has caused a lot of hurt and pain. Is that right?
2. If one of you denies any pain, this indicates the presence of a serious problem. It may be that a structured enrichment program cannot be used until after some family therapy. Tell how this issue has hurt each of you.
3. Each member must describe his or her own hurt and pain.
4. If one of you denies any hurt, then that person might be the one who produces pain and hurt. Is that right?

B. *Recognizing Strength.* It takes strength to ask for help. Strong people don't cry. Could you tell how that statement applies to this family?

C. *Previous Attempts to Resolve the Issue That Brought the Family Together*

1. What ways have you tried to work on this issue in the past?
2. How have those measures worked out? Discuss successes and failures of earlier approaches.

D. *Seeing the Good*

1. What does "seeing the good" mean to this family?
2. What do you think it means to see the good in yourself and the other members of your family?

3. Discuss the similarities and differences in proposed meanings.
4. Could you agree that seeing the good means playing up the positive side, the good side, of those we love?
5. When we love someone, we accept the bad things about that person as things that are overshadowed by the good in him or her. What do you think of that?

E. *Interference*

1. How do you show that you see the good in yourself and in one another?
2. What is it about this family that makes it hard for you to see the good in the others?

F. *Practicing Good*

1. Say something good about each member of your family.
2. Look each person in the eye and tell that person about a good trait or quality he or she possesses.
3. How did it feel to tell the members of your family about the good in them?
4. How did it feel to be told good things about yourself?
5. Were you surprised to hear how much good there is in this family?

G. *Both Sides of a Coin*

1. Speak or write about a situation that has both good and bad aspects.
2. Is it better to work and think about mainly the good or the bad aspects of this situation?
3. Why?
4. Do you see any relationship between what you said and the old story about the optimist and the pessimist looking at the half-filled glass? Remember that the optimist said the glass was half full, and the pessimist said it was half empty. What do you say?

H. *Seeing Good Better*

1. How could you do a better job of seeing the good in yourselves and one another?
2. Respond to and discuss each other's answers.
3. Tell each other something good that you recognize in him or her.

I. *Caring*

1. What does it mean to care for someone?
2. Discuss similarities and differences in proposed meanings.
3. Could we agree that to care is to understand the importance of one's self and the selves of one's family? If you care for someone, you see both yourself and that person as being important. What do you think about that?

J. *Showing Care*

1. How do you show that you care for each other?

2. Tell each other one way in which each member of the family shows you that he or she cares for you.
3. If some family members show care in a destructive manner, how does this family react to show that you care?

K. *Self-Care*

1. Each of you in turn stand up and say: "I am a person, and I am important." Then go up to each member of your family and say: "I care for you, and you are important to me."
2. How does it feel to tell your family that you care for them?
3. How does it feel to have your family say that they care for you?
4. Go to every family member and do something that shows that you care for that person. You might give that person a kiss, a hug, a handshake—anything that feels right to you.

L. *Caring Better*

1. How could each of you do a better job of letting the other members of your family know that you care for them?
2. Think of all the ways you care for and show your care for the members of this family. Tell how each of you could show you care in better ways than you might have done in the past.

M. *Sharing of Hurt Feelings*

1. What does "sharing of hurt feelings" mean to this family?
2. What does it mean to share your hurt feelings with someone?
3. Could we agree that sharing of hurt feelings means telling the people you are close to not only about your victories and happiness but also about your pain and defeats?
4. We can share victories with anybody, but our defeats belong to the family. What do you think of that idea?

N. *Sharing How?*

1. How do you share your hurt feelings with one another?
2. Tell each other how you talk about your pains and defeats in this family.
3. Does it make you feel better to share your hurt feelings with each other?
4. Is there anyone who does not share his or her hurts in the family?
5. Why does anyone not share feelings with those who love him or her?
6. What do you think would happen if the one(s) who have chosen not to share their feelings in the family did it now?

O. *Practicing*

1. This is going to be very hard, but tell something that is hurting you at this moment.
2. How does it feel to tell your family about your pains and defeats?
3. How does it feel to hear about your family's hurts?

P. *Responding to Sharing*

1. Go to each family member, touch that one, and say, "I am glad that you are willing to share your hurt with me. I want to know about your defeats and pains because I care about you and hope that I can do something to make things better for you."

Q. *Sharing Hurt Feelings Better*

1. How could each of you do a better job of sharing your hurt with each other?
2. How could this family better use sharing of hurts to make each member and the whole family happier and stronger?
3. If necessary, think about how this family shares its hurts. Tell each other about something that hurts you. When someone tells you about his or her hurts, try to respond as you would want that person to respond to your hurts.

R. *Forgiveness*

1. Talk about "forgiveness" and what it means to this family.
2. What does it mean to forgive someone?
3. Could you agree that forgiveness means not demanding that we and others be perfect? As human beings, you know, we really can't be perfect.
4. Forgiveness also means not allowing the past to ruin the present. Just because someone may have goofed yesterday doesn't mean that that person will have to do wrong today. What do you think about that?
5. Another way to look at forgiveness is to give up expectations of perfection in self and others. What do you think about that?
6. When someone in this family has hurt someone else, how do you go about forgiving?
7. What do you think it means that you have difficulty forgiving?

S. *Practicing Forgiveness*

1. If someone in this family has done something that is still hurting you, pretend to write that thing on a sheet of paper.
2. Look down at your imaginary paper and say: "It's crazy for me to have to carry this nonsense around with me all the time." Now throw the "papers" into the middle of the floor.
3. Will one of you now please pretend to set the pile of nonsense on fire? It wasn't as big a fire as you thought it would be, was it?

T. *Practicing Some More*

1. Go to each member of your family, touch that person, and say: "We are both human, so we can't be perfect. But I'm not going to let the past ruin the present. I forgive both of us."
2. How does it feel to be forgiven by the members of your family?
3. How does it feel to forgive?
4. You don't have to forget to forgive. Can you learn from what has gone wrong in the past?

U. *Forgiving Better*

1. How could each of you do a better job of forgiving?
2. If you cannot forgive yourself, you cannot forgive others. The best way to forgive oneself is to change one's behavior.

Homework: During the next week, every time you think of an instance when someone has hurt you in the past—this doesn't include ongoing conflict—write down what happened, tear the paper into little shreds, and flush it down the toilet.

INITIAL FAMILY ASSIGNMENT

The purpose of this assignment is to elicit as much information as possible from a family. The issue here is: What kind of information? The focus of this initial family assignment is directed toward how family members feel about themselves and each other. Questions asked in this assignment are to be answered in writing by individual family members, or they can be asked verbally by the interviewer, if this assignment is administered as a structured interview. If answers are in writing, then each family member can read the answers of other family members to share them. If answers are given verbally, it will be up to the interviewer to ask each family member how he or she feels about what other family members have written.

1. Why are you here today?
2. What is the major issue (concern, problem) in your family?
3. Most of the answers are very likely to be expressed in negative terms about the misbehavior or misdeeds of one family member, very likely the identified patient (IP). It will be necessary to reframe positively the family's reasons for being here: "I beg to differ from whatever each of you has written (or said), but isn't the major reason for being here the fact that you love each other? There are many families who have the same issue (concern, problem) as you do. However, they would not come near this office to help themselves. Furthermore, it takes a lot of love and strength to ask for help. Many families who hurt a lot do not have enough strength to ask for help." What do you think about this last statement?
4. What would you say is your family's motto or theme? For instance, "You must do it my way," "If I do not win, you won't win either," "No matter what you say, I'll do as I want," "No one listens to anybody else."
5. How does it feel to live in your family?
6. How would you like to feel in your family?
7. What needs to change in your family to make it feel the way you want it to feel?
8. What is the most powerful positive feeling you share in your family?
9. How do you share this feeling?
10. How often do you share it?
11. What is the most powerful negative feeling you share in your family?
12. How do you share this feeling?

13. What do you like most about Dad (or male caretaker if there is one)?
14. What do you like least about him?
15. What do you like most about Mom (or female caretaker if there is one)?
16. What do you like least about Mom?
17. What do you like most about (name of firstborn)?
18. What do you like least about (name of firstborn)?

19–20. Ask the same two questions (like most and like least) about each child in the family.

21. How might Dad (or male caretaker if there is one) change to be happier?
22. How might Mom (or female caretaker if there is one) change to be happier?
23. Ask the same question for every other member of the family.
24. Are you willing to look at yourself to make changes in yourself rather than expecting others in the family to change?
25. What is the greatest hurt you have felt (or experienced) in the past?
26. Note to interviewer: After each member has had a chance to express and share his or her hurts, contract for two more sessions of "evaluation," saying: "Before we agree to work together, we will need to evaluate each other. You will evaluate me and I will evaluate you. By the end of the third session, we will discuss how we shall proceed, whether we want to work together, whether you want to work with someone else, or whether you do not want to work at all. You should know, however, that my practice is different from that of other mental health professionals. I require families to spend one hour on written homework assignments and family meetings for each hour of therapy with me. You do not have to complete any written homework assignments and have these family meetings, however, if you have a lot of money, you like me a lot, and you want to see me for a long time. I want you to think about how I practice, because, if we want to work together, I will need to have you sign an Informed Consent Form about completing written homework assignments."

Homework: "The hurts that you have just expressed can be used to make this family better or make this family worse. It's your choice how you want to use these hurts. During the coming week, before I see you again (at whatever time has been agreed upon with the family), I would like for each of you to write down all the hurts that you have experienced in your life. Write for 20 minutes a day for four days. OK?"

Note to interviewer: Depending on the family, the interviewer has the choice to have them set a family meeting (on a specific day and at a specific time for no longer than one hour) to share these hurts with each other or to have them bring their lists of hurts to share during the next "evaluation" meeting. Please note, contrary to many other family interviews produced in the literature, which stress a rational approach about interviewing families, this initial family interview stresses the importance of feelings in the family. Consequently, expect either crying, anger, or other intense feelings to be expressed either during the interview or immediately after the interview. If either anger or crying is expressed, comment to the effect that the expression of these feelings is an indication of strength and caring because people who do not care do not express any feelings; they are indifferent.

PROGRAMMED WRITING

Systematically Written Homework Assignments: Self-Administered Workbooks for Individuals, Couples, and Families

While the enrichment work was going on, L'Abate, Wagner, & Weeks, (1980) became aware of the power of the written word (Esterling, L'Abate, Murray, & Pennebaker, 1999). Because of constraints in his time (and energy), the first author started to rely more and more on written homework assignments with individuals, couples, and families in his private practice. This practice became another standard operating procedure for at least three reasons, to (1) facilitate respondents' assuming more responsibility for changes in their relationships, (2) save professional time and energy, and (3) save money and make psychotherapy more cost-effective. This process ranged from non-systematic, generally ad hoc homework assignments to the creation of systematically written workbooks that required writing at home rather than direct contact with a therapist or intermediaries (L'Abate, 1986, 1992, 2002a, 2002b). They could be administered in addition to face-to-face psychotherapy or as an alternative to psychotherapy when dealing with relationships that did not need psychotherapy but that could use some different and less expensive form of help.

The most inexpensive and mass-produced medium is the written word, provided that it is programmed to lead troubled individuals and their mates and family members to face each other at pre-set, pre-determined appointment times to complete in writing questions in homework assignments submitted to them in writing. After years of public and private practice, overwhelmed by teaching, research, and writing demands, the first writer found it useful to start requesting respondents to complete homework assignments in writing. During the last 15 years of clinical practice, this request became a sine qua non to be accepted into a therapeutic contract. Respondents, whether individuals, couples, or families, had to agree to complete written homework assignments to match one hour of homework with one hour of therapy. They did not have to fulfill this requirement if they had plenty of money to pay for fees, wanted to stay in therapy forever, and liked the therapist a great deal (L'Abate, 1986). An objective evaluation of the intensity of the depression using either the Beck Depression Inventory or an inventory developed to distinguish between depression as self-criticism and depression as overdependency (Evaluation of Concerns—Appendix A) was administered before and after therapy (Blatt & Homann, 1992; Blatt et al., 1982).

On the basis of Pennebaker's work and research (1997), the first author started routinely to ask all clients, whether individuals, couples, or families, from the very outset of therapy, to write about their hurts for 20 minutes a day for four consecutive days. In couples and families, they had to make an appointment with each other to share, compare, and discuss what they had written about their hurts. Variations on this assignment consist of listing "hurts given" and "hurts received," including also targets of given hurts and sources of received hurts. On the basis of these homework assignments with clinical couples, it could be readily seen that the process of intellectualization was still present. Often, even though they may be cognizant of the inflicted hurts, partners were not ready as yet to share hurt feelings in an affective fashion. Hence, when couples brought their lists of hurts to the therapist, this homework assignment was very informative from the outset of therapy. However, most couples were not yet ready to share their mutually inflicted hurts in a cathartic fashion, at least not in front of the therapist and not at the beginning of therapy. The area of sharing hurts through writing is completely open to clinical and preventive applications (Esterling, L'Abate, Murray, & Pennebaker, 1999; L'Abate, 1997a, 1997b). More than 100 workbooks for individuals, couples, and families are now available on the Internet (L'Abate, 1996, 2002a).

Theoretical Assumptions. The bases of this approach were originally strictly pragmatic. To make time count and to use time more effectively with respondents in crisis, it was found convenient and useful to them to prescribe (through a written informed consent form) one hour of homework for each hour of therapy from the very outset of therapy, using the written rather than the spoken word. Each couple was administered written homework assignments from the very first hour of therapy after three evaluation sessions. Eventually, workbooks were developed that derived from theoretical models about depression, negotiation, and intimacy (L'Abate, 1986; L'Abate, Johnston, & Levis, 1987) and other models.

This approach was expanded by designing additional workbooks that can be administered to respondents either through the mail or through personal computers. This approach was first used with jailed felons, because they could not be seen face-to-face. Feedback about each assignment took place through the mail (L'Abate, 1992). This approach, however, made the first writer aware that completely new kinds of tests were necessary for this practice, creating *prescriptive* rather than solely *descriptive* or *predictive* instruments. Through the use of prescriptive instruments it is possible to link evaluation with programmed writing homework assignments in ways that are either difficult or expensive to obtain through talk (L'Abate, 2002a, 2002b).

The need for prescriptive instruments came about from the administration of structured enrichment programs, where an instrument, the Family Profile Form (Kochalka & L'Abate, 1997; L'Abate, 2002b; L'Abate &

Weinstein, 1987), was created to make the process of program administration more objective and quantifiable. This process led to thinking that we need finite and specific areas of intervention if prescriptive instruments are to be constructed. Through writing, either in enrichment or in written homework assignments, one creates a finite intervention realm where prescriptive instruments can be applied. As long as the spoken medium is the basis of intervention, it will be difficult and expensive to achieve the priority of linking interventions with evaluation.

Ultimate Outcomes Expected and Intermediate Client Objectives. The priority for respondents is to decrease a debilitating condition, like depression, anxiety, or impulsivity. Ultimately, these workbooks or facsimiles could be applied to high school populations. These workbooks were administered to over 350 undergraduates who admitted to being depressed (L'Abate, in press-b; L'Abate, Boyce, Fraizer, & Russ, 1992; L'Abate & Lambert, 1996).

Workbook Content. Content derives from the topic at hand. For instance, the workbook on depression contains eight assignments about the Drama Triangle (Model[13]), Distance Regulation (Model[14]), positive reframings of depression, achieving control through pre-arranged appointments, and writing down what is depressing to respondents. An impulsivity workbook requires weekly behavioral tasks practically with each assignment.

Targeted Populations. In addition to the workbooks mentioned above, workbooks for a variety of clinical and non-clinical conditions were developed from single or multiple score tests, like the Beck Depression Inventory, Hamilton Anxiety Scale, or the MMPI-2, the Personality Assessment Inventory (PAI), or through clinical conditions (anger, loneliness, moodiness, social phobia, etc.).

Format. Each workbook consists of a varying number of homework assignments, from a minimum of three (prescriptive, standard, and follow-up) to 20+ for the Problems in Relationships workbook. Each assignment consists of varying questions about different derivations and implications from the assignment title.

Session. In actual clinical practice, homework assignments were discussed during the therapy hour. For research purposes, any feedback that was administered was conducted in writing without personal contact, to see whether these workbooks produce any positive changes in and by themselves (L'Abate, submitted-a; L'Abate et al., 1992).

Training Methods. Here training is instantaneous, provided the trainee is acquainted with the rationale and background of programmed writing (L'Abate, 1986, 1990, 1992, 2001a, 2002a).

Example. The purpose of this section is to describe the rationale for a depression workbook that is administered as written homework assignments to depressed individuals, couples, and families as a standard operating procedure in my clinical practice and research (L'Abate, 1986; L'Abate et al., 1992; L'Abate & Lambert, 1996). The background for this workbook will serve as an example for the creation of other workbooks dealing with a wide range of clinical conditions in individuals, couples, and families (L'Abate, 1996). Depression is one of the major debilitating conditions present in human existence. It is present in various forms and differs in degrees of intensity. In many cases, it remains undetected and unexpressed, making it difficult to treat. Psychotherapy and medication alone will not be sufficient, although necessary, to deal with the many people affected directly with this condition as well as those (relatives and family members) who are indirectly affected by it and who are sometimes responsible (without meaning to do it) for generating and maintaining it. Depression, no matter how many professionals insist on its physiological genesis, does not grow in a vacuum. It is the outcome of definite and often deliberate family interactions (L'Abate, 1994b, 1997b). There are never going to be sufficient numbers of therapists who will be able to deal with it directly and with those afflicted by this condition, as well as those who are indirectly responsible for and affected by it. If, as some conservative estimates tell us, at least 15% to 25% of the population suffers from depression at one time or another, it becomes imperative to develop alternative ways—inexpensive and mass-produced—to help people suffering from this condition as well as those who are indirectly affected by it (see Chapter 11).

What was originally a general, "focused" assignment ("Write about your depression for one hour every other day [or once a week or at predetermined times].") became a more specific and systematic program ("This is the first homework assignment in an eight-assignment workbook.") that paralleled a theoretical model developed over the years (L'Abate, 1986). Since the creation of this program, many other depression workbooks have been developed: (1) an empirical one, based on the Minnesota Multiphasic Personality Inventory-2 (MMPI-2; L'Abate, 1992); (2) a depression program developed on the basis of Beck's cognitive model of depression (Beck & Young, 1985); and (3) two depression programs developed on the basis of Blatt et al.'s model of depression as self-criticism; and (4) depression as overdependency (L'Abate, 2001a, 2002a, in press-a, in press-b; L'Abate & Lambert, 1996).

Development of a Theoretical, Interactive Model of Depression

The theoretical model developed over the years of clinical practice is an interactive one; that is, depression does not develop and is not maintained in a vacuum but develops and is maintained within the context of intimate (close, prolonged, and committed) relationships, mostly familial. Many depressions take place or are exacerbated within the context of the marital relationship. Hence, this workbook took into account the presence of another partner or other family members, who affect and are affected by the depression.

Isomorphism between Theoretical Model and Assignments in the Workbook. A reciprocal process took place between the creation and clarification of the model and assignments to be administered. Having to break down the theoretical model allowed to clarify the nature of each assignment as well as the component parts of the model and of its isomorphic assignments.

Sequencing Assignments as an Important Component of the Workbook. In addition, it became necessary to specify the developmental and situational antecedents of depression, making sure that assignments followed a natural, rational, and effective sequence that paralleled the condition in the client.

Description of Rationale for Each Assignment. Assignments 1 and 2 are based on two theoretical models, Models[13 & 14] about the Drama Triangle and Distance Regulation, respectively. The rest of the workbook (Assignments 3 through 8) is based on clinical practice, mostly paradoxical (Weeks & L'Abate, 1982), that includes a positive reframing of any clinical condition as an antecedent for its prescription. What was originally a paradoxical, circular rationale eventually became a rationale based on straightforward, linear principles of control (L'Abate, 1986, 1990, 1992, 2001a, 2002a). Respondents answer each assignment independently from intimate others. Then, an appointment is made for couples or family members to meet together at home to compare and contrast their answers, keeping notes of what happened at this meeting. These notes, together with completed assignments, are shared with the therapist and become part of the therapist's file folder. If respondents want to keep their records, they may make copies of their assignments.

Since publication of the first work (L'Abate, 1992), a whole technology based on systematically programmed, self-instructional materials has developed (L'Abate, 2001a, 2002a, 2002b). Workbooks and distance writing can be administered in addition to therapy conceived as tertiary prevention or in addition to primary prevention, as defined earlier. Workbooks, therefore, are defined as para-preventive and para-therapeutic (L'Abate, 1990, 1992).

Programmed materials include questionnaires and tests for evaluation. Workbooks range from loose, three-assignment programs, to workbooks made up of a series of 8 to 20 assignments related to a specific topic (depression, impulsivity, negotiation, intimacy). Each assignment is made up of questions (the Socratic method) that respondents need to answer in writing. Typically, one assignment a week would be assigned for as many weeks as there are assignments, from 2 or 3 to as many as 20, depending on the condition being dealt with. Respondents would receive feedback from the therapist (in addition to the monologic feedback that they receive from answering questions). Couples and families would compare and contrast their answers with each other as well as the therapist, thus producing three change-oriented feedback loops (to use a systems cliché): (1) individual or monologic, from questions to respondent; (2) dyadically interactional or dialogic, from one to other respondent(s); and (3) between respondents and the therapist, for corrective and assumedly therapeutic feedback.

For instance, in answering questions in the individual assignments, each respondent increases the monologic function. Thus, one hopes to increase internal introspection and reflection or move, according to Schwartz and Garamoni (1989), from an internal monologue to a more functional and constructive internal dialogue. This process means going from just one part of an issue to another part previously ignored. Once this task has been accomplished, respondents need to discuss their answers with partners or other family members on a regular basis, at an appointed time and place, comparing their answers and therefore increasing the intimate dialogue. When the completed assignments and the ensuing discussion are presented to the therapist or counselor, the professional adds a third feedback loop, the corrective interpretation, explanation, or connections that respondents may have missed, individually, dyadically, or as a family.

TOWARD A CLASSIFICATION AND A TECHNOLOGY OF WRITING

Writing comprises at least four different degrees of structure (see Table 7-1). The first is a relatively open-ended, unstructured format, as in autobiographies, diaries, and journals. The second consists of relatively more structured, focused instructions, such as suggesting, "Write about your autobiography (depression, fears, deceptions, your breakup)." The third is guided, as for instance, "I have read your autobiography, and I have written down some questions that need to be answered in writing." The fourth level of a structured format is programmed, as in workbooks.

Toward a Classification of Workbooks

Workbooks, by definition, are programmed in more or less systematic fashion (see Table 7-2). They were written with the following criteria in mind: (1) explicitness of instructions and format, asking concrete questions that are simple to understand and simple to answer; (2) specificity of content, focusing on objectively definable conditions, such as depression and impulsivity for individuals, negotiation for couples, and negativity for families; (3) cost-effectiveness, requiring little professional time and a great deal of involvement, time, and energy on the part of the respondents rather than on the part of the therapist or trainer; (4) mass-production and delivery, relying on written materials that can be mass-produced and -delivered, pro-

Table 7-1
Toward a Classification of Writing*

Expressive/Instructive versus Creative-Spontaneous (Contextual, Constructive of Stories) versus Contrived (Vocabulary, Spelling, Style, Syntax, Logic, Sentence Construction and Combination)
Structure, ranging from Unstructured to Structured
Open-ended (journals, diaries)
Focused (one topic, as in autobiographies and Pennebaker's expressive format)
Guided (written questions about written compositions)
Programmed (as in workbooks)
Goals (prescriptive/cathartic)
Specificity (general/specific)
Content (traumatic/trivial; various categories)**
Abstraction (high/low)

*I am indebted to Professor Deborah Brandt (Department of English, University of Wisconsin) for her help in developing the background for the present classification, which she correctly characterized as a "hybrid of several of these approaches" (personal communication, November 27, 2000).
**See Table 7-2 for an elaboration of this point.

vided, of course, that (5) the professionals administering these materials follow ethically and professionally responsive and responsible practices. These materials cannot be administered without stressing the importance of therapeutic feedback for each written assignment. This feedback can be given orally or in writing, even through the mail under certain conditions, as with persons who are incarcerated or with families who are at risk rather than in need or in crisis (L'Abate, in press-b).

Types of Workbooks

Of course, there can be as many workbooks as the need and ingenuity of therapists warrant. At this time, workbooks can be classified according to at least three origins: (1) from eclectic descriptions that derive from general, impressionistic, clinical approaches; (2) from theory-derived models, and (3) from a phenomenally large literature of self-help books.

Eclectic, Clinically Derived Materials. These programs and workbooks are not derived from any particular theory. They were or are being written eclectically, according to what is available in the literature on the subject, without any particular model. Thus far, the following eclectic workbooks have been produced: (1) Social Training, for impulsive, acting-out individuals; (2) Social Growth, for anxious individuals or those who cannot afford

Table 7-2
Toward a Classification of Workbooks

A. *Composition* of Respondents:
   1. Individuals (children, adolescents, adults)
   2. Couples
   3. Families
   4. Groups of individuals, couples, or families
B. *Theoretical orientation* (behavioral, cognitive, humanistic, etc.):
   1. Theory-derived
   2. Theory-related
   3. Theory-independent
C. *Format*:
   1. Fixed (nomothetic)
   2. Flexible (idiographic)
   3. Both fixed and flexible
D. *Derivation* from:
   1. Referral question and clinical experience
   2. Single-score psychological tests (like the BDI and others)
   3. Multiple test scores or profiles (like the MMPI-2, PAI, and others).
   4. Factor analyses
   5. Pop literature
E. *Style*:
   1. Straightforward linear
   2. Paradoxical, circular
F. *Level* and *Type* of Functionality-Dysfunctionality:
   1. Normalizations
   2. Internalizations
   3. Externalizations
   4. Serious Pathologies
G. *Content*: addictions, affective disorders, aggression, conflict, intimacy, grief and loss, etc.

Sources: L'Abate, 1992, 1996, 2002a, 2002b.

psychotherapy or whose motivation for psychotherapy is unclear or questionable; (3) Building Relationships for Couples, an eclectic workbook with no particular theoretical ax to grind but with emphasis on negotiation and intimacy (L'Abate, 1992).

Theory-derived Workbooks. These workbooks, especially designed as theory-testing instruments, are based on theoretical models derived from a developmental theory of interpersonal competence or to test any other theory (Chapters 2 and 3). Depression, for instance, can be treated according to three workbooks. One, devised by this author, uses a paradoxical interpersonal approach (L'Abate, 1986). Another workbook was derived from Beck's (Beck & Young, 1985) well-known cognitive approach for depression, which has been reduced to workbook format (Levis, 1987). A third depression program was derived from the revised Minnesota Multiphasic Personality Inventory (MMPI-2). With these three workbooks one can compare one theoretical approach with another. L'Abate et al. (1992), for instance, administered all three workbooks to undergraduates with high scores on two paper-and-pencil, self-report tests of depression. The Negotiation workbook is based on a model of negotiation derived from the original theory. An Intimacy workbook was derived from Model^{12}. The Problems in Relationships workbook tests the major dimensions of Reactivity, which is part of Model^{8} (Chapter 2).

Workbooks Derived from Self-help Books. The field is wide open for all sorts of possibilities, for instance, designing and deriving workbooks from self-help books, whose help remains questionable at best. Self-help books do not seem to offer the active and interactive involvement or the monologic and multiple feedback functions offered by workbooks. There can be as many workbooks as there are self-help books and more. Instead of having undergraduates write notoriously boring term papers as part of a class requirement, this author had undergraduates reduce some existing self-help books to workbooks.

Workbooks Developed from Single- and Multiple-Dimension Tests. In the last few years the first author has developed many workbooks from single-dimension tests, like the Beck Depression Inventory, the Hamilton Depression Inventory, and many others. Among the many workbooks developed from multiple-dimension tests, one can find the Minnesota Multiphasic Personality Inventory-2, the Personality Assessment Inventory, and many other (L'Abate, 1996, 2002a).

Workbooks Developed from Research Studies and Factor Analyses. Many other workbooks have been developed from research studies that have produced a list of items derived from either factor analysis or other methods. By using test- or research-derived workbooks, the link between evaluation and intervention becomes more direct than is possible using talk.

Theory-Independent Workbooks. Workbooks are the software of computer-assisted interventions (CAI). Both are the wave of the future in the delivery of mental health services (L'Abate, 1990, 1992, 2001a, 2002a, 2002b). There are too many people in need of mental health help who cannot be reached through the spoken word alone. We need all three media of intervention (non-verbal, verbal, and written) to reach as many people in need of help as we possibly can. Among these three media, writing and computer-assisted interventions are by far the cheapest to administer. In the long run, as already elaborated elsewhere, it may even be the most cost-effective. If cognitive psychology is indeed correct, writing should improve those rational processes that are so fundamental to human adjustment. Many respondents need a written prescription to take home and systematic homework assignments for CAI to become a cost-effective addition or an alternative to face-to-face (f2f) psychotherapy. One could argue that such personal f2f contact may be necessary for the relationship aspects of psychological interventions (warmth, unconditional positive regard, empathy), even though very intimate relationships have been established through the Internet. Nonetheless, the written word is necessary to structure and address most symptoms and symptomatic behavior (L'Abate, 1994b, 1997b, 1999b, 2001a, 2002a, 2002b).

Furthermore, while talk is infinite in its unlimited expressions, the written word can be programmed toward a finite, limited topic. This specification allows evaluation to be linked with treatment. Through writing, this link can be achieved much more specifically and effectively than through talk. Writing, when programmed, can be made isomorphic with parallel theoretical models (L'Abate, 1986, 2002a, 2002b; L'Abate & Harrison, 1992). In this fashion, one could assert that the written medium becomes a method of testing and validating theoretical and clinical insights that cannot be substantiated as long as these insights rely on the spoken medium.

Functions of Workbooks

Workbooks fulfill a variety of functions (see Table 7-3). First, they serve as preliminary preparation for therapy. Considering the needs of many families in crisis and in need who drop out after a few sessions of therapy, we need to ask ourselves whether it would be less expensive to request that they work among themselves on workbooks designed to elicit reactions from each of them. Considering the number of individuals, couples, and families on the waiting lists of many mental health clinics and hospitals, would it not be better to have them start working on a workbook rather than just wait? By decreasing or minimizing the probability of failure and of attrition, which is so common in psychotherapy, the professional will not have spent so much time and energy on a loss.

Second, programmed materials and workbooks are helpful in assessing motivation and competence to enter and stay in a personal, possibly prolonged and close, professional relationship, requiring self-disclosure, con-

Table 7-3
Advantages of Workbook Administration

Specificity: match between referral problem and workbook
Explicitness: clarity of plan, sequence, and instructions
Interactivity: instead of respondents being or becoming passive recipients of therapist's wisdom, they become actively and interactively engaged, involved, and responsible for the outcome of treatment
Versatility
Straightforward, written homework assignments administered in addition or as alternatives before, during, or after talk-based, f2f prevention, psychotherapy, or rehabilitation
Written treatment plans
Structured interviews for beginning mental health students or professionals who are not familiar with treatment for a specific condition
100% documentation of treatment plans
After traditional interventions, workbooks could follow up unfinished business
Co-morbid conditions
Training professionals
As software for computer-assisted interventions
Decreasing dependency on professionals and increasing sense of self-mastery and autonomy in respondents
Cost-effectiveness compared to f2f talk-based approaches
Mass-administration in prevention and rehabilitation
Verifiability in research
Hypothetical Meta-functions of Workbooks: Change Feedback Loops from written answers to comparisons or feedback from others (partners, family members, group members) or from professional helper
Illiterates can profit by receiving tape-recorded instructions answered in a tape or read by volunteers who then record answers in writing

Sources: L'Abate, 2002a, 2002b.

frontation, and support (L'Abate, 1986). Evaluating and possibly increasing the respondents' involvement in change through programmed materials and workbooks are a way to paraphrase Broffenbrenner's (1979) dictum: "If we want to know how a family works, try to change it!" If respondents are really motivated to change, they will work for change. Consequently, respondents can learn to work with each other through workbooks better and faster among themselves and with a modicum of professional time and effort. Of course, the more dysfunctional, clinical, or critical the condition, the more difficult it will be for respondents to start working together, at least at the beginning of the therapeutic relationship. As therapy normalizes the condition, after the referring symptom or crisis has been taken care of, respondents will become more able to work with each other, using the structure demanded by programmed materials. In fact, systematically written workbooks have a much greater degree of structure, specificity, and clarity than the spoken word. A workbook presents a definite, concrete, and positive plan, often a structure that cannot be found in the spoken word.

Third, workbooks add to traditional psychotherapy by using a different modality (i.e., the written modality) from the oral or even the non-verbal. Traditional psychotherapy still suffers from the myth of uniformity (Kiesler, 1996); that is, it is supposed to treat every psychological dysfunction known to humanity, and, if people cannot profit by it, it is because of their extreme dysfunctionality rather than deficiencies in the method of treatment. We can no longer subscribe to this possibility. How about considering, instead, the possibility that the oral modality may not be the most appropriate modality for certain, yet to be identified respondents? Workbooks at least offer an alternative route through which many respondents can relate, as an addition or as an alternative to the oral and to the nonverbal modalities. Of course, it will be another task to identify which respondent(s) profit(s) by this type of approach rather than by another. After all, the idea that any form of psychological treatment based on the spoken word would be applicable to any deviant condition, as psychoanalysis assumed in its early days, is no longer tenable. Given a variety of treatment modalities, even with differentiations within each modality, which respondent will benefit from which modality, at what cost, and with what kind of therapist, trainer, or facilitator?

Fourth, workbooks have the potential to increase generalization from the office to the home, because the respondents are required to spend as much time working on weekly assignments as they spend in therapy. With respondents in need, it should be possible to minimize the spoken interchange and maximize their working together as a unit (couple, family, group) through workbooks. In this way respondents are made more responsible for change, relying more on their internal resources and less on the resources of the professional.

Finally, one of the main functions of workbooks is research. Programmed materials and workbooks have the potential to help us deal with issues that cannot be dealt with or are very expensive to deal with through traditional psychotherapeutic approaches. For instance, workbooks can help us control treatment and therapist variables that are too complex and too difficult to control in research. Also, they can help us verify theoretical and therapeutic approaches in cost-effectively fulfilling the criteria of explicitness and specificity, characteristics that are usually not found in traditional therapeutic approaches, for instance, (1) studying the differential effects of workbooks versus role-playing versus lecturing or verbal interpretations; (2) studying the effects of face-to-face relationship skills versus the effects of specific "therapeutic" feedback (i.e., structuring skills); (3) being able to deal with the matching hypothesis in psychotherapy; that is, which problem or symptom needs which form or type of treatment at what cost? This hypothesis can now be verified directly through the use of specific versus general workbooks rather than through generally vague, oral psychotherapeutic practices; (4) comparing the outcome of specific workbooks produced by the author and coworkers versus the outcome of other workbooks produced by other authors; (5) comparing group versus individual administration of workbooks with high-risk populations, such as adjudicated criminals or juveniles; and (6) identifying polarized dimensions in couples, using two self-report tests derived from the status and selfhood model described in Chapter 2.

In addition to dealing with (if not solving!) the whole issue of specific condition-treatment match, which will remain insoluble or expensive to solve, as long as two humans come together verbally, workbooks help us deal with another crucial therapeutic issue: generalization from the therapist's office to the home or wherever our respondents reside. How can we make sure that our directives, suggestions, and prescriptions will make a difference to respondents? How is a respondent able to transfer skills and knowledge from outside the home to inside it? Workbooks link the office and the home, thus increasing generalization, that is, transfer of learning from one setting to another.

Furthermore, workbooks can help us deal with the common problem of dual diagnoses. Face-to-face therapy can be directed, for instance, toward the whole family, while selected individuals work on specifically assigned workbooks, either dyadically or individually. This advantage will become clearer as different types of workbooks are described.

To sum up, workbooks can be administered (1) before any face-to-face therapy takes place; (2) at the beginning of therapy; (3) in parallel with ongoing therapy, either with dual diagnoses, such as alcoholism and depression, or when the therapist is on vacation; or (4) after termination of traditional crisis therapy, to deal with loose ends. Workbooks can be administered also as an alternative to existing psychotherapeutic practices: (1) with respondents (individuals, couples, or families) who may not be as proficient with the oral modality as required by most psychotherapies; (2) with individuals who are resistant or unable to deal with face-to-face interpersonal confrontation (acting-out individuals, addicts); (3) with populations that cannot be reached through any other means, such as incarcerated individuals, missionary or military respondents, and handicapped and shut-in respondents.

These functions and advantages should not blind professionals to inevitable dangers and shortcomings of workbook administration (see Table

Table 7-4
Dangers and Possible Shortcomings of Workbook Administration

Sudden and unexpected discovery or uncovering of extremely painful, heretofore avoided past traumas
Mismatch between problem and workbook (perhaps because of incomplete or inadequate evaluation)
Confidentiality, especially if there is the possibility that online communications can be intercepted
Vicarious liability (the producer of a workbook is still responsible, even though he or she did not administer it)
Cheating; the respondent is not the one he/she claims to be, or someone else is completing homework assignments
Poorly written workbooks (hortatory, verbose, etc.)
Biases and resistance of mental health professionals, who may be frightened to work at a distance from respondents without face-to-face contact
These and other potential dangers will not be discovered unless we take the risk of helping respondents at a distance without talk or f2f contacts

7-4) as well as necessary ethical and professional issues, discussed elsewhere (L'Abate, 2002a) and available in the extant literature on Internet interventions.

MATCHING MODELS WITH WORKBOOKS

As already indicated, there are assignments and workbooks that match some of the theoretical models presented in Chapter 2. However, the reader should keep in mind that whatever research has been conducted thus far has dealt with the short-term outcome workbooks as a whole and not as parts.

Negotiation: Model[1]. A workbook matching the ERAAwC model includes also Models[5 & 6].

Modalities: Model[6]. Is included as an assignment of the Negotiation workbook.

Continuum of Likeness: Model[7]. Ambrosini, Cusinato, and Scilletta (2002) combined the likeness continuum with the selfhood model by using both in one workbook and by including important others in teaching family psychology. Within the course of family psychology for undergraduate psychology students (academic year 2000–2001), at the University of Padua, a workbook was administered on the different modalities used by individuals to modulate likeness to people close to them. The structured intervention was articulated over seven homework assignments and intended to increase awareness of attitudes and behaviors in this area and find a more satisfactory relational mode. The theoretical approach referred to the theory of relational competence proposed by L'Abate (1994b). Students could choose among four attendance groups, and all were evaluated on a pre-post basis with a battery of tests: (1) Group 1 (n = 55) individual workbook and a discussion work group with every assignment; (2) Group 2 (n = 42) individual workbook alone; (3) Group 3 (n = 11), no workbook or work group intervention; (4) Group 4 (n = 19), individual workbook and a higher-level, theoretical seminar (with final examination). An experimental computer task (Relationship World Test, Version 1), operationalizing the likeness and selfhood models[7 & 8], was used for the pre-test and post-test evalution with 104 students completing all the required work. Pre-test and post-test data analyses, comparing the four groups, highlighted a statistically significant change in subjects using forms 1 and 4, in the sense of a weakening "oppositeness" stance. Process data consisted of qualitative analyses of writings, and minutes of the debriefing sessions of work groups helped in discussing results, so that useful hypotheses can be proposed both at didactical and dialectical levels.

Included later is the first assignment of the "Who Am I?" workbook that is isomorphic with the model.

Styles in Relationships: Model[8]. Included as an assignment in Negotiation workbook.

Selfhood and Personality Propensities: Model[9]. Included in Self-Other workbook given below.

Priorities: Model[10]. Included as an assignment in the Negotiation workbook.

Negotiation: Model[11]. Evaluated through the Negotiation workbook (L'Abate, 1986).

Intimacy: Model[12]. Theoretically, this workbook was based isomorphically on an early model of intimacy that made love and caring (Assignment 1), seeing the good in self and partner (Assignment 2), and forgiveness (Assignment 3) prerequisites to the sharing of hurts (Assignments 4, 5, and 6). Preliminary results from a study evaluating the usefulness of two negotiation and intimacy programs are found in L'Abate (1992). A review of research to evaluate these programs is available in L'Abate (in press-b). Esterling, L'Abate, Murray, and Pennebaker (1999) reviewed the research that supports the use of distance writing (away from the presence of a professional) in prevention and psychotherapy.

To help respondents become more intimate with their partners or family members, six homework assignments were developed, matching isomorphically the theoretical model exposed by L'Abate (1986). After answering each assignment individually, partners or family members are required to meet at predetermined times to share, discuss, and comment on each other's answers. They also are required to bring to the therapist their completed assignments as well as notes taken during their appointment times.

In the first three assignments, "Love and Caring," "Seeing the Good," and "Forgiveness," respondents are asked to define these terms and to express practical applications of them. In the fourth assignment, respondents are asked to answer questions about their completion of homework related to forgiveness of self and others, and then are asked to define "Intimacy." After answering this last question, respondents are asked whether they would subscribe to a definition of intimacy "as the sharing of hurts and of fears of being hurt." Respondents are then asked to give examples of how intimacy thus defined applies to them and to their partners. The fifth and sixth assignments essentially require respondents to become increasingly involved in dealing with and sharing their hurt feelings with each other.

Drama Triangle: Model[13]. The first homework assignment of the Depression workbook (L'Abate, 1986) is devoted to the different variations that stem from each of the three roles. For instance, for the Persecutor role, there are variations like the "Judge," "Jury," and "Executioner," among others. For the Victim role, there are variations like the "Poor Little Me," the "Martyr," the "Saint," and similar others. For the Saviour role, there is the "Therapist," "Daddy Big Bucks," the "Nurse," and similar others. Respondents have to circle those variations in which they recognize themselves. After this recognition, they are asked to expand on how they play those roles in greater detail "to keep the family together."

Distance Regulation: Model[14]. This model is found in the second homework assignment of the Depression workbook (L'Abate, 1986). Respondents are asked to check which of the three roles they play more consistently and then expand on how they play that particular role in specific spheres of their relationships.

Homework assignments presented below are illustrative of how practice and theory can be used together once a workbook is based on a theoretical model. Note that only the first assignment is presented here as an example. Qualified professionals will need to access L'Abate (1996) to obtain the whole workbook on which these examples are based.

Note: Workbooks For Better Living (WFBL) must be administered by qualified mental health professionals. WFBL is not responsible or liable for their inappropriate use.

WHO AM I? VARIOUS ASPECTS OF IDENTITY FORMATION

The purpose of this workbook is to help you clarify and identify in greater detail who you are and who you want to be.

Assignment 1. Definitions of Identity Aspects

We are all the products of many identities acquired since and before birth. The purpose of this assignment is to expand on various aspects of the many identities that we all acquire over the years. This workbook aims at pinpointing which aspects of your identity are more important to you than others.

1. Below you will find many aspects of possible identities. For each aspect explain what it is and what it means to you. Define each aspect and give two examples of how that identity is applied either in your life experience or in general.

Aspects of Identity **Definitions and Examples**

a. Gender
   Example 1
   Example 2
b. Sexual Orientation/Preference
   Example 1
   Example 2
c. Body: No examples necessary. Just state information:
   Shape ____ Size ____ Height ____ Weight ____
   Any other body characteristic
d. Geographical (where you were born)
   Example 1
   Example 2
e. Geographical (where you have lived the longest)
   Example 1
   Example 2
f. Geographical (where your heart is)
   Example 1
   Example 2
g. Son/Daughter
   Example 1
   Example 2
h. Brother/Sister
   Example 1
   Example 2
i. Partner
   Example 1
   Example 2
j. Parent
   Example 1
   Example 2
k. Caregiver
   Example 1
   Example 2

l. Homemaker
   Example 1
   Example 2
m. Provider
   Example 1
   Example 2
n. Grandparenthood
   Example 1
   Example 2
o. Ethnic/Cultural
   Example 1
   Example 2
p. Religion/Spirituality
   Example 1
   Example 2
q. Educational
   Example 1
   Example 2
r. Occupational/Work/Job
   Example 1
   Example 2
s. Political Affiliation or Ideology
   Example 1
   Example 2
t. Leisure-Time Activities
   Example 1
   Example 2
u. Sports Fan
   Example 1
   Example 2
v. Military Experience and Identity
   Example 1
   Example 2
w. Any other identity not mentioned above that is important to you (write what it is)
   Example 1
   Example 2

2. Now that you have defined various aspects or facets of your identity, you need to rank them according to how each aspect is important to you. Rank as No. 1

your most important aspect. Rank as No. 2 the aspect that is next in importance. Rank as No. 3 the aspect that is next in importance to you and so on, giving a rank order to each aspect until you reach an aspect that does not apply to you at all (N/A).

Aspects of Identity	**Rank**
a. Gender	____
b. Sexual Orientation/Preference	____
c. Body	____
d. Geographical (where you were born)	____
e. Geographical (where you have lived the longest)	____
f. Geographical (where your heart is)	____
g. Son/Daughter	____
h. Brother/Sister	____
i. Partner	____
j. Parent	____
k. Caregiver	____
l. Homemaker	____
m. Provider	____
n. Grandparent	____
o. Ethnic/Cultural	____
p. Religion/Spirituality	____
q. Educational	____
r. Occupational/Work/Job	____
s. Political Affiliation or Ideology	____
t. Leisure-Time Activities	____
u. Sports Fan	____
v. Military	____
w. Any other identity not mentioned above that is important to you (write what it is)	____

Homework: During the next week, think about how you have rank-ordered your many identities and whether you need to change the rank order you have completed. Feel free to make whatever changes you want to make to the rank order.

THE SELF WORKBOOK

This workbook is to be administered after testing with the Self-Other Profile Chart to determine whether assignments should be administered to Self or to Others. The purpose of this workbook is to help you improve your sense of self-importance.

Assignment 1. How Important Am I?

The purpose of this assignment is to understand how the characteristics listed below are related to your sense of self-importance.

1. Write how each characteristic listed below is related to your sense of self-importance:
   a. Intelligence
   b. Physical Attractiveness
   c. Sports Success
   d. Sense of Humor
   e. School/Job Competence
   f. Sociability/Popularity
   g. Morality
   h. Self-worth or Self-esteem
   i. Any other characteristic not listed above (write what it is)
2. Rank-order the characteristics listed above by how much they contribute to your sense of self-importance. Rank as No. 1 the characteristic that contributes the most to your sense of self-importance. Rank as No. 2 the characteristic that contributes second to your sense of self-importance, and so on, until the characteristic that does not contribute at all is ranked 8 or 9 or is just not applicable (N/A) to you.

Characteristic	**Rank**
a. Intelligence	____
b. Physical Attractiveness	____
c. Sports Success	____
d. Sense of Humor	____
e. School/Job Competence	____
f. Sociability/Popularity	____
g. Morality	____
h. Self-worth or Self-esteem	____
i. Any other characteristic not listed above (write what it is)	____

3. What guided your thinking as you rank-ordered these characteristics?

Homework: During the coming week, think how each characteristic could affect your sense of importance in a positive way.

THE "OTHERS" WORKBOOK

The purpose of this workbook is to help you develop a better understanding of people who in one way or another, positively or negatively, have affected your sense of self-importance.

Assignment 1. Who Are the "Others"?

The purpose of this assignment is to understand better who the people are who affected your sense of self-importance.

1. Explain in great detail who these people are by giving their names and more information about the nature of their relationship with you:
   a. Close Friends ______________________________
   ____
   b. Boy/Girlfriend or Partner/Mate ______________________________
   ____
   c. Children (if applicable) ______________________________
   ____
   d. Mother or Mother substitute* ______________________________
   ____
   e. Father or Father substitute** ______________________________
   ____
   f. Brothers/Sisters (list all of them by name and age) ______________________________
   ____
   g. Coworkers or fellow students ______________________________
   ____
   h. Neighbors ______________________________
   ____
   i. Other relatives (list only those who were close to you) ______________________________
   ____
   j. Teachers/Mentors ______________________________
   ____
   k. Write the name of anyone else who affected your sense of importance ______
   ____

*Female caretaker could be biological, stepmother, or other institutional caretaker of feminine gender (check which).
**Male caretaker could be biological, stepfather, or other institutional caretaker of masculine gender (check which).

2. Now that you have identified further those people who in one way or another affected your sense of self-importance, rank-order these people according to how they compare in how they affected your sense of self-importance. Rank as No. 1 the person who, in one way or another, had the greatest effect on your sense of self-importance. Rank as No. 2 the person who was second in how much he or she affected your sense of self-importance. Rank as No. 3 the person who was third in how much he or she affected your sense of self-importance, and so on, until the person who ranked the lowest among these people in affecting your sense of self-importance.

Person	**Rank**
a. Close Friends	____
b. Boy/Girlfriend or Partner/Mate	____
c. Children (if applicable)	____
d. Mother or Mother Substitute	____
e. Father or Father Substitute	____
f. Brothers/Sisters	____
g. Coworkers	____
h. Neighbors	____
i. Relatives listed above	____
j. Teachers/Mentors	____
k. Anyone else (write the name)	____

3. Now that you have rank-ordered all these people according to how much they affected your sense of self-importance, explain why you ranked them in the way you did.

Homework: During the next week start thinking about whether there are other people who affected your sense of self-importance.

CONCLUSION

This chapter has illustrated how interventions can take place at a distance from respondents, provided a duly signed Informed Consent Form and a test battery are completed by respondents before these interventions are administered.

Chapter 8

Theory-Derived Interventions for Clinical Relationships

The purpose of this chapter is to link interventions for troubled (clinical, critical, chronic, dysfunctional) relationships with models of the theory (Chapters 2 and 3).

ERAAwC MODEL[1]: TOWARD A CLASSIFICATION OF PREVENTIVE AND PSYCHOTHERAPEUTIC INTERVENTIONS

The first purpose of this model is diagnostic. It serves to classify problems in relationships according to its five components. For instance, in addition to the five possibilities, there are 25 possible combinations among the components of the model. One exemplary source or school of therapy will be given for each component, as in Chapter 1, but without explanation about this model.

1. *E*motionality-dominated and -oriented or *E*-based relationships, where *E* is rampant in one or more members of the relationships, to the point that the relationship cannot go forward without *E*'s being reduced and diminished in its impact on relationships. When one component of the model is used excessively, the other components of the model are diminished, either not used properly or used very little. The humanistic school, as represented by the work of Greenberg and Paivio (1997) with couples, would be exemplary of this approach, which stresses the importance of helping multi-relational systems using *E* more constructively and selectively.

2. *R*ationality-dominated and -oriented or *R*-based relationships, where logic and *R* dominate to the point that *E* is avoided and belittled, are possible. Among the various schools of therapy using a predominantly ra-

tional orientation are psychoanalysis, reality therapy, rational-emotive therapy, and behavioral-cognitive therapies, including EPM (Chapters 4 and 5; Westen, 1995).

3. *A*ctivity-dominated and -oriented or *A*-based relationships, where one or more than one party in the relationship is compulsively driven to action (*A*), as in workaholics, compulsive sport addicts, and the like, to the point that other components of the model are underutilized or used very little. Here is where behavioral approaches, through the use of consequent reinforcements and consequences, make their contribution (Dobson & Craig, 1998; Nathan & Gorman, 1998).

4. *Aw*areness-dominated and -oriented or *Aw*-based, relationships, where parties indicate awareness of the problem ("Yes, I know.") but are helpless in changing and doing anything about solving the problem. Here is where the Gestalt school and Rogerian non-directivism have made a contribution.

5. *C*ontextually-dominated and -oriented or *C*-based relationships, which are context-driven, stressing external influences and avoiding looking at internal, individual determinants of the relationship. Here is where couples and family therapies can be classified according to the four previous categories (Hansen & L'Abate, 1982).

The issue of matching one component of the model with a similarly oriented intervention approach or school of therapy raises the question of whether each modality should be matching with a similar approach. Should an *E*-dominated relationship be matched by an *E*-based approach? Or should that kind of relationship be matched with a more *R*ational- or *A*ctivity-oriented approach? Hence, the question is: Should an intervention match the most dominant component of the relationship, or would a mismatch be more helpful? For instance, matching a specific intervention or approach with the prevalent or dominant component present in a relationship would produce the following possibilities:

1. Match *E* with *E*, or mismatch when *E* is paired with either *R*, *A*, *Aw*, or *C*.
2. Match *R* with *R*, or mismatch when *R* is paired with either *E*, *A*, *Aw*, or *C*.
3. Match *A* with *A*, or mismatch when *A* is paired with either *E*, *R*, *Aw*, or *C*.
4. Match *Aw* with *Aw*, or mismatch when *Aw* is paired either with *E*, *R*, *A*, or *C*.
5. Match *C* with *C*, or mismatch possible by stressing an individual rather than the parties involved in a relationship.

Implications of these possibilities for improvements in interventions are completely open to investigation. Thus far, each therapeutic approach would advocate its own as the cure-all for any troubled relationship, regardless of diagnostic considerations about the major characteristic of relationships. A model-oriented approach using differential ERAAwC components would raise novel diagnostic and interventional issues that require serious study before finding specific answers for the match-mismatch problem. Of course, this problem can be studied when workbooks matching each component can be administered in a match-mismatch design using functional subjects rather than patients. The RAQ developed by Cusinato (Chapter 3) would be one way of evaluating which component is higher than the other four.

Table 8-1 lists interventions based on each component of the model, as suggested originally by Karasu (1996) and many other contributors.

HELPING FAMILIES TO LOVE

Love is an emotion, and as such, this section deals with how to enter the area of intimacy and introduces therapeutic tasks that can be assigned to couples and families. Questions and tasks may increase their intimacy and teach them how to love without having to Do or Have anything. As simple as this goal may be at first blush, it will take all the ingenuity of the professional helper to carry these tasks to completion. Before dealing with intimacy (Model[12]), however, one needs to deal with all the various aspects of problematic relationships that characterize them, namely, the ability to negotiate, unclear or ill-defined personal identities, personality propensities, and priorities. Only when these issues have been taken care of can possible issues of intimacy be dealt with (Firestone & Catlett, 1999; Praeger, 1995).

Face-to-Face Approaches: Three Exemplary Applications

Three clinical applications that derive from the previous definition of hurt and closeness are (1) drawing lines, (2) hugging, holding, huddling, and cuddling, and (3) sharing of hurts.

Drawing Lines in Co-dependent Individuals (Model[7])

This structured interview is the third homework assignment from a workbook on co-dependency (Jordan & L'Abate, 1995; L'Abate, 1996, 2002b; L'Abate & Harrison, 1992). The purpose of this structured interview is for co-dependent (i.e., selfless) respondents, individuals who are married or living with an addicted partner, to learn to set clear, definite limits to protect themselves from abuse or neglect from their partner or anybody else.

1. What does drawing lines mean to you? Please tell me or write down your definition. Give me two examples of how drawing lines applies to your experience.
2. As a result of past and present training, the overly dependent person is usually unable to draw lines to assert her or his importance. How does this conclusion

Table 8-1
Matching Components of the ERAAwC Model[1] with Similar Interventions

***E*motionality-Based Interventions**

1. fantasy trips
2. awareness exercises
3. hurt-sharing
4. empathy-training
5. body work
6. being together physically (to be explained below)

***R*ationality-Oriented Interventions**

1. relabeling and positive reframing
2. cognitive reconstruction
3. correction and interpretation of "irrational" beliefs
4. explanations
5. written homework assignments (combining both *R* and *A*)

***A*ctivity-Oriented Interventions**

1. task assignments
2. paradoxical prescriptions
3. homework assignments
4. straightforward directions
5. ordeal directives
6. art and drawing work (overlap with *Aw*)

***Aw*areness-Oriented Interventions**

1. Awareness exercises
2. Body work, calisthenics, physical exercise, sport activities
3. Consciousness-increasing exercises
4. Non-verbal exercises
5. Diet
6. Medication

Context-Oriented Interventions

1. Couples and family therapy
2. Couples and family psychoeducational skill training programs
3. Couples and family life education

apply to your experience? Were you ever able to draw lines on your partner's or anybody else's behavior?

a. If no, why not? Explain in detail.

b. If yes, how were you able to do it? Explain in detail.

3. If the experience of not being able to draw lines concerning your partner's behavior does not apply to you, let us skip this part of our interview, unless you feel you still would like to learn how to draw lines with your partner or anybody else. Perhaps you may need a different way of helping you.
4. Please answer the following statement: "Drawing boundary lines as to what you will or will not put up with from your partner refers to what is acceptable and unacceptable to you. If you do not know what will be acceptable or unacceptable to you, how will you be able to draw any lines? How do we learn to set boundaries? Setting lines or boundaries starts at the condom line. If a woman, for instance, does not know how to set a boundary to protect herself and her body from the very outset of a relationship, she has lost it. By the same token, a man should use a condom to protect both himself and his partner. Lines need to be drawn before sexual intercourse in either a casual or a committed relationship either to avoid an unwanted pregnancy or to avoid many, some now deadly, diseases. If one cannot set boundaries at this point, it is doubtful whether one can or will be able to set firm and clear boundaries on any other issues from then on in the relationship. The selfish partner usually could not care less. She or he wants to get what she or he can get when she or he can get it, and *how* she or he gets it is not important! His or her immediate needs are more important than the partner's needs! If you do not care about your importance, why should your partner care?" What do you think about the above statements? Note: This statement or its facsimile could be printed and given to the respondent to read as a homework assignment and to respond to in writing.
5. This table (hand to respondent a copy of Table 8-2 or give as homework assignment to read and to answer in writing) lists different ways a co-dependent may be unable to draw lines with the partner from the very beginning of the relationship, perhaps because of giving more importance to the partner rather than to one's self. This first line of defense ("the Condom Line") deals with how one protects and safeguards his or her body during courtship or after marriage: "Read this table and check which of these statements applies to your experience."
6. After you have checked them, pick the three most important statements and write in detail how they apply to you and what the outcome was for you as a person and as a partner: (a), (b), and (c).
7. In addition to the list of this table, are there other abusive or neglectful behaviors that you were not able to deal with in your partner? List as many as you can remember.
8. Which of these abusive or neglectful behaviors of your partner are similar to behaviors of either of your parents? Explain how they were or were not.

Table 8-2
Relationships between Abusive and Overly Dependent Individuals

Partner	Overdependent
1. Not taking "precautions" during intercourse before marriage _____	Allowing it to happen _____
2. Not taking responsibility if and when one's sexual partner gets pregnant _____	Allowing it to happen _____
3. Not holding a steady job and expecting to be taken care of by others, including spouse, partner, or live-in companion _____	Allowing it to happen _____
4. Using work or work pressures to avoid taking responsibilities in the home _____	Allowing it to happen _____
5. Not sharing in household chores _____	Allowing it to happen _____
6. Watching TV or drinking or whatever while other partner is still working _____	Allowing it to happen _____
7. Not taking initiative in child's care _____	Allowing it to happen _____
8. Having to be reminded of duties and responsibilities relevant to the role of partner and caretaker _____	Allowing it to happen _____
9. Spending leisure time away from home, with friends or in projects that are not related to the family and home _____	Allowing it to happen _____
10. Being or becoming addicted to work, TV, alcohol, gambling, or worse _____	Allowing it to happen _____
11. Verbally, sexually, or physically abusive of partner and/or children _____	Allowing it to happen _____
12. Running around with other "friends" _____	Allowing it to happen _____
13. Buying more clothes than the rest of the family to look good and make a good impression at work _____	Allowing it to happen _____
14. Any other behavior that takes place at the other's expense _____	Allowing it to happen _____

Source: L'Abate & Harrison (1992). Reprinted with permission.

9. Which of the abusive behaviors listed in the table are the opposite of behaviors of either of your parents? Explain how they were or were not.
10. Would you conclude (from everything that has been presented thus far in these assignments) that one of the major problems with your relationship is an inability to draw lines? If you agree, write down why. If you disagree, write down your reason for disagreeing.
11. Does your partner match your inability to draw lines by his or her ability to push the limits? How is it (pushing the limits) done? Describe all the ways your partner pushes the limits, if indeed she or he does.
12. Whether you agree or disagree with the conclusion, are you willing to learn how to draw lines to safeguard yourself? Please write your answer.
13. How and when do we draw lines? First of all, to draw lines verbally with an addicted partner means that "words are cheap," and are often useless. Words, most of the time, lead to escalations and into explosive arguments and fights. Before speaking and trying to talk sense with your partner, you must avoid engaging him or her in another round of useless and destructive arguments, unless you have thought an issue through and the rule of three has been used successfully. If you cannot come up with at least three good (appropriate, relevant, positive, helpful, etc.) reasons, it means that not enough thought has been given to the issue at hand. What are your reactions to the statements above?
14. If you are ready to learn how to draw lines, read the instructions in Table 8-2 using a blank, unlined piece of paper. Draw these lines using a yellow or black pen or pencil for lines a, b, and c and a black pencil or pen for lines d and e.
    a. Draw one straight, interrupted, dotted black line, like this: - - - - - - - - - -
    b. Draw two straight, parallel, uninterrupted black lines, like this ═══════
    c. Draw one straight, uninterrupted line, like this ____________________
    d. Draw two straight, parallel yellow or black lines with one (just one!) break in between, like this ════════════ ════════════
    e. Draw two straight, parallel, uninterrupted, yellow or black lines, like this:

    ════════════════════════════════════

15. What do these lines remind you of? If your answer is "Highway" or "Road" signs, you are absolutely correct. Applied to your life, these lines indicate what you will put up with and what you will not put up with.

    Line a. What problems are taken for granted by both of you that are already set up and accepted and that do not require talking over? Here you may list things that have already been solved or that do not need any talking over. They do not present a problem to either one of you.

    Line b. What is still unclear in the relationship that would require further, continued, and prolonged talking over? Some of these problems may have been dealt with under line c. Other problems are still unresolved and are still affecting the relationship. Here you may find problems that need upgrading to line c, to keep in line b, or downgrading to line e.

Line c. What would you put up with over an extended period of time? Everyday decisions? Who is going to take care of the house? What chores should be taken up by whom? Who is going to clean what? Who is responsible for doing what? Who will draw a budget? Who will follow it? How are disagreements going to be settled? By fighting? By sitting down at a table at a pre-set time with an agenda? How are purchases to be made? Separately? Jointly? How should vacations be talked over, with relatives, away from relatives? How is money to be spent, etc.? Ideally, *both* of you should be working, talking, and solving problems without blaming and without using abusive behaviors.

Line d. What behavior would you put up with just once, not to be repeated *ever again*? Running around with other people? Rape? Incest? Violence? Physical and verbal abuse? Getting drunk or hitting you more than once? Failure to draw a firm line the first time does not mean that you cannot draw a firm line now. Write down exactly what you would do if your partner were to do something to you that legally, morally, emotionally, and personally would be hurtful to you or to those you love. Make it very clear that the first time you were hurt, it was the responsibility of your partner. However, if you are hurt again, then the responsibility belongs to you to protect yourself. We have only two cheeks!

Line e. What do you put up with? Infidelity? Violence? Rape? Incest? What would your partner need to do for you to draw a line? Commit murder? Is anything and everything your partner does acceptable or unacceptable? Are you trying to make excuses for his or her behavior and allow him or her to get away with murder? Here, list all of the behaviors that you find completely unacceptable under any conditions and that you will not put up with.

Homework. Once this assignment is completed, put it aside and sleep on it for one or more nights. Then go back to it and see whether it needs any improvement, changing whatever needs to be changed. Once you have a final draft, you should make at least two copies, one for yourself and one for your counselor (or friend). Discuss your answers with your counselor (or whoever cares for you enough to be willing to talk about it) and change whatever needs to be changed on the basis of your discussion. Make three copies of your final draft. If it is important, it needs to have more than one copy made.

Being Together (Model[6]): Hugging, Holding, Huddling, and Cuddling (3HC) in Couples and Families

Loving someone means being together in a way that allows direct, frequent, and consistent physical contact. This contact is necessary to feel emotionally available to and close with another intimate in a non-verbal fashion, in addition, of course, consistently with words. As already expanded in Chapters 2 and 3, the modality of Being or Presence (importance and intimacy), together with Performance or Doing (services and information) and Production or Having (money and possessions), composes what is exchanged among human beings, intimate or otherwise. Major referral problems faced by marriage and family therapists, therefore, stem from clients' inability to Be Present Together physically and emotionally, in order to assert reciprocally their importance. Closeness and affections need to be taught to these couples and families directly through prescription of 3HC, with more than just words (L'Abate, 1999a, 2000a).

Background Rationale for This Prescription

In terms of Model[6], visually, this triangle is equilateral in functional relationships with Being at its base, where all three modalities are of roughly equal size. In functional relationships all three sides are balanced appropriately and flexibly, according to various stages of the family life cycle. This equilaterality decreases or is lost when Performance and Production are given greater importance than Presence. This imbalance reduces the size of its base (i.e., Being), transforming the triangle into an obelisk instead. The image of an obelisk, like the Lincoln Memorial, with the two sides of Doing and Having being much larger than Being, comes to mind. Under these circumstances, where Being/Presence is restricted, narrowed, and perhaps defective or even absent, dysfunctionality develops. Hence, if this triangle is valid, most couples and families who seek professional help need it in the area of Presence more than in areas of Performance or Production. The modalities Model[5], as represented by the Triangle of Living, will suffice for the purposes of this task prescription, which is directly derived from that model.

As a culture and as a profession, including, of course, this writer, stereotypically, we in the United States seem obsessed with Doing (i.e., performance) and Having (i.e., production). According to Spiegel (1971), the two latter modalities characterize some aspects of the American culture, while Presence or Being characterizes some Mediterranean and Latin cultures. We forget to stop to show and share affection toward and with loved ones without intimation or the implication of sexual overtones, that is, Being Together. Our lives are so busy and so overscheduled that our priorities are oriented toward survival first. When we do have surplus time, we are secondarily oriented toward enjoyment by doing something, very seldom doing nothing (L'Abate, 1994b, 1997b; Spiegel, 1971). In fact, we have individuals who are tremendously afraid and are unable to "do nothing."

For instance, traditional treatment approaches, whether behavioral or otherwise, are directed usually toward "doing something" or "performing," requiring problem-solving ability and activity, on the part of either the professional, the identified patient (IP), or the IP's caretakers and family. These approaches mirror the pragmatic orientation of American culture to act, perform, and "do something" to produce and solve problems. Why not teach families how to enjoy doing nothing together, instead, as the Italians call *dolce far niente* (sweet doing nothing)? Instead of acts, actions, or activities that seem necessary to solve problems and treat intimate relationships in distress, why not use a task that requires no solution or activity whatever? On the contrary, this task allows intimates, instead, to learn by being available to each other non-verbally, without doing anything except hugging, holding, huddling, and cuddling (3HC).

Of course, this possibility runs counter to not only our cultural heritage of "Learning by Doing" but also therapeutic needs to do something immediate, and sometimes complex, to confront and "solve" issues raised by referral questions. This task prescription (3HC) is completely generic and nonspecific. It is not directed in any way toward "solving" any specific issue, including separation anxiety disorder (SAD) or any other condition. It is directed instead toward hopefully improving the emotional climate of couples and families. If this goal is achieved, adding any other specific procedures that may help "solve" the problem may become easier.

The close physical presence of all family members without demands for performance, production, perfection, or problem-solving (i.e., "unconditional love") defines "presence" as being the major glue that holds couples and families together and makes them function well. Inadequate presence in a couple or family (i.e., the incomplete or negative attribution of importance to self and others and not sharing intimacy) produces an emphasis on Performance and Production at the expense of Presence. When this process happens, there may be an increase in symptomatic behavior in any one member of the family.

Clinical Background

The need to intervene in systemic ways with separation anxiety disorder (SAD) families, some of them with limited emotional, educational, and financial resources, brought about the search for a simple-to-administer, non-verbal prescription that would bypass talk as the major vehicle for change (L'Abate, 1999a). Such a therapeutic orientation, systemic in nature, derives directly from the modality of "Being" or "Presence," as described above. Physical contact is necessary on a daily basis to stress continuous emotional availability and closeness with other intimates in concrete, immediate, and non-verbal ways. This closeness is best achieved through direct and continuous showing and sharing of affection rather than just words. Affection is shown through touching and 3HC.

The purpose of the task prescription described here is to suggest how a theory-derived and seemingly simple but apparently powerful prescribed task, 3HC, seems to affect positively persistent and pernicious couple and family interactions. Originally, this task was used to deal with SADs in children. However, the impressionistically powerful results obtained by prescription of this task with a few SAD families suggested its expansion to couples as well as to families with different referral questions. The admittedly anecdotal results from this task, of course, need to be replicated by other couples and family practitioners as well as evaluated objectively by external researchers other than the first author.

Literature Search and Background for Task Prescription

The practical inception of this task at the outset was due to the need to treat SAD in children. This disorder is one of the most common developmental symptoms of depressed emotional development. In the first author's opinion, SAD finds its roots in the family's functioning, in spite of contrary opinions as to its etiology (Barrett, 2000; Bowen, Offord, & Doyle, 1990; Donovan & Spence, 2000; Gullone, 2000; King & Tonge, 2000; Last, 1992; Ollendick & Huntzinger, 1990; Schniering, Hudson, & Rapee, 2000; Tonge, 1994). SAD has been subjected to a variety of approaches, mostly behavioral or behavioral-cognitive (Beidel, Turner, & Morris, 2000; Compton, Nelson, & March, 2000; Firestone & Silverman, 2001; Francis, 1990; King, Tonge, Heyne, & Ollendick, 2000; Lease & Strauss, 1993; Mansdorf & Lukens, 1987) or pharmacological (Albano & Chorpita, 1995; Graae, Milner, Rizzotto, & Klein, 1994; Klein, Koplewicz, & Kanner, 1992).

These traditional approaches have followed a strictly linear, acontextually monadic model, without reference to family factors in the etiology or treatment of this condition. Behavioral approaches are often coupled with pharmacological treatments (Lease & Strauss, 1993). For instance, in selecting optimal treatment strategies, Thyer, Himle, and Fischer (1993, pp. 151–152) stated that

> behavior therapy is the first choice treatment. . . . Marital/familial dysfunction can exist independently of a child SAD, but if assessment reveals a clear relationship, then therapy directed toward the parent, couple, or family as a whole may be indicated to address SAD *indirectly*. (emphasis added)

At best, these approaches may have added the mother or maternal substitute in their treatment. These approaches have been subjected to critical reviews (Bernstein & Borchardt, 1991; Pilkington & Piersel, 1991).

Only recently, Kashdan and Herbert (2001), in a review about

> the current status of research on the phenomenology, etiology, assessment, and treatment of children and adolescent social anxiety disorders (SAD) [concluded that] [d]espite being one of the most prevalent disorders of childhood and adolescence, SAD paradoxically stands as one of the least recognized, researched, and treated pediatric disorders. . . . Future directions are suggested . . . [like] incorporation of "positive psychology" constructs in treatment and prevention. (p. 37)

While references to the behavioral and pharmacological treatment of SAD abound, as illustrated by representative references cited above, only two references concerning systemic approaches for the treatment of SAD could be found to date (Dadds, Heard, & Rapee, 1992; Hamilton, 1994). In spite of including families in their treatment approaches, neither of these two references included the whole family in their treatment. Dadds et al., for instance, focused on the interaction of parents with their child during a display of anxiety, their management of emotional upsets, and family communication and problem-solving skills. Five of seven children who received treatment no longer met the criteria for an anxiety disorder after the 12-week program. Hamilton, on the other hand, claimed to use a "Family-school behavioral treatment model," which consisted of direct confrontation of what the child feared and avoided, with in vivo exposure. She used a strictly behavioral approach, even though it attempted to link contextually family and school in the overall approach. Two recent treatises on family therapy (Gurman & Kniskern, 1991; Mikesell, Lusterman, & McDaniel, 1995) and one on child psychotherapy (Shirk & Russell, 1996), for instance, failed to contain any reference to the systemic treatment of SAD.

The paucity of family therapy references in the treatment of childhood SAD is similar to the situation in the treatment of adolescent depression. As Kutcher and Marton (1996) concluded on this matter:

> There is little empirical literature regarding the effectiveness of family therapy in treating adolescent depression, probably due to the lack of attention given by family therapists to diagnostic issues and the underdeveloped state of family therapy outcome evaluation. Nevertheless, this is an important research area. (p. 115)

From this brief review of the literature, one is led to believe that more specific and systemic treatment approaches are necessary to deal with SAD and related childhood disorders. Consequently, a therapeutic task consistent with the modality of Presence = Being Together was devised as a way to deal with SAD or other childhood disorders that have roots in the whole family and are not "inside" the IP alone. With seemingly successful results, this prescription was extended to couples.

Limits of Task Prescription

This task can be prescribed whenever a referral question or problem meets the following requirements: (1) the task is defined and identified clearly and precisely, (2) the identified patient (IP) and his or her family are interested in solving the problem, (3) the task chosen to deal with the problem is accurately chosen in view of the needs of the IP and the family, (4) the task needs to be justified and explained for its use to the family; that is, it flows directly from the stated needs of the IP and the desires of the family to be together more often "without doing anything," and (5) the task needs to be straightforwardly simple, concretely non-verbal, and easy to administer in order to be followed by any couple or family, regardless of cultural or ethnic background and educational or socio-economic levels. It would be a responsible professional procedure to have couples and families sign an Informed Consent Form that would specify conditions of administration as well as its possible pros and cons, which are yet to be identified.

This task should not and must not be prescribed whenever there are indications or even hints of sexual, physical, or verbal abuse, as in the case of past incest. It should not be prescribed in symbiotic conditions, where closeness is already so tight and extreme that asking or prescribing 3HC to such couples or families would seem counter-therapeutic. It should not be prescribed when there is evidence or suggestions of substance abuse or any other type of dependency or any other boundary issue between parents and child, unless these issues are resolved first. Furthermore, this task should not be administered until a great deal of information about a couple or a family has been gathered and evaluated. It could be administered whenever other prescribed "solutions" do not seem to work, or when the emotional climate of a couple or family needs a boost. On these bases, this task could be prescribed perhaps toward the end of therapy, as a diagnostic way to evaluate whether the couple or family is ready to be "really" close.

Preliminary Preparation for Task Prescription

As part of information gathering preliminary to this task prescription, defenses and negative reactions should be dealt with before this task is administered. Partners or caretakers should be asked how affection was shared in their families of origin and how affection is presently shared in the family of procreation. Are there hugging and kissing? Who is affectionate toward whom? Who does not want and even fights affection? How are dependence and denial of dependence taking place here? For instance, A-type, obsessive-compulsive, driven personalities are extremely threatened by this task. Consequently, one might have to deal with the fear of intimacy and other issues of closeness before administration of this task. The sharing of hurts task could be used to assess how hurt feelings are shared in the relationship.

The initial administration of this task in one's office will yield a great deal of information about whether the family is ready to undertake practicing it at home. It is to be expected that, for every willing participant, there are going to be some resistant partners or family members. Adequate preparation for the administration of this task may take four or more sessions, depending on how couples or families are functioning in the area of sharing affection and being emotionally available to each other.

Characteristics of Task Prescription

This task consists of four parts, usually but not necessarily administered in the sequence given below. For instance, explanation, which is listed as a fourth part here, could be used as a starting point and introduction to this prescription:

Part 1. Performing the Task in the Professional's Office. Before prescribing this task, it is imperative for therapists to administer it in their office, in front of their eyes and ears. Therapists must be sure that the task is followed to the letter and that the couple or family is ready for it. Parent(s), caretaker(s), or partners should be seated on a sofa large enough to accommodate the whole family ("I would like to see how you all together hug each other. Go ahead [IP and siblings], go and hug [mother, mother and father, or caretaker[s])." Here the therapist must observe the reactions of all family members to this direct prescription.

For instance, in response to an IP (retarded) child draping himself on her, his mother picked him up immediately and shook him, telling him rather angrily, "Don't do that! Just hug me!" The message to this child was quite contradictory. More information and therapy would be necessary before this task would be administered to this mother and child to perform at home. Therapists must be observant to reactions of every family member with subtle and not so subtle resistances to this task administration. Do partners or family members comply eagerly? Do they smile while huddling together? What are the caretakers' reactions? For instance, a great deal of preparation took place in one case to convince the mother to follow this task, after a certain degree of trust and confidence in the therapist was established with the whole family.

Part 2. Prescribing Duration, Frequency, and Rate of Application. Duration of this task should be determined at the outset by the therapist together with the couple or family. Subsequently, depending on results obtained after the first administration, this period of time can be changed to meet the family's consensus. Family members (including, of course, the IP) are asked to agree on (1) what time they will perform this task (in the mornings, when parents come back from work, after supper, before going to bed), (2) how long it will last (from 10 to 20 minutes), and (3) how often they will perform it (once a day, every other day, on Mondays, Wednesdays, and Fridays, or Tuesdays, Thursdays, and Saturdays). After two weeks, if this task seems to work, the time duration can be reduced to 15 or even 10 minutes per session. Duration and frequency about Being Together through 3HC can be changed depending on the needs stated and agreed upon consensually by partners or most, if not all, family members. A kitchen timer or alarm clock can be used to determine beforehand the length of time desired by each family.

Part 3. Describing the Task. If the task is performed relatively well in front of the therapist, and the couple/family is ready, willing, and able to perform it, they are instructed to (1) make an appointment at least 24 hours ahead of its performance, with everybody knowing and agreeing as to the time, duration, frequency, and place, (2) close all the windows to have a certain degree of darkness that will maximize concentration on the task, (3) disconnect the phone to avoid being disturbed, (4) turn out all the lights in the house and, if necessary, leave a message outside the house door to keep out any possible, unexpected visitor, (5) sit together on a sofa embracing, hugging, holding, huddling, and cuddling with each other in semidarkness, and (6) not talk during the complete duration of this task (from at least 10 to at most 20 minutes for the first two weeks).

Part 4. Explaining the Task. Explanation for the application of this task is straightforward in terms of the experimental nature of this task:

> "I do not know whether this exercise (task, prescription) will work. However, if you are willing to try, let's see what happens in the next two weeks. If this task does not work within a month, we will try something else."

The importance of emotional needs for all family members, especially for the IP, is stressed by mentioning how difficult it is to fulfill these needs when everybody is so busy that there is little, if any, time for caretakers to satisfy these needs. Various historical and developmental events may be presented to illustrate how important emotional needs are and how they can be fulfilled simply by Being Together in the way described by the prescribed task.

The experimental nature of this task should make its administration very tentative ("I don't know whether this is going to work. Why don't we try it and see what happens?"). If its administration is unsuccessful, it should furnish grounds for further questioning as to the "causes" or "reasons" for its failure. If the task is successful, it is important, in some cases, for the therapist to express surprise and skepticism ("It might be a fluke. Why don't we try it again and see whether it really works?"). If the second trial is also successful, then the couple or family should consider it an everyday occurrence that needs to be performed to reassure everybody in the system on a continuous basis.

Case Study No. 1 [1]

This case consisted of severe separation anxiety in an 11-year-old son of an upper-middle-class family consisting of parents, IP, and a younger daughter. This anxiety bordered on panic even when the mother went to the bathroom. She could not go anywhere without the son going with her. When the possibility of a therapeutic summer camp to "treat" this condition was suggested, the IP became agitated and could not even sit still in his chair. When the task was implemented in the therapist's office, the whole family seemed to enjoy huddling and cuddling together ("We have never done this before."). On the basis of this positive reaction, the family was instructed to perform 3HC every other day for at least 15 minutes. Over a period of two weeks, the IP started to become less anxious and even allowed the mother to take brief trips to the grocery store, provided she came back home within a clearly stated period of time.

In the meantime, while this task was being performed at home, the parents, seen without the children, were beginning to disclose their unexpressed feelings, even with each other, about the death of the husband's father and the wife's traumatic separation from her mother. After two weeks of completing the task prescription on an every-other-day basis, the IP was able to attend summer camp, where occasional anxiety attacks were dealt with by camp counselors with telephone support from the therapist. After returning from two weeks of camp, the IP seemed to have become more sure of himself, indicating his wanting to attend the camp again the next year. School was started in the fall without any incident. On a one-year follow-up, according to his independent report and the report from his parents, he seemed to have forgotten about his past anxieties and was heavily involved in Boy Scout activities.

The apparent success of this case, as well as similar cases of separation anxiety, resulted in trying it out with two somewhat different cases.

Case Study No. 2

This 8-year-old IP was referred for frequent assaults on other children in school. He was in the second grade and is the second of a three-children, single-mother family. His father, divorced from the mother, was in the penitentiary. The mother was worried that the IP would follow in his father's footsteps, especially as far as aggression was concerned. She showed and gave to the therapist a whole stack of "expelled" notes from school, with the danger that the IP might have to repeat second grade. A 10-year-old sister and a 5-year-old brother completed the family. The mother worked in a job that required her to be up at 5 A.M. five to six days a week. She would dress and feed the children and drive them to a babysitter, who would then see that they got to school for the two older children and nursery for the youngest.

The IP was a thin, articulate child who was less than forthcoming in admitting his aggressive behavior both toward his siblings and in school. For the first two weeks, the mother was instructed to have the IP punch an inner tube or something similar for at least 30 minutes a day. She used the mattress instead, but even though there were no expel notes received from the school, she felt that no drastic change had occurred. Consequently, the therapist had the children go and hug the mother sitting on a sofa. All three children concurred in happily hugging the mother. The IP especially seemed very happy in his facial expression in doing so. Hence, on the basis of this spontaneous demonstration of need for affection from the children, the mother was instructed to follow up with the practice of being together for the next two weeks, at least every other day for 10 to 15 minutes or however long the family could tolerate. In the next session, she reported then that they had performed the task for 10 out of 14 days and that no notes had been received from school. She was asked to continue the practice for at least two more weeks, when we would evaluate the results. The jury is still out on this case, because there was no way to determine whether the mother, who went to sleep at 8:00 P.M., was following this prescription. The children were often left on their own at home without the mother. During this time they would spend time calling people at home, including the therapist.

After three months, with one session a month and without any school notes, the mother terminated therapy with the proviso that they would call if it became needed. At the end of three months the mother called, very upset, to inform the therapist that the IP had attempted suicide through hanging a cord around his neck from the doorknob. Fortunately the cord broke, but it left a scar on the IP's neck. When questioned about the reasons for this attempt, in session the IP reported that it was an "accident" that took place while "we were having fun." When asked whether the task prescription had been followed, the mother reported that she had had no time or energy at the end of the day but that the children would hug each other on their own. She did not have a car and could not take the children to the therapist's office. Consequently, the IP was instructed to call the therapist every day for the first three months to report how he was doing. This prescription brought forth strong rivalrous reactions from the younger brother, who wanted to know why he could not call and talk with the therapist as well. He was told that he could. After three months of daily calls except on weekends, with no further trouble in school or at home, the IP was asked to call the therapist at the end of the school week on Fridays to report whether any trouble had taken place at school or at home. These weekly calls lasted for one year, during which the mother reported that the IP was doing well and seemed happy and that the children were continuing hugging on their own, without her help.

After one year without any communication, the therapist received a call from the IP, who in a mischievous tone, with the other two siblings snickering in the background, asked whether he was still remembered. When he was reassured that he was and was asked how he was doing, he reported that "everything is all right." His younger siblings then got on the phone reporting that they were doing "OK" and that they were still hugging each other.

Although not completely successful, this case illustrates that 3HC had a limited impact on at least this family and that, when discontinued, it seemed to produce deleterious reactions, especially in the IP. The most relevant aspect of this case was the need of the children to seek comfort and reassurance from each other, since the mother was able to provide only survival skills (Doing and Having) but was too tired to furnish affection and 3HC (i.e., Being Present Together).

Case Study No. 3

This middle-aged couple was devastated by their 33-year-old son's accidental death. They reported many ups and downs in their 35-year marriage due mainly to the husband's workaholic behavior and his frequent business trips out of town. Their son's death triggered a whole host of past, unresolved issues in their relationship that needed immediate solution because the wife demanded and had started legal divorce procedures. This crisis brought the husband into therapy for his depression and to keep the marriage intact and "better than in the past." The wife accepted begrudgingly coming into couple therapy, since she questioned whether the husband wanted "real" change and whether therapy was a ploy to avoid divorce.

She saw coming into therapy as another of her husband's frequent manipulations. During the first visit together, after the husband had been seen alone for 12 sessions, they were administered the "Sharing of Hurts" exercise in the therapist's office. This task has been described repeatedly as another task derived from the same developmental and contextual theory of personality socialization in the family from which 3HC was derived (L'Abate, 1994b, 1997b, 1998b, 1999a). This task, described in greater detail below, consists of partners holding hands, closing their eyes, and expressing and sharing hurts accumulated before and during their marriage. As a result of this sharing they were able to cry together and comfort each other through hugging and holding. After completion of this task, the wife, who up to this point had been quite reticent in speaking about herself, confided that there had been little affection in her family of origin as well as in their marriage. The husband concurred in reporting the lack of affection in his family of origin. In spite of their critical situation, they were willing to follow the 3HC task on an every other day basis for 15 minutes a day. This task, according to their joint report a week later, allowed them to grieve and cry together about their past mistakes in their relationship as well as in their parenting of one son and two daughters.

They liked the 3HC task so much that they, completely on their own and without any suggestion or instructions from the therapist, decided to perform it "every day come hell or high water." The wife reported that if it wasn't for this task, their marriage would have dissolved. They considered themselves "hooked" on hugging, holding, huddling, and cuddling with each other every day, either not talking or sharing pleasurable and non-pleasurable past and present experiences ("Whatever comes down the pike.").

On a one-year follow-up, they reported practicing 3HC every day, and, if they missed it for one day, they would need a double session the next day. Even though they still admitted to infrequent "ups-and-downs," they were able to travel together for fun rather than for business, which the husband had discontinued unless the wife joined him.

Discussion

This task prescription could conceivably be explained also by object relations and attachment theory concepts. Theoretically, only two textbooks in the vast attachment theory literature (Atkinson & Zucker, 1997; Cassidy & Shaver, 1999) mentioned "holding." Josselson (1994) credited the object relations theory of Winnicott (1965) as stressing the importance of holding. However, these references dealt with the importance of a generic and nonspecified "holding environment" for the child to grow with a sense of self-security. Furthermore, these and other attachment references in the extremely large literature on attachment theory did not mention this task at all, nor did they present illustrative case studies to illuminate the importance of this behavior (Bowlby, 1988; Crittenden & Claussen, 2000).

Given some similarities between L'Abate's Selfhood Model[9] (see Chapters 2, 3, and 5) and attachment theory, both the Selfhood Model[9] and attachment theory stress the importance of behaviors designed to increase a sense of security and self-importance. Only the theory presented here, however, stresses the importance of 3HC as a way to increase affection and physical contact, emotional containment, reassurance, validation, sharing, and reduction of stress. These correlations notwithstanding, this task prescription could be used to reassure with direct, immediate, and concrete availability children and adults who show "insecure" attachments with their caretakers. Just body contact in itself may be very reassuring to a baby, child, and adolescent, as well as to an adult. Unfortunately, many adults, especially men, deny the need for such contact. Attachment theory, however, even though similar in some respects to the Selfhood Model[9], as far this writer knows, has failed to produce task prescriptions that are directly connected with and specifically derived from that theory itself (L'Abate et al., 2000).

As with any intervention, it is important to find out under which conditions this task prescription is useful and under which conditions it is useless, if not harmful. For instance, we need to ascertain whether this task prescription would work better with internalizing rather than with externalizing children. This determination cannot be achieved by this author alone but can be achieved by other clinicians and investigators who will be more objective than a single clinician could ever be. Premature enthusiasm for the implications of this task not only for children with SAD but also for children of families that are emotionally spent, neglected, and impoverished —as well as for couples in distress—must be tempered by objective evidence external to its author. It is crucial to verify whether this task is clinically and empirically useful and valid. If valid, its simple application to countless families who need emotional reassurance might be quite significant.

INCREASING INTIMACY IN COUPLES AND FAMILIES

A specific and concrete definition of intimacy leads to structured distance as well as less structured f2f interventions. Intimacy grows in close, committed, and prolonged relationships. It does not grow in short-lived, superficial, and uncommitted ones. Once intimacy is defined as the sharing of joys as well as the sharing of hurts and fears of being hurt, then specific and concrete methods can be designed to improve intimacy in couples that find it difficult to become intimate (Cusinato, Aceti, & L'Abate, 1997; Cusinato & L'Abate, 1995; L'Abate, 1994b, 1997b, 1999a, 2002b). Hurts are defined as the accumulation of traumas, abuses, losses, stresses, strains, rejections, put-downs, and offenses that are inevitably received throughout the course of life. One cannot be alive and not be hurt, as the research of Becvar (2001), Bohart and Greenberg (1997), and Pennebaker (2001) shows.

Admittedly, some receive more hurts than others. Some may be more sensitive to certain hurts than others. Some hurts may be more intense and long-lasting than others. Nonetheless, being alive and loving and being loved mean receiving and giving some hurts, no matter how small. We are all vulnerable to hurts from others, and we all fail by hurting others intentionally or unintentionally. We are more vulnerable to being hurt by loved ones than by strangers. Strangers do not have the power to hurt us emotionally the way intimate others do. They may produce physical harm, but emotional hurts produced by physical harm lessen more quickly when they are shared with those whom we love and who love us. To protect ourselves from being hurt, we develop defenses that keep us distant from the very people whom we love and who love us. Fear of intimacy is frequently found in troubled couples because the necessary ingredients for an evolving and deepening relationship are missing or insufficient.

Diagnostically, the relevant questions to ask couples and families, in the process of facilitating their intimacy, are (1) "Did you ever see your parents cry together?"; (2) "What happened when one of your parents cried?"; (3) "What did the other parent do?" More in the present, both partners and family members need to be asked (1) "What do you do when one of you cries?" For men, it is usually relevant to ask (2) "When was the last time you cried?" However, here one should be careful not to fall victim to sex-gender stereotypes, making sure to avoid precipitous conclusions about which partner is able to cry. Stereotypically, of course, in terms of culturally traditional norms, we expect women to find crying easier than men. It seems easier for men to get angry and to withdraw from painful confrontations.

However, what is relevant here is finding whether there is a polarization in the expression of feelings; for instance, whether one partner gets mad and walks out whenever the other partner cries. The relativity of stereotyped generalizations about being "strong" or "weak" needs to be explored and exploded by indicating that being "weak" is actually much more constructive than being "strong" in the stereotypical sense. Being "strong" and stoic is a very destructive (inhuman, unrealistic, unnecessary) position to take and to maintain in intimate relationships.

It follows from the above that asking for professional help means being strong, because "weak" people deny the need for help. Hospitals, jails, and cemeteries are full of them. Consequently, the rationale for asking for help is "love and strength," to the point of contradicting the couple's or family's negative reasons for referral:

> You should be congratulated for asking for professional help. It takes guts to ask for help. It takes a lot of care and strength to ask for help, because those who do not care for themselves and each other prefer to spend good money to pay a lawyer rather than ask for professional help. It is much easier to destroy a marriage than to build a new one.

SHARING HURTS AND FEARS OF BEING HURT (MODEL[12])

A specific and concrete definition of intimacy as sharing of joys, hurts, and fears of being hurt has been productive, if not successful, in creating distance and face-to-face approaches to improve intimacy in couples and families. The next step consists of determining the validity of the present formulation.

The Hurt Exercise was developed to use in therapy sessions (L'Abate, 1986, p. 235; 1997b, pp. 320–321). This exercise requires partners to face each other on a sofa or two chairs, to close their eyes, and to hold each other's hands. They are asked to concentrate on their physical sensations first, such as those elicited and expressed by holding each other's hands, before concentrating on their hurts. Once the request to concentrate on their hurt is made, the professional is to wait for the outcome. One may repeat the request for a second time, but no more than twice altogether. Once partners are in touch with the hurts that are dwelling inside their bodies, partners are asked to acknowledge and, if possible, share them ("I hurt, I am hurting").

Often one partner is unable to express these hurts, and, consequently, he or she is unable to empathize with the one who is acknowledging them.

This task is primarily diagnostic because it gives clues about what is not working in the couple or family. In a way, one could argue that therapy is completed when partners and family members are able to share their hurts by crying together to share them congruently.

CONCLUSION

This chapter contains illustrations of how models of the theory encompass most interventions requiring face-to-face contact with a professional helper. The major issue raised by these interventions is where to match or to mismatch an intervention with each of the five components of Model[1]. Two task prescriptions to be conducted first in the professional helper's office and later at home, sharing and hurts and 3HC, derive directly from at least two, if not three, models of the theory. The major shortcoming of both prescriptions is that they are based strictly on anecdotal evidence gathered by the first author. Whether these interventions are valid in the hands of other professional helpers remains to be seen. Both prescriptions are behaviorally concrete and specific enough to be replicable in the laboratory as well as in the clinic.

NOTE

1. Parents or partners for these case studies gave their written permission to publish them provided that complete anonymity would be observed. Some characteristics were changed to further disguise each family and assure complete confidentiality.

Chapter 9

Model-Derived Preventive Interventions for Non-clinical Relationships

Over the last few years, following his application of the EPM to himself and to others, the second author has developed structured programs or workbooks to administer in clinical and non-clinical settings. Some were developed directly from the EPM, and some have a loose connection with the EPM, even though they owe their existence, in some way or another, to the EPM. The programs presented here apply to relatively well functioning individuals and to selected, clinical individuals as adjuncts to ongoing psychotherapy and psychiatric medications.

A PROGRAM TO INCREASE COGNITIVE FLEXIBILITY

This is a computer program (published also in English) in a CD-ROM format attached to a book by De Giacomo (1995/1999). It has been used as a method to develop problem-solving creativity in students attending classes devoted to that topic. It is based on the 16 functions of the EPM. The purpose of this program is to offer respondents (readers or CD-ROM users) the possibility of observing themselves and the world around them using additional cognitive tools that might expand their awareness. They are trained step-by-step to resort to 16 different ways of constructing relationships by applying the 16 different mental constructions of the EPM. It is like putting on a pair of special lenses by which one can observe phenomena that occur inside and outside ourselves from 16 different points of view. Next, readers are encouraged to recognize and to master these 16 styles by reconstructing them in their minds and to interact with them and practice using them by choosing different sequences. These sequences are

Figure 9-1
Sixteen Artistic Styles and 16 Styles of the EPM

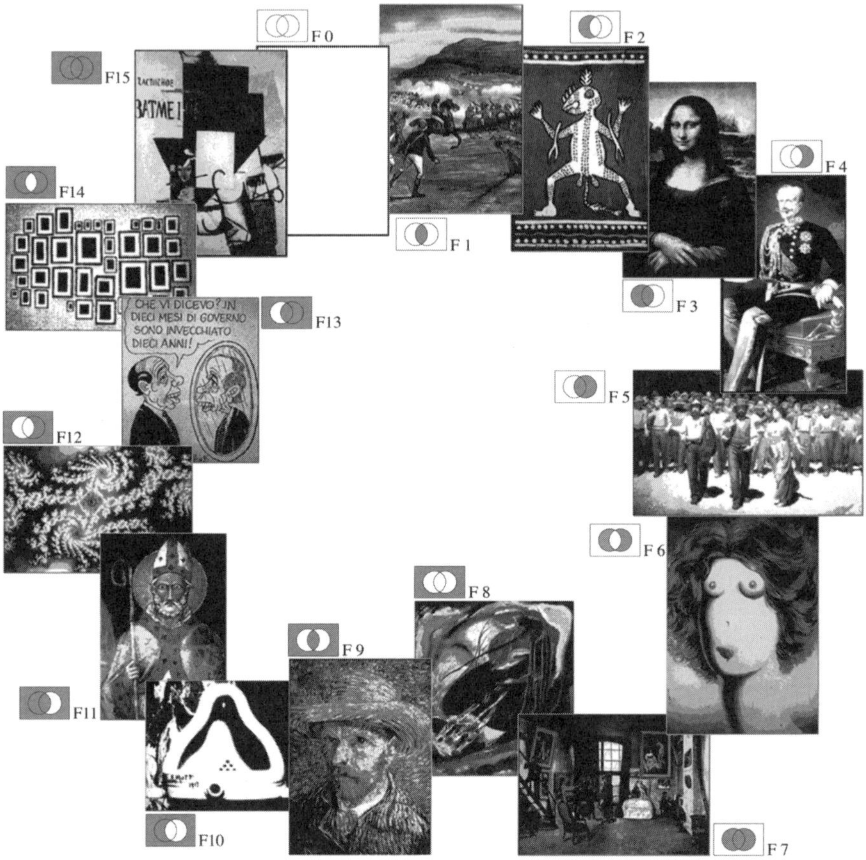

like cognitive gymnastics. They are meant to amplify the mind's potential and to make it more flexible.

Moreover, this program pushes respondents to multiply ideas by 16 different possibilities and thus increase cognitive flexibility. This program was explained in general outline form in Chapter 4 to give an idea of its practical use. We send the reader back to that section of Chapter 4. Here we show Figure 9-1, where 16 different artistic styles represent 16 ways to see reality.

Besides this program in English, the CD-ROM contains several other programs in Italian and English. One of them includes figures that appear in Figure 9-1. They are presented one at a time in a sequence, either in a rigid order or at random, as the respondent may choose to see them. Viewing rate and time can also be controlled by respondents. In yet another program, the sequences of figures reproduced in Figure 9-1 are accompanied by a pleasant and stimulating musical sound.

This program has been administered to several samples of medical students attending a course in general psychology and to groups of university graduates from various branches of science and arts who were instead attending courses on theories and techniques for the development of creativity. This program was rated favorably by over 70% of its users. Various tests administered on a pre-post program basis also showed that the program could be used by relatively well functioning participants without any major problems and that a wealth of interesting ideas was produced (De Giacomo & De Nigris, 2001).

This program has also been used clinically with 10 patients suffering from mental disorders. The results obtained (as yet unpublished) were positive.

COMPASS SENTENCES

Another tool originated by the EPM is the Marine Compass Sentences, or Passwords of the Mind (De Giacomo & Iadicicco, 2001). By compass sentences is meant statements likely to produce a strong psychological impact on the receiver. The idea was born in the clinical experience of the second writer. He happened to see again, after many years, some of his patients, who had relapsed or who were accompanying relatives who needed the second author's help. These patients reported that a sentence that they had heard from him years earlier had been very important and crucial in their lives. The sentence had acted on them like a grain of sand inserted in a pearl oyster, a process that creates the core in the growth of the pearl. From these repeated experiences with various patients, the idea to utilize sentences for preventive and psychotherapeutic purposes was born.

To understand the passage from Compass Sentences to the EPM, we have to be aware that this model is a four-floor building (refer to Figure 4-2). At the first floor, the simplest one, there are three-element situations (triads) based on the question: When an individual with his or her own world encounters another individual with his or her own world, how does the former individual transform himself or herself? At the second floor there are four possibilities (tetrads) that derive from the preceding triads: acceptance of one's own world, acceptance of the other's world, sharing of one's own world, and rejection of one's own world and of the other's world, the world of the two interacting subjects. On the third floor there are 16 possibilities, that is, 16 relational styles that derive from the combination of the above tetrads. These 16 styles can be read as adjectives or couples of adjectives. The fourth and last floor envisages 256 possibilities that result from the permutations of the 16 styles of the third floor among themselves.

Figure 9-2
How These Phrases Develop from the EPM

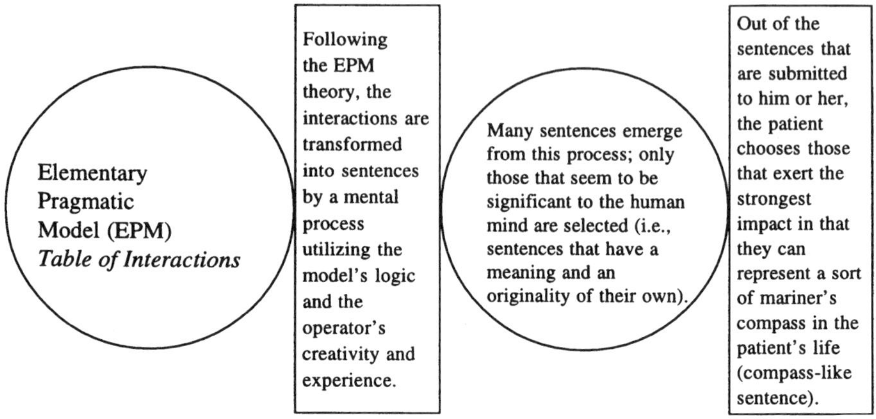

The sentences presented below derive from the last floor. To go into the detailed logic of this model, one is referred to Chapter 4 of this book.

These Compass Sentences, therefore, originated from the fourth level of this building, that is, from the transformation of the 256 rules generated by the permutations of the 16 relational styles with the same 16 relational styles, as found in Table 4-19. The procedure that led to the creation of the sentences is illustrated in Figure 9-2.

Over 100 sentences obtained in this manner underwent a series of selection with different groups of subjects (students, psychiatrists, psychologists, graduates in various disciplines, psychiatric patients). This process has resulted in the following 31 "cryptic" sentences. Under each sentence there is the interactive EPM formula from which it is derived.

1. Much unhappiness derives from the fact that you want to do one thing *and* the other, whereas in fact you can do one thing *or* the other.

   F6 × F6 = F0

2. If you meet a deliberately contrary person and you adopt a creative, sharing attitude, they will feel doubt.

   F10 × F9 = F6

3. Being a perpetual poet is incompatible with life.

   F8 × F7 = F0

4. If you are hostile to yourself, any attempt to solve a problem creatively will be transformed into doubt and uncertainty.

   F10 × F9 = F6

5. Wear dream-tinted glasses.

   F9 × F8 = F14

6. Project yourself toward the other person's world.

   F9 × F5 = F3

7. Enter the world of doubt.

   F5 × F6 = F6

8. The way you see my relationship with you is not necessarily the way I see my relationship with you.

   We are all the products and producers of relationships.

9. Having a goal is already achieving a goal.

   F9 × F15 = F9

10. Hurting someone hurts yourself.

    F5 × F10 = F10

11. If you are a doubter and you want to become an upholder of your world, give yourself gifts you really like, do things that lead toward your world.

    F6 × F5 = F3

12. Uncertainty, doubt, ambivalence, doubtfulness are being swayed by the waves. If this is a state that repeats and repeats, in the end it nullifies you and kills your mind.

    F6 × F6 = F0

13. In every situation there is one way already ready, organized in an uncertain way that has to be organized, but sometimes it is difficult to find that first way.

    F9 × F5 = F3
    F9 × F6 = F0

14. There are negative things that fascinate you.

    F14 × F10 = F5

15. When a situation is against you, you will have to go through a phase of doubt before taking the direction of the search for the solution.

    F10 × F6 = F9

16. Wear worry-tinted glasses.

    F9 × F0 = F6

17. Give me a hand by not giving me a hand.

    F14 × F0 = F1
    F8 × F0 = F7

18. If the starting point is not clear, all the next steps will be unclear.

    F15 with whatever function = F15

19. If you pursue a goal creatively and if the outcome is positive—in other words, leads toward your world—this will make you stronger.

    F9 × F5 = F3

20. Saying that they are better would make them worse; saying that they are well would make them ill (this is because you are afraid that this statement could provoke a reaction in the other person that would nullify you or make the

other person hostile to you or cause them to withdraw into their world).

F5 × F0 = F0

21. When you think you are a great person, the almighty or a genius, or your work seems to you very important and headed for great results and great successes, tell yourself, I'm in a dream-attack.

    F14 × F14 = F1

22. What seems definite is not in fact definite if it is seen only as a content and not as a container; that is if it is put in brackets, let's say in a certain frame.

    F(F)

23. True luck is when you get something unexpected that you like.

    F9 × F13 = F11

24. The problem is to wear or not to wear suspicion-tinted glasses.

    F9 × F10 = F6
    F9 × F12 = F10

25. If you want to keep your creativity, feed on chaos.

    F9 × F15 = F9

26. Teasing is a way of attacking that is softened by a component of pseudoaltruism and that hides a way of using teasing to strengthen one's own position.

    F12 with whatever function = F3

27. Losing control of yourself is sometimes like becoming your own enemy; forgetting something (emptying your mind completely) is sometimes the same as becoming your own enemy.

    F5 × F0 = F0
    F1 × F0 = F0
    F9 × F0 = F6

28. Hang some abstract pictures on the walls of your home and add some abstract constructions to the construction of your mind.

    F9 × F8 = F14
    F6 × F8 = F14

29. If you are a contrary person, confusion kills you.

    F10 × F15 = F0

30. If you want to make a contrary person uphold his or her world, show yourself to be a pseudoaltruist.

    F10 × F12 = F3

31. Sequences are interrupted by nullification or by absolute inflexibility or by total confusion.

    Think about the three final states of EPM (F0, F3, F15)

These sentences may be used in both clinical and non-clinical settings to help respondents reflect on certain aspects of their own or others' lives. For instance, they can be said right at the end of a therapy or prevention session, either with one individual or with a group of individuals, or they may be administered in writing as a tool to help respondents in any setting reflect on themselves and on their lives.

The simplest way to utilize these sentences is to ask respondents to rate them by giving three points for the most impacting, two points for less impacting, and one point for the least impacting. Then, among all sentences, ask respondents to choose just one as the most impacting of all. Then professionals may interact with respondents by asking why the respondents rated the sentences the way that they did, why one sentence was chosen over others, how that chosen sentence impacted their beliefs, what associations were generated in their minds by that sentence, which episodes in their lives were brought to mind by the sentence, how they would rewrite the sentence, which history they would construct from the sentence.

The most structured procedure to administer these sentences online was published quite recently (De Giacomo et al., 2002). The intervention has the purpose of "increasing knowledge about yourself."

After respondents are registered online, they receive two tests: the Self View Questionnaire (SVQ: Appendix C) and the 31 sentences listed above. Respondents have to choose one of the 31 sentences, complete the test, and complete a grid about the impact that the chosen sentence has had on them. (The grid is based on the 16 functions of the EPM, as shown in Figure 9-3.) Then respondents have to answer in writing the following items:

1. Write freely about the sentence of your choice.
2. Write why you made that choice.
3. How does this sentence fit into your belief system?
4. What associations does the sentence create for you?
5. Now re-elaborate on the sentence as personally as you can.
6. Create a history around the sentence.

After completing these six items, respondents can ask to receive feedback from the e-therapist or proceed automatically to the next session. If respondents decide to receive feedback from the e-therapist, they have to state that they are very eager to receive it. In this case, the e-therapist opens a chat line and answers whatever questions may arise according to the EPM. In the 2nd session, respondents have to choose a second sentence and follow the same procedure given above, except for completing the initial SVQ (which is repeated only at the last session). This process is followed for 8 sessions for a total of 10 sessions, the first to pre-test and the last to post-test. In the 10th session, respondents also have to write a general synthesis of what has emerged from this process, with the focus about what has been understood about the self. They have to give an evaluation of the intervention on a four-point scale: very good, good, modest, poor. Because of the

Figure 9-3
Framework for the Impact of Psychological Interventions of Phrases in Respondents According to the EPM

It nullifies you F0	It just encourages you to read the text F1	It forces you to shut yourself away F2	It confirms your way of thinking F3
It leads you to passive acceptance F4	It leads you to full acceptance F5	It leads you to doubt F6	It leads you to mediate points of view F7
It seems strange to you F8	It makes you understand and think of other possibilities F9	It leads you to oppose it F10	It seems like an imposition F11
It leads you to accept because it is worth your while F12	It leads you to accept with surprise and enthusiasm F13	It leads you to think in metaphorical terms F14	It leads you to confusion F15

novelty of this program, with only a few experimental cases, thus far the feedback from respondents has been positive. However, the second author and his collaborators are aware that this feedback constitutes only consumer satisfaction. Future analyses will be devoted to whether any changes have taken place because of pre-post administrations of the SVQ.

THE WHEEL OF WISDOM AND THE TAPE OF THE MIND

The human mind works according to limited models, some clear, some unclear, some fuzzy, some confused. Hence, it is necessary to use as many models as possible to overcome this limitation, at least up to a certain point. We can recognize limitations of the mind when we attempt to introspect, when we try to make our mind turn toward itself, or when we listen to others reporting on their own personal experiences, their own states of mind, or events of their lives. We do, for example, in psychotherapy, or even when we ourselves try to communicate the contents of our own minds to others. The limitations of the mind can be recognized especially when it works spontaneously and automatically, that is, when it does not use any of those special tools that we refer to as "models."

To help the reader realize what we actually mean when we talk about the limitations of the mind, we can try a very simple exercise that we have often performed with several psychiatric and psychology colleagues who are experts in human relations. If we ask somebody, "What happens, in your opinion, if a person withdrawn in his or her own world meets another person who is a mediator?" Or, again, "If an abstract and absentminded person meets someone else who is an altruist, what do you think will happen?" "What happens if an acceptor of the other's world meets another acceptor of the other's world?" It is only too obvious that the overwhelming majority of respondents whom we have queried will find it difficult to answer these questions, yet these questions sound quite legitimate and important in our everyday interactive life, that is, in our relational life.

The very fact that questions like these are difficult to answer shows that the human mind usually works only when it follows certain fixed courses, and it finds itself in trouble as soon as it departs from them; it is here that its limits become apparent. We are now facing the problem of whether we can construct any tools or models by which these narrow limits can be overcome. Can we suggest that alternative paths can be taken, paths that will enable people to think of things that would otherwise never cross their minds? Obviously, the purpose of discovering and using these new tools is to improve knowledge by expanding one's horizons, hence, among other things, to furnish more tools for use in primary, secondary, and tertiary prevention.

Our assumption that, in order to get out of a certain kind of automatic and limited functioning of the mind, one has to use models needs further explanation. The usual criticism about models is that they are only an impoverished version of reality, but, while this is certainly true, it is also true that they allow an exceptional expansion of the possibilities of our mind and of its practical applications. An aircraft, for example, is only a poor model of what has been created by nature, the bird. Still, while it is indeed an impoverished copy of a bird (which in any case exhibits much more flexibility in its behavior than does the product of a person's technology), really the aircraft can fly at terrific speed and carry much heavier loads than those produced by nature could ever do. If, then, the models' function is to expand the human mind, they must be further refined and developed to a point where their potential has been fully exploited.

Our choice has been to try to identify, from among the tools that we have been describing so far, a model by which it would be possible to provide "containers." The word "containers" is to be understood as meaning conventional and arbitrary indicators. As we are going to see at a later stage, we are talking about regulators of the mind, like organizers, definers, formulators, perceivers, surveyors, designators, representers, translators, analyzers, configurators, mental constructors, invariants.

The mental process that we are illustrating here and that provides the foundation for our work on models is based on two aspects:

1. Transferring ideas toward ideas at a higher logical level, transferring concepts into broader concepts, transferring from contents to containers, bearing in mind—as we will mention again later on—that the containers that we are talking about are the 16 functions of the EPM, and 10 empirical constructions that we have defined (see below for details) as "constructions of comedies," "constructions of tragedies," "operational construction," "construction of a triumph," "construction of indifferent recollections from the past," "construction of dreams for the future." This transfer from contents to containers can also be defined as a reframing of contents into higher-level cognitive organizations (i.e., containers).
2. Identifying the temporal and spatial organization of containers in an attempt to identify structures at a still higher logical level, in an attempt to identify some metacontainers. To better understand what we mean, it is useful to read about Bateson's zigzag ladder between form and process in Chapter 1.

The following is a brief outline of the method that we are proposing and that was described in the preceding paragraphs; various mental contents that emerge when we interact with our patients, our families, or our intimate self when we observe ourselves are introduced into certain containers. Once they are inside the containers, the elements lose most of the characteristics that they possessed as elements and take up instead the characteristics of the container; the characteristics of the elements after they have been placed into containers become the background for the container's own characteristics.

In turn, as the containers organize themselves into sequences, they arrange themselves in time and in space and take up specific features so that they can be viewed as containers belonging to a higher logical level (i.e., as metacontainers).

Figure 9-4 is a simple, schematic representation of the four concepts described above as elements (first row), containers (second row), elements inside containers (third row) and container sequences, or metacontainers (fourth row) (De Giacomo & De Giacomo, 1997).

This notion will become clear as the reader follows our line of reasoning.

Containers

As was mentioned earlier, the most important containers used by us are the 16 functions of the EPM and 10 empirical mental constructions. These 10 constructions arise in the attempt to answer the following question:

Figure 9-4
Contents, Containers, Contents in Containers, and Pattern of Containers with Their Contents

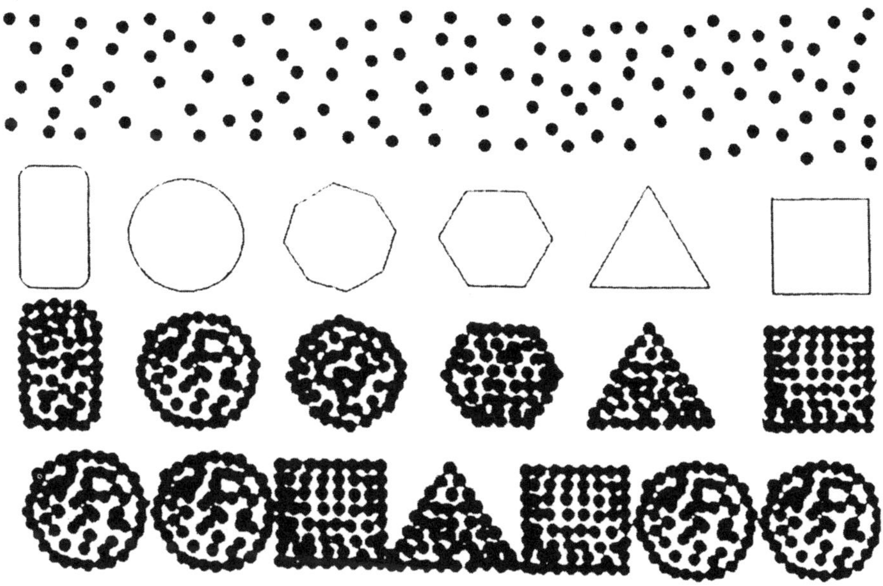

What does it mean to enter the world of the other (F5)? Thinking about how to reach the world of a person, we invented, with the help of the first author, the 10 constructions of the Wheel of Wisdom. The idea was that our mind works like a series of mental constructions succeeding one another (either due to continuous interior motion or due to external factors acting upon us) and is similar to a continuously running tape on which the mental constructions, as well as the emotions and feelings linked to those constructions, are recorded. Therefore, by "constructions" is meant the products of our mind as we perceive them while we are reflecting about ourselves.

In the following paragraphs we report the 10 mental constructions and explain briefly what they mean. For a more complete description of the mental constructions and how they can be used, the reader is referred to a special computer program available in the CD-ROM attached to a work by De Giacomo (1995/1999).

1. Constructing a big tragedy: this means that our mind is thinking, with great intensity, of tragic, sad, anguishing, desperate events; it seems as though there were no way out: severe losses, major disillusionments, heavy remorse, serious mistakes made by ourselves, frightful experiences, and so on.

2. Constructing a moderate tragedy: unlike in the big tragedy, intensity is lower; darkness is not absolute; there is at least some dim light; and one can bear it, though only hardly so. The themes are the same: losses, errors, awful experiences, and humiliations, though less intense.
3. Constructing a minor tragedy: unlike in the big and in the moderate tragedies, the level of intensity is very low, and it is quite tolerable; losses, errors, humiliation, and so forth attain only a very low intensity. These first three tragedies in various degrees of sorrow correspond to what the first author calls "hurts" in Chapter 2.
4. Constructing a very amusing comedy: the mind thinks of very amusing things, pleasant situations that make us laugh and put us in a good mood.
5. Constructing a moderately amusing comedy: unlike in the case of a very amusing comedy, here the mind thinks of fairly amusing, though not too amusing, events, which certainly put us in a good mood but do not make us roar with laughter.
6. Constructing a hardly amusing comedy: unlike in the very amusing and the moderately amusing constructions, the mind thinks of things that are just a bit pleasant, just a little amusing, hardly gratifying, which make us smile just a little. These comedies would constitute what the first author (Chapter 2) calls joys or enjoyments.
7. Operational construction: this means that the mind is engaged in carrying out a certain instrumental task, as when one thinks, "Now I'm going to do this; now I've got to do that." For instance: "Now I am typing on a computer; now I'm going out to buy some bread."
8. Constructing a triumph: we feel we are so very clever, so proud of ourselves; we are riding a high horse; we feel we are invincible—a triumph of our ego.
9. Constructing indifferent recollections of the past: we recall something unimportant that translates neither into tragedies nor into comedies; we are just dealing with plain recollections.
10. Dreams for the future: this means daydreaming, fantasies, aspirations, and hopes for the future about what we would like to happen in our future lives to make us feel happy.

Here again, as with the 16 functions, one will easily realize that each construction, just like each function, corresponds to a way of "setting" or of organizing the mind to perceive "reality" (note that the word "reality" is in quotation marks to stress the relativity of this term.

The Tape of the Mind has been patented in both its Italian and English versions. The wheel of Wisdom is represented in Figure 9-5.

These constructions and their sequence have led the second author to patent a device named the Wheel of Wisdom which, in addition to being a good-looking tool (of the type of an Eastern mandala), is meant to facilitate the task of its users.

The device is made of a hard cardboard base containing a pin on the back in which the method is described. An upper circle is subdivided into

Figure 9-5
The Wheel of Wisdom

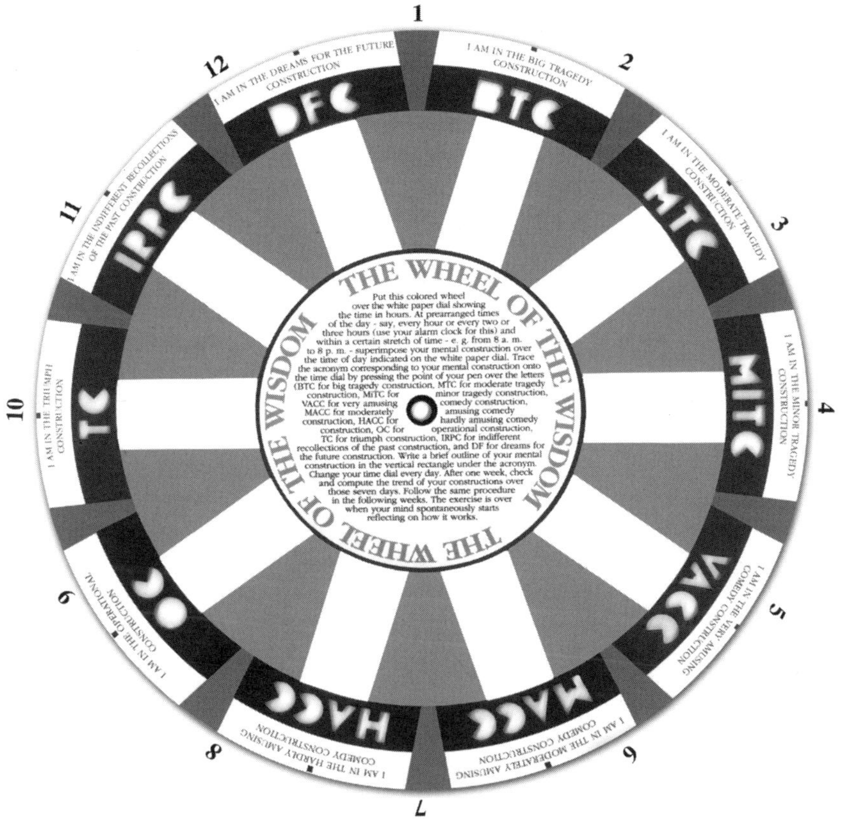

Source: PLANSERVICE SRL, via Somalia 146, Roma, phone no. 011-39-06-8632-8620.

10 slices with the acronyms of the 10 constructions written at the periphery of the circle. The space around each acronym is empty so that it is possible to write with a pen in the underlying space.

In addition, each slice contains an empty rectangle placed perpendicularly to the wheel. Inside this rectangle, one writes on the underlying space that is covered by a round sheet of paper. Between the base and the sliced wheel there is a circular sheet of paper indicating the 12 hours of the day, like a watch, placed as if it were the contents of a sandwich between the sliced wheel and its base. These sheets have a central hole for them to be hung to the pin. Seven such sheets (which correspond to the seven days of the week) are hung. The outlines (contours) of the initials of the 10 mental constructions are reported on the sliced wheel and between its perimeter and each rectangle. The inside of the initials is empty, like the rectangles. The rectangles are 10 in all, one for each mental instruction.

The procedure is as follows: at pre-arranged, pre-determined hours, with the help of an alarm clock (for example, every hour or every two hours), during a certain span of time (say, from 8:00 A.M. to 8:00 P.M.), one writes the initials of his or her own mental construction (great tragedy, average tragedy, little tragedy or very funny comedy, average funny comedy, slightly funny tragedy, operational construction, triumph construction, neutral past memory construction, or dream-for-the-future construction). The choice of one-hour, two-hour, or three-hour intervals depends on our desires and on our possibilities. The initials of these constructions coincide with the corresponding hour in the space underneath. One spins the wheel at the hour established and for the initials of the mental construction he or she is in, to be followed with the tip of a pen so that they remain printed on the sheet beneath. In addition, users must write a short description of the construction in the vertical rectangle below each acronym. Each single sheet underneath the sliced wheel represents the pattern of the day. The hour sheet, therefore, has to be changed every day. Day after day, one has to focus on the pattern and on the content of the 10 constructions at the end of the day.

After a week, the pattern of the constructions in the course of the seven days should be observed and, if desired, assessed. The same procedure has to be followed in subsequent weeks. The exercise ends when respondents feel that they are trained and able to reflect spontaneously on their cognitive functioning, when they learn to recognize the rhythm and melody of their own minds.

Results

Since the only objective of the Wheel of Wisdom is improving understanding of oneself and of the other, any kind of experimentation would be tautological because it would confirm the assumption of the method.

In the clinical experience, instead, we were able to register positive results in hospitalized patients. Depressed patients who completed the written tasks following the organization of the Wheel of Wisdom showed significantly better results in both the Beck and Zung Depression Inventories in comparison to in-patients who did not participate in the same task. The rationale for administering the Wheel of Wisdom was that in depression the wheel is blocked in tragedy constructions, and the wheel helps to overcome this block. The efficacy of the method, in our opinion, is that it gives the possibility to create an interaction between feelings and classifications of feelings by changing the mind-set. One will easily realize that each construction corresponds to a way of "setting" or of organizing the mind to perceive "reality" (note that the word "reality" has quotation marks to stress the relativity of this term).

Moreover, the 10 constructions of the mind's "continuous tape" change as time goes by and depending on different circumstances. If, for example, we mark the succession of our constructions in time, we will find out that we are experiencing a given mental construction at eight in the morning, another one at nine, and very likely still another one at ten, and so on. So we must realize that we are dealing with something that moves along all the time, a sort of mental wheel (the "tape") that never stops.

A WORKBOOK TO INCREASE SELF-AWARENESS

The following workbook is based on the previous constructions about the Tape of the Mind and the Wheel of Wisdom. A single-subject application of this workbook is available in English (Jordan & L'Abate, 1999). A description of the first assignment follows.

SETTING APPOINTMENT TIMES AND CHOOSING THE ORDER OF ADMINISTRATION

The purpose of this assignment is to set times and choose the order of administration for all future homework assignments.

1. *Set Appointments First.* Before you start working on this workbook, you must organize a schedule about how to work on it. This schedule will consist of pre-set, pre-arranged, pre-determined appointment times when you will be working on this workbook for no longer than one hour at one time. These appointments could take place once, twice, or three times a day and once, two, or three times a week, according to the instructions from the mental health professional who is administering this workbook to you. It might be up to you to choose how often you want to work on this workbook or up to the professional who is helping you with this workbook, according to the initial contract (informed consent form) that you have signed to complete this workbook.

What is important is that you must make sure that you choose the specific times on which you are going to work on this workbook beforehand and that you will stick to those pre-set times that you have chosen no matter what (Monday at 9 A.M., Tuesday at 10 P.M., etc.). If, for whatever reason, you are unable to work at the time that you chose beforehand, make an appointment with yourself at least 24 hours ahead. Never work on this workbook on the spur of the moment but always by appointment at least 24 hours ahead of time or even longer.

2. *Defining the Contents of Your Thoughts.* Homework assignments are made up of at least 10 types of thoughts:

(T1) Extremely Painful Tragedies are made up of very tragic, extremely sad experiences and events of great intensity to you that did not allow any escape or solution, like great losses, terrible traumas, major hurts and defeats. These experiences may have produced and provoked intense feelings of shame and guilt in you and may have taught you to become aware of errors and mistakes in your life, influencing your mood very negatively.

(T2) Very Painful Tragedies are experiences or events whose intensity is minor in relationship to extremely painful experiences. One does not deal with total darkness here; there is a light at the end of the tunnel. The themes may be the same, that is, errors, painful experiences, humiliations, losses, defeats, and so on; however, these experiences or events are of lesser importance to you than extremely painful tragedies. Nonetheless, these tragedies influence your mood negatively.

(T3) Somewhat Painful Tragedies are experiences that, although of lesser importance to you than extremely painful and very painful ones, are still somewhat vivid in your mind, including minor losses, small errors, slights and humiliations of lower intensity than the two previous types of tragedies, having little, if any, effect on your mood.

(C1) Extremely Enjoyable Comedies are extremely funny experiences and events in your life that can still make you laugh uproariously and keep you always in a very good mood.

(C2) Very Enjoyable Comedies are different from extremely funny experiences because, even though they may keep you in a good mood, they do not make you laugh.

(C3) Somewhat Enjoyable Comedies consist of enjoyable experiences or events that are pleasant and pleasing but do not make you laugh or keep you in a good mood.

(TD) Things You Have or Need to Do, like going to the grocery store, calling a friend, or paying an overdue bill, and so on, to deal with practical matters that are necessary for daily living.

(TT) Thoughts about Triumphs consist of events or experiences in which you feel victorious, proud of your achievement, indestructible, invincible, and positively full of yourself, making you feel on top of the world.

(MP) Memories from the Past that do not fit into any of the previous categories of thoughts or memories and that are neither tragic nor comedic but that, nevertheless, represent simple memories of rather simple events or experiences in your life.

(DF) Dreams about the Future consist of daydreams, fantasies, aspirations, and hopes for the future about what you would like to see happen in your life to make you feel happier and in a better mood.

3. *Choosing the Order of Assignments.* Now choose in which order you want to work on the homework assignments defined above. Rank which assignment you want to work on first by writing 1 in the proper place, which assignment you want to work on second by writing 2 in the proper place, then third, fourth, and so on until the last assignment is ranked 10.

Title of Assignment	**Rank**
(T1) Extremely Painful Tragedies	____
(T2) Very Painful Tragedies	____
(T3) Somewhat Painful Tragedies	____
(C1) Extremely Enjoyable Comedies	____
(C2) Very Enjoyable Comedies	____

(C3) Somewhat Enjoyable Comedies ____
(TD) Things You Have or Need to Do ____
(TT) Thoughts about Triumphs ____
(MP) Memories from the Past ____
(DF) Dreams about the Future ____

YOU, I, AND THE UNIVERSE: A CARD GAME

You, I, and the Universe is a card game derived from the EPM. By playing this logically based game, one can learn how to reflect on human relations and view them in an original light. To fully understand the logic of this game, one should refer to the description by De Giacomo (1999). However, the rules are summed up in the table of interactions that is provided together with the cards in two versions, a numerical and a graphic version. Players should use the tables only for a short time until they have grasped the logic of the game, then forget about them.

The main point about the game is that it consists of a pack of 16 cards, each of them numbered sequentially from F0 to F15 and each carrying a diagram reproducing one interactive style or characteristic (e.g., Mr./Ms. "Accepter," Mr./Ms. "Mediator," Mr./Ms. "Antagonizer," Mr./Ms. "Pseudoaltruist," etc.).

The game can be played by a single person, like solitaire or else by a number of players who do not, however, play against each other but who alternate in selecting the cards, one from the player's own set of cards and one from the pile placed at the center of the table. Choosing the two cards (from one's own set and from that on the table), hence choosing the two styles represented in those cards, produces a change in accordance with the table of interactions. If the change leads to F0 (i.e., to Mr. or Ms. "Blank"), the player loses one point; if it leads to F15 (i.e., Mr. or Ms. "Total Accepter"), the player gains a half point; if the result is F3 (Mr./Ms. "Aloof"), the player gains one point. If none of the three conditions have been attained, the game goes on (always according to the table of interactions) until the conditions are achieved.

The game can also be played by two persons playing one against the other trying to achieve a higher score. In that case, each player has one set of cards, and the two players play one card at a time, alternately. Each player tries to gain points in such a way that he or she will end up in F3 (+ 1 point) or at least in F15 (+ ½ point), but not in F0 (− 1 point). The turn is concluded when all of the 16 cards in each set of cards have been used. The players may choose whether they want to play a single turn (so the game will be very brief) or several turns (e.g., 10 turns).

Using the same deck of cards, the following alternatives are also possible:

The Altruistic Game. Unlike the game described above, each player tries to make his opponent gain points (clearly, if there is a prize to be won, the game becomes "pseudoaltruistic").

The Endless Game. Players can use an endless number of the 16-card sets, out of which they can choose whichever card they like best. During the game, they must never end up in F0, F3, or F15 and must instead use as many different styles as they possibly can; in other words they will have to avoid, as far as possible, using the same style that they have used before.

All of the above games can be played by teams.

Many more games can be organized depending on the creative ability of the individuals or groups. The card game can be adapted to become a parlor game or as rehearsals for stage actors who could work on the characters described by the cards and on their interactions or could even offer cues for comedy plots. Unfortunately for English-speaking readers, these cards are written in Italian.

RELATIONSHIP STYLES WORKBOOK

Lastly, from the SVQ, the EPM has been translated by both authors into a workbook (L'Abate, 1996, 2002a). This workbook invites respondents to learn how to recognize the 16 styles, one by one, and explains what they mean exactly by giving two examples for each pair of adjectives:

> Once you have understood them thoroughly, you will have to apply them to your own self, having arranged them in an order corresponding to what you believe you are really, starting with number one (a), namely, with the style you use with most people. You then go on to the second style (the style you feel comes next in a classification depicting yourself, i.e. a style that corresponds to the way you are, the third style in the same way, etc.; then you proceed with styles that do not apply to yourself in any way (N/A). Once you have done that, you may ask your spouse or other significant person/persons to classify you (i.e. the workbook user) on the basis of the 16 "terms" listed above. This will enable you to compare your own points of view on how you relate with the point of view of other people who know you well. From this comparison and from the differences that will emerge from it, you will acquire a better awareness of yourself. You can hide your ratings to avoid influencing unduly other raters.

In addition, the workbook suggests a number of procedures that the user can develop either freely or else following certain patterns proposed by its authors. This assignment will give a clearer understanding of the way in which the user perceives self with views of self that may contrast with those of others.

ASSIGNMENT 1. UNDERSTANDING RELATIONSHIP STYLES

The purpose of this assignment is to help you understand various types of relationship styles.

1. There are 16 styles in intimate relationships. Using a dictionary, your partner, a relative, a friend, or a mental health professional, define each pair of words according to what each pair means to you. Please add two examples of your own to make sure that you understood these definitions:

Definitions and Examples of Relationship Styles

a. empty/absent

____

____

Example 1

____

____

Example 2

____

____

b. participant/sharing

____

____

Example 1

____

____

Example 2

____

____

c. solitary/reserved

____

____

Example 1

____

____

Example 2

____

____

d. tenacious/egocentric

____

____

Example 1

____

____

Example 2

____

____

e. docile/surrendering

____

____

Example 1

____

____

Example 2

____

____

f. altruist/involved

____

____

Example 1

____

____

Example 2

____

____

g. mysterious/ambiguous

____

____

Example 1

____

____

Example 2

____

____

h. collaborative/mediator

Example 1

Example 2

i. abstract/unpredictable

Example 1

Example 2

j. sharing/innovative

Example 1

Example 2

k. rebel/antagonist

Example 1

Example 2

____

____

l. dominant/dictatorial

____

____

Example 1

____

____

Example 2

____

____

m. two-faced/false altruist

____

____

Example 1

____

____

Example 2

____

____

n. unpredictable/altruist

____

____

Example 1

____

____

Example 2

____

____

o. inconclusive/disorganized

____

____

Example 1

____

____

Example 2

____

____

p. confused/chaotic

____

____

Example 1

____

____

Example 2

____

____

2. Now that you understand various types of relationship styles, it is important to find out how they apply to you. Rank-order them according to how much they apply to you. Rank as No. 1 the style that applies to you the most. Rank-order as No. 2 the style that applies to you next, and so on until you reach a style that does not apply to you (N/A). If you have trouble ranking these styles, ask your partner to help you out in this ranking and make yourself available to your partner to help with his or her ranking of these styles in his or her assignment. Often one who is outside us is able to see us more accurately than we can. By the same token, you may be able to see your partner more accurately than he or she can.

Styles	**Rank Orders**			
	First	**Partner***	**Other****	**Final**
a. empty/absent	____	____	____	____
b. participant/sharing	____	____	____	____
c. solitary/reserved	____	____	____	____
d. tenacious/egocentric	____	____	____	____
e. docile/surrendering	____	____	____	____
f. altruist/involved	____	____	____	____
g. mysterious/ambiguous	____	____	____	____
h. collaborative/mediator	____	____	____	____
i. abstract/unpredictable	____	____	____	____
j. sharing/innovative	____	____	____	____

k. rebel/antagonist	____	____	____	____
l. dominant/dictatorial	____	____	____	____
m. two-faced/false altruist	____	____	____	____
n. unpredictable/altruist	____	____	____	____
o. inconclusive/disorganized	____	____	____	____
p. confused/chaotic	____	____	____	____

*Indicate here who your Partner or Relative is: ____________________

**Indicate here who Other is: ____________________

3. Ask your partner (if you have one), relative, or friend to help you by ranking how these styles apply to you, independently of your ranking. Ask your partner (relative or friend) to rank-order these styles independently of your rank order. Write or type this list on a separate sheet of paper and give it to your partner, relative, or friend, without their seeing the rank order of your styles as you see them in yourself. By the same token, help your partner by rank-ordering his or her relationship styles.

4. Now you need to ask Other, who knows you very well (parents, siblings, relatives, close friends), to rank-order these styles as they apply to you. To make sure that this rank order is independent from yours, type or write this list on a separate sheet of paper.

Homework: During the next week, compare and contrast your rank order with the two rank orders of your partner, relative, or friend and write down (under Final) how you would re-rank these styles on the basis of the feedback that you received from your partner, relative, and Other.

CONCLUSION

This chapter includes examples of preventive and psychotherapeutic applications that derive in part from the EPM.

Chapter 10

Model-Derived Interventions for Clinical Relationships

Before going any further into this chapter, we need to understand what is meant by psychotherapy and what kind of process is followed in practicing it.

DEFINING PSYCHOTHERAPY

By psychotherapy we mean the medical treatment of illness by psychological means. However, this definition appears to be too generic and limited to a medical vision. Another definition is that psychotherapy is an interpersonal process aiming at modifying feelings, knowledge, attitudes, and behavior that have proven disturbing for the person who is seeking aid from an expert professional. A criticism of this definition is that it does not take into consideration psychotic patients, insofar as most of them are not aware of their illness and do not seek aid. Furthermore, not everybody agrees with the claim that psychotherapy is the exclusive domain of expert professionals. Finally, it does not take into account the interactive perspective in which one works not only with one person but with the system as a whole (e.g., the family), and one operates as part of a team of experienced professionals, rather than as a single psychotherapist.

A very recent definition says that psychotherapy is an intervention based (almost) exclusively on an interpersonal relation, prolonged in time, with a more or less explicit program, aimed at alleviating psychological distress, at modifying a behavior or interpersonal relation or an existential condition.

An analysis of this definition leads us to a fundamental distinction; first, there are psychotherapies in which the therapeutic program is agreed upon by psychotherapist and patient, and others in which the program is not defined. Second, some psychotherapies are prevalently aimed at modifying psychological distress, and others are aimed at modifying behavior. Thus, at least in a heuristic sense, the difference emerges between therapies aiming at solving a problem ("problem-solving") and therapies aimed at increasing awareness ("insight therapy"). For example, faced with anorexia nervosa, the therapist can take two fundamentally different attitudes, that is, aim at solving the problem of anorexia or work with the subject so that he or she might achieve a greater self-knowledge. The first attitude is typical of behavioral therapy and of some models of interactive therapy like ours; the second is typical of orthodox psychoanalysis. The first leads to the possibility of quantifying, while the second one doesn't.

A second possible distinction is between therapies that intervene mainly on the cognitive level and those that intervene on the affective level; for example, cognitive behavioral therapy (e.g., Beck's depression therapy, in which depression is traced to a belief system that acts on a cognitive level). Also, certain types of interactive therapies (prescription of the symptom and of rules, positive connotation, etc.) act on a cognitive level, while psychoanalysis, by definition, works on the unconscious (i.e., on the affective) level.

It seems to us that a definition of psychotherapy according to the vision adopted by this chapter should contain the following elements:

1. a model of human relations,
2. a model of the process of change of these human relations,
3. a temporal map, and
4. an invariable element. While the first three points have been discussed, point 4 has not yet been treated. Our viewpoint is the following.

In order to introduce predictability, it may be useful to introduce an invariable element. Theoretical considerations that we cannot expound here indicate that in order to know and modify a system, introducing a fixed formula of intervention is of great importance. It, in fact, allows us to observe how the system organizes itself around this fixed point. Through this information we can pick out the characteristics of the system and therefore organize the instruments to modify it. In other terms, by introducing a standardized perturbation in the system, we force it to change; the manner in which it changes is a clue to its organization and functioning. It is a route to understanding it and to modifying it. It is a key, a passe-partout, opening black boxes and complex structures.

Creativity, Metaphors, High-Impact Statements

Beyond all these considerations and whatever model one follows, there is always an emerging process that can be defined as creativity. The model adopted by the therapist is an important element in our work, but it is certainly not sufficient for doing psychotherapy. There is always the successive and unpredictable step of the dialectical passage from form to process. Peseschkian reports an old Persian proverb that says that one cannot fly with only one wing; theory and creativity are the two wings that allow us to carry out our task as psychotherapists in an adequate manner.

At this point it would be interesting to introduce the issue of metaphor, which we do not intend to treat in this book but promise to discuss in a later publication. One could also discuss the many phrases that we use in our work that belong to a language shared by the group belonging to our "school," as, for example, when we say, "the feeling of guilt is the cement of the family." We instead report a series of therapeutic pointers, drawn from our experiences, that emerged in our consciousness as brilliant ideas capable of solving extemporaneously a small or large therapeutic impasse. On the issue of Compass Sentences, see Chapter 9.

A GENERAL OUTLINE OF RELATIONAL PSYCHOTHERAPY

Working with a lot of cases, we thought of a general map to organize sessions to increase the strength of each single session. In several cases presented before, we saw that the fifth session (a session characterized in our model by the presence of a supervisor behind the one-way mirror) was particularly meaningful. We will see how this idea was transferred also in the simple psychiatric visit. A general set of interventions may be the following.

First stage—acquisition of therapeutic power through the "pact with the devil" or "the empty box."

Second stage—giving a prescription that (1) involves the family, usually the whole family and sometimes only a spouse, (2) interacts with the patient focusing on the symptom, (3) according to an interactive mode, goes toward the world of the patient (i.e., toward the problem presented by the patient), and (4) amplifies paradoxically (i.e., according to unpredictable modes, i.e., according to a modality that does not exist in the conscious world of interacting subjects) and according to certain temporal methods (following certain "temporal maps").

Many interventions that we mentioned before took place in a certain psychotherapeutic setting, constituted by cycles of 10 sessions at one-week intervals, each lasting one hour, carried out by a member of our clinical group, with supervision on the 5th session (half cycle) and at the 10th session (end of cycle) by the senior therapist of the group, who is usually entrusted with particularly powerful interventions.

Such interventions, however, can be utilized outside a given therapeutic

Figure 10-1
Optimizing the Psychiatric Visit

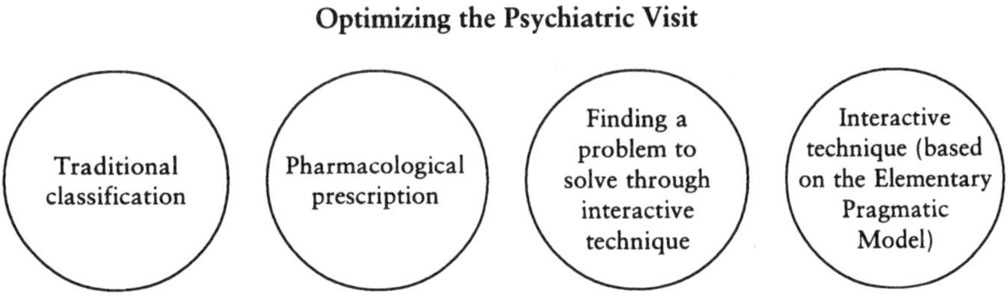

setting. In fact, we hope that, far from remaining the exclusive domain of psychotherapists, they will also be adopted by, for example, physicians who usually, for professional reasons or due to a personal propensity toward pharmaceutical treatment or on account of their traditional training, and so on, see patients only for a very limited time.

In other words, professionals benefiting from these techniques could also be psychiatrists or physicians who see their patients in their office or clinic, make a diagnosis, and set up a pharmacological intervention. They could utilize these techniques in those cases in which their usual treatment (and the usual support interview) fails to obtain good results or when through these brief interactive interventions they want to increase the efficiency of the results obtained with medications.

OPTIMIZING THE PSYCHIATRIC VISIT

The way we operationalize our work makes it easy to integrate our approach with the traditional psychiatric visit (De Giacomo, Margari, & Rutigliano, 1997 [Appendix D]). "Optimization of the psychiatric visit" means that the psychiatrist during the visit, in addition to diagnosis based on DSM-IV and medical prescriptions, should pick a specific problem of the patient and his or her family and give a behavioral prescription as described before in this chapter or give some workbook, as, for example, the "Wheel of Wisdom" or a statement with psychological impact like those described in Chapter 9 (see Figure 10-1).

In a broader sense, schematizing and optimizing the psychiatric visit mean improving our diagnostic capability, our capability in using medication, and our capability of using ourselves as agents of change and establishing a therapeutical relation, for example, developing efficacious tools for interventions.

The way the second author works is based on the following points:

1. Give advice and prescriptions when you have the power to do so. Such power derives from:
    a. Transference with the patient and with the patient's family (e.g., patients who have been reporting to him or her for years).
    b. Specific interventions such as "the pact with the devil" and "the empty box."
2. Work on the crisis. If the patient declares that he or she feels bad, right then encourage him or her to feel as bad as he or she can, so that one can realize what is really the matter, by causing the crisis to occur during the session.
    a. For example, a lunch session with a girl with anorexia nervosa (consisting of letting the parents make the daughter eat during the session).
    b. Another example: a patient is complaining about a sense of dizziness: make him or her stand on the table with closed eyes.
    c. One more example: a patient cannot swallow: make him or her eat a cookie.
    d. Invite the patient to try to feel as bad as he or she can.
    e. If the patient calls you on the phone, saying that the medication that you prescribed made him or her feel sick, summon him or her to your office and find out if he or she really feels bad. In most cases, treatment need not be discontinued. Trying to carry on with the same therapy is in itself an important therapeutic intervention (F3).
    f. We can also use the information that fear is something that increases initially but then declines and eventually disappears.
3. Use spatial arrangements in your office or therapy room.
4. Use unpredictable therapeutic moves (enlist creativity).
5. Acting is often better than talking.
6. Place the problem into your intimate relationships.
7. Use the timing technique (e.g., prescribe medication and tell patients that unless you find some benefit when you see him or her again in a month's time, the next prescription will be for a very difficult exercise. When prescribing medication, cross out on a calendar the 30th day since the beginning of medication and give it to the patient).
8. Transmit to patients the ability to equip themselves with mental constructions that can help them out of the problem. For instance, a patient learned to avoid states of excitement through a technique that he had discovered.
9. Learn from the patient.
10. Small moves are useful.
11. Keep note of sentences that the patients will recall (e.g., "she was developing muscles in her mind"; while husband and wife are having an argument, say that "they where having an intercourse" or that "depressed mothers have good children").
12. Be enigmatic (as suggested in Chapter 9 using Compass Sentences).
13. Let time work.

14. Solving the symptom does not mean that the patient is satisfied.
15. Some patients recover, whatever the intervention.
16. Some patients will not recover, whatever the intervention.
17. Some patients recover with us "in spite" of another colleague who worked with them earlier.
18. Some patients recover later on with other colleagues "in spite of" our interventions.

THE PRACTICE OF RELATIONAL PSYCHOTHERAPY

In this chapter a number of examples are described about how our group works clinically on the basis of the EPM and the 18 contextual considerations just given. The first step (the first floor) of the model consists of triads of reality as seen by the world of the first party, reality as seen by the world of the second party, and the change in the world of the first subject after the interaction (see Figure 10-2). Let us give as an example the reading of a patient's dreams. The subject of the dream was in a given internal or external situation (he or she was in a certain state of his or her world); he or she interacts with another person, with another situation, within another set, or within another world; what happens?

Example 1. I dreamed I was the secretary of the Psychiatric Department. During a meeting there was a big mess, but in the end I was able to draw up the minutes of the meeting very clearly.

Reading of the dream: I was participating in the department meeting to pursue some objectives (I was pursuing an aim creatively) (set A) (for EPM experts F9). There was a big mess; the voices of all the participants were overlapping, and it was impossible to understand anything (set B) (for EPM experts F15). In the end, I was able to draw up the minutes of the meeting in a very clear and clever way (result of the interaction of set A with set B) (for EPM experts F9 that leads to the following formula F9 × F15 = F9).

Example 2. A young lady reported that she had met a dear friend of hers on the beach. She got near her to greet her very warmly and have a chat with her (she creatively pursued a goal) (set A) (for EPM experts F9) and suddenly realized that her friend had grown older and uglier (a negative answer from the world) (set B) (for EPM experts F0). So, the young lady entered a state of doubt (set C) (for EPM experts F6) and, finally, of deep depression (she felt down—in EPM terms, F0) (for EPM experts F9 × F0 = F6 that gives F6 × F6 = F0).

The second step (floor) of the model is represented in the four coordinates of the interaction. An example of its use in practice is the intervention represented in Figure 10-3.

However, most interventions arise from the third step (floor) of EPM,

Figure 10-2
The Triads of the EPM

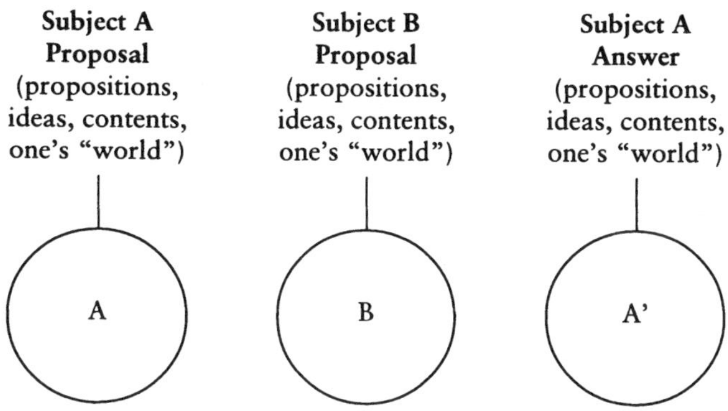

Figure 10-3
The Four Coordinates of the EPM

It should be explained that to function properly, a couple must achieve a harmonious combination of four aspects: entering the other person's world, maintaining their own world, recognizing shared aspects, and learning how to create something new and unexpected.

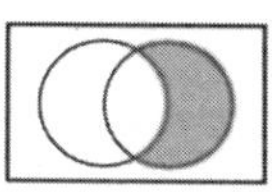

Entering the other person's world, recognizing the other's world.
For example: asking the husband to say what his wife likes; what her world contains, what gifts she would accept, what actions she would appreciate on his part, etc. Then the wife would answer the same question.

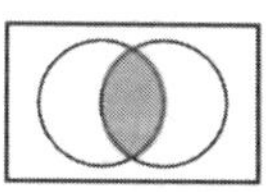

Recognizing shared aspects.
Asking them to mention those aspects that are common to both, the goals they share, the aspects of life that both enjoy, the activities they can do together, etc.

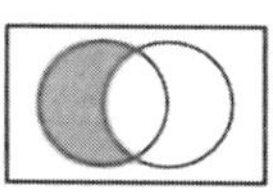

Recognizing their own world and maintaining it.
The characteristics of that person's world should be defined, their ideas, aims, preferences, philosophy, tendencies, etc. Each member of the couple should give these definitions clearly in turn.

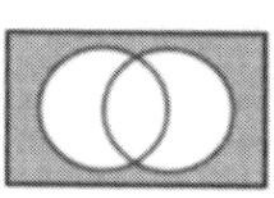

Creating something new and unexpected.
They are asked to demonstrate their creativity by means of proposing unusual, unexpected things to do, deciding to do something strange or crazy, and also to find solutions to problems based on creativity, problem solving, etc. The program "The Tape of the Mind" may be used (De Giacomo, 1995/1999).

the 16 relational styles or functions. They inspire most interventions by taking into account the meaning of the interactive styles of patients and the interactive styles that therapists need to use in relating with them.

In Figure 10-4 summarized interventions are linked with the 16 styles of the model. Later in this chapter we describe some of them.

THE EMPTY BOX

Before describing interventions with a variety of psychiatric disorders, an overall interventional stance to increase the therapeutic power of the therapist will be described: the "empty box." This is a prescription generally used as an alternative prescription to Jay Haley's (1976) "pact with the devil." In the first session, after the phase of socialization and presentation of the problem, the therapist has already acquired a considerable amount of power with the family (generally around the last 15 minutes in a one-hour session). The family is asked whether they are ready to do anything to solve the problem. When they ask for explanations, one can vaguely answer that by "ready to do anything" one means ready even to "stand on their head and put their feet up in the air." If the family answers affirmatively, then there is no problem, and one can go on with a usual prescription. If, instead, the family appears to have any doubts (or if they are ambiguous in their answers), we proceed with our prescription.

The prescription consists of saying that the therapist knows what the family must do in order to solve the problem (i.e., he knows the solution to the problem), but he cannot reveal it because the family is not ready to receive it yet, and the family is sent away until the next week, without a prescription.

Generally, at the next session, one sees that the family has mobilized itself to understand what the therapist's mysterious solution is. They ask if the solution is this one or that one, proposing a series of solutions of their own (which, by the way, are very useful in understanding the world of the family). However, the therapist does not reveal the solution, claiming that the family is not "ripe" enough to receive it and that she or he wants guarantees before saying it. Such guarantees consist of the fact that they must show their readiness to accept the solution by doing this or that. They are given traditional prescriptions, which are effective in modifying the system's dysfunction.

In some cases we proceed with this track for a certain number of sessions, giving various prescriptions but not the "final" one. At a certain point, due to the combined effect of the traditional prescriptions and of the "empty" prescription not yet given, the symptom disappears. At this point the problem of revealing the mystery, of opening the empty box that the therapist had given the family, presents itself. There are various solutions about what the therapist can say:

Figure 10-4
The 16 Functions of the EPM and Interventions Arising from Them

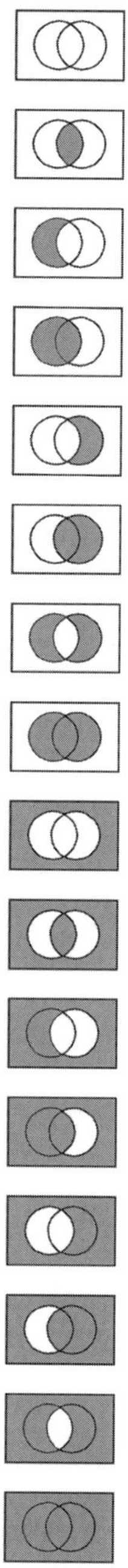

Function	Description	Interventions
F0	Characterized by the impossibility of a relationship	Periodic withdrawal
F1	Characterized only by sharing	Tabulation of complaints Fill in the intersection List of thoughts
F2	Withdrawal into one's own world	Periodic withdrawal
F3	Maintaining one's own world	Pact with the devil Space distribution Strengthening the weak member
F4	Giving in to the world of the other	Sculpturing the parents Entering into the other's world Entering into delusion Form-process intervention Von Domarus intervention Acting the problem Tabulation of complaints List of thoughts Massage
F5	Entering the world of the other	
F6	Maintaining one's own world and accepting the world of the other, but not of the shared elements	
F7	Maintaining one's own world, accepting the world of the other and sharing	Filling in the intersection by broadening the interacting subjects' world Act like go-between in the communication Act like participating witnesses Sculpturing the parents
F8	Impossibility of engaging in a relationship with the tendency to use elements belonging to neither one's own world nor that of the other	Speaking pure "schizophrenese" Speaking partial "schizophrenese"
F9	Sharing and using elements that are outside of one's own world and that of the other	Appear united like body and soul Prescription of the four rules
F10	Mary, Mary quite contrary	Pact with the devil Holding Training to put up with the problem Exercise of the rules Bringing the world home Looking at oneself in the mirror
F11	Maintaining one's own world and using outside elements	
F12	Total renunciation of one's own world and using outside elements	Entering into delusion Form-process intervention Von Domarus intervention Acting the problem Paying attention to the attention of others Mourning session Tabulation of complaints Prediction of worsening List of thoughts Going around two chairs Massage
F13	Entering the world of the other and using outside elements	
F14	Accepting everything except what is shared	
F15	Total acceptance	Empty box Imitating repressed troubles

1. Now that the family has solved the problem, it is useless to talk about it.
2. The family has understood the solution that the therapist had in mind, but it is best not to talk about it.
3. The solution is X (corresponding to one of the solutions proposed by the family).
4. The solution is X and can cite what is truly the "knot" (problem) that has brought the family to therapy.

ANOREXIA NERVOSA

Anorexia is an eating disorder prevalent in adolescence that almost always manifests itself in females. It is characterized by (1) fear of getting fat (which does not diminish with weight loss); (2) disorders in body perception (like feeling fat even when emaciated); (3) loss of weight until cachexia sets in due to the reduction of food intake (especially fats and carbohydrates). In certain cases there are episodes of bulimia, induced vomiting, use of laxatives and diuretics, and almost constant physical hyperactivity and lack of sexual interest. As for physical disorders, it causes amenorrhea and lanugo. In the advanced phases it causes hypothermia, bradycardia, edemas, and metabolic imbalance. The mortality rate is from 15% to 21%, generally induced by cardiac arrest.

As far as the characteristics of families with an anorexic member are concerned, the extant literature is readily available to English-speaking readers. The four characteristics that can be observed in psychosomatic families are (1) enmeshment, (2) overprotectiveness, (3) rigidity, and (4) avoidance of conflicts.

1. *Enmeshment*. This term means the high resonance with which the system reflects even the smallest change in a member. The consequence of this characteristic is little differentiation in boundaries both between the subsystems and between individual members. In the enmeshed family, one observes, in a very redundant manner, that a member speaks about what another member thinks or feels, a very frequent use of the first person plural next to a clear difficulty in using the first person singular, a high percentage of interference in dyadic interactions, and so on. The tendency to share everything obviously implies an obstacle to individual tendencies toward differentiation and autonomy and to the definition of roles that are functionally and structurally adequate.
2. *Overprotectiveness*. This term means that the component members of the system appear excessively interested in and/or worried about the welfare of each other. Such overinvolvement appears as an interactive style of the system, considered both globally and in its individual components.
3. *Rigidity*. This term means the difficulty experienced by the family in finding and carrying out new interactive possibilities in response to stress or change. The family seeks, at any price, to maintain the status quo, opposing any biological, economic, social, and cultural event that could lead to a recalibration. The symp-

tomatic behavior can mask, for example, the ineffectiveness of the adaptive abilities of the system toward the old age decline of the parental couple.

4. *Avoidance of Conflict.* This term means that a family considers tension and conflict "catastrophic," so it adopts various modalities of avoidance. In this type of family, conflict is generally implicit and denied, but when it reaches a certain level, although usually a very low one, that is deemed dangerous, there is an immediate mobilization of the members of the system, who through an interactive game of alliances, marginalizations, interest, or faulting of the sick member, submerge and cover up the conflict again.

As far as the second author's experiences are concerned, one of the things that has constantly struck him in families of anorexic patients is the presence of a peripheral father, generally considered as a non-entity by the family (even if very successful in his professional field or generally outside the family). Our quick technique focuses on untying this knot. It can be synthesized in the formula father F5 toward the daughter. Presently, the intervention has been greatly standardized. If applied in an optimal manner, in several cases it leads to a positive result in just one session. In the following session, in fact, it is ascertained that the girl has started eating again and has gained weight.

The intervention is as follows: The whole family is called into the office. The father and the mother sit facing each other. The therapist is in front of the parents, behind a desk. The children are sitting next to each other behind the parents with the chairs leaning against the wall.

After the usual joining, the family presents the case. Generally the voice of the mother prevails, and the worry of the family and the severity of the situation are stressed. The therapist agrees with the severity of the case and even tries to accentuate it, by claiming that a life is at stake. He states that the situation is extremely difficult even at the therapeutic level, and he doubts whether anything can be done.

The family looks very anxious. The therapist asks, one at a time, each member of the family, including the patient, whether he or she is ready to do anything, truly anything, to overcome the problem. Everyone says yes. At this point the therapist and the patient's father go into a nearby consulting room, where the patient is asked to undress, almost completely, and she weighs herself on a scale. The father checks her weight personally. Generally, the father seems shocked in seeing his daughter reduced to a skeleton, and even the daughter appears anxious because of the situation.

Then they all go back to the therapy room, where the rest of the family has remained. Father and daughter are placed facing each other, near the therapist's desk, while the mother is invited to sit in the chair previously occupied by the daughter. Then the father is invited to make a detailed inquiry of the daughter's eating problems: what she prefers to eat, what she wants to eat, what she feels, what type of menu she would prefer, if

Figure 10-5
Interventions in Anorexia Nervosa to Increase the Interactions between Father and Daughter

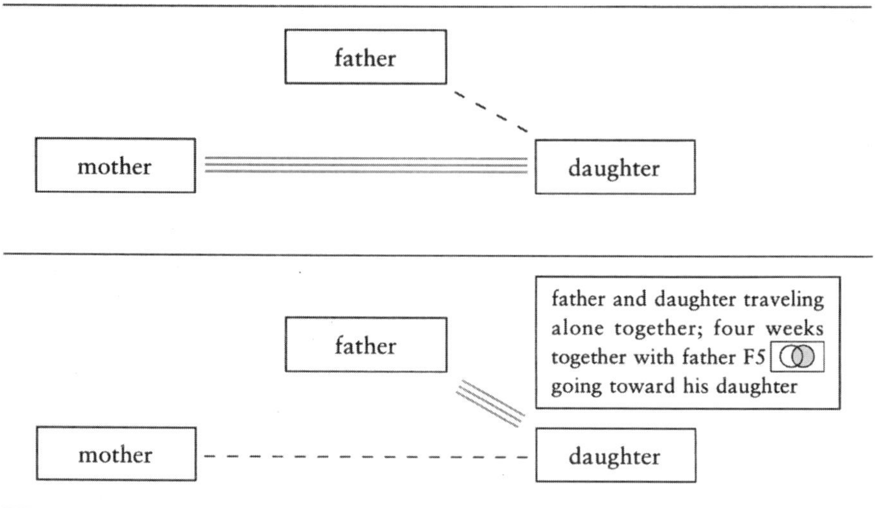

she vomits, and if so, when, where, and how, if she takes laxatives, and so on.

At this point the therapist pauses, full of suspense, and asks everyone if he or she is ready to do anything to help the girl, because what he is about to ask is extremely difficult to carry out. Once the therapist receives the assurance that they are all ready to do anything, with appropriate pauses, he asks the father and the daughter to take a one-month trip together to a different city or place where they have no relatives or friends and to be together 24 hours a day. They will be able to phone home only once a day. During this long period of togetherness, the father will try to enter the daughter's world, and the daughter will help the father to enter into her world (interactive style F5) (see Figure 10-5).

As an added element, one can encourage the mother by saying that one realizes what a sacrifice one is asking but that it is necessary for the daughter's sake. During the month, she will be able to devote herself to the other children or to herself. In the brief lapse of time before the departure, she will be able to advise the father on how to behave toward the daughter during the absence, given the husband's lack of experience with the daughter's needs. In the minds of mothers of anorexic girls, there is almost always the idea that the father is an unrefined man, incapable of interacting with the mother herself and, of course, the daughter.

BULIMIA NERVOSA

In bulimia, interventions, besides bringing closer the father and the daughter, are more articulated and complex than in anorexia nervosa (see Figures 10-6, 10-7, and 10-8).

SCHIZOPHRENIA

This section presents how schizophrenic disorders are treated. Results from this process (De Giacomo et al., 1997) compared a group of schizophrenic patients treated only by medication and another group treated by medications plus 10 sessions of family therapy utilizing interventions of the kind described below.

A Patient Suffering from Hallucinations: Whispering Voices

Here we are dealing with a family with a schizophrenic patient who has greatly improved but is still suffering from hallucinations. The whole family is present, including an uncle who is a physician. The therapist is F. Margari, and the supervisor is De Giacomo. It's the usual fifth session in which De Giacomo comes into the therapy room and organizes the prescription of going toward the patient's problem, to be followed by all family members.

The prescription consists in ordering that, in turn, all family members speak to the patient, but in such soft voices that he or she cannot hear. On the other hand, the patient will commit himself or herself to grasp what the relatives are whispering to him or her. The explanation given for the exercise is that it aims at reducing the "overlistening attitude" of the patient. At the sixth session the patient reports that the voices have disappeared.

A Schizophrenic Patient Who Was Worried About His Family Being Worried Over Him

This case involves a family composed of father, mother, a brother, a young male paranoid schizophrenic patient, and a younger sister. They are part of an experimental program of family therapy involving schizophrenics. The therapist is psychologist Antonietta Santoni-Rugiu. The intervention comes from the patient saying that what worries him the most is his family worrying about him.

The intervention consists in asking parents, and brother, and sister to work hard at pretending that it is not a problem whenever the patient behaves in such a manner as to create a problem. The son, on his part, must pay a lot of attention to discern from the family's attitude, even the smallest sign that he's creating a problem.

Figure 10-6
Interventions in Bulimia Nervosa (1)

Optimizing the Psychiatric Visit: Bulimia Nervosa

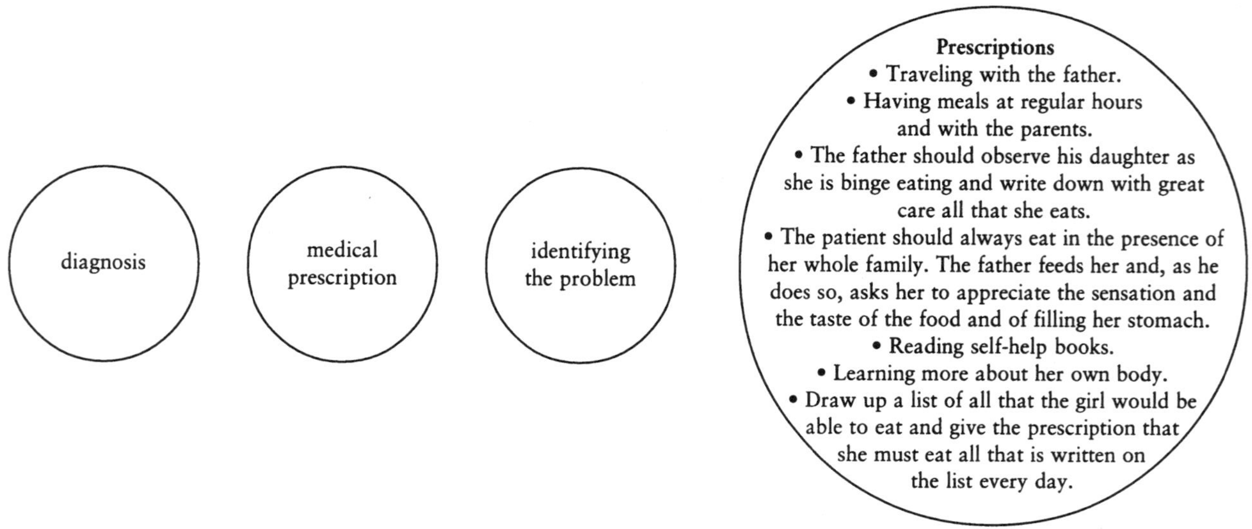

Figure 10-7
Interventions in Bulimia Nervosa (2)

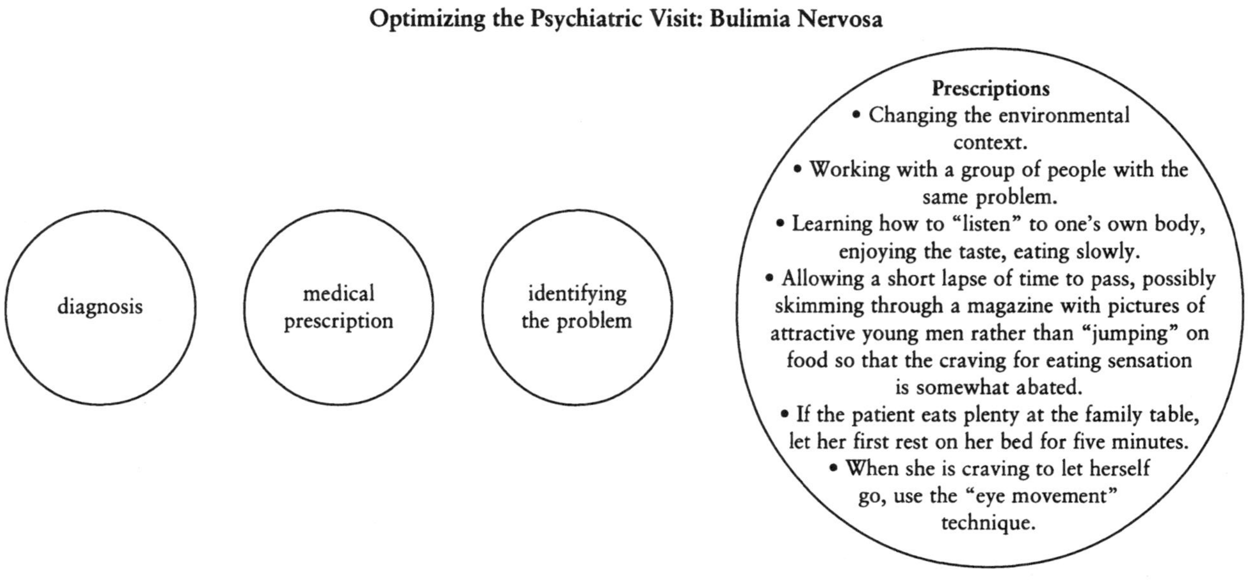

Figure 10-8
Interventions in Bulimia Nervosa (3)

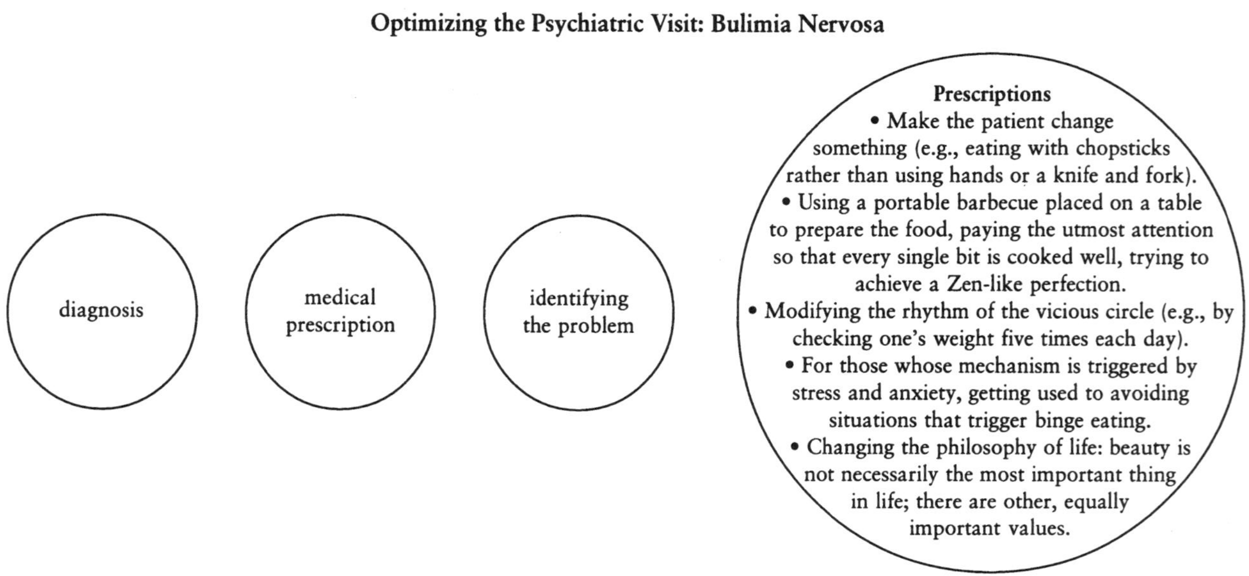

In the next session, after one week, it is reported that the family atmosphere is a lot more relaxed than usual; the patient has started working again and has never noticed any signs of worry in his family members.

Other Interventions in Schizophrenia

The previously described interventions, based on the function F9, are a fundamental component of the therapeutic strategy that we use in schizophrenia. Of course, other therapeutic maneuvers seem useful in certain cases of systems with a schizophrenic member. They are interventions that, in contrast with the previous one, involve the patient. The difficulty encountered in working in a way that directly involves the patient is that often the prescriptions are not carried out. This problem arises from the fact that the schizophrenic patient "does not accept rules." That is, it seems that the basic rule of the schizophrenic is not accepting rules.

To give an example, a schizophrenic woman would kneel to pray because she said she heard the voice of God telling her to do so. I instructed her to kneel and pray for a half hour each day, which she did not do, even if she spontaneously ceased to kneel (we do not know if this improvement was due to drugs that we prescribed). Then I asked her to concentrate her thoughts on "religious things" for 15 minutes three times a day. At the next session, she said she had not done it. Then I asked her if she wanted to learn to control her own thoughts so she could escape the "influences" of others (almost all schizophrenics have the idea that others can influence their thoughts, can command them to steal, etc.). The patient answered that she wanted to carry out the prescription but that it was difficult for her.

This rule of not following rules seems more true the more the patient appears to be fragmented. In instances of serious fragmentation one has the impression that there is no solid point to gain leverage in order to obtain a change. It seems that the degree of entropy is too high, that the dialectic of form-process is most often blocked on the process side. In these cases, it is absolutely necessary to work with the context (i.e., with the other members of the family). There are, however, some cases, less serious ones, sometimes in a phase of remission, with a lower degree of entropy, mostly blocked on the level of form (i.e., the patients are capable of creating mental constructions) in which it is possible to involve the patient directly in the therapeutic intervention.

We present, then, a series of examples of therapeutic interventions that are possible when there is a minimum of structure, compatible with the execution of prescriptions (i.e., the acceptance of the fact that it is the therapist who assigns the rules).

A young schizophrenic patient had auditory hallucinations. She perceived a woman's voice coming from behind her head that would say, "Fuck you!

Fuck you!" In spite of the fact that she had been under a drug treatment she had shown no improvement. The patient was hospitalized in a psychiatric clinic with a high dose of psychotropic drugs. The family was composed of the father, a weak and submissive man; the mother, a South American woman who seemed as if she could no longer stand the sight of her daughter; and several brothers and sisters. The situation seemed extremely difficult, because the mother absolutely did not want to take her back into the home. The father had no power to make his voice heard, the drugs were having no effect, and the symptoms, in spite of the in-patient milieu, were stationary. At this point I delivered my intervention, and it resolved the situation with three sessions.

During the joining, a good relationship had been established between myself, the girl, and the mother which certainly contributed to their acceptance of my prescription. The first prescription regarded the daughter only; she was instructed to carry it out at the clinic. She was to make a tabulation of the voice, that is, write down in a notebook the beginning and end of the voice, with a great degree of accuracy, timing it with her watch. The girl carried out the prescription scrupulously. The second prescription, which was given during the session and then continued at home after her discharge from the hospital, was that the mother was supposed to put herself behind the daughter and whisper to her, with the same tone as the voices, "Fuck you! Fuck you!" When I gave this prescription the mother laughed for the first time since she was in therapy, and the daughter was perplexed, as it did not seem right to her for a mother to insult her daughter. The prescription, however, was carried out.

Since the mother could not stand the daughter, so much so that she had explicitly said that she did not want her at home, the prescription should be interpreted as going toward the world of the mother by amplifying (F13). The effect of the intervention was certainly positive, because it finally led to the disappearance of the hallucination, to an overall improvement in the clinical picture, to the discharge of the patient, and to a good level of reintegration in society, so much so that one and a half years later the situation seemed satisfactory.

An intervention that we frequently used in the course of sessions with schizophrenic patients is that of the "triangle." It was used the first time with a catatonic patient who never spoke spontaneously. He truly seemed completely devoid of will, as catatonics are described in psychopathology textbooks. During a session, we prescribed that the parents speak through the son. The father would suggest to the son the words that he wanted to say to the wife, and the son would repeat them to the mother. Then the mother would say to the son the words that she wanted to say to her husband, and the patient repeated them, and so forth. Thus, a kind of therapeutic echolalia was created, producing positive results.

Of course, it is possible to prescribe different types of triangles besides the one mentioned above. For example, if the son is allied with the mother against the father, we ask the father to question the son; the son, in his turn must answer what his mother prompts him in his ear to say, using the same tone and words of the mother. In other words, the son must be the mother's voice, and vice versa if the son is allied with the father. The example that we mentioned before referred to a case of equidistance of the son from his parents.

These interventions can be classified as "interventions about process" rather than about form, and in terms of functions they correspond to different styles, sometimes F1, sometimes F5, at others F11, and at others yet, F13, according to specific cases and interacting subjects.

An example of F11, an intervention in which the therapist appears to be very demanding and hardly interested in considering the world of the family, even if he has an interest in overcoming the symptoms, can be found in the case of a young psychotic who was annoyed by the noise made by the upstairs neighbors (up to the point of forming delusional persecutory interpretations). We gave the prescription that all family members, gathered together in specific periods of the day, in turn make a noise (which the patient had selected as the most annoying), so as "to train the patient to increase his threshold of resistance." The patient was supposed to signal when he could not take the noise any longer, and at this point the family members were supposed to stop, let him rest, and then start again for the amount of time prescribed.

Another intervention based on the same therapeutic function (F11) was used in the case of a young autistic patient. The symptom was not relieved at all until we thought of a strange prescription; that is, given that the patient did not feel like facing the outside world, the outside world must be brought home to him. The father, an amateur filmmaker, and the mother were given the task of filming the places that terrified the boy the most (the street near the house, the inside of the supermarket, a stadium full of people, etc.). It was then prescribed that the parents and the son watch the film together for three hours a day until the next session. At the next session the parents announced that the boy had finally gone out of the house.

An intervention characterized by the reduction of interactions (which can be seen as an F0) is that of prescribing to stay far away from one another for a certain amount of time, that is, to stay together only for a certain period of time determined during the therapy. An example of this process was the Rubini family. This family had an obsessive son, a pre-psychotic daughter, and a husband with atypical depression. The principal problem was the daughter's violence. In this family, usually in the afternoons, there were big fights due to a series of reciprocal interferences in which each sought to control the activities of the others. For example, the father would enter the daughter's room and reproach her because her room was messy, the daughter expected the mother to stay at home all day at her complete service and complained if she did not help her do her homework, the mother went to check the daughter's homework, and the brother would then hit the sister because he could not study on account of the noise that she made. In short, it was a big mess. We gave the prescription that every afternoon, for two hours, each one was to stay locked up in a different room.

As the reader may have already noticed, we have a preferential line of interventions for schizophrenia based on the style of appearing "bound like body and soul" on the parents' past, but many other styles can be proposed. It is not possible for us to describe them all.

We conclude this section by mentioning that when parents do not follow the therapist's prescription (e.g., the "four rules" quoted above), or even just when we want them to preventively decrease the "resistance" (i.e., the non-acceptance) to their executions of the four rules), we tell them that "schizophrenic disorder" implies, on one hand, the patient's disorders and, on the other, the disobedience of the parents to the therapist's advice.

PARANOID DISORDERS

In these cases, patients exhibit delusions (erroneous and incorrigible ideas) of persecution, reporting that someone wants to hurt them or their family, someone wants to kill, damage, or ridicule them, without serious signs of mental incongruity or of hallucinations or organic problems. Under this heading we can place some jealousy delusions (unjustified certainty of a spouse's infidelity).

Some clinical cases treated by the second author are summarized below.

In 1981 a couple came to my office, Giorgio, aged 37, and Claudia, aged 31, married, with two children. They were accompanied by his mother, her brother (a priest), and his brother-in-law. Giorgio had been working for nine years in a manufacturing industry, he had always been a well-liked and a scrupulous worker, and she was a housewife. The reason for the visit was the family members' concern for Giorgio's behavior. He seemed very frightened and had told people that stolen goods had been stashed in his house to frame him (in reality there had been a burglary near their house). Furthermore, he had torn to pieces a 100.000 liras bill without explaining his gesture. That had been a bad period for the couple; they had been forced to tear down a veranda that they had built on their balcony with many sacrifices, the factory management had threatened to reduce or even take away his overtime (here we must clarify that, in reality, firms were going through difficult times because of the economic crisis), and finally, there had been a quarrel with his brother for business reasons, and he, Giorgio, had given in.

In that first session I limited myself to listening, and I prescribed some neuroleptics. In the second session, after nine days and only with the wife's participation, the patient had gotten worse. A large delusional system emerged that involved his supervisor and other coworkers at his office, the brother, the aunt who lived with his mother, and perhaps even the mother herself. According to him, one of his children had been given drugs. On this occasion my attitude was not one of simple listening or passive acceptance but rather an interested and active one. I asked who was at the head of this organization, and I hinted at the possibility, in a rather implicit way, that I could exert my influence on the head of the plot or in some way mediate the situation. I obtained answers by asking for very detailed information about the person (first name, last name, address, people he socialized with, political affiliations, whether there was someone near him whom he would listen to or who could influence him), and also through non-verbal behaviors (eye movements and facial expressions).

At the end of the session, I told him to pay a lot of attention to even the smallest signs generated in his environment so as to perceive if there was even the smallest decrease in hostility toward him, and suggested to the wife not to block the husband's ability to express himself freely, not to contradict his point of view but rather to listen to him and even stimulate the exposition of the husband's thoughts and worries. At the next session, after 15 days, the symptoms had disappeared, and the patient criticized his delusion and appeared to be re-integrated in his life and work. His wife agreed about the normalization of the situation.

In reconstructing what had happened in the days following the second session, I was told that the patient had attempted suicide by swallowing an excessive amount of the medication tablets that had been prescribed for him. This attempt had followed the disappearance of the delusions, which had happened almost immediately after the session.

From this experience, I concluded that I had a very powerful weapon in my hand but that it had to be used with caution. I found that family members stay very close to the patient in the days following the prescription reported above.

After a few months I chanced upon another case that corresponded to my desire to try out the aforementioned intervention. It was a couple in which she, the patient, B. C., was a teacher at a technical junior high (for 31 years) and he, G. H., was an employee of a public institution (for 39 years). They had three children aged 25, 23, and 14, without any problems. In the reconstruction of the patient's history that I obtained over several sessions, it emerged that when she was 18, she had had a nervous breakdown (due to fright caused by a bomb explosion). She had felt very weak and depressed, her periods stopped, she had a fever, and for a certain amount of time she had been unable to move the left portion of her body. This had led to the suspicion of a stroke, but this diagnosis had been proved wrong by her quick and complete recovery.

After this episode, she had been well up to a month before, with the exception that for a certain period of her life she had been jealous of her husband. Then, gradually, she had become indifferent, and finally, in the last 10 years, she had become so sexually detached as to not have sexual relations with her husband in the last six years. The husband appeared to be open to cooperation in whatever manner to aid the wife, whom he seemed to care for a lot.

It had been a few months since B. C. had begun to notice that people looked at her in a certain way and insulted her ("bitch," "whore," "fucking whore") and that she had begun to feel physically harmed by electrical phenomena and by various illnesses; once she had collapsed; she also heard the noise of a tape recorder.

My intervention was articulated on several points. First of all, during the interview, I helped her express her delusionary construction by predicting the various contents of these events by helping her to report them; for example, by asking who the person was who started it all, asking her, as in the earlier case, first name, last name, address, and the person's social ties and possibilities of being influenced. She gave me a great amount of this data. The head of the organization was an old lady who lived in the same building, who wanted to avenge a lady who had left a few months before and whose husband used to look often toward B. C.'s balcony, thus causing his wife's jealousy.

B. C. was not to try to stop "communications" with people; rather, she was to accentuate them. She had to keep ties with the old lady.

Starting the next day, she had to pay attention to even the smallest signs of a decrease of "influence" toward her. When she heard the voices that insulted her, she was to report it to the husband, and if he was present, he was to violently insult her with the same words as the voices, for a certain amount of time.

At the next session, a week later, B. C. had greatly improved, and at the third session afterward, the delusions had completely disappeared. The illness caused by "electrical devices" had transformed themselves into hypochondriacal worries about her health, in particular, the fear of a breast tumor. The fourth session, the last, took place a month after the third; the situation had become normalized to the satisfaction of both. After four years, I had a chance to see this couple again, because of a relapse. The situation, though, was a lot less serious; the delusion was centered on fear that her daughter would be kidnapped for ransom. It was rapidly resolved by hinting at the technique used previously. In reconstructing what had happened in the previous four years, it emerged that, after the last session of the first cycle, she had gone to Lourdes. From then on, everybody had been convinced of her morality, and she had learned to avoid harm to the brain and vital organs. The old story was over. I said in a whisper, "We have taken care of that thing," and B. C. started to laugh, leading me to believe that we had reached a double level of communication both on the "disease" and on human understanding.

From 1981 to today the intervention has been tried on numerous cases and almost always with a positive result. For this reason it is used by myself and by my group, either in a "light" or "strong" version, in all cases of paranoia. One proceeds this way:

- Call the couple or the family, never the patient by himself or herself; this is done in order to make the spouse or the family change their attitude toward the patient, passing from a position of opposition toward him or her, in the sense of wanting to make their world prevail (the world of logic and of the commonly accepted), to one of entering and accepting the world of the other. Furthermore, they become active members of the therapeutic prescriptions, often paradoxical ones, so that the total interactive pattern may change radically.
- The therapist shows himself to be very interested in the world of the patient, wants to understand him or her deeply, and helps the patient clarify all aspects of his or her construction. In this work, the head of the plot must always be discovered. One asks precise information about him or her: work, home address, work habits, social and business contacts, and ways of influencing the patient.
- The therapist sends out the message that he will help the patient and, in an implicit manner, lets it be known that he will influence the key person in a favorable direction to cease making problems.
- The patient must be careful in the following days to see if there is a decrease in the signs of persecution.
- The use of medications is justified by the necessity to decrease the patient's sensitivity to the external world.

It is clear that all five of these points are directed toward one goal: to establish an interactive modality toward the patient of the F5–F13 type.

BE PSYCHOEDUCATIONAL BY USING THE EPM: "PARENTS BOUND TOGETHER LIKE BODY AND SOUL"

The common denominators of psychoeducational treatments are

1. Schizophrenia is most likely a biological disease.
2. Stress has a negative effect on the functioning of the schizophrenic's mind.
3. Giving the family information about the nature of the disease and specific suggestions on the manner to confront it can decrease family tensions, thus reducing the chances of relapses and the emergence of mental disorders in other members of the family.

Both educational sessions and therapeutic ones take place in most research programs. However, the methodology differs in the number of sessions (educational ones ranging from 1 to 3, therapeutic ones from 5 to

40), in length of time, in place (at home or at the hospital), in number of families present (from one to four in the educational sessions, usually one but in certain research groups, up to three for the therapeutic sessions). On the patient's participation, it also varies with regard to the beginning of the treatment during or after hospitalization and in the session's format and characteristics.

As far as this latter aspect is concerned, these approaches are very different and range from the behavioral one, combining the training session on communication and social skills, to those containing many elements of the structural approach.

This fascinating approach defines itself, implicitly or explicitly, as impervious to the theorization and thus not very transmittable or quantifiable. This interactive style was chosen on the basis of the model's predictions and on the basis of a series of trials and errors made by our clinical team.

The intervention takes place according to the following sequence.

At the time of our first contact with the patient, either at the hospital or at home, with the patient in either an acute phase or a chronic one, we ask all family members who usually live at home to be present. The session can be held at the patient's house, but generally it takes place in the therapist's office or at the Mental Health Center or at the hospital.

On the day of the first session, the entire family is present, and generally there are two therapists, one working with the family in the therapy room, the other located in the supervision room behind the one-way mirror. The latter sees the system at a different logical level. However, even if the therapist is only one, the procedure of the session is the same.

It starts off with careful joining in which the therapist shows a great deal of interest in each family member's way of thinking; that is, he or she enters into the world of each of the family members. Then, the problem is discussed (and inevitably, the patient). All information concerning health care is accepted without criticizing the family or colleagues. This information includes periods of hospitalization, the work of mental health professionals, medications, and so on. The biological aspects are never underestimated.

After this, all the children are sent away, and a discussion with the parents begins. Now the parents are free to express themselves, and usually they give a more serious picture of the child's; for example, the son's "disease" and the symptoms that he exhibits. Second, they show a constant characteristic exhibited by parents of schizophrenic patients, an explicit or implicit reciprocal opposition. They reproach one another for being the cause of the child's pathological behavior, and they list the negative characteristics of the other partner, even in reference to their marital relationship. At a certain point, they ask if it is their fault that the child is sick. The therapist reassures them on the subject by saying that it would be against nature, and in fact in so many years of experience he or she has not ever seen a father or a mother who wanted to harm their child. At the same time, however, the therapist emphasizes that only the parents can help the child to improve, that medication by itself is not sufficient, and that it is necessary to act on both the biological and the psychological level, that is, on the world of matter and on the world of communication. "Are you, parents, willing to do all that is possible to help your son?" They declare that they are totally willing, and they ask what they can do to help the boy.

At this point the therapist explains to them that mental dissociation consists in the fact that the patient feels as if he or she is torn into two parts and that the only way to unite the separate parts of his or her mind is to see the parents really united. By contrast, any disagreement, no matter how subtle, increases the split. The therapist gives examples of disagreements on both the verbal and non-verbal level.

According to what we have said, ultimately, the best way to help the son is to be bound together like body and soul. In case, as it generally happens, the parents start to refer to their personal situation, the therapist encourages them to think in abstract terms, to think about an ideal couple rather than of themselves. Generally, each parent gives a different view of what they understand the expression "bound together like body and soul" to mean. The therapist then expresses his or her opinion that they cannot be united like body and soul and that therefore the only possible solution to the problem is to at least appear bound together like body and soul. The therapist adds that this certainly requires a great deal of sacrifice on their part, even a greater one that the ones that they have made in the past, but that it is necessary for the son. The more they appear bound together, the more the son will take steps toward normality. The following sessions are held on the subject of practicing to appear bound together, and the sessions are enriched by the constant improvement of the patient. In what we call "to appear bound together like body and soul" we include behavior like the parents' going out together without the child for a certain amount of time, three times a week, keeping where they go and what they do a secret. In addition, they must keep their participation in and the contents of the sessions a secret. They must make general decisions together, and they must reach a consensus and decide what attitude to take toward the son's behavior.

In the last few years, we have introduced two strengthening maneuvers to our intervention: *a family sculpture and periodic parents' meetings*. The former takes place either during a special session in which all the family participates or during a session with the parents, in which, as it inevitably happens, they take the patient with them. In either of the two circumstances we ask the children (or the schizophrenic son) to position the parents as though they were statues, according to how they see them in their marital relation as a couple. Once the sculpture has been made, we ask the children to once again position the parents as though they were statues, but this time not as they see them in real life but rather as they wish they could see them. Almost always there is a great difference between the sculpture representing their real-life relation and the one that the children would wish them to have. The "real-life" sculpture is almost always characterized by detachment, whereas the ideal one is characterized by closeness. Thus, the parents receive a confirmation of the necessity to appear bound together in the eyes of the children.

The other change that we adopted in the last few years is that of organizing sessions with four or five parental couples, always mainly centered on the subject of how to appear bound together, like body and soul.

Summary of the Interventions

Briefly, the intervention unfolds as follows. After joining with the whole family conducted in such a manner as to allow the therapist to achieve great prestige and full-fledged cooperation on the part of the family (i.e., they are willing to do anything that is necessary to resolve the problem at hand), we proceed by working only with the parents.

Phase 1. Tell the parents that the only thing that they can do to help the patient is to be "bound together like body and soul."

Phase 2. What does the husband mean by "bound together like body and soul"?; what does the wife mean by "bound together like body and soul"?

Phase 3. The two of them have completely different worldviews because for him "to be bound together like body and soul" means one thing while for her it means another thing.

Phase 4. We realize that it is impossible for them "to be bound together like body and soul." So we are asking of them a great sacrifice for the patient's sake.

Phase 5. Having acknowledged that they cannot be "bound together like body and soul," they must at least appear to be "bound together like body and soul." According to the husband (and then according to the wife), what does it mean to appear "bound together like body and soul"? Based on what elements does one conclude that they are so bound? If they think about a couple with whom they are acquainted whom they perceive to be "bound together like body and soul," based on what elements have they come to that conclusion? If they were to picture a movie in which two characters, a couple, are "bound together like body and soul," by what elements? What signals does the husband (and then the wife) use to draw the conclusion that they are "bound together like body and soul"?

Phase 6. Each of them must write down a list of elements that make two people appear to be "bound together like body and soul."

Phase 7. They must agree on common points by writing a single list of the elements that make two people appear to be "bound together like body and soul."

Phase 8. They must transform into concrete behavior what they wrote on the common list.

Phase 9. They must practice!

This intervention was used for the first time only a few years ago, and that is why we know only its short-term results. On 31 cases that were treated in this way we have seen a consistently positive result, in the sense of a quick improvement of the patient. There have been no cases of suicide. Only in two cases was hospitalization necessary.

The "Prescription of the Four Rules"

This prescription is a short version of the maneuver "to appear bound together like body and soul" (F9). We (the second author and his group) use it when we cannot carry out a complete cycle of psychotherapeutic sessions, even though it is certainly less effective than the complete intervention, which has been described. However, it is useful in many instances, especially when adequately delivered.

Usually, it is presented at the end of a single session, after joining with all family members has taken place, and after the problem has been analyzed. All the members of the family except the parents are asked to leave the room. We address the two of them, asking if they are willing to do everything that is necessary to help their child (the usual "pact with the devil" developed by Haley). Having had a strong, affirmative answer (in the case of a dubious consensus, one should make recourse to the "empty box" maneuver, mentioned earlier). We emphasize that the only way to help the child is to do what will be prescribed. After we advise them to keep what we will say a secret from their children, relatives, and friends, we go on to the four rules.

Starting from tomorrow, the two of them as husband and wife will behave in a certain manner.

1. They will close the bedroom door (which almost always is kept open in the families of schizophrenics).
2. Three times a week the couple will go out alone without telling anyone where they are going and what they are doing.
3. In their children's presence, they will show a lot of reciprocal affection (the wife toward the husband and the husband toward the wife). They will sit next to one another, they will look at each other in the eyes, they will walk arm in arm, they will hug, kiss, and so on.
4. Every day they will assign a small task to their children, and they will appear completely united in making them carry it out.

This intervention usually elicits surprise in the parental couple. The four rules will then be repeated every time we phone or have contact with one or both of the parents.

DISSOCIATIVE IDENTITY DISORDERS

We are treating here a certain rather severe psychological disorder, which has great theoretical interest. Two years ago, a family composed of five people came to see me. The father and the mother were about 40, good-looking, and they were the owners of a perfume shop. The three children were Lucrezia, 17, Carlo, 14, and Cosima, 10. The reason for their visit was that Lucrezia would fall into periods lasting from a few minutes to several hours in which, from an intelligent and mature young woman, she would be transformed into a very young girl. She would speak like a little girl, she would move like a spoiled little child, she would throw tantrums like a small and immature child, to the point, for example, of throwing objects at family members.

The mother appeared as a totally powerless woman in regard to the husband and children. The father was a man who during the sessions appeared very calm but who, as he himself admitted, was often nervous. Sometimes he would lose his patience and become violent, and one day a little before the onset of the symptoms in the daughter, in a moment of rage he had hurled her motorbike down the stairs, destroying it. The mother was very afraid of him and thought he was very selfish (he preferred outside "company" rather than his family), but she was incapable of rebelling.

The precription that I gave right away, during the first session (in which the girl had arrived in a full crisis) was that the mother force the daughter to behave like an adult. Initially, the mother was hesitant, but with the help and the insistence of the therapist she put herself to work. A physical fight ensued between mother and daughter, during which I prevented the father from intervening. At the end the mother won out, and by the end of the hour the girl seemed to have slightly improved. This intervention, based on very few elements picked up in the chaotic situation of that first encounter, was aimed at a detriangulation.

I hypothesized that in that system the mother was really down, that she was absolutely incapable of transmitting clear messages (communication patterns that were not flat but with specific characteristics) to the daughter, and that, therefore, she was not able to control her. Due to this, the father had to take on the task, but he exercised control in an unrefined manner that was certainly looked down upon by the mother. Therefore, if the mother had been able to increase her ability to maintain her point of view (F3), also thanks to the therapist's prevention of the father's "help," this would have been an important first step in making that system more functional.

At the next session, a week later, there had been an improvement. I then worked on the couple, leaning in favor of the mother or, better yet in elementary-pragmatic terms, in the direction of making the husband enter into his wife's world (the husband as an F5 relation toward the wife). After a few sessions the problem seemed solved.

Unfortunately, after three months the family came back because the symptoms had appeared once again. This relapse gave me the possibility to carry out an intervention that I think is more effective in attacking hysterical psychoses. This time, after the usual joining, I asked the girl, who in that moment appeared to be normal, to show me how she behaved during the crises. Lucrezia answered that she was not able to do so because she could not remember anything that happened during those periods. Then, I asked all the family members if they were able to imitate Lucrezia's crises. They tried but with unsatisfactory results. I gave them the prescription that they carefully observe Lucrezia's crises at home so that, in the following session, they could imitate her perfectly. In fact, at the next session, they were very good at imitating the pathologic behavior of the girl. At this point I asked Lucrezia to observe carefully her behavior during the crises as being reproduced by her family, so as to be able to imitate it herself. Lucrezia observed her behavior during the crises as it was being imitated by the others, and she herself began to imitate it, at first rather badly, then at the therapist's insistence (he was very demanding!) with ever greater improvements. I gave the prescription during the week to improve on imitating the behavior that she could not remember, with the help of the family. At the next session the girl gave a splendid performance of her crises. At this point I was able to give the prescription that three times a day, every single day, in the family's presence, she was to imitate her crises. Thus, her symptom rapidly disappeared and this time permanently.

Let me repeat the sequence, as it was also carried out in other cases:

1. Joining.
2. Presentation of the problem: the crises.
3. The patient is asked to enact the crises during the session.
4. The patient declares that he or she does not remember what happens during the crises.
5. Family members are asked to observe carefully the pathological behavior of the patient, so as to be able to imitate it perfectly.
6. The patient is asked to observe the imitation by the family of his or her pathological behavior (which he or she cannot recall), so as to be able to imitate it in turn.
7. The patient is asked to imitate the behavior that he or she cannot recollect, in the presence of the family.
8. The prescription is given to imitate systematically one's own recollected behavior, in the presence of the family.

In these cases, it is difficult to establish which function was used, but I am inclined to believe that it was basically the F14.

It is also interesting to me to draw a parallel with the Freudian approach. In fact, in our intervention we do not force the defenses with hypnosis, nor do we achieve the raising of consciousness through free associations; we make a totally "external" intervention (I could not define it differently), and yet the results leave no doubt. Furthermore, the result can be achieved by following different therapeutic strategies (in the preceding example, first with a structural approach and then later with an elementary pragmatic one).

This multiplicity of possible interventions leads us to take a position in respect to the symptom. In fact, our model does not imply any explanation of how one passes from the interactions to the symptom and from changes in interaction to the disappearance of the symptom.

The hypothesis that we make in order to explain the positive effects of the use of certain interactive styles on the part of the therapist or on the part of one or more members of the family due to the therapist's input is the following: each person is an element of a system and is showered with a pattern of communication that is the global result of all the interactions that surround him or her. This pattern of communication puts him or her either within a range that allows an acceptable psychological life or outside this range, in a context that generates a state of ill-being. The interventions that we adopt, which can even be different from one another but cannot be random ones (in the sense that certain interventions lead toward a functional area while others do not, and others yet draw away from it altogether), allow the individual to re-enter the physiological area.

Strictly in terms of the EPM, the hypothesis is that the global communication pattern sent and received by anyone, in order to be optimal, must have a certain minimum or maximum of each of the four coordinates and also of each of the 16 functions and of the 16 functions in relation to one another. These percentages lead to the formation of an optimal space. When one goes out of the optimal space, a mental dysfunction appears. The use of appropriate functions on the part of therapist or of elements of the context makes it conducive to the re-entry of the respondent by modifying the global pattern.

DISORDERS OF CONVERSION AND SOMATIZATION

Irritable Colon

Patients affected by irritable colon suffer abdominal pains and intestinal disorders (mostly associated with other gastroenteric disorders, disorders of other organs and systems, and psychological disorders).

The therapy that we use (see Appendix D) is based, as previously stated for other disorders, on a combination of the structural approach, aiming at changing the boundaries between the subsystems and thus allowing the individualization of the members, and of the EPM. A therapeutic move that we now use very frequently in treating these types of somatization disorders was used, for the first time, 18 years ago. The couple in question consisted of a 35-year-old wife who was clearly unhappy with her marital relationship with a very passive husband, who was very detached from her both emotionally and physically. The patient complained of a very evident intestinal syndrome, which at times involved vomiting. For years she had been treated with drugs and diets, and she landed in my office as though it was her last resort. As a first step, she was asked to monitor the symptom, with the aid of her husband, who was supposed to prepare the appropriate chart. She was to record, with great accuracy, the beginning and the end of the symptoms, checking her watch.

At the next session they were asked if they were willing to do whatever was needed to overcome the woman's disorder; having received a clearly affirmative answer, the lady was asked if she felt ill at the moment. The woman said that she felt very ill and was about to vomit. She was told that the bathroom was next door and that any type of purging was not a problem; in fact, it was an advantage that she felt sick during the session.

Then the husband was asked to massage his wife's abdomen. Such massage had to be done in various manners: superficially, deeply, at various depths, horizontally, circularly, and so on according to the feedback given by the wife. In other terms, she was to concentrate on the disorder and at the same time evaluate the husband's action while guiding it according to the sensations that she felt, because, she was told, there was a particular type of massage that would make the pain diminish or disappear.

Both spouses expended a lot of effort, and after about 20 minutes the wife declared that the pain, which usually lasted for hours, had disappeared. At this point they were given the prescription to do the massage for exactly half an hour (checking her watch) three times a day, every day, morning, noon, and evening, at the time they agreed on during the session ("like taking a medicine three times a day"). This prescription led to a quick disappearance of the symptoms. The therapy then continued, focusing on their marital relationship.

The positive effect of the intervention can be interpreted in the sense that through this bodily approach the spouse enters into the patient's world (F5); these alexithimic subjects, in fact, accept more easily an entrance into their world through a bodily route than through a symbolic one.

Another possible interpretation, which is not ours, is that contact with the spouse is so unpleasant for the patient that she prefers to abandon the symptom. Simultaneous administration of medication is useful.

The Woman Whose "Vocal Chords Sang of Their Own Accord"

A few years ago a Calabrian family came to my office: a 45-year-old lady, her 50-year-old husband, and a 23-year-old son. The woman was the patient; I had successfully cured her two years before from a manic state of insomnia. The symptom that she exhibited was very pronounced; continuously, for two months, in spite of the different treatments given by local doctors, she emitted a guttural sound, a kind of eeeeeeee, which was interrupted only when she spoke. Because at that moment I did not have much time at my disposal, I prescribed some drugs and sent her back home, giving her an appointment in a week. After a week the disorder had not changed by one iota, and the patient asked to be hospitalized in the clinic.

The disorder was extremely irritating to the family and also, parenthetically, for me. I decided to stop it at any price. First of all I asked why she would not stop, and she answered that she could not, that it was her "vocal chords that sang of their own accord." At this point I feigned optimism, saying that if the vocal chords spoke involuntarily, then they would automatically stop, if one triggered the appropriate reflex. I made the lady sit comfortably, the husband behind her. I made her close her eyes in order to concentrate on the sensations that she would feel, and I invited the husband to massage her neck in various ways: circularly, vertically, horizontally, superficially, deeply. After 10 minutes the annoying sound continued to be emitted by the patient without interruption. Then I made the son go out of the room, and I asked the husband to massage lower along the trachea toward the breast. Another 10 minutes went by, without any positive results. Then a thought crossed my mind: I was not supposed to go toward the patient's world (F13), but rather, I was to make difficult for her the continuation of her symptom through a prescription opposed to the previous one (F11).

I said that they had to change positions: I put her on all four limbs, on the floor, with her body leaning forward, a rather hard position (that the patient tried to change, but on which I firmly insisted), and the husband, sitting on the floor, continued the stimulation. After a few minutes the sound ceased first for a few moments and then it seemed to stop permanently. At this point I asked them to get up, I opened the door and invited the son to come in, and I declared that his mother was cured. At this point she began again to emit the sound, and I repeated the operation; the son was ushered out, the door was closed, she was put on all fours, and the husband, sitting on the floor, massaged her. After a few minutes the disorder ceased completely, this time permanently.

As for a therapeutic move, this case resembles the irritable colon case, with the difference that it is based to a greater extent on a function in which one takes the symptom into account while showing little consideration for the world of the patient, with the therapist playing a tyrannical and demanding role (F11).

This second solution was adopted after the first one (F13) had not been effective. Therefore, this intervention is a good example of a change in therapeutic style during a session.

The Retarded Beauty with Self-Aggressive Crisis

This was a family composed of the father, a 50-year-old taxi driver; the mother, a housewife; and three children, a 21-year-old girl and two boys, one aged 17 and one 10. They had come on account of the mentally retarded girl, who was affected by cerebral palsy. Michela—this was the young woman's name—in spite of her handicap had a pleasant appearance: she was dark, tall, and slender and had a certain verbal expressivity; in fact her soft yet stentorian tone of voice and her rhythms in speech were pleasingly musical. They had discovered her handicap when she was 3, and they had fought very hard to make Michela lead the most normal life possible; in fact, she had received a junior high diploma, and she had completed a sewing course.

The reason they had come to see me was that for some time the girl had been having some "worrisome" crises. She would beat her hands rhythmically and violently against the furniture's corners, causing some wounds; she would throw herself on the floor; and she would bang her head against the pavement violently and repeatedly.

The mother seemed very anxious and worried; the father was more detached. Before the session was over, I asked the girl and all the family members if they were ready to do anything whatsoever to overcome the problem for which they had come to see me. The girl answered yes, and so did all the members of the family. I ended with the prescription that the family pay a lot of attention to the girl's crises, so that they could describe them with the greatest accuracy in the next session. Furthermore, the parents were to accurately record the beginning and the end of the crises.

In the next session, I asked all the members of the family to imitate the crises in the girl's presence, and she had to imitate herself, in a manner analogous to the case described earlier. Then I gave the prescription to re-enact the crises at home for a quarter of an hour three times a week under the parents' supervision (because of the father's work schedule the re-enactment of the crises had to take place between 11:00 A.M. and 11:15 A.M. and from 4:00 P.M. to 4:15 P.M. under the mother's supervision and from 8:00 P.M. to 8:15 P.M. under the father's supervision).

Later, during the same session, I clarified that the re-enactment of the crises had to be perfected in the following manner: that the father had to understand what thoughts crossed the girl's mind right before and during the crises, by interacting with the daughter for as long as necessary, and he was to help her repeat these thoughts during the "exercises."

At the third session, 20 days later, they reported that the crises had completely ceased, that they had done the exercises but then they had stopped because the girl had improved. I insisted that they continue, and I started to work with the parents only, with the intention of establishing appropriate boundaries between the parents' subsystem and that of the children and in particular between mother and daughter. It was clear that things were not going well between husband and wife.

At the next session, I invited only the parents, but at the last minute they called to say that they were not coming. The next time that the mother called I explained that they had to schedule about 10 sessions, involving only husband and wife. They were to do these sessions with a colleague of mine and under my supervision. They told me that they would let me know, but they never called back.

After seven months, wishing to hear how the case had evolved, I phoned their house. The girl answered and said that she was doing very well. I asked to speak to her mother, who confirmed that the girl had not had any more crises and that, inexplicably, she had become more sociable (thus reducing the other great source of anxiety for the mother, i.e., her daughter's tendency to have few social contacts). She explained that they had not re-contacted me because the girl had overcome her problem, and they did not feel like starting a new series of sessions.

This very short psychotherapy, as the reader will have noticed, is a concentration of structural and elementary pragmatic interventions. The structural component consists in bringing the father and daughter closer together through the prescription to listen to the thoughts crossing the daughter's mind before and during the crises; and in this there is also the elementary-pragmatic style of entering into her world (F5). Again, on the structural side, there are the therapeutic prescription and the program of 10 sessions with the two of them only (this never happened but was equally valid, as was the program that would have made the husband open to entering the wife's world—F5). This is the style of reaching a limited goal (the recording of the disorder—F1), with the addition of going beyond the prescription's predictability by telling the girl to practice her own disorders (F9, F11, F13).

The Man Who Was No Longer Able to Write

In June 1983 a couple, parents of two daughters aged 25 and 24, came to my office: Edoardo, 59, an elementary school teacher, and his wife, Antonietta, 50. They had come on account of the father, a pleasant person who was anxious by temperament and had worsened in the last few years. His appetite had decreased, he did not want to see people, he felt fearful, and he was even afraid of school, in spite of his 20 years' teaching experience.

Apparently everything had started with a robbery at home. The wife had become very demoralized, and he had given her strength, only to fall apart once she had recovered.

Marital relations were not good; she was a very vivacious person with modern views, also toward the daughters. He instead was quiet, retrograde (to the point of demanding that the girls must not go out by themselves, at the cost of making personal sacrifices to accompany them), and he was also rather tight with money. In short, both of them admitted that there was a great distance between them, both psychologically and physically.

For a year now, he had been checked by many specialists who had administered different types of anti-anxiety and antidepressive drugs, but with no appreciable results. I set up the therapy according to the modalities described for anxious depression, prescribing, among other things, the chair exercise. At the next session, about a month later, the patient had notably improved in both his tone and mood. By the next session, he appeared to be totally cured except for one disorder, to which I had previously not paid attention, "the trembling." I asked for information about the trembling, and Edoardo told me that it was evident mainly on the right side. In order to clarify the nature of the symptom, it came to my mind to ask him to write something down. At this point it became clear that he had a very serious writing disorder. Prompted by curiosity and by the suspicion that it was the notorious "writer's cramp," I tried a very simple interactive approach; the wife had to try in various ways to help the husband write, for example by raising his arm (which he tended to lean too heavily on the table) while he was writing or in any other way that they might experiment with. To my great surprise Edoardo rapidly improved during the session.

In fact, after 10 minutes of help by the wife, his writing had become much better. The improvement continued in the following days. After two years there have been no further episodes, neither of the depressive type nor in the writing.

I think that the therapeutic result was due to the prescription that the wife go toward the husband's world, amplifying it (F5, F13). This outcome was possible only through the somatic channel and particularly through contact with the non-functioning limb, which almost completely handicapped his abilities as a teacher (teaching was for him his purpose in life, what gave him prestige and preserved his self-esteem).

After a few months I tried to use the same technique of intervention with a housewife who was no longer able to sew, and I obtained similar results.

A Case of Psychogenic Pain

In April of 2001 a family came to our office. The therapist was Antonietta Santoni-Rugiu. The therapy took place in 10 sessions, and I supervised the fifth and the tenth sessions. The family was composed of a father, a small factory entrepreneur aged 47, a 45-year-old mother of a foreign nationality who was a collaborator in the management of the firm and held a key role, and an only daughter, aged 10, in grade school.

The problem was an intense pain in the daughter's neck that forced her to hold her neck in a particular antalgic position (with left rotations and a strong adduction) reminiscent of the position characteristic of spasmodic torticollis. Maria was a beautiful child, with a suffering face, and with a compulsive head posture; she walked cautiously, turning her eyes around with a look of pity in her eyes as though searching for a confirmation of her suffering.

The mother was overweight and rather unattractive but very intelligent. She related that Maria had started to show that symptom after a fall, a year and a half before. They had consulted numerous specialists, and she had even been hospitalized in Switzerland. At the end, everybody had agreed that there were no organic causes, and a psychological treatment had been advised.

The father, who in contrast with the mother was a rather good-looking man, had remained silent during the mother's exposition but at the end intervened to express his doubts about the lack of organic causes in his daughter's illness. Concerning Maria's behavior, the mother further related that at nighttime the daughter would wake up crying on account of strong pains in her head and neck. Lately she had become oppositional toward the mother and showed affection only for the father.

Shifting the focus from the child to the parents, we learned that the couple had not been sleeping together for some time because he went to bed late while the wife and child went to bed early. The child could not be left alone, and while at first she had gone to sleep in her mother's room (with the father sleeping alone in Maria's room), lately things had changed because the child had asked and was allowed to go back to her own room, with the father sleeping in the same room, always because of the pains that would wake her at night.

Observing the interactions, it was noticeable that none of the three were able to speak directly with the person they referred to; they did so indirectly, through the third person. For example, the father complained to the daughter about the wife's shortcomings, or, the mother would complain with the husband about some of the daughter's shortcomings. Maria would ally at times with the father and at times with the mother, trying to create a bridge between the two.

The first intervention, following on the footsteps of the ones previously described, was that the father had to massage the daughter's neck for half an hour twice a day. At the next session, the father reported that he was not able to carry out the prescription because, being too sensitive, he was not able to withstand his daughter's crying. Thus, he asked to be relieved of the task and that it be given to his wife, who had a stronger alliance with the child. The therapist insisted on the prescription, proposing to carry it out during the session, but this time the mother was to help him out by giving him advice. Reluctantly, the father began the massage; as soon as he would graze the child's neck she would start screaming and imploring her father to stop, because the massage was too painful. The father was ready to stop, but the mother, mindful of the therapist's wishes, encouraged him to continue. The father showed signs of resentment against the wife, and thus a skirmish ensued between the spouses, in which the daughter served only as a pretext, allowing them to define themselves pragmatically in respect to each other. Meanwhile, the daughter continued to cry and calmed down only when, finally, father and mother committed themselves to carry out the prescription together. At the end of the session they were given the prescription, for the week, to proceed according to what they did in the session.

At the next session (the third) the father had not carried out the prescription once again, with the mother's complicity, as she justified the husband by saying that he was too busy at work, and she had taken his place in the execution of the exercise. She reported that they had had some good results, and that the daughter had in fact improved. The therapist showed skepticism and gave no prescription.

At the following session (the fourth) the parents reported that Maria was doing very badly and that she had even begun to be troublesome at school. The mother seemed desperate; the father seemed very tired and said he was not able to sleep at all because Maria was crying all night long. The doubts started coming back: was it really a psychological condition? The therapist asked Maria to put herself in front of the mirror and to concentrate so that the pains would come. Maria executed the prescription in a masterful way, reproducing perfectly the screams, the crying, and the gestures typical of the moments of highest suffering. The parents were left dumbfounded—so it really was a psychogenic thing! From this moment on, the system began to vacillate. What had happened during the session was prescribed at home, as an exercise that she had to perform in front of the father twice a day.

At the next session (the fifth) the parents reported that the child had improved a little but that it had been necessary to give her two doses of feprazone (zepelin). The father stated that he had mustered his courage and that he had witnessed the dramatic performance of his daughter. We took advantage of this initial collaboration on the part of the father to prescribe that father and daughter take a weeklong trip together, by themselves, to a destination undisclosed to the mother. Any communication between the two and the mother was to be interrupted.

At the next session (the sixth), the father reported that the girl had never cried during the trip and that she had played with other children they met during the trip. However, it was revealed that en route, in contradiction to the therapist's prescription, the father had secretly phoned the mother several times to communicate Maria's suffering to her.

In contrast with what usually happens with this prescription, the father appeared to be fully satisfied with his trip with Maria, while the mother was rather nervous. The girl, on her part, from this moment on stopped being oppositional toward her mother.

The therapist realized that the moment had come to work with the parental couple, in order to move to the other side of the triangle. This was now possible because Maria finally accepted remaining outside the therapy room, which was impossible before because of her crying. Maria, in fact, could not bear leaving her parents alone.

The therapist began the maneuver of "appearing bound together like body and soul." The father and the mother were forced to go back to sleeping together, to go out together alone, to show more affection toward each other. The assignment was carried out with the utmost diligence.

At the next session, however, things went very badly; the father said that an old ulcer had come back, the daughter cried day and night, and the mother's leg had swollen because of lack of rest. They were very discouraged for they had done everything they were told, but with no results. Once again skepticism about the psychogenic causes of the disorder emerged; in fact, she was doing better when she was taking feprazone (zepelin). They wondered whether there were other drugs that were more effective. The supervisor, who is a physician, intervened; there was a very new and very powerful drug, and she had some samples, in suppositories, right in the office. The problem was that the suppositories were for adults only; therefore, they were rather large. The father, then, was to make them smaller and then to administer them to Maria. During the session itself, the father began to make the suppository smaller in order to get an idea of the right size. Of course, the suppositories were to be used only in case of need. At the eighth session, they reported that it was not necessary to use the suppositories because the girl was doing fine.

Uncautiously, the therapist said that if in the following days the girl was continuing to do well, there would be a three-month summer break in the sessions. At the ninth session, after a two-week intermission due to holidays, the family came back in a disastrous condition; the girl was doing very badly; not only did she feel pains in the neck and head but also in the arm and a tingling in the right leg, she cried almost uninterruptedly, and she had problems going to school. The parents were desperate, for all they did had not been useful.

It seemed clear that the symmetry that existed inside the family had now shifted to the family and the therapist. This outcome revealed that the family had understood and knew what was the correct path to the solution of the problem. Thus, the therapist admitted her defeat and the family's victory approximately in these terms: I cannot do anything else, only you can help her, and by now you know what you are supposed to do. If you are not able to do it, or if it is too dangerous for you, the girl will get increasingly worse up to the point of not being able to move. You will then have to put her in a wheelchair and spend the rest of your life always taking care of her. The parents protested, they implored her not to abandon them, but the therapist remained firm in her position. She would see them once again in three months, just to conform to the contract that had been set for 10 sessions. While the therapist expressed herself in the terms reported above, the little girl stopped crying and moved more freely, and, going out of the therapy room, she muttered, "I'll show her, the doctor, if I can get better or not!"

After three months the family came back. The situation had improved enormously (80% according to both parents); the girl was now in junior high, had made new friends, socialized a lot, played on a volleyball team, slept regularly at night, and did not need drugs. However, the family insisted on another series of sessions, this one not directed to the daughter but to the couple, to deal with another problem that was never confronted in the prior sessions: the mother's inability to ever close the bedroom door! This was presented by her as a kind of "claustrophobia."

Insomnia

Four years ago, a Mr. Z. G., from a small town in Apulia, came to my office with his wife. They were desperate on account of his insomnia. They had consulted more than 10 specialists, some of whom were very highly regarded ones, and he had been prescribed all sorts of drugs without any results. They were coming to me as their last hope. I had a moment of hesitation; it was not the case to even think of drugs, nor was it appropriate to send them to some traditional psychotherapist. They had already seen more psychodynamically oriented therapists, but the patient had not become "engaged." The situation seemed urgent; I had to find an immediate solution. Suddenly, the strategy I had to use came to mind. I turned to the irritated and anguished wife and told her that it was not true that the husband was not sleeping; actually he was always half awake and half asleep. I explained that what had happened to him was that sleep and awakeness had gotten "mixed up," due to which he was never either totally awake or totally asleep. She was to watch her husband carefully. It was clear (and obviously it was true) that the fixed expression of the eyes, even if they were opened, revealed that he was partly asleep. She was to try to slap him right then, and she could see how he would change his demeanor and see what kind of expression he really had when he was awake. She laughed but obeyed. Having been slapped, Z. G. took on a very awake expression, and the theory seemed very acceptable to both (why could it not be so also for academic science?). Then, the problem was that of completely separating sleep from wakefulness. I made a pause and asked if they were willing to do all that was needed to achieve the result. They answered strongly that, yes, they were willing. Then I said that the only way to separate completely sleep from wakefulness was for him to stay awake for a long time, completely awake for 72 hours. In order to achieve this, it was necessary to mobilize relatives and friends, besides his wife and children, so that everyone would take turns, day and night, to keep him completely awake by talking, stimulating, even pinching him and making him wash his face. The family asked, "What happens after the 72 hours?" After 72 hours he would be allowed to rest or sleep for 8 hours; after which he had to stay awake 42 hours, then 8 hours of rest or sleep, then 24 hours awake and finally sleep and wakefulness as desired. If the problem was not solved, then they would have to do a second cycle, eventually a third, and so on. They expressed the fear that Z. G. might collapse, and I answered that there was no danger of a collapse because, as they had said, he had already not been sleeping for a long time.

This intervention was very successful. At a later checkup, after a few weeks, the insomnia had completely disappeared, and they showed me their gratitude not only with words but by referring several friends and acquaintances to me.

I saw them again after about a year. They told me that since the time of the intervention the problem of insomnia had completely disappeared; this time they were coming to me because Z. G. was depressed. This problem, too, was solved easily. His depression corresponds to my experience that in the great majority of insomnia cases, depression is really the problem. However, it is important to overcome the problem of insomnia so as to be able to work on the real problem.

Since then, this technique has been successful in numerous cases. In certain cases it was enough to lay out the modality of the intervention to obtain results. For example, benzodiazepines or other medications were administered. The subject would show his doubts as to their effectiveness by citing the numerous medications taken without any results. Then they were told that if the medication did not work, they had to follow a much more difficult route. Which one? Seventy-two hours of complete wakefulness, 8 hours' rest or sleep, 48 hours of continuous wakefulness, 8 hours' rest or sleep, 24 hours of continuous wakefulness, rest at will. If there were no results, the cycle had to be repeated. At this point the insomnia disappears without the previously ineffective medications or with no drugs at all.

A blander type of intervention, which seems just like a piece of advice, is to tell them not to stay in bed if they are not sleeping, because this generates a mixing of wakefulness with sleep with deleterious effects. In fact, it does not allow the subject to stay either completely awake or completely asleep.

Finally, I wish to mention those cases in which a true insomnia does not exist, cases of subjects who want to sleep more than their physiology allows. There are, for example, subjects who complain they are waking up at 4 A.M., and then, in the course of the interview one learns that they go to sleep at 8 P.M. If in counting the hours of sleep, one decides that they are sufficient, one must explain that they should not sleep beyond eight hours because it could lead to serious problems. One must also advise them to sleep in the night hours and enlist the help of others to remain absolutely awake at least until 11 P.M.

According to our model, the interventions mentioned above are mainly based on the F11 function.

AFFECTIVE DISORDERS

Severe Anxious Depression

In this section, we refer to an emergency intervention used in those cases of serious anxious depression, in which the patient appears very agitated. Usually, she or he uses expressions like "Oh, my God!" "It's over!" "I'm finished!" "I can't take it any more!" and so on and is not able to sit still, shifts around on the chair, gets up, walks around.

As I always do in my work, I ask the patient to come to my office with his wife if he is married or with significant members of his family if he is unmarried. They appear to be very distressed. The global atmosphere is highly dramatic. After a brief and difficult joining and the gathering of some information obtained with great effort (the whole context seems to emphasize the uselessness of talking) there is no choice but to attack the symptom. The alternative, in fact, would be hospitalization, which is in fact what the family and sometimes even the patient asks, even more so because the patient (as always happens to me!) has already been unsuccessfully treated by other colleagues with antidepressive and anti-anxiety drugs.

In intervention, the psychiatrist gets up and puts two chairs at a certain distance from each other. The distance is necessary to prevent the patient from getting vertigo; then he asks the patient, in the presence of the spouse or of the family, to go around the two chairs, moaning very loudly and walking at a faster pace than what corresponds to his anxiety. The "exercise" goes on for a certain length of time (15 minutes, half hour, one hour, three hours!) and is very carefully monitored by the therapist, who urges the patient to carry out the exercise in an optimal manner, encouraging him and spurring him to action. The intervention shows its effectiveness in the session: the patient relaxes, the expressions of family members change from tense and worried to relaxed and smiling.

The rationale given for the exercise is that it is designed to free the patient from anxiety ("to let the anxiety out") and is prescribed at home. The patient must carry it out three times a day (in the morning, at noon, in the evening), every day, for a certain amount of time (usually half an hour at rigorously set times (e.g., from 6:00 A.M. to 6:30 A.M.; from 3:00 P.M. to 3:30 P.M., from 9:00 P.M. to 9:30 P.M.) "just as though it were medication." It is the task of the patient's wife or other significant family members to check that the patient carries out the exercise according to the agreed-upon modalities, whether he feels like it or not.

The meaning of the intervention in its initial stage is to go toward the world of the patient, amplifying it. His world, in fact, is a world of tension and desire to free himself from it. The patient's inability to stand still and the tendency to moan aloud are tied to this tension.

The therapist's prescription, then, goes toward the patient's world. However, in asking the patient to move in a certain way, at a greater speed than his anxiety, and to complain in a very loud voice, the therapist adds something that is outside the patient's ability to predict, something that belongs to a space external to the "ring" of interaction; thus, the function used by the therapist takes the form of an F13.

Afterward, in the prescription at home, one can add other functions, such as pursuing the goal (F1), and strongly introduce the world of the therapist to the patient (a shade of "ordeal") and indirectly strongly introduce the world of the spouse or other significant family members to the patient (F11). It is important that the exercise be done with the spouse's collaboration or that of significant family members, because of its configuration of shared experience.

It must be stressed that in all cases, a single intervention was used, and all patients were suffering from very serious anxiety, as previously described. Furthermore, when they came to me, they were already being treated with benzodiazepine, an antidepressant, but during the session no medication was administered. In all cases there was a follow-up four days after the session (before the effect of the tricyclics would show). The last follow-up took place after a time span ranging from a month to a year.

In many cases the result was an immediate one. Already by the end of the session, the patient appeared to be calm, and the family members, who previously were worried, by the end of the session were relaxed and smiling.

In a later attempt to quantify the effectiveness of the intervention, we compared the results that we obtained with those of a group of patients who had been treated with tricyclics and benzodiazepine according to a purely pharmacological setting, by impersonally filling out a rating scale. The statistical analysis of responses gave good results in 91.6% of patients against 61.5% of patients using only medications.

Since that time, we have treated tens of cases with the same success rate.

Among the cases treated, I will cite one that has a follow-up longer than one year and that seems to exemplify well the approach that we use.

On December 19, 1984, a family came to my office: a father, A, 58 years old, a professional; a mother, B, 54 years old, a teacher; and two siblings. C, a very good-looking 28-year-old woman, a librarian, was engaged and had great intellectual interests. The second sibling, D, was a 26-year-old-young man who also had great intellectual interests and was a college graduate, employed, and close to getting married.

What had motivated their visit was that since 1982, in a discontinuous manner, C, the young woman, had been ill. She was silent, with little vitality, sad, and with a lack of enthusiasm. Furthermore, in the morning she felt anxious. The symptoms had gotten much worse in the last three months. From the interview with the family, it emerged that the father was affected by a bipolar disorder and that he was being treated with lithium by a very famous specialist. The mother was afraid that the daughter had the same illness as the father, and the young woman was obsessed with that idea.

The parents, interviewed alone, said that their marital life was anything but rosy and that for the past five years, since B's hysterectomy, they had not had sexual relations. This had caused a great unhappiness on the part of the husband, who had always been very active sexually and was now reduced to express his virility with wet dreams. Relations between father and children had always been very difficult because of A's illness. However, the relation between father and daughter had improved since her illness. It also came out that the mother had suffered from a phobic-obsessive disorder and that 20 years earlier she had been through psychotherapy. B had kept this a secret from her children.

Speaking alone with the children, it emerged that C had the idea of wanting to save the family. In a later interview, alone with C, I learned that in 1982 some very important events had taken place. Her fiancé's mother had died. She had accepted living with him for a certain period of time. Later, she had had a relationship with another young man, and later she recalled it to her fiancé. The fiancé, on his part, had had a brief relationship with another young woman. Later, I held a session with C and her fiancé, a junior high school teacher, who made it clear that their relationship was in a very serious crisis. By now, they were fighting over any little thing, and anytime she appeared desperate he would draw away. In short, he thought the possibility of a marriage was absolutely remote.

I told them that it seemed to me that they were doing a little dance, in which first they came together, and then they came apart. Spurred by my statement, he asked how he was supposed to behave when C appeared to be desperate. I advised him to be a participant (silent) witness (see the section titled "Other Interventions in Depression"). The situation seemed to me to be too complicated for family therapy, and I asked C if she was willing to do individual therapy. I told her that I would send her to a colleague of mine whom I fully trusted. Her answer was that at the moment she did not have any money to do psychotherapy and that she did not have any trust in all those psychotherapies subsidized by state mental care. I was thus put into a corner; I could not do a brief family therapy because of her parents' horrible psychological condition and because of her fiancé's disengaged attitude. He, in fact, seemed to be leaning in the direction of leaving her to her fate. The individual approach was not an option because the young woman was not willing. At this point I decided to play my last card.

At the next session I asked whether she was willing to do anything necessary to overcome this difficult moment. She sincerely answered yes. Then I asked her to give me an accurate exposition of her ideas. She expounded a series of sad ideas. I asked her to write down these thoughts clearly as they were surfacing, and I helped her write them. I gave her the assignment to complete the list at home, making sure not to leave out any thought. At the following session she presented me with the following list:

1. I have a seriously ill father and therefore I too will get seriously ill, because it is almost surely a hereditary disease. Owing to this, I will no longer be able to work, to fulfill any plan and I will not even have the means to support myself. I will be reduced to a vegetable. I'll end up locked up in a room. I will become only a thought separated from my body, and a sad thought at that.
2. The others don't care about me, I don't exist, whether I am there or not is the same thing. I am as important as a piece of furniture, as an object, I am withering away.
3. Nobody likes me anymore, nobody has the slightest interest in me physically or psychologically.
4. I am not loved, I cannot make people feel passion or affection for me.
5. I don't have any interests, no enthusiasm, no human warmth.
6. I feel guilty, rather than bringing happiness to the house I am like an owl.
7. I am almost nothing to my boyfriend, he is leaving me and he is right, because why should he stick around? As a partner I am worthless, my maternal function is non-existing. Surely, he will find a happy, warm, sensual, concrete woman.

At this point I gave her the prescription to memorize what she had written on that piece of paper she had shown to me and secretly, three times a day, to practice repeating these thoughts (in the hours she had chosen from 7:30 A.M. to 8:00 A.M; from 2:00 P.M. to 2:30 P.M.; from 11:00 P.M. to 11:30 P.M.) while walking between two chairs, set at a certain distance from one another. She was to get back to me by phone after three months or a year.

After 13 months I received a phone call from the young woman. I perked my ears because I was really interested in the evolution of that situation. She told me she had tried contacting me before but had not been able to reach me, and she told me that things were going very well. The depression had gone away, and she had finally gotten married. I gave her my congratulations and I asked her whether she had done that exercise. She said that she had done it regularly. Then I asked her if her economic situation had improved, and she answered affirmatively.

I suggested, then, that she start individual psychotherapy, and she answered that she would think about it.

Other Interventions in Depression

The therapy of depression constitutes an important chapter in the evolution of psychotherapy. It requires a series of interventions that are linked together. In this section we deal with interventions that we use continuously and that almost always produce positive results. We are referring to certain advice given to the family of a depressed patient about how to behave toward that person, to a certain theory of depression that is explained to the patient in the presence of the family, and of the approach we use when a patient expresses suicidal ideation.

When we treat a family of a depressed patient, we always give the following advice. The attitude that the spouse and family members should take is not that of downplaying it, that is, of telling him or her that the disorder is not that big, that the symptom will go away easily. They should not spur the patient to pull himself/herself together. Instead they must behave like "participant witnesses"; that is, they must watch, listen, and not say anything. When they can't take it anymore, when they have had it "up to here," they should leave the house. In fact, we explain, it is precisely the consoling attitude that prevents the patients from getting out of a depression. Everyone is subject to depression. Such intervention creates in the family a state of stupor and is usually accepted with satisfaction by the patient. The depressed patient sees the downplaying and consoling attitude on the part of the family members as lack of understanding and shutting off in his regard; this irritates him and depresses him. The therapist's intervention then can be described as generating an F5 style on the part of the relatives toward the patient. All of these are important changes in the network of relations, in the reference point of a person.

The skills that are required to repair and form a new network are generally different from the ones that the person had previously utilized.

Depressive symptoms must be seen as a set of messages requiring reassurance, for the subject, that he or she will be able to maintain the network of interactions. It also requires action on the part of the others to reconstruct the network.

The initial sequence of interactions with other significant people is a determining factor for the evolution of the subject either further toward depression or toward a return to normality. Depressive communication aims at ascertaining the nature of the relation or the context in which the interaction is taking place. The error that is usually made is that of giving instead a literal answer. For example, when a subject says that he is not feeling well, a literal answer would be the advice to go to the hospital. Grinker has observed that giving a literal answer to the various hows and whys asked by kids or depressed people creates the feeling of being rejected, neglected, or discarded.

The change undergone by the normal subject in speaking to the depressed remains hidden; that is, the depressed is given few indications of his or her impact on the others. The information given by the depressed of troubles and suffering is very strongly capable of causing a feeling of guilt in the other, as well as the inhibition of a direct expression of boredom or hostility. This can be observed both in the families and in the therapists.

The dilemma confronting the depressed is to decide whether the others are reassuring him that he is worth something and that he is accepted based on genuine feelings toward him or rather because he has elicited these responses by his depressed behavior. On his part, the interlocutor answers in an ambiguous manner, and this prevents the depressed from getting out of the dysfunctional cycle.

If communication took place at a single level, then depression would be a less ubiquitous problem. The fact that human beings not only communicate but communicate about communications, (i.e., they metacommunicate by qualifying and labeling what they say) makes it possible for a person to offer support and reassurance with a tone of rejection or to offer criticism with a tone of reassurance and support. One can state that he cares to be with a person and in fact draw away from him or her.

The ambiguity, indecisiveness, and confusion of the interaction lead the depressed person to elicit continuous feedback from others, in order to be able to ascertain the nature of the relationship. But it is exactly these continuous feedbacks that have an ever-increasing negative effect on the relationship. The persistence and repetition of the symptoms are hard to understand and cause a negative response in the social context.

The members of the social context are in fact irritated but inhibited and increasingly guilt-ridden, but they continue to give verbal support and assurances of acceptance. However, slowly and progressively, the discrepancy between verbal content and the affective level of the answers, parallel to the escalation of the depressed's symptoms, leads to a clarification of the interactive situation to both. At this point, some members of the social context abandon the field, finding unconvincing arguments for their drawing away. Others remain in a mutually manipulative pattern that is self-perpetuating. It is a kind of "game" in which members of the social environment manipulate the depressed person with reassurances, support, and denial of the process that is taking place, thus reducing the aversion and guilt. In turn, the depressed person manipulates the environment so that it may yield sympathy and reassurances. At this point, though, he or she knows that the elicited response is not genuine.

The cycle can remain chronic at this level, or it can have a further downward development with the passage to physical symptoms of the type "I am tired" and "My stomach feels weird," and once again the environment is given the responsibility of making changes.

At a certain point, the depressed person, no longer capable of rebuilding his or her living space, asks for a "suspension of the rules," a moratorium in the network of obligations. The person and the environment legitimate the sick role. Once again, with hospitalization, the answer is a literal one, but it obviously does not solve the problem and signals a further withdrawal on the part of the environment.

Another route that the depressed person can follow is that of a declaration of failure and of guilt, and in this case, too, generally, the result is the withdrawal of the members of the context and eventually hospitalization.

In the case of a stable relationship, like that of husband and wife, this withdrawal acts as a cushion against depression. But when stability is not accompanied by adequate support and assurance, it results in a chronic depressive cycle. In fact, if the depressed is convinced that the wife tolerates him more than what can be reasonably expected without protesting, he can start to believe that she sticks by him only out of a sense of duty and not because of a genuine acceptance of the relationship. At this point, through his symptoms, the depressed person can put his wife to the test and see if he is really accepted, up to the point of leading the other person to separation. If the wife passes the test by continuing to tolerate the annoying behavior, the depressed husband is not necessarily reassured about being accepted. In fact, he will lean in the direction of convincing himself that she remains with him because she is incapable of leaving. If, instead she makes an effort to abandon the situation, this can be read by him to mean that the relationship was a truly desired one and that he had been accepted.

After the reconciliation, however, the wife can once again appear excessively tolerant, thus causing a new series of tests, doubts, contests to be put in motion. This cycle can cause chronic troubles but could also be an alternative to a straight-down depressive spiral. In essence, the depressed person finds himself in the difficult situation of wanting to avoid rejection and at the same time fearing acceptance.

This theory is briefly explained to the family as follows. The patient has the right to his sad feelings, and the more one seeks to shut them out, the more one will be trapped by them. Normal people can be defined as such because they come in and go out of depression; they leave the door of depression open. He who wants to close it instead remains trapped inside (Weeks & L'Abate, 1982). In line with this principle, one can ask to try to concentrate on the depression. One can say that depression has become chronic because one has stopped halfway and that only by touching the rock bottom of depression can one get out of it. If the issue of suicide comes out, one must say that suicide is precisely a way of avoiding touching that rock bottom that would allow the cure.

Finally, as to the approach to the patient who expresses suicidal thoughts, it is our opinion that it is necessary to fill the intersection, that is, to discuss the issue openly rather than avoid speaking about it.

In dealing with depression, which at times is a very serious psychiatric problem, it must be stressed that, aside from the technique of interaction, the therapist's experience plays a fundamental role. The interventions must be prescribed in proper doses and must be used only when one is sure they will not have a negative effect.

BIPOLAR DISORDERS

The basic premise of this section is that we do not claim the ability to cure manic-depressive psychoses with exclusively psychological means. The prescription of medication, particularly lithium and antiepileptics, is almost always indispensable. However, there are some cases in which some patients do not respond to medication or in which the exclusive use of medication yields unsatisfactory results. In these cases, psychotherapy becomes an instrument of intervention of the greatest importance. Finally, in our opinion, psychological interventions are a useful supplement for all patients. If we observe patients treated only with medication and those treated with both medication and psychotherapy, the difference in favor of the latter is evident.

Facing bipolar disorders, one inevitably runs into some very interesting theoretical aspects concerning the relationship between medication and psychotherapy and the possibility that a single mechanism subtends two diametrically opposed clinical configurations, depression and manic disorders.

Let us briefly examine the interactive intervention that we used during the stage of depression, then the intervention used during the manic phase, and finally during the symptom-free period. As the reader will have noticed, most of these cases have already been described in other parts of the book; however, we think it is useful to group them together in order to give a vision of continuity, parallel with the cyclical course of psychosis.

Interventions during Depression

"Going toward the world of the other by amplifying it" (interactive style F13) as an interactive style surely proved effective in interrupting episodes of depression. That is, the intervention goes toward the world of the depressed patient, toward feelings, thoughts, and behavior without opposing them but rather by amplifying them.

An example of this type is the so-called maneuver of the chairs mentioned earlier. We usually resort to this intervention in emergencies and in forms with a heavy anxiety component, and we are almost always successful. During the family therapy session we place two chairs in the middle of the room at a distance designed to prevent vertigo, and we ask the patient to walk around them moaning and expressing his sadness. While the therapist incites the patient to continue reframing the exercise as an "outlet, a relief of anxiety," the relatives witness the exercise quietly. After a certain amount of time, varying from a few minutes to more than an hour, we witness the relaxation of both patient and family members.

The session concludes with the prescription to carry out this exercise three times a day, at fixed hours (morning, noon, and evening), for a fixed duration (usually half an hour), "as though it was medicine." The task of the spouse or of other significant relatives is to preside over and check the manner in which the patient carries out the exercise according to the agreed modalities and up to the complete control of depression.

A second example of this type of intervention is the so-called maneuver of concentrating on depression. We explain to the patient's family that he has the right to his feelings; the more they try to close the door on these feelings, the more the patient will be trapped in depression. Normal people can be defined as such because they come in and out of depression and leave the door open; people who want to close it end up trapped inside (Weeks & L'Abate, 1992). In keeping with this principle, one can ask the patient to concentrate on depression. For example, during a session we ask the patient to write down on a piece of paper in a complete and precise manner all his sad thoughts. At the end of the session the piece of paper (filled by him or by the spouse or a family member under dictation) is given to the patient, who will complete it and memorize the contents. Then, in a manner analogous to the chair exercise, three times a day, at fixed hours and for a fixed duration, he or she will recite them to his or her spouse or the assembled family, concentrating on his or her depression.

The effectiveness of these interventions is tied both to the interactive style prescribed and to the proposal of a temporal map different from the family's, as far as the four parameters are concerned: (1) structure of successions (writing, memorizing, repeating); (2) fixed duration (half hour of exercise); (3) frequency of occurrence (every day, three times a day); and (4) standard temporal setting (morning, noon, evening).

According to the "Tabulation of depression" (interactive style F1 or F9, according to the EPM), the shared focus is maintained on the symptom (F1) and at times unpredicted by the two interacting subjects' behavior (F9).

We ask the patient to write down on a temporal diagram (with days on the abscissa axis and the 24 hours divided in quarters on the ordinate axis) the beginning and the end of depression, eventually making it more detailed by making marks to indicate the intensity. Also in this intervention, so briefly summarized, we prescribe a temporal map even if the parameters have not been previously fixed. The temporal diagram described above will force the patient to modify his or her temporal map in the framework provided by the therapist.

In "Night awakening" (interactive style F11, according to the EPM), manipulations of the sleep-waking rhythms are often utilized in the treatment of depression. We sometimes ask the patients to wake up at a certain hour of the night and to stay awake for a certain amount of time, generally with good results, at least temporarily. Such a type of intervention reminds one of Haley's ordeal, (i.e., a prescription so difficult that the patient withdraws from the symptom). The therapist interacts according to a demanding interactive style, tending toward and leading to the preservation of his or her world. One or more family members are involved in the prescription.

Interventions during Mania

The lower incidence of manic episodes, their briefness, and their more frequent control through drug treatment make an interactive approach less prevalent in this type of disorder. However, even while having a smaller number of case studies compared with depression, in certain cases we do use therapeutic maneuvers both during a session or as a prescription at home. These interventions, even if their effects are limited in time, are certainly useful, at least in eroding the interactive rigidity exhibited by the patient, insofar as they facilitate the acceptance of a later psychotropic and psychological therapy.

The Switching Chairs Maneuver. Frequently a manic patient will put himself or herself in symmetry with the therapist or challenge the rules of the setting by creating disturbances, interrupting, or incessantly speaking. Sometimes, in these cases, we ask the patient to exchange seats with the therapist. Then, the latter will begin acting like a madman and say, "I feel insane, and how are you feeling?" At this point, the patient's mood shifts, and he or she becomes depressed and silent.

Standing on a Chair. When the patient's euphoria is openly reinforced by the family context, by the fear of contradicting and thus defining oneself in the interaction, we usually ask that the patient stand on top of a chair, and we continue the session normally with the patient displaying this peculiar position.

Gym Suit and Tennis Shoes. The patient used to go out very early and run through his town, then would return home, sleep a little, and then would go out again running through town, repeating the pattern until night. We gave him a prescription to carry out at home; he was to buy a gym suit and a pair of tennis shoes, so as to be able to run more comfortably all day long. Actually, given that this was the patient's sole occupation, he was to be encouraged to run all the time. We advised family members to inform their acquaintances in town about this prescription and to ask for their collaboration in encouraging the patient to run.

Creating a Carnivalesque Context. An intervention that we have not used up to now and is therefore totally imaginary (but one that we plan to experiment with as soon as we find a family that is very open to collaborating) is that of creating a carnivalesque context for the euphoric-manic patient, a context in which the whole family conforms to the patient's state of mind by wearing masks, dancing, and displaying lively and festive decorations.

Interventions during Symptom-Free Periods

Paradoxical Prediction. This type of intervention was developed in the form of a counterparadox given to the family that asks for a change without changing. The prediction of a worsening or of a relapse is in part a prescription not to change, thus asking the family not to change in order to be able to change. In our experience, such a technique is effective both in the immediate sense and during the therapeutic cycle in overcoming an impasse, but until now we have not been able to ascertain an interruption in the occurrence of bipolar disorders.

Making the Expectations Explicit. This approach has proven very useful in discussing the expectations of a relapse in a thorough way with the patient's family (this in itself is a therapeutic intervention based on the style F5, entering the world of the other, or filling the intersection F1, when the message is not made explicit by the family, F6). Generally, families build concrete expectations about the issue of relapse. They develop fears as well as implicit and explicit attempts at solutions that end up, instead of keeping the status quo, as a homeostatic mechanism. These attempted solutions serve as preludes to a new episode, as described below. The therapist will then be able to build and propose a way out, as, for example, the attempts that we will now describe.

Periodic Imitation of Behavior during Depressive or Manic Phases. During a session, the therapist gathers and/or makes people gather detailed information on symptomatic behavior. Then he or she asks the patient to reproduce them "voluntarily." The family is to collaborate by offering suggestions, until the patient reaches a perfect imitation. Finally we assign the prescription that once a month, for a fixed duration, for example, for an entire day, the patient is to act out his or her symptomatic behavior at home. Family members will make sure that he or she carries it out or, in other cases, will be directly involved performing their own role during the agreed-upon period.

Attention to the Early Signals of Steering toward Depression or Mania. During a session one will undertake a detailed investigation of the very early signs, those first moments that precede the onset of mania or depression. For example, the wife of a patient identified as the very first sign of her husband's veering toward mania his ceasing to be tolerant or accommodating, his tendency to react toward others (in the sense that he would get angry with both family and strangers, attributing problems and troubles to them, thus exhibiting a projective tendency). The husband instead hinted that the first signal of mania was the appearance of insomnia.

This intervention usually ends by asking the patient to immediately start over again or strengthen his drug therapy at the appearance of the first symptoms of a relapse.

ANXIETY DISORDERS: OBSESSIVE COMPULSIONS AND PHOBIAS

In this section we deal with some disorders that the DSM-IV classifies in the diagnostic category of "anxiety disorders." Phobias consist of a persistent and irrational fear of objects and situations. One has obsessions when ideas and thoughts become persistent against the will of the subject and in spite of the attempts to eliminate them; they are generally associated with repetitive behavior ("ceremonials") carried out with subjective compulsion and a desire to resist (see Figures 10-9 and 10-10).

The therapeutic moves that we use with the families are basically of four types:

1. Let the father enter the daughter's world (F5);
2. Let the spouse go toward the patient's world, amplifying it (F13);
3. Let the therapist ask the family to carry out difficult and complex actions, related to the problem that has been presented but that needs the acceptance of the therapist's world in order to be carried out. The therapist appears central beyond measure but not very open to taking their world into account, except for what pertains to the solution of the problem (solution that belongs also to the world of the therapist—F11).
4. Let one focus on the goal, but in an excessively conspicuous manner or with bizarre nuances so as to induce a shift to the corresponding antifunction (F1 → F9).

Type A Interventions. Five years ago a small family came to my office, composed of the father, a big, illiterate, non-talkative peasant; the mother, a petite woman, dignified in both dress and speech and rather talkative; and a small and skinny 13-year-old daughter. The problem that they presented was that for some time the girl had been afflicted by strange fears: she was afraid that objects would go into her mouth. She feared that her father's medicine, sputum, and hair would end up in her mouth. Furthermore, she washed her hands very often, and she ate very little.

It became clear right away that, in that family, the father was totally peripheral ("my function is to bring home the bacon") and that there was an over-involvement between mother and daughter. After the process of joining with the family was achieved, and after a deflation of the over-dramatized symptom was achieved by making the mother put a hair into her daughter's mouth (without any show of considerable anguish on the daughter's part but also without immediate therapeutic results), we proceeded, in the second session, to make the father interact with the daughter.

Figure 10-9
Intervention in Obsessive-Compulsive Disorders (1)

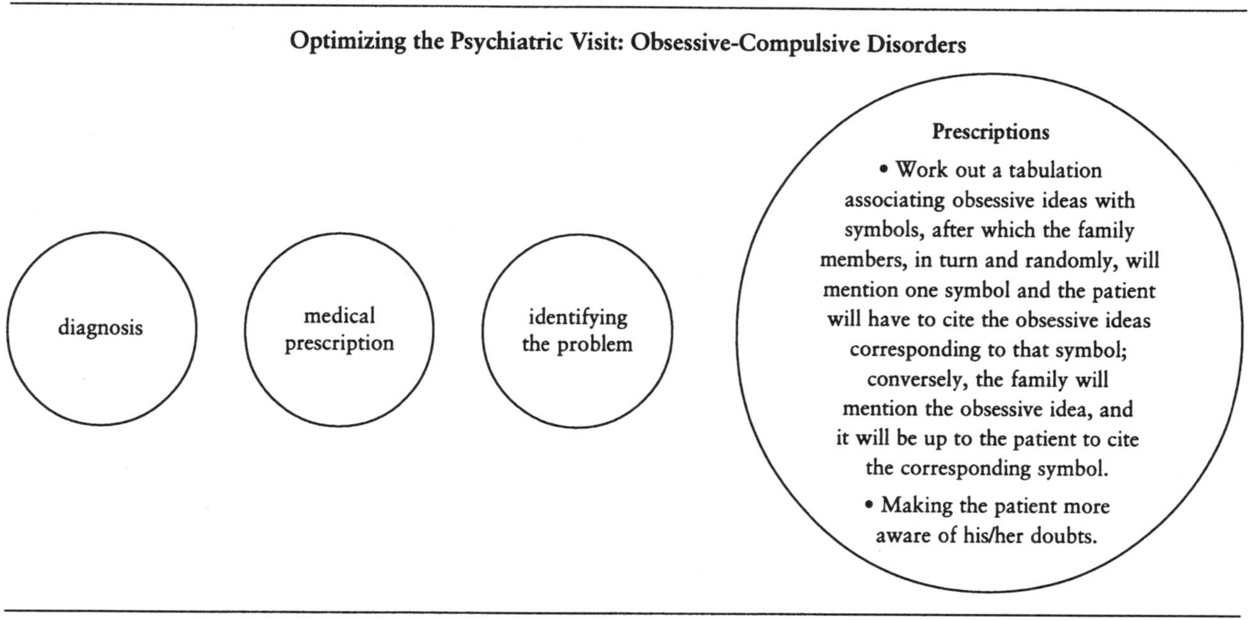

Figure 10-10
Intervention in Obsessive-Compulsive Disorders (2)

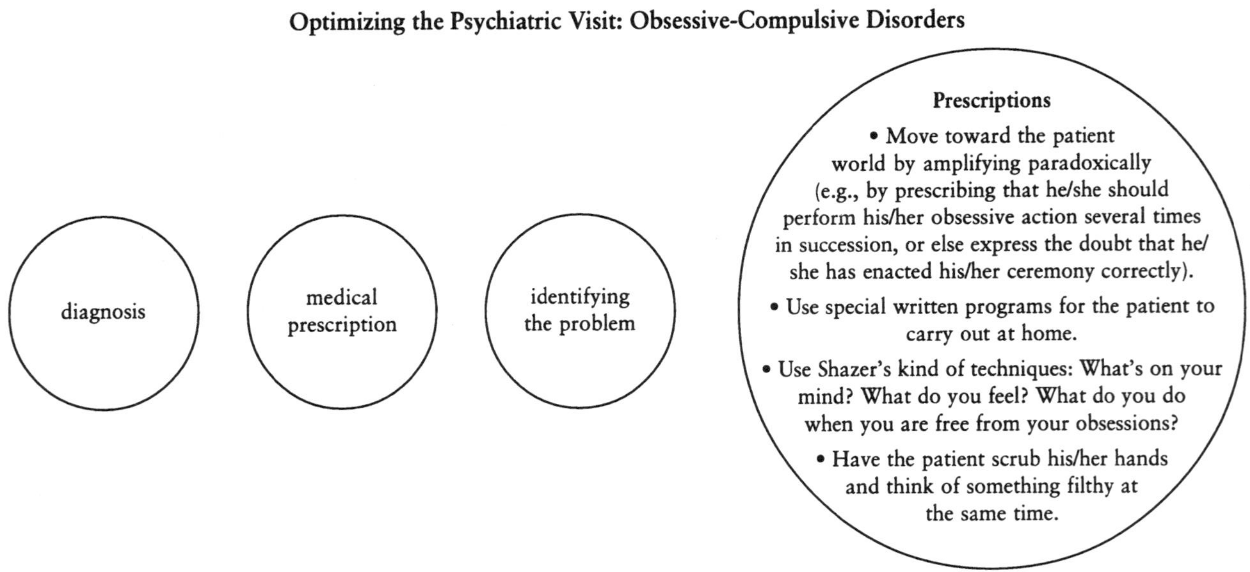

The interaction followed the line of "let the father enter into the daughter's world." It was not easy because of the difficulty on the peasant's part to operate at a symbolic level. In fact, we had to go so far as to make him touch his daughter's face and body (something that he had never done before) in order to make him carry out what we intended. Such interaction was also prescribed at home. By the next session (the third one, after a week) the girl's disorders had practically disappeared.

From then on this type of intervention has been used in many cases of young families, almost always with good results. In some cases, a single, well-conducted session was sufficient to solve the problem in a final manner, as we have been able to ascertain by checking after some years.

For example, in April 1982 I saw a family composed of a 54-year-old storekeeper, the father; a 51-year-old mother, who worked in the same store as her husband; and three children, aged 25, 23, and 17. The identified patient, F. B., the second daughter, was a very scrupulous, studious, and serious girl (who had never had a boyfriend). At a certain point in the year before, owing perhaps to the "tiredness caused by university exams" or due "to a prior threat of parental separation" (the father accused the mother of talking too much), she began to develop an obsession. This consisted in the belief that the university registrar was not reporting her grades correctly and that her student registration number was incorrect, so she had to check very often.

Subsequently, other "obsessions" appeared such as becoming a drug addict, stealing, killing, losing control. I prescribed to the father to enter into his daughter's world, that is, to understand what existed in her mind, what desires, fears were there, what she thought of certain circumstances of her life; in other words, to introduce himself to the world of the daughter. They agreed on the hours that they should spend together; and the meetings were to take place daily. In the next session, after 17 days, I was able to ascertain that the prescription had been scrupulously followed, that there had been a great improvement in the father–daughter relationship, and that the symptom had disappeared. During telephone contact made after more than three years, we learned that the problem had been completely resolved without additional contacts with mental health professionals.

Among these cases, we must mention one indicating that this type of intervention is effective not only when the symptom concerns the children. In 1980, I saw a family in which the mother was obsessed by the idea of killing the daughter. I prescribed to the father to enter the daughter's world. This therapeutic move caused a rapid disappearance of the symptom in the mother. Upon checking three years later, we ascertained that it had not reappeared.

The reader must have noticed that this style of intervention greatly resembles the one prescribed for anorexia. This observation is correct, which leads one to think that in many cases there are some affinities between the anorexic system and the obsessive one. Comparing the two interventions, the difference is that in the case of anorexia, the intervention is organized in a different way; it is more incisive, the emotional response is much stronger, and there is more emphasis placed on bodily aspects.

Type B Interventions. Some years ago I cured a family composed of two spouses around 40 years old and two small children; the wife had a serious case of chronic obsession. The husband was very jealous and intolerant toward the wife's disorders. For many years, the wife had been obsessed by the idea that the children could get infections caused by the many small scratches and abrasions that they would accidentally inflict on themselves during their daily activities. For this reason she would check them very carefully, and she often disinfected them with rubbing alcohol. These ceremonies would make the husband furious, but his violent reproaches had no effect on the wife, who even felt compelled "to repeat them more often." Clearly, the therapy took one step forward when the following maneuver was prescribed, first during a session and later at home. The husband was to inflict minuscule scratches on his legs. The wife, in the dark with a small spot flashlight, was to explore the husband's skin inch by inch, and if it seemed to her that there was even the smallest cut, she was to proceed immediately to a careful disinfection with alcohol. The husband was to encourage her to carry out the exercise with care and within the prescribed time.

A simpler example is that of a pair of old maid sisters who had always been very religious, especially the patient, who in her life had been the unluckier and uglier of the two. The symptom consisted in the very intense desire to utter blasphemies directed to Jesus, the Virgin Mary, and Saint Joseph; the insults concerned their origin and morals. In vain she had turned to her priest to relieve her anguish, and the priest himself had sent her to me. The prescription was that for half an hour, three times a day, in the presence of her sister (who was to supervise the exercise), she was to say these blasphemies that obsessed her aloud and with the greatest of expressivity. Actually, she was to try to make them more elaborate. When we checked on her one month later, the symptom had already ceased.

Type C Interventions. These are interventions analogous to those of Erickson (Haley, 1976) with the patient with the driving phobia. For example, in one of our cases, a very seriously obsessive patient spent her time dusting some household objects. She was a middle-aged woman, married and with children, whose own nuclear family, however, had been totally re-absorbed in the family of origin. They had no autonomy. They lived in the parents' house and shared with them the meals, the rooms, the problems, the children. She was asked which household object gave her the strongest urge to dust, and she pointed to a certain chair. She was asked to bring the chair along to the session. A week later the prescription was given that father, mother, and husband, in turn (for 15 minutes each), spill chalk dust that we provided on the chair and that the patient was to dust. This prescription was later given at home, for the duration of three hours daily. The result was clearly positive, in the sense that there was a clinical improvement and that they left the parents' house to return to their own house, which had been abandoned for years.

Type D Interventions. An atypical example of this category is the one that we practice for agoraphobia and that I will describe in greater detail. The disorder consists in the inability of certain subjects to go out of the house, because of the anxiety that this causes and for the connected fear of falling or fainting in a crowd. As usual, in most of our interventions, we ask the patient's family or the couple if they are willing to do everything possible to overcome such a handicapping disorder. Once we receive a positive answer, without ambiguities, from each member (in the case of an ambiguous answer we make use of the "empty box" technique), we ask the various members of the couple or of the family to take a week off from work, because what we are about to propose is a very intensive treatment requiring total commitment. Once we obtain this second agreement, we give the prescription that the patient—say, a man—must take a notebook and a watch and get out of the house. He is to stay outside until he develops a rather strong state of anxiety, strong but not unbearable. At this point he should go back home. As soon as he is back, he will check the watch and record with great accuracy how many minutes or seconds he was able to stay out. Right away (i.e., leaving no intervals) he will again check the watch, go out, and stay out until intense anxiety appears again; then he must go back in, check the watch, record it on the notebook, and then go out again; and continue this way for the whole day and for all days of the week.

The partner, if it is a couple, or the family if it is an unmarried person, will remain home all day supporting the patient's action in the sense of encouraging him to carry out the task and will eventually have the function of "bouncer." It will be explained to them that we are trying to help the patient achieve his freedom but that we are aware that this freedom can cause fear to the family (having said this, one generally receives a reaction of reassurance on the part of family members that they are ready to do anything to free their relative). Continuing, we say that it is clear that any leniency on their part (in appearance a benevolent act in its form but an insidious one in the substance) as far as the patient's attempt not to dutifully carry out his prescription is concerned will be nothing else but an act of sabotage against the patient's liberation. Therefore, it will be an act of collusion of the entire family against the efforts of the therapist. Having thus overcome the greatest obstacle to the curing of the symptom, we then proceed to give an appointment for the following week, so as to verify the results.

As for the joint prescription of drugs, in these cases it is useful. We always jointly prescribe chlorimipramine and an anti-anxiety drug.

Compulsion to Rummage

A young woman of about 30, a housewife married to a municipal employee and mother of a three-year-old girl, complained of an irrepressible compulsion to rummage through the trash and take out little things like used-up matches or pieces of paper, which she would then hoard. Both spouses, husband and wife, appeared to be hyperinvolved with their family of origin, both of them having experienced conflicts with each other before the couple's marriage.

For this reason, they insisted that the husband's parents not participate in the sessions, while the wife's parents, who lived in the same apartment building as the couple, in an adjacent apartment, did participate. The patient had been treated with chlorimipramine and benzodiazepines for several months without noticeable results.

The theme of the first four sessions was the reconstruction of the family context, while the symptoms were left in the background. In fact, they were only the object of homework assignments and were listed in order of "importance," tabulated and shifted in their "time" placement (e.g., shifting from the hours in which the husband was absent to the hours in which he was present).

The most effective intervention took place in the fifth session. The therapist reconstructed in detail the symptom that was most disturbing to the family (i.e., that the patient picked up and hid objects that were meant to be in the trash). Then the supervisor came in, renewed the "pact with the devil" (see above), emphasizing that the crucial moment of the therapy had arrived. He used some expressions and a tone of voice that increased the tension in the session and finally asked each of the family members present, in turn, to throw something on the floor that the patient had to pick up. The session ended with the prescription that for three hours a day, always at the same time, the family was to carry out the exercise demonstrated in the session.

In the sixth session the patient and the family said that the symptom had almost disappeared. She was re-contacted some months after the end of the 10-week cycle and said that the problem had ceased.

Psychic Obsessions

Another case is that of a family with a young woman exhibiting an obsession of a purely psychic character, that is, one that did not lead either to rituals or to manifest behavior, a fact that made the therapeutic intervention particularly difficult. She had been treated with chlorimipramine and benzodyazepines for a long time, but the problem had not been solved at all. The patient had fallen prey to several obsessive roles, among which were having to think about Jesus' penis, having to think about having steel lungs, having to think about cemeteries, having to think that shampooing one's hair is the equivalent of brainwashing, and having to think about being a cog in a big organization similar to a machine.

The following prescription was given in two stages. In the first stage, the patient was supposed to keep track of her obsessive ideas (i.e., every day she was supposed to mark on a special table the beginning and end of each obsessive idea). In order to do this, she had to connect each obsessive idea to a graphic symbol, for example, the obsessive sexual ideas connected to a triangle, the steel lungs to two circles, the cemetery to a cross, brainwashing to a circle, a big organization to a square.

As is well known, the tabulation of symptoms usually leads to the decrease of the symptoms themselves, but this did not happen with our patient.

In the second stage, we gave the prescription to the whole family (parents, brothers, sisters) to carry out the following tasks: for three hours a day they all had to meet, and each of the members had to mention, in turn, one of the symbols (what came to mind first—triangle two circles, cross, etc.), and the patient had to say immediately the thought to which it corresponded or, vice versa, the family members had to mention the thought and the patient was to say immediately the corresponding symbol.

The family and the patient carried out the prescription with great accuracy, and the following week a great improvement was reported.

After a month, the patient reported an overall improvement, which she quantified as an 80% improvement (and we all know how difficult it is to get an obsessive subject to admit to any positive effect whatsoever of a therapy).

Sexual Disorders

In the interactive perspective, sexual symptoms are placed in a broader context as one of the elements of interaction between people. Often, in fact, we see that the same modalities that develop in numerous other daily situations are perpetuated in sexual relations. Sex cannot always and totally be seen as a neutral area in respect to all other interactive modalities of everyday life. On the contrary, the field of sexuality often represents one of the clearest expressions of the general rules existing in the couple.

A symmetrical relationship can develop between the couple; in sexual relations a battle can be perpetuated between the spouses over the children's upbringing, household expenses, friendships, and so on. Two spouses can set up their life as a couple on the model of soldiers of opposing armies. It is obvious that in these cases sex can become a very destructive weapon.

In other cases a complementary relationship develops. One can arrive at extreme situations in which all the enjoyment is due to one of the two members, while the other becomes a passive object.

Between the extremes of total symmetry and total complementarity there is a development of a series of intermediate modalities. Our group (Silvestri et al., 1980) has criticized the concepts of symmetry, complementarity, and parallelism as being too vague. Actually, as we have seen in preceding sections of the book, those three interactive modalities can be proposed, from a much less ambiguous perspective, as the encounter of 16 basic functions or interactive styles of a subject or of a system with the 16 basic functions of another subject or system.

According to the EPM, the different techniques of traditional sexual therapy acquire a different perspective. Let us give some examples. In the so-called Sensate Focus I and II, clearly a situation is created in which only one part of the whole sexual sphere of the two partners is shared. Thus, in vaginismus, one establishes a very limited interaction that extends gradually by the prescription of introducing first one's own finger into the vagina and then that of the partner. In the "non-demanding coitus" we witness an interaction in which the partner tries to maintain an attitude of passive acceptance.

The prescription to patients not to have sexual relations when they come to us precisely to resolve the problem of sexual relations that they cannot have, is an antifunction.

However, in this section, I do not spend time describing all the modalities of sexual relations and the therapeutic prescriptions in terms of function, so as not to make the treatment more difficult.

Having One's First Orgasm at Forty. This is exclusively a couple therapy, held in two months' time, with sessions spaced every seven days for the first three weeks and with longer intervals later on, making a total of seven sessions. The couple consisted of two people a little over 40, of humble origins but with a great wealth of energy and abilities. From a simple factory worker the husband had become the head of a successful firm that repaired industrial products. The wife had been an outstanding organizer of the home, a support for the husband, and the mother of four very healthy children. The first was 23 years old, married and working in the father's firm, the second was 21 years old and also worked with the father, and the other children were 17 and 12 years old.

The father defined the children as lazy and disrespectful, while the mother defended them, saying that he did not know how to relate to them. She accused the husband of being harsh and tactless (this interaction allowed us to make the hypothesis that the lady considered the husband to be unrefined and pushy, starting from the concept of children as metaphor of the parents).

According to the wife, the 17-year-old daughter had psychological problems; she was rather withdrawn and looked sad (metaphorical reading: the lady was expressing her own sadness and introvertedness). We also spoke about Rome, their city of origin, and Mrs. X said that she would like to go back; she even made a burning question out of it. In fact, their interactions with the people of town Z (in Apulia, southern Italy) were very few, because she feared that she would be betrayed in her friendship and trust, as had recently happened. This request to go back to Rome was in contrast with the fact that actually they had been living in town Z for over 20 years. The husband pointed out that in Z they had reached a very good economic and work position, not only for them but also for their children, while if they went back to Rome, they would have to start from scratch.

However, the wife vehemently insisted that they leave Z. The very intense tones of the discussion made us understand that we were missing something. The therapist asked what the problem was. At this point a great feeling of embarrassment was shown, especially by the woman. The reason of the visit was that in sexual relations she did not feel, and had never felt, anything.

We expressed our skepticism on the possibility of a successful therapy and even of obtaining small improvements. However, they insisted in wanting to go on with the therapy, declaring that they were willing to do anything that we would ask them to do. We wondered what was urging this couple to confront this problem of frigidity at such a late time. The reason surfaced clearly in the next session. The husband had had an affair with a 19-year-old secretary working in his firm. The affair lasted for at least a year and had ended only a few months earlier. To tell the truth, the husband had had affairs in the past. The wife knew about them, even if not in an explicit manner. The husband, on the other hand, even while saying that he was very much in love with his wife, claimed that as a male he had the right to satisfactory sexual relations. He stressed that he had often suggested to the wife to go to a specialist, but she had always refused. The wife seemed to feel guilty on this point and attributed her sexual coldness to previous experiences going back to her early adolescence. When she was 11 years old, her mother died, and she concentrated all her affections on her father. But one sad day she surprised the father in bed with her aunt (her mother's sister), and she was deeply disturbed by it. On that occasion she told her father in a beseeching manner never again to bring that hateful woman in the house. In spite of this, the father had shown himself indifferent to the daughter's prayers and had decided to live with the "wretched" one. But the day before the aunt was supposed to move in and live there permanently, the father died in an accident.

We asked her why at other times she had closed her eyes to her husband's escapades, while this time she thought that it was such a serious matter. She answered that this time had been different because the husband had truly lost his head. He had resorted to underhanded tricks and lies, and only after one year of battle after battle and of unspeakable suffering was she finally able to tear him away from the powerful rival's hooks. The husband said that the episode was now over and that they had to concentrate on solving the problem of her frigidity.

Initially, we set up the therapy according to a classical, sexual approach for anorgasmia, but the husband put on airs of a super-expert, saying that he had already tried everything, while the wife, even if seeming to be open and willing, was very embarrassed and expressed her doubts about the modalities of the approach, which she felt to be a little artificial (they had been together for 25 years!). It was clear that the wife preferred to talk about the family, and we went along with it in order to go along with her frame of mind (moving in the direction of her world).

We decided to work on the boundaries between parents and children, mainly between the mother and the 17-year-old daughter. We also worked a great deal to make explicit (filling the empty intersection) what was implicit in that couple, that is, that the father was isolated and opposed to the remaining members of the family (mother and four children). Instead, they were as tight as a fist; and we also worked on the different modalities of interaction existing between the family members.

We made it clear to the mother that she was supposed to change her attitude toward her children; for example, toward her 17-year-old daughter, in the direction of making the daughter more autonomous. She herself had to become autonomous in respect to the daughter. Toward the end of the third session during a husband-wife interaction we made the husband ask Mrs. X what she would like as a personal present. She asked for the record *Moonlight Sonata* by Beethoven. Mrs. X, in fact, loved classical music. In the course of the following week the husband made sure to buy a number of records that the wife particularly liked.

In the next session we suggested that during the upcoming week they should change the bedroom in a way that was particularly pleasing to her. They were to close the bedroom door, and the husband had to limit himself to caressing her affectionately. This latter request caused protests, which were then withdrawn, on the part of the husband, who was used to getting straight to the point.

At the fifth session the wife expressed her gratitude for what the therapist had done. Things in the family were going very well; the 17-year-old girl had changed a lot and seemed freer and more autonomous. Mrs. X felt stronger and more self-assured, and even the relationship between husband and wife had improved quite a bit. She really enjoyed his caresses, even though she had not been able to reach orgasm.

We set up the session as a bland "mourning session." By now it was clear that we would not be able to achieve our goal and that the wife would be unable, for the rest of her life, to experience the great pleasure of orgasm. However, we concluded that it is possible to live without orgasm; perhaps it was even a blessing in disguise that she had this limitation, because no one could predict what would happen if she, a mature woman, were to experience such new sensations. The husband stuck to the position that what was important to him was that his wife "had tried to do it." At the end of the session, we did not set up any other appointment.

After a couple of weeks we received a phone call from them. They wanted another appointment, which we set up for them a few days later. When they arrived for the appointment, both of them were radiant. They had left for a trip alone, a thing that they had never done in 25 years of living together, and in the quiet of a hotel room the miracle had happened: she had experienced a pleasure never felt in the past. We put on a skeptical and incredulous expression, but the description the woman gave us was very clear, and the husband, "the expert," attested to its truth without a shade of doubt. They added that it was not an isolated success but that she had reached orgasm even in the following days. She stated that some block had been removed.

One last consolidation session marked the end of the therapy.

Interpretation of the Positive Result of the Therapy. Paradoxically, we attribute a great part of the therapeutic success to factors outside the therapy. The threat of destruction had come down heavily on that family. The father, who was increasingly more peripheral, at the end had formed a tie outside the family system. The only possibility of saving the situation was the disappearance of the wife's frigidity. A homeostatic maneuver triggered the success. As far as the therapeutic technique that we used is concerned, it came from the interactive perspective, utilizing the mixture of three models: the structural, the elementary pragmatic, and the paradoxical. From the structural model, we used the setting of boundaries between parents' subsystem and children's subsystem. This allowed the patient to become a wife, a function that in the past she had never fulfilled because of her enmeshment and confusion of roles with regard to the children.

From the EPM, we mainly took the function that can be defined as "entering into the world of the other" on the husband's part toward the wife: the music she liked, the attitude of kindness, petting without penetration. We also took the function "to fill the empty intersection" and the use of antifunctions that can be identified in certain paradoxical interventions.

From the paradoxical model (Weeks & L'Abate, 1982), we took the attitude of skepticism displayed at the beginning of the therapy, the declaration of powerlessness in the fifth session, together with the prescription not to change, and the incredulity at the result in the sixth session.

CONVERSION, SEXUALITY, AND INTERACTIVE DISORDERS

The case that I present now represents in a certain sense the reverse of the preceding case. In contrast to the previous one, the therapists' references to sexuality were instrumental to overcoming the different problems. The premise of the presentation of this family and the connection to the one quoted above are that what characterizes the interactive approach in sexual dysfunctions is seeing them as part of a larger context. At times, in fact, couples consult a specialist, saying they want to solve a sexual problem, while actually they are asking to reorganize their relationship. At other times, they do not ask for the solution of a sexual problem, but proposing to confront this issue is an important element for the therapist and could lead to the overcoming of dysfunctional situations that manifest themselves as nonsexual symptomatology.

Therefore, the approach chosen initially by the couple about sexuality can be the key leading to the modification of dysfunctional rules of a system. Vice versa, the therapist's secondary choice to make sexuality the area of intervention can be useful, always through the modification of dysfunctional rules, in overcoming other problems presented by the couple as primary problems.

The explanation of this interexchangeability of the primary objective of intervention is easily understandable if we think of the distinction existing between content and process. The content of the intervention could be sexuality or other disorders, but process must be understood at a higher, logical level. Then, the choice of what symptoms to treat is in certain cases only the starting point, the means through which to modify the system.

In November 1985 a couple came to our office, composed of a 23-year-old lady (a housewife, good-looking with northern features but with an infantile expression) and her husband, a physically average type, 31 years old, who seemed older than his chronological age and in fact could pass for the patient's father. They had been sent to the senior member of the team by a woman neurologist to solve Anna's diagnostic and therapeutic problems. In fact, for the past two months she had been suffering from symptoms that had been previously diagnosed as epilepsy, and now she was being treated with anti-epileptic drugs and had undergone numerous X-rays, electroencephalograms (EEGs), computerized axial tomographies (CATs), and so on.

The crises were described as loss of consciousness from a fall, at times causing a cranial trauma and drooling. These crises over time had increased to a frequency of two or three times a day. During this first visit, the patient had one of these attacks, which turned out to be of a hysterical nature. She felt a very intense tingling that rose from her limbs to her trunk; she turned pale and collapsed on the chair. The anti-epileptic therapy was halted, and we prescribed an anxiolitic therapy with benzodiazepine, as well as couples therapy.

The first therapy cycle consisted of 10 sessions held one week apart, lasting one hour, with one therapist and supervision at the fifth and tenth sessions, a practice that we have successfully experimented with for a couple of years. The supervision took place with the use of a one-way mirror, communicating through an intercom, but also with direct interventions by the supervisor.

The couple had been married for three and a half years and had a son born a year after their marriage. The woman's symptoms had appeared after a serious problem with legal ramifications concerning her father. Anna's involvement in this situation had been significant, as she had never really separated herself from her family of origin. This caused further enmeshment with regard to the past and the onset of not only intense crises of anxiety with somatization and conversion but also episodes of diffidence and suspicion toward other family members. With the passing of time, Anna had developed an agoraphobic attitude, secluding herself in the home, from which she would go out only in her husband's company and only to go to her parents' house.

The first session ended with the prescription to monitor (accurately recording on forms that had been prepared for that purpose) the beginning and the end of the crises, day by day, in such a manner as to quantify their duration and frequency.

In the second session we prescribed the symptom, indicating the times of day during which Anna, in her husband's presence, was supposed to concentrate and do everything possible to induce the "crises." These two prescriptions led to a visible improvement in the hysteric manifestations.

The second phase of the therapy concentrated on structural family problems, in the sense of defining boundaries in relation to the family of origin and the extended family. In fact, the perception that her family had of her was that of a little girl in need of care and attention.

The third phase concentrated on resolving the problem of agoraphobia, which was certainly a serious one but which was overcome quite rapidly with the prescription described earlier.

During the 10th session, in which the supervisor participated and in which the issue of sexual relations was confronted, it was learned that Anna, in spite of her middle-class background, her high school diploma, and the fact of already being a mother, was greatly ignorant in the field of sexuality. She was ignorant not only at a physical level but even at a purely theoretical one. Not only had she never experienced orgasm, but also she did not even know the meaning of the term, nor was she aware of the existence of such a thing. On his part, the husband testified that Anna had never reached it.

A repression of sexuality was clearly evident, and it amazingly agreed with hysterical organization as conceived by Freud. The therapists showed great surprise at such great ignorance and prescribed an educational assignment, providing two books. One was given only to her (a feminist book), and she was supposed to read it by herself, and another one on couple sexuality was intended to be studied by them together.

At the end of the session and after six months, at the checkup session, Anna was decidedly doing better. She no longer suffered from hysterical crises, was no longer under medication, was able to leave her home alone, and had acquired a theoretical education on sex. But the couple's sexual problem had not been solved; thus, it was decided to go on with a cycle of sessions focused on the sexual difficulties.

The husband had had several sexual experiences before marriage with other partners, had no problem of early ejaculation, and after a certain time span reached orgasm, while his wife was not even minimally aroused.

In the first stages we prescribed sensorial focalizations I and II. Furthermore, according to the elementary pragmatic model, we tried to make the husband enter the wife's world (F5), trying to find out her desires, fantasies, and so on. At a certain point in the course of these sessions Anna finally said she felt a certain desire to get physically close to her husband. However, such desire appeared in circumstances in which the husband could not have sexual relations with her.

A significant turning point, in our opinion, took place during the eighth and last session of the second cycle, when Anna related with great anguish a dream that she had had recently but that was a recurring one also in the past: she dreamed that she had felt pleasure masturbating a woman.

The intervention consisted in giving a positive connotation to the dream as it revealed a desire on Anna's part to be active in the relation. Consequently, we prescribed to the husband to be a passive object in her hands (F4). She had to take the initiative. The prescription was begun in a manner mentioned during the session itself. Anna was supposed to be caressed by her husband's hand, which she herself moved, concentrating on the sensations that she felt in carrying out this task.

After a year and a half we followed up this case through a long telephone call to Anna. From the conversation we learned that the sex life of the couple had distinctly improved. Sexual relations were, in fact, characterized by them as mature and satisfying. Anna reported that even without a "prescription" she was able to take the initiative and not merely submit to her husband's desires. Together they decided to face a second pregnancy.

Finally, what gave her the most satisfaction was the fact that she had become independent and autonomous even in small aspects of daily life.

ADDITIONAL MODELS USED IN THERAPY

The Prescription of "Temporal Maps" and Interventions on the Form-Process Dialectic

As the reader has most likely observed in this chapter, our psychotherapeutic interventions always have three components. The first refers to the change in interactive styles among the various members of the therapeutic system and to what we have explained in the preceding chapter. The second component refers to temporal prescriptions, and the third, to the form-process dialectic. Thus, before we proceed to the clinical cases, I briefly discuss these two aspects.

Time Prescriptions

Every psychotherapist, beginning with Sigmund Freud, the pioneer of the discipline, knows that the time distribution of the sessions, their duration, and the number of sessions that are planned are very important for his or her work. We feel that it is impossible to carry out a therapeutic process without giving a temporal structure. Furthermore, we feel that the organization of time is an integral part of the therapeutic process. In our prescriptions and in planning our sessions we use the map proposed by sociologist Zerubavel as a theoretical reference point. He proposes the following distinction:

- Rigid, successive structures
- Fixed durations
- Standard temporal settings
- Uniform frequencies of recurrence

By rigid, successive structures we mean that two events can follow one another only in a certain order of succession; that is, they must be separated in such a manner that one must occur before the other; they cannot be simultaneous, nor can there be an inversion in their order of occurrence.

By fixed duration we mean that the event must have a certain duration (either by necessity, by agreement, or by shared expectation). An example of this is the 50-minute therapy session.

By standard temporal settings we mean that specific temporal reference points are established. For example, lunch is at 1:00 P.M., and dinner is at 9:00 P.M.

By uniform frequencies of recurrence we mean another type of temporal reference such as birthdays, holidays, and other occurrences that have uniform intervals.

These four parameters constitute the temporal frame, the reference model of individuals, families, and society. They constitute the temporal map belonging to family systems and also, obviously, to therapeutic systems. Thus, therapists can prescribe a temporal map that is different from the family's map as far as one, two, or all four parameters are concerned. If, for example, we prescribe that a family carry out a task on Monday and another one on Tuesday (rigid structure of succession), at time x (standard temporal setting), for the duration of 30 minutes (fixed duration), and to repeat the task every Monday and Tuesday of every month (uniform frequency of recurrence), we have prescribed a temporal map to the family. At present, we tend to prescribe maps that include all four parameters.

Interventions on the Form-Process Dialectic

Concerning interventions on the form-process dialectic, we must refer to Bateson's viewpoint. For Bateson (1972, 1980), people, like other living beings, perceive the world through differences. "All receipt of information is necessarily the receipt of news of difference" (Bateson, 1980, p. 32), and "no new order or pattern can be created without information" (p. 50).

In the world of ideas there needs to be a relation, either between two parts or between one part at moment 1 and the same part at moment 2, in order to activate a third component that can be called the "receiver." The receiver (e.g., an organ in the sense of a terminal) reacts to a difference or to a change. Ideas, according to Bateson (1980, p. 250), are "a difference or distinction, or news of a difference."

Another important element in this discussion on the formation of mental constructions is what Bateson defines as the fifth criterion of the mental process: "The effects of difference are to be regarded as transformations (i.e., coded versions) of events which preceded them" (1980, p. 102). In very simple terms this indicates that the mind works through maps ("a map is not a territory," as Korzybski said); in other words, reality can be perceived only as a derivative of the mental process ("the name is not the thing named, and the idea of pig is not the pig," p. 210). The mental process, in turn, originates and works according to two modes, the analogical and the digital. "As I see it, the root of the matter lies in the contrast between the digital and the analogic or, in another language, between the name and the process that is named" (p. 205).

Another important aspect of Bateson's discourse is what he defines as "the zig-zag ladder of dialectics between form and process" (p. 215), which he compares to Mittelstaedt's concepts of calibration and feedback (p. 216). This means both that "the structure can determine process, and that, conversely, process may determine structure. It follows that here must be a relation between two levels of structure mediated by an intervening description of process" (p. 217).

This alternating dialectic between form and process must be seen as the process of processes. One, then, can posit a mental process based only on analogical communication or only on digital communication. Both must necessarily alternate.

To summarize, referring back to the concept of process as the dialectic between form and process, we can then think that in pathology this process is blocked either at the level of form or at the level of process. To understand better what we are referring to, we can present two aspects of pathology, paranoia, on one side, and hebephrenia, on the other. In the first, in fact, we can observe a mental construction (a form) that cannot be modified, while in the second there is an impossibility to construct ideas (forms). In the first case we are dealing with a block at the level of form, while in the second, at the level of process.

The problem arises of why—or better, how—this blockage in the form-process dialectic originates. Our answer is a simple one; the obstruction is born from the context or, more precisely, the relation. All mental pathology could be seen as a function of problems in this zigzag process.

A Case of Inverted Belle Indifference

Last year I treated a family in which the identified patient, A, a young and beautiful divorced lady, had been hospitalized for two suicide attempts. She was very determined to commit suicide, as she had tried to throw herself under a truck, being saved only by the skill of the driver. She later had tried to drown herself at sea, but this attempt failed thanks to the intervention of her individual psychotherapist, who had followed her after the session, worried by her behavior during the session. What was strange about this patient was that when I saw her in the clinic, she did not show any signs of suffering. She claimed that she suffered very intensely and asked to be freed at whatever cost from the desperation that seized her, but she gave no external sign of such desperation. There was a schism between her mask and her internal experience. This attitude had an interesting equivalent in the general attitude of her family (a mother, a sister, a brother) who appeared to have little tolerance toward expressions of suffering.

My intervention carried out during her hospitalization was based on the idea that if I had been able to act out to A her internal persona, I would have interrupted the schism between the two characters. Thus, projecting the suffering character onto the indifferent one, I would go toward her world (which emerged as the desire to halt the suffering and at the same time as a hysterical component of appearing on a stage). Furthermore, going toward her world was to happen through an unpredictable request on my part (the entire intervention then was shaping up as an F13). In the family's presence, I addressed the patient and at times other family members, saying that from what A had told us and from what we had been able to observe, there was no congruence between what was inside her and what she projected externally. There was a problem in A's making her feelings manifest. She was not able to express what she had inside, or she had a great ability to appear different on the outside. In her there were two personae, an internal and an external one, even if she was a single being. During the week preceding the next session, A was supposed to think about her internal character, observing it in such a manner as to be able to perform it during the following session. In fact, her assignment in the next session was to act, express, and imitate her internal character. A, who was a very intelligent woman, for a whole week thought of how she would express her internal character in the most convincing and most realistic (or real?) manner. In the next session she was good at "acting" the internal A and was amply praised by the therapists. After this session there was a clear improvement.

In the next two sessions we worked to expose the mother's and siblings' true attitude toward her, which was not one of intolerance for her affective manifestations but rather one of true indifference toward her. The empty intersection (F6) was then filled. From then on there were no suicide attempts.

The Case of the Wife with Paranoid Jealousy and of the Husband's Paranoia toward his Wife's Paranoia

One day, as a supervisor, I saw a couple at their fifth session in which the wife was convinced that her husband was unfaithful, but apart from this belief she was calm and cooperative. Vice versa, the husband appeared to be very aggressive, not available to listening and non-accepting toward therapy. We had the strange feeling that the wife was expressing the content of the delusion, while the husband was manifesting it in his behavior. In other words, the wife communicated the content, and the husband the behavior that was supposed to be connected to the content. One expressed the delusion, and the other one acted it out. In terms of the dialectic form-process mentioned earlier, she represented the form, and he represented the process.

We also had the impression that the husband interpreted as signs of her jealousy even phrases or behaviors that were totally innocent and that had nothing to do with her delusion. Because of this, among ourselves we spoke of the "husband's paranoia toward his wife's paranoia." Beyond these considerations we decided to do an articulated intervention based on the attempt to break the couple's interactive situation. The therapist, Dr. Margari, after having consulted me behind the mirror, went back to the therapy room and said,

> I spoke with Professor De Giacomo behind the mirror, and he told me that this morning he had a discussion with a colleague of his concerning the case of a subject affected with delusions of grandeur—he thought he was a great inventor. This colleague was not at all able to make the patient give up his delusion. Discussing among colleagues, they reached the conclusion that the subject could never have been cured of his delusion because the cure would have meant recognizing that he was a fool.

The therapist made a pause that allowed us to observe that the message had been received and that it caused a certain attitude of openness toward the prescription that we were about to propose.

The prescription was the following:

> We observed that the two of you have a problem in common. Both of you have a threshold of reception that is too low. You [addressing the wife] as far as your husband's thoughts and behavior toward women are concerned, and you [addressing the husband] in an excessive perception of jealous attitudes on your wife's part toward you. Then, the problem is to raise the threshold for both of you. However, in order to do this, we must start with the one who is stronger, more willing to sacrifice, the one that can be relied upon more, the more flexible one.

Because we had reached the end of the session and the two seemed perplexed and undecided, they were given another appointment with the prescription of deciding between themselves who was the one who could be relied upon more. What we had in mind was an intervention in which if the husband had been chosen as the more available of the two, we would ask the wife to nag him three hours a day, from time x to time y, from Monday to Saturday, with themes of jealousy in order to raise his threshold; if the wife had been chosen, we would tell the husband to nag her, interpreting every gesture and action of hers as signs of her jealousy, sharply denying that there was any truth to it (i.e., proposing and negating contents of jealousy invented by him and attributed to her, only with the purpose of raising the wife's threshold of sensitivity, (intervention F11 and partly F13). Actually, at the next session a week later, the couple had greatly changed. Both of them seemed depressed and did not speak of jealousy anymore.

Jealousy and Acceptance of the World of the Other

In two cases of acute jealousy we made recourse to the following maneuver: we asked the jealous member of the couple if he or she was willing to forgive in his or her world the spouse's infidelity, even if the betrayal had not been confessed. Then we asked the other if he or she was willing to accept forgiveness for something that in his or her world he had not done. The effect was a positive one. Furthermore, in one of two cases, the husband, who had been unjustly accused of infidelity but who had accepted to be forgiven for something he had not done (on equal ground with the wife who had accepted to forgive him for an infidelity that he had not confessed), asked a very interesting question, one that opened the way for a new prescription.

As we shall see, through the introduction of a temporal factor we created a change at the level of logic. He asked if the act of accepting was supposed to be a single one, once and for all, or if he had to repeat it in the future. We complimented him quite a bit (and sincerely), for his question opened new and unforeseen horizons. If they would be able to make this change from a sporadic one to a continuous one, not a *una tantum* but an uninterrupted one, this would mean a greatly different change. In fact, in this case, the prescription would be the beginning of a whole different manner of interpreting their way of being a couple. Definitely, it represented the introduction of something that could be defined as a philosophy of tolerance and acceptance.

On the Theme of Uncompromising Opposition

In cases of uncompromising opposition (where two subjects are both F10) we intervene in the following manner. We say that we have discovered that when there is such a drastic opposition between two people, when people are like cats and dogs, when one always says white and the other one always says black, there is always something that exists in both people's worlds but is not talked about; there is something that is known to one and is also known to the other that both know but is never shown (F6).

Prescribing Narcissism

A woman dragged her husband and teenage daughter into therapy. She literally lived to care for them, while it was clear that the two of them cared neither for her nor for one another. After a few sessions this was clear to the mother, too, due to which the sessions were halted. During the period of suspension the mother came to me asking me what she was to do now to live independently from her husband and daughter. It was clear that she was absolutely incapable of envisioning an autonomous life for herself. I gave her the prescription to look in the mirror, to observe, to think, and to describe her body point by point, starting from her hair tips to the tip of her toes, according to a certain temporal progression. The interactive style that I saw missing in the patient and that I wanted to develop in her was the style to circumscribe and preserve her own world (F3).

The "Whirlpool" Technique (How Does One Inspire a Patient to Open Up with the Therapist) and the "Searchlight" Technique (How to Get the Patient to Listen to You Selectively)

In this chapter we have dealt with aspects of art, besides the science of psychotherapy. When we speak of art, we mean what each of us puts of our own (which is not transmissible in a formal manner) into the activity that we carry out. The concept is valid not only for psychotherapy but also for surgery, for medicine, and for every field of knowledge involving intervention. How can one transmit these individual behaviors of the therapist? Certainly, it is very difficult; they can be presented in the clearest of ways only to colleagues and to pupils, and perhaps they are useful only in denoting a certain way of working of a particular therapist.

Let's take as an example the technique that is used to increase a person's desire to make another one enter into his or her world (to predispose the person to interactive style F5), which we defined as the "whirlpool." If we receive the message, explicitly or implicitly, that a particular member of the family, for example, the patient, wants to be heard by the therapist alone, we can make contact with all family members, one at a time, including the identified patient (first as personal acquaintance, then asking for information about the problem) according to age, and after having finished the round, we ask that the other members leave the room and that only the patient remain in the room, adding, if it seems appropriate, that what the patient will say will be protected by confidentiality. When we remain alone with the patient, we can ask him or her what he or she does not want to say in the family's presence and say that what the patient says will remain a secret. This modality of approach favors the opening up of patients who resist disclosing themselves with the therapist and accepting the therapy. In certain cases, we had the impression that during the phase of making contact with other members, important contents had come to the patient's mind and that he could not express them because he was held back by the others' speaking, or because he did not want to express them in public.

The "searchlight" technique consists in talking to the patient and/or the family in a cryptic, unintelligible, vague, confused manner, making a "word salad" for a certain amount of time. Later, one says something important in a clear manner. The listener in the phase of confused speech tries desperately to give a meaning to what the therapist is communicating and therefore increases the receptivity of his or her mind. When finally, in the second phase, the therapist transmits a clear message, this is perceived with great clarity.

Closing Sessions Enigmatically

We make recourse to a closure akin to the "empty box" to close a cycle of sessions when the family recognizes that some changes have taken place but not others, or with families whose various members disagree on the changes that have occurred. Also this is used if one wants to accentuate the change that has happened in the system or when the family asks the therapist's opinion about the changes that have taken place in the system. We tell the family that the therapist knows what has changed, the knot that has been untied, but it is necessary for them not to reveal it because it is much more important and productive that they understand it by themselves. It is a type of closure that predisposes to the filling of the empty intersection (it tends to bring the family toward the F1 style). This consideration is drawn from a conceptual extrapolation; if we must prepare a specific theme, for example, a lecture, there is a precise goal. Between the "other" and me there is something specific to be shared. There is a well-established goal. But if I must prepare myself on a given day at a given hour for a discussion whose subject I do not know, the mental configuration will be different. In all likelihood my mind will get prepared to share something that at this moment I do not know yet; therefore, I will have a predisposition toward the intersection, to share elements in common with others, a predisposition without objects, elements, or contents. In the form-process dialectic it would correspond to the process of predisposing to the construction of form. "Enigmatic closures," just like "empty boxes," are presumably techniques predisposing to sharing.

Reinforcing the Messages

Once a path has been identified, it is easy to increase the intensity of the message (or the intensity of the interactive style) that one wants to propose. Actually, it is exactly in the ability to adjust the message that the art of the psychotherapist resides. For example, if the therapist decides to use the sociobiofeedback maneuver with a couple in which one of the members suffers from "irritable colon," if he wants to accentuate the maneuver, he can increase its length or its quality (changing the position of the two, making it more comfortable or less comfortable). If the therapist wants to increase the intensity of the maneuver "father F5 toward daughter in anorexia nervosa," one can ask the father to touch the daughter, in addition to looking at her. If one wants to strengthen the parents' style of appearing bound like body and soul, if, for example, they already close the door in their bedroom (a prescription for this action cannot be given), one can ask them to play records that both of them like, at such a volume that the children could hear them, thus receiving the information that between Mom and Dad things are going well.

Symmetry and Complementarity, Complete and Incomplete Fitting, Complete and Incomplete Symmetry

The EPM leads us to dispute the traditional concept of symmetry and complementarity as too limited. In fact, if we observe the four spaces of Venn's diagrams, we can deduce that, when coupled, there are at least four possibilities. One member fills some spaces, and the other the remaining ones, due to which none of the four spaces or the whole remains empty. This represents an absolute complementarity, a perfect joining, a complete fitting. But there is also the possibility that one member fills some spaces, and the other, other ones (different from the ones filled by the first subject, i.e., without any overlapping), but that both leave some empty spaces. In this case, we are in the presence of a fitting that is incomplete. There is also the possibility that both subjects fill exactly the same spaces, and this is a complete symmetry, while, if the overlapping is only partial, we are in the presence of an incomplete symmetry. The clinical consequence of this concept is that we can single out, as a therapeutic goal, the transformation of a couple from a relation of complete fitting to one of incomplete fitting, from one of complete symmetry to an incomplete one, from a complete fitting to one of incomplete symmetry.

In a couple in which she was creative but illogical and he instead was very organized but not at all creative, we gave the prescription that he take on attitudes and behaviors that his wife would not foresee. This meant the passage from a complete fitting to an incomplete symmetry.

Furthermore, because in that family each one interfered too much with one other, we added that each one should withdraw into his or her own world, remaining silent for an hour every day (in the hour in which everyone usually remained home). This meant passing from one type of symmetry to another.

Entering into the World of the Other

Because this function, as we said, has a distinct therapeutic value, it is the subject of additional discussion. First of all, we must specify that the term "entering the world of the other" does not have anything to do with the theory of object relations in psychoanalysis. In the latter, we are dealing with a concept of energy related to libido, while in the case of the elementary pragmatic model we are dealing with communication and information theory. Furthermore, we must not forget that, according to a pure interactive vision, we are interested in the contents only as a means to know and modify processes, that is, the modality of interaction of the subjects, "the connecting structure," according to Bateson.

In conclusion, we are interested in the overall behavior of the system. For example, when we speak of symmetry between two subjects, we mean that the system overall functions in a certain manner, that is, that the two subjects in interacting exchange the same behavior. While psychoanalysis deals mainly with the individuals, our greatest interest is centered on interaction. Our intervention must be seen as a programmed disturbance aimed at modifying the modalities of interaction of a subject vis-à-vis the modalities of interaction of other subjects. It aims at modifying interaction. Having clarified this in relation to the theory of object relations, we must answer a question that often surfaces in discussions with colleagues. The term "to enter the world" means to know the worldview of the other. By worldview we mean the attitudes of a subject, which are made up of beliefs, traditions, myths, shared interests, moral values, goals, objectives, ambitions, motivations, family histories.

This means that if we work with a peasant family, we use language and metaphors coming from their world. In the case of delusions in which a subject manifests an imaginary world, for example, mystical ideas, perhaps as a consequence of the frustration received from the husband, we prescribe to the husband to read the Bible to her (or some other religious material) for an hour every night.

Sometimes the communication modalities of the patients are such that it is difficult to understand what their world is. In these cases, one can attempt, as Erickson does, to use the same modalities as the patient, thus establishing some type of intersection, that is, at least a partial overlapping with their world, with shared elements. For example, if a patient expresses himself or herself in illogical rhymes, we must use the same language with the patient or prescribe to the family members to try to speak in the same manner for x amount of time.

A case in which we used the Ericksonian style was that of a family who complained that the identified patient would walk up and down and never speak with his mother and sister. The boy loved music. I prescribed that for an hour, three times a day, they play records that the three of them particularly liked and that the boy dance with the two of them.

Another Ericksonian intervention was practiced by me on a young man who came to my office with a series of anxiety and phobic disorders, which disappeared with interventions that I described in the section on obsessive and phobic disorders. Once the most elementary symptoms ceased, he expressed a problem that I would define as being at a higher level. He realized that he had the shortcomings of being an impatient person. He wanted to do everything in an accelerated manner; he wanted to reach results immediately; he could not wait. I knew that he was an extremely strong-willed boy, which had been instrumental in his overcoming the symptoms. I gave him the "clock prescription." For a quarter of an hour, three times a day, he was supposed to observe the movement of the clock hands.

Besides using Ericksonian interventions, we tell patients to visualize something that corresponds to their state of mind or to a given mental content. For example, I asked an anorexic who vomited to close her eyes and to visualize this act. After a few minutes I asked her what she saw with her mind's eyes, and she said that she saw herself in the act of vomiting. I asked her if, with her eyes closed, she could always visualize herself vomiting in the bathroom. She said that she could. I asked her if she could see herself vomiting in the bathroom while wearing very elegant clothes. She said that she could. I asked her if she could visualize herself in the act of vomiting in a "flirtatious" position. Again her answer was affirmative. At last I asked her if she could visualize her vomit being of a beautiful color, and she said yes. At this point, I complimented her and added that many people have the erroneous idea of being at the mercy of their mind, as if they were swept by a current, while in reality the mind can be programmed, as she herself had demonstrated a little earlier. I concluded giving her the prescription to practice at home according to a given temporal map. After six months at a checkup visit, she reported that her vomiting had ceased.

For those of us with a systems orientation, punctuating is an arbitrary fact that clearly has a pragmatic meaning; for example, to punctuate in the same manner as the other is different from punctuating in an opposite manner. If I punctuate in the same manner, I use different functions than if I punctuate in the opposite manner.

Since we have focused our interest on the form-process dialectic, a certain problem of interpreting what we have defined as "entering into the world of the other" arose. This problematic aspect, however, has led to an interesting direction of research. I begin with a clinical example in order to make the reader understand in what perspective we found ourselves.

A schizophrenic patient claims that he feels stings. These stings are a way for a girl whom he loves and who wants to help him to make contact with him. He thinks that she wants to help him because, after feeling the stings, his ideas become clearer in his mind. I prescribe to the father to sit in front of the patient and to observe the son. Every time he shows signs of having been stung (by his abrupt body movements, by rubbing) or whenever the son signals to him that he has received the sting, the father is to actually sting him. He must do it according to his son's instructions, stinging him with the same intensity as the imaginary sting. The question arises if the prescription refers to form or process or if it represents or not an example of "entering into the world of the other" (is it an F5?).

Going back to Bateson, the sting represents perceiving difference (between before the sting and after the sting and between a part of the body that has been stung and one that has not). Receiving the stimulation and perceiving the difference are the process. The sting is then placed in a certain referential scheme, a certain mental construction according to which a certain girl sends a message that "clears his thoughts." This is a way of classifying events coming from the world. Thus, he builds a form. When we prescribe to the father to sting his son, this means, in our opinion, working at the level of process, while if we disputed the boy's theory of external influences on his mind that he attributes to the girl we would have acted on his mental construction (i.e., mainly at the level of form). I realize that this distinction, as is true for the majority of distinctions, is a conventional one. It is only an arbitrary map, but interesting and useful therapeutic approaches can be born from these arbitrary maps, from these "differences." The problem remains if a prescription like the one given to the father is an "entering the son's world" (F5) by amplifying (F13) or something else that is outside our model.

1. We must warn the reader that we use medication only starting from late adolescence.
2. Symmetry is different from a difference in perspective; in fact, almost always, at the beginning of the therapy, the systemic perspective of the therapists is different from the linear perspective of the family.

Follow-Ups of Cases after Therapeutic Interventions

After having described numerous interventions of brief therapy, I feel the need to write something about the evolution of the cases that we treat in our professional work. What I am describing is the result of many years of experience, in a context of limited dimensions, where many patients can be easily tracked again. This easy access is proven by the contacts that I was able to have with many former patients of mine in writing this book.

An initial consideration can be made as to the value of the therapist's intervention. Is it useful or not? The answer to this question is clearly in the affirmative. By working with some quick techniques, we witness changes under our very own eyes. There are short-term changes that are undoubtedly the result of the therapist's work. In the various sections of this chapter I have reported many examples of dramatic changes. This happens in the great majority of cases. The change is sometimes permanent (i.e., it becomes a long-term change). These are the luckiest changes, and they correspond to the goal that we have set as our ideal.

A second consideration refers to those cases that improve rapidly but then relapse. In these cases, evidently, the forces of the system are modified only temporarily by the intervention; then, later on, they prevail again. However, in some ways the intervention makes a crack, even if a temporary one, which reveals a certain vulnerability, a certain flexibility, and this must make the therapist optimistic. Almost always, in fact, a second, well-aimed intervention again obtains good results, at times permanent ones as, for example, in the case of the girl with the hysterical psychosis.

A third consideration refers to other cases in which after 10 sessions there is no result. In these cases we postpone therapy to a later series to be started after a few months. In my opinion, this technique is preferable to the one of continuing the sessions for years. Chronic treatment, in fact, goes against our philosophy; as we said earlier, in order to help the families, it is not at all a sure thing that continuing the sessions for years will solve the problem. Or if the problem disappears, one cannot say with certainty that it is due to the great number of sessions. It could simply be due to external events that modify the system or the impact of the passing of time on the system. It could even be that making the therapy chronic will lead to making the disorder chronic.

In fact, in my investigation over the years it emerged that numerous families had solved their problem without going through an infinite number of sessions. They solved their problems simply after a brief therapeutic input, by relying "on their own strength" or with external help. In my opinion, this external help often had the meaning of a compromise for the family. I defined this latter situation as the "magic cure." Let us look at some examples.

The Magic Cure

In May 1976, a family came to see me. The family was composed of a 50-year-old father, who was a teacher; the mother, a 41-year-old housewife; and three daughters, aged 16, 14, and 12. The identified patient was the middle daughter, Giovanna. It was a typical case of anorexia nervosa, but the situation was serious because the girl was 1.54 meters (5 feet) tall and weighed 29 kilos (64 pounds). We undertook a 10-session series, apparently without positive results. When the first series had finished, the parents, without waiting for the second, went to a biological psychiatrist, who immediately asked the girl to take some tests. These tests required about 15 days, and they revealed that the girl was anemic. Fleboclysis was prescribed. The first fleboclysis treatment was done exactly 20 days after the end of our sessions, and as soon as the fleboclysis was finished, the girl asked for a sandwich. Her anorexia was gone forever. I say forever, because I was able to gather this information after nine years, and the girl has overcome the problem. She is working, has had a relationship with a young man for a number of years, and is about to get married. In gathering this data from the mother by phone, I asked her if in her opinion it was the fleboclysis that had cured her daughter or instead if it had been a change in their behavior toward the daughter. The answer was that, of course, it was not the fleboclysis that was responsible for the daughter's recovery. However, they had no idea of what had really happened. To them, it seemed like a miracle.

This case resembles one whose development I was able to follow very closely, as the family happened to have close ties to kinship with mine. The family consisted of the father, a very intelligent man who was extremely patient, the mother, a dissatisfied woman who was full of energy and overcontrolling, a socially integrated sister who was married and had a decent job, and a young man, the identified patient. He was a drab fellow in spite of his intelligence. He had a modest job and a girlfriend to whom he had been engaged for years but whom he never married, continuing to just live together.

The symptoms of the patient were very serious. He had started with Oriental mysticism, and then he had joined a yoga cult. He had broken all contacts with the world and did not eat for a long period of time, thus risking starvation. Gradually, he progressed to symptoms that were clearly schizophrenic, with delusions and hallucinations. I entrusted him to a colleague of mine whom I knew to be excellent, certainly one of the best in the field of family therapy. This colleague took the boy's fate to heart and worked with the family for two years, going through all sorts of problems, among which were serious breaches of trust, suicide attempts, difficulties in getting paid, and so on.

After two years, during which the parents, especially the mother, would often contact me to express their doubts on the therapy and on the colleague to whom I had entrusted them, they phoned me to say that they had decided to stop the sessions with the family therapist. They also asked me to refer them to someone else. The morning when they phoned I was not in full control, I became irritated, and without thinking about it I gave them the name of another colleague, a traditional psychiatrist.

After a few days I received another phone call from them, and I prepared myself to hear further complaints and degradations of my profession. Instead, to my surprise, the mother fell all over herself in thanking me. The traditional psychiatrist had performed the miracle; with a few drops of a certain medication, he had solved the problem. After a few days, the boy was cured! I asked the name of the medication. It was the same drug that had been administered by the previous colleague in addition to psychotherapy, except that its commercial name was different! Of course, I was careful not to tell them that it was the same medicine. Being that he is a relative of mine, I have always kept myself informed about his health. Indeed, he has no longer shown any signs of abnormality.

The following case seems even more appropriate to the subject of miracle cures and is, in a certain sense, even more perplexing and enigmatic in relation to our profession. In August 1982, a family came to my office. The 67-year-old father was a retired farmer and in a poor state of health on account of prostate problems, for which he later had surgery. The mother was a 49-year-old attendant in a nursery school, and they had a 15-year-old daughter. She was an only child, very cute but very spoiled and tendentially oppositional toward the people with whom she interacted. She was studying to be a nursery school teacher and was officially engaged. This engagement met the approval of the mother, but not that of the father, who thought that the girl was too young to be seriously engaged. Sometimes when the couple went out alone, the father followed them. But aside from this concern for the girl's love life, the relationship between father and daughter was rather lacking. Around July of that year she had developed phobicobsessive symptoms focusing on dirt. According to the family, this coincided with her having found a worm in her chest of drawers. The symptoms were serious, according to her; her freshly washed underwear was dirty, she herself was dirty, she would wash her hands constantly, and she did not want to touch doorknobs. In her overly scrupulous washing she did not use the sink or the bathtub but rather a special washbasin of hers. In addition, she had become very nervous and at times even violent to the point of beating up her parents when they did not give in to her wishes (which at times were rather absurd considering their economic situation, for example, the time when she asked to buy five pairs of pants).

In contrast to the previous cases, this time the family had come to us after having been under the care of a traditional psychiatrist, who was very good. He had given them chlorimipramine (certainly, a highly effective medication in this type of disorder) and some anti-anxiety drugs. Given that he had not seen any improvement, he sent her to me for family therapy. In turn, I referred the family to the Family Therapy Center of the Psychiatric Clinic (where my group works and which is also the location of the university's school of interactive therapy). Here we went through 15 sessions, 5 more than usual. It took great effort, and we faced critical moments such as the girl's escapes, her threats of suicide, beatings, and so on. By the end of the 15 sessions, the positive aspect was an improvement in the girl's aggressivity. By then we had arrived at the summer break, so we gave the family leave. From then on, we did not hear from them.

I contacted the family again after two years. The mother answered in a very friendly manner. I asked her how things were going in the family. She said that the girl was doing very well, and that she was completely cured. I asked then, if after our sessions they had gone to other specialists. The answer was negative. I asked her, then, how was she cured. At this point the mother seemed embarrassed but then told me what had happened.

A few days after our last session, one that had caused her great discouragement, she had run into a friend of hers to whom she confided all her family problems. The friend advised her to go to a sorceress whom she trusted. Thus, they immediately went to the sorceress, who told them that the problem could not really be solved by doctors because it was not an illness but an evil spell. She then proceeded with the appropriate liberatory and protective rituals. Since then, the girl steadily improved until reaching a fully satisfactory state of health. When our conversation was over, she insisted that I talk on the phone with her daughter. The girl, too, was friendly and cordial, a very different person from the one I remembered. She promised to come by sometime and pay a social call.

There are some cases in which the magic cure happens through surgery given for a physical illness, as in the case of a female member of a couple who had symptoms of depressive neurosis. The relationship with the husband was clearly dysfunctional. We went through 10 family therapy sessions, all characterized by a high degree of tension. Four years after the session had finished, I fortuitously met the couple. They told me that a few days after the end of the sessions, the wife had had surgery to remove her gallbladder. From that moment on, she was completely cured. Of course, they attributed the end of the wife's illness and therefore all of the couple's problems to the surgery.

These four examples, taken from a rather large pool of analogous case studies, pose problems of great interest. One of these concerns is the issue of time, that is, the time necessary for the therapeutic effects to manifest themselves. In fact, as we said previously, there are the following possibilities:

1. The problem is solved during the sessions and disappears permanently.
2. The problem is solved during the sessions but surfaces again after varying amounts of time.
3. The problem is solved after the sessions stop, after varying amounts of time, without the further aid from the specialists.
4. The problem is solved after the end of the therapy sessions, by other specialists.
5. The problem is not solved either by our sessions or by the intervention of other specialists and lasts forever.

In the four cases mentioned above we are in an intermediate position between points 3 and 4 in the sense that the intervention of an outside person has in itself little or no value. In fact, it was not the fleboclysis of the first case or the change in the medication label in the second or the sorceress' intervention in the third or, finally, the surgery in the fourth that was the true cause of change. Different explanations are possible. One explanation is that in the time lapse following the sessions, in all four cases a brief one, the time necessary for the system to change had elapsed. Systems change happens slowly. To this, we add that it manifests with a different rhythm depending on the change of structure, which we determine with our input. We find this aspect an interesting one to pursue.

With this explanation, there is simply a coincidence between the time necessary for the system to change and the apparent, valueless intervention of the psychiatrist, the sorceress, or the surgeon. However, our interactive and model-based perspective urges us to look for another solution. For one thing, one could make the hypothesis that the change is due to the end of the sessions, that is, to the separation of the family system from the therapeutic team. In our own work, this separation is previously agreed upon by contract. Generally there are 10 separate sessions if my group leads them while, as the reader must have gathered by now, a much smaller number (sometimes even just 1) if I lead them.

In the case of the usual 10-session approach, we certainly act upon the system also through the time coordinate, thus modifying the rhythms belonging to the system (understood as the combination of all the interactive aspects of the various members of the system each with his own time clock). This is less evident but also possible in cases with a smaller number of sessions, like the ones that I conduct.

Another possible interpretation is to make the hypothesis that a family does not gladly embrace the idea of change caused by an expert in the family therapy field. Which father, mother, or responsible member of a system is ready to acknowledge that he or she is not very good in managing his or her own family? Certainly not many. On the other hand, in my opinion, the changes that happen in a family must be attributed to forces inside the family itself, even if these forces are unleashed by the well-aimed or less well aimed input of the therapist. Furthermore, the punctuation given by the members of a family, in spite of all efforts to the contrary, is interpreted by them as blaming, that is, that they are the cause of the "illness" of one of the members. Therefore, in many cases a symmetry between therapist and family is created. Thus, the family is searching for a compromise, for a lifesaver like that of the "empty box" of the magician so that the sick family member is cured without gratifying the therapist (i.e., without accepting his or her philosophy) or even disqualifying him or her. In this light we can explain the "curing" contribution of the biological psychiatrist in the first two cases, of the sorceress in the third, and of the surgeon in the fourth.

In the first two cases, the psychiatrists were probably people who communicated verbally or extraverbally their triumph over their defeated colleague, or, more in keeping with our elementary pragmatic model, they confirmed, without personal participation in their conviction, that mental illness cannot be cured psychologically. In the third case, the sorceress decreed the defeat of all official medicine, both of traditional psychiatrists and of the psychotherapists. Finally, the surgeon solved everything on a completely different level.

In terms of our model, what was the interactive style of these four characters—the two psychiatrists, the sorceress, and the surgeon—toward the family? According to what we said previously, in the world of the family there was the proposition that the ecological philosophy of the therapist was erroneous, that the family had nothing to do with the "son's illness," that the suggestion to change reciprocal behavior compared to the past did not make any sense, and so on. Now, the two psychiatrists, the sorceress, and the surgeon were unmistakably going toward the world of the family, exhibiting toward the family an interactive style with a high therapeutic significance. In the future one could plan an intervention that takes this aspect into account. For example, at the end of an apparently unsuccessful therapeutic series, one could send a previously instructed colleague to perform the function mentioned above. Or one could plan a special session at certain intervals of time after a series that was apparently without positive results.

In the present state of the art among us mental health professionals, this process of referral is always operational whether on a conscious, subconscious, or unconscious level, as demonstrated by my sending my relative to a second colleague of mine with a biological orientation.

To close this chapter, I present one last case in which the improvement took place in a more complex manner, because the external intervention was linked to another member of the system. The carrier of the symptom was a 33-year-old lady, Rosaria, married to a professional in his 40s and mother of three children, who came to see me in June 2001. For many years she had had serious problems focused mainly in her digestive system. She had problems swallowing, an annoying feeling of inflation after eating, vomiting, and she weighed 40 kilos (88 pounds). Furthermore, she was not able to stay alone at home, she could not drive, her relationship with her husband and even her sexual rapport were not satisfactory. The therapy took place in only two sessions.

During the first session the husband talked constantly and defined his wife as an irresponsible person. I intervened, telling him to give her here and now the responsibility to speak for herself that is, I unbalanced the couple in her favor. Later, I asked each of them to define the wishes of the other and to predict what wishes the other would not have mentioned, and finally I gave them some advice about their sexual problems.

At the end of the session I asked them which of the numerous symptoms they wanted to solve. They answered that the reason for which they had come was her problem swallowing. In particular, Rosaria had never been able, in her whole life, to swallow meat. It would stop in her esophagus and would not go down. I asked them to come next time with a dish of cooked meat.

They arrived at the next session punctually with their meat dish. I asked Rosaria to cut it into small bites and eat it. If she were to have problems, the husband would massage her in the spot where the meat stuck.

By the end of the session, with her husband's help, she was able for the first time in her life to eat meat. There were not any digestive problems thanks to the husband's preventive massage. They did not come to the next meeting that we had set up after 20 days. After six months I gave them a phone call to find out the evolution of the situation. Rosaria answered, and she sincerely apologized, saying that they did not show up because her husband had a serious problem with his ear, which had required a lot of tests and eventually surgery. For this reason, her own problems had been put on the back burner. I asked her then how she was doing, and she said that she had considerably improved in all of the symptoms; since the last session she was eating meat regularly, she was no longer vomiting, and she had gained a few pounds. She was able to stay at home alone and to drive. The relationship with her husband had considerably improved.

CONCLUSION

This chapter has illustrated how creativity can be applied to the therapeutic enterprise. Whether this creativity would exist without the EPM remains to be seen. The second author ascribes creativity in part to the EPM and in part to the excitement of discovery and improvisation implicit in the process of improving relationships, like an actor on the stage. This art, however, needs to be coupled with rigorous evaluation, lest the therapist become enamored of his or her power and forget that humility is still necessary in helping troubled relationships. There are still too many failures that need to be understood and new ways to improve troubled relationships to be found.

Chapter 11

Practical Integration: Using Computers and Internet Technologies for Clinical and Non-clinical Relationships

Applications of both the theory and the EPM in prevention (Chapters 7 and 9) and psychotherapy (Chapters 8 and 10) lend themselves to computer-administered or -assisted interventions for both clinical and non-clinical relationships. As the results of Marks et al. (1998) and of Jacobs et al. (2000), among many others reviewed elsewhere, indicate (L'Abate, in press-b), interventions based on distance rather than face-to-face (f2f) contacts will be how most mental health services will be administered in the future. Consequently, reliance on distance technologies is another area where both theory and EPM are similar as well as complementary (De Giacomo & De Nigris, 2001; L'Abate, 1992, 2001a, in press-a, in press-b).

As the results of the Pittsburgh Youth Study indicate, among many others, Loeber, Farrington, Stouthamer-Loeber, Moffitt, Caspi, & Lynam, 2001), many adolescents as well as adults with character disorders do not receive the kind of help that they need: "[M]any youngsters who need help for mental health problems do not receive it or do not receive it in a timely manner" (p. 292).

As already pointed out in previous publications (L'Abate, 1990, 1992, 2001a, 2002a, 2002b), there is no way that the f2f verbal paradigm is going to take care of the countless emotional and mental health problems facing this and other nations. The results cited above speak to the bankruptcy of that paradigm. More cost-effective, mass-oriented approaches will need to be implemented if a contribution to the mental health problems covered by the report of the Surgeon General of the United States (1999) is going to make a difference. The f2f talk-based approach will continue to be a drop in the bucket if no new approaches will be implemented. Computer-assisted online interventions are the logical and ultimate approach to deal with so many problems preventively as well as therapeutically. If someone can come up with a more cost-effective, mass-oriented solution, these authors would like to know about it.

THE STRUCTURED VERSUS UNSTRUCTURED DISTINCTION

Here is where this distinction made in Chapter 3 comes into sharper focus. By structured is meant pre-written, already systematically organized workbooks, instructions, and prescriptions administered as homework assignments. By unstructured is meant responses made by professionals to respondents on the basis of what respondents say or do. Hence, workbooks represent a constructive, conductive style of intervening with relationships, while unstructured interventions, whether verbal or written, are reactive and therefore, if Model[8] is valid, tend to be repetitive and relatively inefficient. This conclusion, of course, is bound to arouse controversy, unless we specify that structured interventions, like workbooks, can be administered at a distance, that is, through the Internet or fax machines with non-clinical relationships, provided an exhaustive online evaluation is completed and an informed consent form is signed (L'Abate, 1992, 2001a, 2002a, in press-a, in press-b). In dealing with clinical relationships, on the other hand, distance technologies may be supplemented with professional contacts as well as medication, both requiring f2f contacts. There is no denying that in crises, people in trouble need the comfort of personal contact and the reassuring presence of a professional.

PREVENTIVE, COMPUTER-ADMINISTERED INTERNET INTERVENTIONS FOR NON-CLINICAL RELATIONSHIPS

Samples of workbooks contained in Chapters 7 and 9 are strictly suggestive. There is an extremely wide range of workbooks available commercially (www.workbooksclearinghouse.com) that cover a wide spectrum of non-clinical, semi-clinical, and clearly clinical relationships (L'Abate, 2002a, in press-a).

COMPUTER-ADMINISTERED INTERNET INTERVENTIONS FOR CLINICAL RELATIONSHIPS

Online, literally thousands of professionals offer their therapeutic services on an unstructured, reactive basis, mimicking on the Internet what they do in f2f psychotherapy. These professionals are extremely resistant to the possibility of what they see as a threat to their livelihood by structured distance approaches (L'Abate, 1997a). These approaches, using programmed and other forms of writing, would deprive them of what they value the most, their personal and professional presence, their verbal expertise, and their assumed intuitive sensibilities that cannot be conveyed through a "canned" workbook. This resistance will furnish the battleground between professionals who favor a structured approach and those who do not, as well as professionals who want to keep an f2f approach from professionals who are comfortable working at a distance from respondents through computers and the Internet. Ultimately, regardless of personal preferences and professional predilections, the marketplace for this type of intervention will be decided by respondents themselves. It will be up to them to decide what intervention to accept and what price to pay for it.

CONCLUSION

Mental health interventions of the future will be increasingly based on distance between professionals and respondents. Which approach is more beneficial than others will be based on newly created professional and ethical issues that will arise from new distance practices and technologies. The question is and remains: Who will profit by which approach at what cost? Here is where the public health paradigm, advocated by both writers, will again conflict with a private practice paradigm. Both will be needed to deal with so many intimate relationships that need help.

Part III

Conclusion

Chapter 12

Integration of the Theory and the Model with Other Models

> [W]e argue that the facts underlying the assumptions of classical theories have changed so radically as to make the theories obsolete. (Barnett & Hyde, 2001, p. 784)

This chapter refers to models, approaches, theories, and schools of thought that are described in Chapter 1 as well as throughout this work. This scrutiny has been conducted as if there were a continuum of approaches, from those that do not accept any kind of theorizing, just empirical evidence, to those that have developed well-organized, seductive constructions without external or empirical evidence. Before going into the details of this scrutiny, an obvious, albeit crucial, premise is necessary. It can be summarized in the following notion: being in an interaction with someone is something totally different from defining, rating, and reflecting on the interaction that one is experiencing. Actually, the way in which the mind organizes itself in the two situations mentioned, being and experiencing, varies a great deal. This diversity, among other things, affects the therapist's way of communicating. For example, consider that the therapist is interacting with his or her patient, and, at a given time, he or she tries to define the type of interaction that is taking place between him or her and the patient. We are going to label this interaction as symmetrical or, according to the EPM, as an interaction of the style that "he or she keeps and maintains his or her own word," or, with a contradictory, oppositional style, the therapist will appear to the patient(s) as one person who has assumed a thoughtful attitude. Reading the map (i.e., resorting to one's own models and theories, varies a great deal according to the different levels of complexity of the same map as well as according to the different levels of familiarity that one has with it. To get oriented in his or her therapeutic plan, if any, the therapist discontinues his or her direct and genuine relationship with the patient. This would be an example of the humanistic professional, being with the patient at the moment with our theoretical biases.

Alternative states of being in and defining the interaction experienced may occur during the therapy session. When a distinction is made between the time one reads the map and the whole interaction, it is necessary to bear in mind that reading the map is a continuous process. Resorting to one's own models and theories varies a great deal according to the different levels of complexity of the same map as well as according to the different levels of familiarity that one has with it. For example, in the case of the authors of this book, the map can be considered as a musical score where the notes almost coincide isomorphically with the music itself; that is, the 16 EPM styles can be compared to the seven notes.

However, the two steps of interaction and reflection on the maps, with the resulting planning of the interventions, can be attributed to two different people. For example, within the setting of the one-way mirror, widely used by therapists following the systemic approach and thought to be the best setting also for EPM, one can proceed as follows. The therapist is in the room with the family, and the supervisor is behind the mirror. From this more detached position (compared to being embedded and taken up by the communication storm determined by various members of the family and by the automatic reactions to them of the therapist), the supervisor is able to reflect on the models and design the interventions (almost as it were desk research) to be transmitted to the therapist, either via intercom or entering the therapy room with the well-designed plan of intervention in his or her mind.

Difficulties encountered in conducting accurate scientific research in the field of psychological interventions not only arise because of differences among different models but depend also on how these models influence the work of professionals when they are interacting with respondents. If it is true that a difference does exist among the models, it is also true that a difference does exist among the models, it is also true that a difference does exist in the way that the theory and the EPM may be put into practice within the reality of professionals during their interactions with respondents. We have to underline that the theory and the model have to be put into practice. To be put into practice they have to be accepted and applied by other professionals.

An additional complication for "accurate" research is that the professional's own model, to a greater or lesser extent, is somehow transferred to respondents, who could accept certain models better than others, depending on how these models match their own perceptions of the world.

Respondents could even construct their own model, making use of inputs that come from professionals and their models.

To clarify what is meant by the influence of models and theories on the work of professionals, an example from an EPM-based intervention in anorexia nervosa will be used. As seen through the lenses of EPM, in the families with an anorexic member, there is a symbiotic relationship between mother and daughter, whereas the father is more detached and unable to enter the world of his daughter (or of his wife, for that matter!). For this reason, in the presence of this situation, it was prescribed, and it is still prescribed with very good results, that father and daughter leave together for a three-week trip out of town. During this period the father tries to enter his daughter's world. In this case, the model led to a strong and clear prescription. The intervention derives from a systemic approach that is made even more precise through the EPM.

HUMANISM

The humanistic model, more than others, does not accept theories, and it favors approaching the other in a genuine and pure relation that is left free to flow. The underlying assumption of this model is that the human mind has in itself, regardless of any theoretical construct, the potentials to help the other to find himself or herself. If put to the extremes, this approach differs a great deal from other current therapeutic approaches. Nevertheless, it still remains an approach that derives from Western thought and does not refute, as is the case for Zen thought, all mental constructs. Zen does not accept any kind of mental construction, even those that appear to be fundamental to Western eyes, including the notions of Self, time, causality, master, servant, and so on.

By definition this humanistic approach is impossible to evaluate. However, those who accept theories and models could place it within notions including, for example, under the theory, the notion of distance defined by the extremes in approach-avoidance between intimates and among non-intimates, and the notion of ability to love, in the sense of being emotionally available, as well as in the modality of being together to differentiate it from modalities of doing and having.

In the EPM this way of working, following a humanistic approach, would mean communicating according to the 16 functions but, above all, the 8 functions that contain an intersection with the other's world (Figure 5-1). Among the latter, the one that deserves particular attention is the function corresponding to entering the other's world (F5). Actually, according to the EPM, the function of entering the other's world, at both a theoretical and experimental level, renders the other "master of his or her own life." Hence, this position reinforces the practice of working with patients in a humanistic manner that becomes a priority for success in therapy.

PSYCHOANALYSIS

As to the psychodynamic approach, unlike the humanistic approach, this approach widely accepts theorizing, even if the notion of an unconscious, albeit vague, accounts for a highly flexible element of the interaction. The tendency to find reference constructs, that is, mental constructions that serve as anchors and connections with other constructions, has been a constant feature of Freud's work. This is clearly exemplified by Freud's theory of id, ego, and superego. The existence of an element of pressure (id), one of control (superego), and one of mediation (ego) originated from the science of those years, namely, from the model of the steam engine with its alternation of thrusts and counter-thrusts to produce power. Also the Oedipus complex could be considered as based on the search for models, but, in this case, it draws on a theatrical metaphor, that of a great-emotional-impact, Greek tragedy. In addition, the "interpretation" tool, as introduced by psychoanalysis, accounts for a continuous creation of co-constructs with the patient, deriving from the interactions between the world of the therapist and that of patients.

Seen from the perspective of the theory and from the EPM, psychodynamic constructs appear to be less defined. EPM followers tend to abandon the notion of the unconscious in favor of a view based on the complexity of the situations to be examined and of the extra-conscious. At a merely hypothetical level, the EPM, put to its extremes, has in itself the notion that the functioning of the human mind relies on some specific mathematical formulas that govern the operation of the mind. Even in the theory the notion of unconscious is not dealt with except through the constructs of Emotionality and Awareness of Self, Other, and Context.

Since, as mentioned at the beginning, theories do trigger operational practice, the attitude of psychoanalysis of (1) giving ample legitimacy to what is unknown (the "unconscious") and (2) favoring small models and theories (the so-called interpretations) has reached a widely recognized but limited usefulness. In essence, one enters the patient's world and provides him or her, at least in part, with the tools of knowledge as well as with a common language meant to help the respondents make sense of their experiences within specific constructs given by the theory.

Psychoanalytic therapy is based on a background where there is room enough to place all the complexity of the human mind and of human systems without, however, pretending to discover rules that govern that complexity. It is anyhow recognized that some rules are required to govern such complexity; one such rule, for instance, relates to the setting. It is quite strict in terms of the duration of sessions and the time that has to elapse between sessions. In determining the setting and the comprehensive way in which the therapy has to take place, the therapist plays the role of rule setter (F3 function under the EPM). From the theory, it appears to be a much more comprehensive and detailed map (in Korzybski's sense).

As is the case for the humanistic approach, also for the psychodynamic approach, some modalities of intervention proposed by the latter are commonly used by professionals who follow other approaches, referring, above all, to the interpretive (i.e., explanatory) process that is so widely used even outside the psychoanalytical approach.

BEHAVIORISM AND COGNITIVISM

This approach may be seen as another extreme of the way of facing problems of the mind and of its changes. It tends also to reject theories and models, but, contrary to the humanistic approach, it tends toward empiricism, scientific experimentation, and data reproducibility. It draws on research on conditioned reflexes, on operating conditionings, and on animal observation both in the wild and in the laboratory and tends to apply to people the results of these observations. A person is essentially seen as an animal that, albeit at the highest level of biological evolution, is ultimately considered in terms of the principles of stimulus/response and reinforcing consequences. The mind and its mental constructions are not to be taken into account because they cannot be verified experimentally; the human mind has been seen as a "black box."

This attitude leads us to consider deductive and inductive thought. Behaviorism owes its very existence to an essentially inductive attitude. Deductive thinking, on the contrary, starts from a model created by our mind that is used to observe and to influence reality. But in that reality a model can hardly be considered mono-directional but rather circular, up-down, down-up, up-down, down-up, and so on. Nevertheless, one cannot deny that the attitude of supporters of inductivism first devises the tools through which reality should be observed, the glasses, the microscope, the telescope, the spectroscope that must be used to observe the world, whereas supporters of deductivism prioritize observation of the world through natural instruments that can also, if necessary, be refined. A distinction, therefore, does exist, even if in practice it is much more blurred. Starting from the dichotomy inductive-deductive, the EPM, if put to its extremes, may be considered just as the opposite of behaviorism as it attaches importance to cognitive organization, even recognizing that models are not absolute truths but rather mental tools to understand the human mind and its functioning in terms of interactions and changes, starting from a general theory of intimate relationships. The theory stands somewhere at the midpoint of this continuum to the extent that it includes both deductive and inductive aspects.

If a theory or model that is followed influences one's practice, the behavioral approach supposedly entails a detached observation of human phenomena, void of personal or professional entanglement. That position is close to that of the scientist or a surgeon, who may be kind but who is also scientifically detached and strictly instrumental. The method of operation over the respondent is all-important. In this model the patient is induced to be passively compliant, following the prescription of tasks and exercises and responding to questions in the most accurate manner.

The EPM tries to go deeper into the patient's world to understand its nature as shown through the 16 relational styles. To speak of relational styles means using a certain language. This language is "better" than other languages because it grasps processes of interaction and change. This language makes it possible to grasp even those aspects that common language is unable to grasp. Indeed, the EPM has the ability to grasp interactions in a very synthetic way.

The effort to use a particularistic mental tool like the EPM means wearing "certain lenses," from which derives a certain scientific attitude on the part of the professional. That attitude remains, however, less detached than the pure behavioristic approach, because it attempts to enter into the patient's world according to a very specific map of 16 styles. In the theory, there is also an effort to translate intimate relationships in terms of a language that maps events taking place before the eyes and ears of the professional.

From classical behaviorism arose cognitivism, which does not reject theorizing. Quite the contrary, the latter appears to be particularly intertwined in it. Mental constructions prevail in this approach to psychotherapy (Guidano & Liotti, 1985).

Obviously, both theory and the EPM, in most of their elements, fall within the field of cognitive sciences. The higher specificity of the EPM compared to cognitivism lies in the search for a formal structure that goes beyond the usual way of thinking. The unusual ways of thinking found in both the theory and the model, and their departure from most common reflections and most common ways of thinking about intimate relationships, also challenge traditional ways of practicing. The EPM is different from cognitivism in its different way of looking at reality. When cognitivists work with "belief systems," they work with traditional mentalistic tools. On the contrary, EPM works with unusual mentalistic tools. The difference between cognitivism and EPM is that, while cognitivists work on belief systems that commonly exist and are grasped by the minds of most people, the EPM searches for and utilizes a completely new original organization of thought. This is a novel way of reading thinking processes that does not make reference to common experiences of what happens in one's mind. The EPM makes reference to an organization of thought that goes beyond common ways of elaborating experiences. It finds its referent basis in the logic and in the processes of interactions.

Once this logic has been found, its products are then placed in an unusual way of conceptualizing intimate relationships. Thus, the logic of the EPM creates an interaction among usual levels of reflection and new ways of thinking prompted by the model. This process triggers new ideas and new paths that we hope will be found useful by clinicians and researchers alike.

As to the integration among the models mentioned thus far, for the humanistic approach and the psychoanalytic one, most therapists, during their work, detach themselves now and then from the interaction with their patients. Supposedly, they want to become scientific and detached observers. This position assumes a behavioral stance. Now and then it assumes a cognitive stance, elaborating and interpreting the constructs of their respondents that they try to improve. Each model corresponds to a particular therapeutic stance and, therefore, a particular therapeutic approach. Consequently, if professionals want to enter into their respondents' worlds and be flexible in this regard, they may become professional chameleons. Even a humanistic therapist may make interpretations, just as a psychodymanic therapist will reflect on feelings and emotions. By the same token, a behavioral therapist may have recourse to interpretation of actions and a reflection of feelings just as much as a humanist. If flexibility is necessary in dealing with intimate relationships, to enter into our respondents' worlds, one cannot maintain one rigid therapeutic stance, only humanistic, only psychodynamic, or only behavioral. No wonder that most therapists define themselves as "eclectic." Both the theory and the EPM cover so many possibilities that they give eclecticism both a needed background and rationale.

SYSTEMS THEORY

When therapists work within a systemic approach, they no longer see the individual but the entire system in which the individual is existing. The systemic approach is characterized by shifting from observations about the individual to its context, the way the network of intimate relationships is perceived by each member of that network. Systems means a set of elements with strong links among them. The direction along which this approach has mostly been applied is family therapy. The three elements on which this perspective is based are (1) the general theory of systems, that is, drawing scientific models from other fields of science ("thermostat") and applying them to the study of the human systems (i.e., families); (2) cybernetics (i.e., a circular vision of events, with its rejection of linear causality in favor of a bi-directional causality); and (3) importance attached to modalities in which communication takes place. The systemic approach proposes itself as a point of view completely different from that of traditional psychotherapy. By placing a psychological situation on a higher logic level, it radically modifies traditional perspectives, putting emphasis on the links and on the interactions among respondents. The EPM owes its existence to the need to work on links, on the interactions that develop among interconnected and interdependent individuals in an effort to define and classify them. Another aspect of the EPM that can be linked to the systemic approach is the fact that they both draw on general systems theories. These theories could be related to any physical or natural entities when there are interactions between objects and, when observed, transactions.

The theory, in some respects, falls within the systemic approach, but at the same time, it gives importance to individuals, in mostly linear terms. This shifting from system to individual and from individual to system might be seen as a more complete way to work clinically. Shifting from system to individual and from individual to system might be considered as a more relevant and valid view of how individuals succeed or fail in the context of their intimate relationships.

In passing from theory to clinical practice, the systemic therapist tends to approach or depart from members of the system (e.g., family members) according to maps that take into account the functioning of the entire system. For example, in the case of a child with psychosomatic disturbances, one could ask parents to sleep with the door of their room closed, to diminish the involvement of the couple with their children, as in the case of some psychosomatic disturbances. Closing the door, however, is often an unsuccessful prescription, because the child will bang on it until the parents give in and let the child in their bedroom. It takes more that a locked door to break down symbiotic relationships!

Here is where the theory and the model come into being as complementary. If symbiosis is controlling a system, what would the theory and the EPM suggest as interventions that have not been included in the repertoires of traditional family therapists? In the first place, the theory would give a model in terms of the likeness continuum, with the EPM giving specific styles that expand on the model. In the second place, in symbiotic relationships, intervening with the 3HC prescription might not work, because it may make the family even more symbiotic. Which relational style(s) given by the EPM might be more helpful? As can be seen from this example, even systemic therapists make use of maps that could be defined as cognitive maps, thus creating a link with the cognitive approach.

In working with patients, the systemic therapist appears as a person who balances interventions and modulates communications among members of the family. The therapist introduces in the system certain logics derived from models that are sometimes perceived by the same families as paradoxical novelties sometimes difficult to be understood. Families often do not understand why the therapist administered certain prescriptions for home consumption or what has been said in sessions. This is why it is important to add writing, in its various structures, to verbally based psychotherapies. This is an important contribution, especially in assigning written homework, when verbally given prescriptions could and will be forgotten, distorted, or misunderstood (L'Abate, 1986, 1990, 1992, 2001a, 2002a, 2002b).

AWARENESS

This component of Model[1] appears to be the common denominator of all the approaches just reviewed. The notion of awareness can be seen as something that clearly emerges from an obscure and blurred situation. The EPM through its function F14 intends awareness as something that is similar to grasping and understanding the mining of a metaphor. Actually, this EPM function is characterized by the absence of one's shared core. When only this intersection is missing, the mind is induced to fill the gap by giving rise to awareness. The metaphor represents a situation where something non-explicit is made explicit, a kind of nucleus that stands out very clearly from a bottom. It is like something emerging from the bottom that was supposed to emerge but that did not emerge before, like a dream that conceals a hidden meaning. Under conditions of uncertainty, insecurity, and inadequate clarity, when something new is suggested, no matter how cryptic, the mind may develop a new meaning and a feeling of greater clarity. This process occurs in creative endeavors, when one, empty of ideas, at last, is able to find the solution that was being sought but not yet found. To facilitate awareness in the EPM, through the use of the interaction table (see Figure 4-5), a series of sentences has been generated that serve as a sort of password of the mind (Chapter 5). These sentences are used to increase reflection about oneself and about one's world. Those sentences should function like a grain put inside an oyster that determines the formation of the pearl. These sentences again may be seen as "Compass Sentences" in that they orient the organization of our mind (De Giacomo & Iadicicco, 2001). The clear consciousness implicit in the notion of awareness can be linked to its being completely inside ourselves, as masters of ourselves. What psychoanalysis defines as "increase in ego strength" can be considered a common denominator among most psychotherapies and most mental health professionals (Wile, 1979).

In conclusion, the purpose of humanistic psychotherapy is to enhance humanness and its unique nature. The purpose of psychoanalysis lies in increasing the strength of the "ego." The behavioral school tries to eliminate disorders of "subjects." The systemic school tries to "individuate" members of the family. The selfhood model and EPM demonstrate that keeping one's own world in the interaction is the function most represented in functional human beings, suggesting that a common denominator exists in different approaches. Awareness, therefore, refers not only to respondents but also especially to professionals. The problem, already considered in the Preface, is the following: Do professionals who use any models, theories, or maps that help them work with greater clarity obtain better results than professionals who do not have these maps? What happens if they receive more encompassing and specific maps? The theory and models presented here have introduced novel ways of thinking and of intervening in intimate relationships, assumedly in a more efficient manner than done heretofore. These ways are, to a certain extent, independent of the particular style of the professional. They imply using replicable methods rather than non-replicable, idiosyncratic techniques, gimmicks, or games.

CREATIVITY

Before closing this section on the differences and the common aspects of the different approaches in the field of psychotherapy, it would be relevant to speak of creativity in both prevention and psychotherapy. Creativity plays a fundamental role in all the fields of human activities. In many situations—when one works in a company or in a research laboratory or in a school or in the building sector or, to a greater extent, in the field of art, creativeness plays a fundamental role in solving problems linked to different activities. Even in the field of psychotherapy creativity plays a crucial role for success of the same, for example, in helping us solve certain problems in our patients or when we have to devise a new psychotherapeutic intervention for a specific kind of mental or emotional disturbance. Actually, all the approaches that we have mentioned make use of creative thinking, starting from the humanistic and ending with the behavioral approach. Therefore, one cannot neglect the essential part that creativeness plays in all psychotherapeutic endeavors as well as in intimate relationships.

Freud made use of the Greek tragedy about King Oedipus as a model for a certain kind of human relation. The behavioral cognitive approach has even introduced a problem-solving technique inspired by Osborn (1992) as a pre-established module of family therapy in the work with families as a constant practice (Miklowitz & Goldstein, 1997). Concerning the systemic approach, Bateson has given a remarkable contribution explaining how ideas are born (see Chapter 10). The theory gives room to creativeness as a central element when placed at the center of functionality in the likeness continuum and the creative-conductive style in intimate relationships.

As far as the EPM is concerned, it has given rise to a full-fledged method of developing problem-solving creativity. It consists of passing from one mental condition to another in 16 possible conditions. This approach, as given in Chapter 4, makes it possible to see a certain topic or issue from 16 different perspectives (De Giacomo & De Nigris, 2001). Starting from one idea, it produces other possible ideas drawn from the 16 functions of the EPM (De Giacomo, 1995/1999).

The theme of creativity in psychotherapy constitutes also a fundamental aspect of the psychotherapeutic work that could be synthetically defined as "the art of thinking." Much as an entire life could be seen as a work of art, our psychotherapies could also be seen as works of art. In most cases it is important to convey to our patients a pragmatic, creative perspective, because without problem-solving creativity no problem could be solved.

Some psychotherapists are particularly keen to use certain metaphors that are full-fledged linguistic works of art. The art of thought is translated into the art of language that, in the case of the EPM, has found an application in a number of sentences (Chapter 5) with high psychological impact. We know that they have an impact because they were chosen from a list of hundreds of possible sentences. The list of phrases given in Chapter 5 is the outcome of statistical analyses that found these phrases to be more frequently chosen by respondents and can be utilized in psychotherapy both by the psychotherapist during sessions and by patients who may select and process them (De Giacomo & Iadicicco, 2002). These sentences are the fruit of the EPM used as the art of thought. These sentences have been made available in online counseling.

GENDER

The variable of sex and gender continues to be an important battleground that mirrors what has happened between the sexes from time immemorial (Acitelli & Young, 1996; Barnett & Hyde, 2001; Chafetz, 1999; Fehr & Broughton, 2001; Seeman, 1995). As Canary et al. (1997, p. viii) concluded: "[L]iterature shows that men and women communicate intimacy and control in more interesting ways than those suggested by sex stereotypes." Women stereotypically tend to cry and express their hurt feelings in ways that men cannot deal with. Men may tend to get angry or find rational solutions or withdraw altogether if the emotionality is too intense for them to handle.

As indicated in previous publications and Chapter 2, the selfhood model makes specific predictions about men-women ratios in the four personality propensities. This is one dimension where the theory and the EPM are complementary, since no predictions have been made about these ratios by the latter. For instance, the selfhood model predicts that in the Selful propensity there should be an equal ratio of men to women because they balance complementarily their similarities and differences. Another way to state the same prediction would be that Selful individuals balance and negotiate their modalities and priorities in ways that would ensure a positive outcome for themselves and intimate others, including offspring and close relatives. They also would combine and share equanimously communal and agentic modes of relating. This prediction is supported by the research of Fehr and Broughton (2001) with college student samples that must be considered "normative" for the time being.

The same ratio of an equal number of men and women should be found in the No-self propensity, but for different reasons. While Selful individuals tend to attract each other for positive reasons and characteristics, No-self individuals attract each other for negative reasons, that is, there is an equality of Abusive-Apathetic (AA) styles from their families of origin as well as in their interactions, and there are the Drama Triangle and Distance Regulation models being operational here. They are unable to negotiate their differences, nor can they profit from their similarities. They are unable, to some degree, to use communal (i.e., love) and agentic (i.e., power) modes of relating.

Reverse ratios, however, are predicted in Selfishness and Selflessness. In the former, men behaved according to stereotyped notions of the agentically assertive, aggressive macho man, while in the latter women behaved according to stereotyped notions of the communally passive, gullibly compliant, homebound caretaker and doormat (L'Abate, 1992; L'Abate & Harrison, 1992). More specifically, most gender comparisons reviewed in the literature cited above are usually based on normative samples of students and not on deviant populations. Once the focus of analysis shifts from normative samples to diagnostically deviant populations, sex and gender ratios tend to become real and distinct (Seeman, 1995), yet they also illustrate the absence of an overarching theoretical framework that could view such differences as extensions of basic personality propensities derived from the selfhood model. Furthermore, among deviant populations, criminals are usually left out of many gender differences (Seeman, 1995). The greatest gender differences predicted by this model lie along the horizontal axis of exernalization (i.e., Selfishness propensity) versus internalization, that is, Selflessness propensity.

In terms of the characteristics of each propensity, Model[9] predicts a preponderance of men over women, up to a 5 to 1 ratio, depending on which criterion is used, in Selfishness or externalizations. In Selflessness or internalizations, on the other hand, a preponderance of women over men is predicted up to a 5 to 1 ratio, depending on which criterion is used. These ratios, however, are influenced greatly by socio-economic and educational levels (Cusinato & L'Abate, 2002). Nonetheless, one needs to look at the gender of most incarcerated felons, who would by definition fall within the externalization category, and find a ratio of about 7 to 1 of men versus incarcerated women. Many in the latter would fall into the internalization/Selfless propensity. Many incarcerated women acted out to help their lovers or boyfriends, even though a greater number of younger women are beginning to show characteristics similar to those of acting-out men. By the same token, the overwelming numbers of moody, depressed, and anxious women over men tend to support this differentiation and the importance of looking at deviant populations before generalizing from normality to deviancy (Nolen-Hoeksena, 1995; Shaw, Kennedy, & Joffe, 1995; Yonkers & Gurguis, 1995).

PERSONALITY SOCIALIZATION, RELATIONAL COMPETENCE, AND INTIMATE RELATIONSHIPS

Now we are able to answer the question: What are personality socialization and interpersonal competence, and how are they expressed in intimate relationships? The answer by now should be clear: It takes all 15 models of the theory and the EPM to define personality in its various intra- and interactional manifestations. Personality socialization and interpersonal competence may be conceived as an artichoke in the theory. The leaves of the artichoke represent the models of the theory that cover up and even defend the core of the artichoke. Even anger, conceived as the prickly choke, functions as the defense for the core; that is, hurts and fears of being hurt. No matter how we look at it, it takes more than one model to understand personality socialization and relational competence in intimate relationships. They are the sum total of how one behaves over time in intimate relationships, not in short-lived, contrived, and superficial laboratory encounters or superficial, one time-only encounters.

With that proviso, we can go back to the models reviewed in the previous pages and integrate them from the viewpoint of an overarching dimension of internality-externality (see Table 12-1).

HYPOTHETICAL INTEGRATION OF RELATIONAL MODELS

The purpose of this final section is to integrate convergences and divergences among three completely different models of intimate (prolonged, close, and committed) relationships: (1) attachment, (2) circumplex (Plutchik & Conte, 1997), (3) EPM, (4) selfhood, (5) Reiss' family paradigms, and (6) Fisher and Ransom's family typology. We endeavor to integrate these models by selecting a representative few and linking them together along a dimension of internality-externality. While internality implies an inference from hypothetical internal states or traits, externality, by the same token, implies visible and observable dimensions. All five models, even though they derive from different theoretical sources, do predict seemingly similar patterns of relationships between and among intimates. Each model has its own peculiar language that has meaning only within the parameters set by the model itself. Possible convergences and divergences among these models have already been discussed conceptually elsewhere but only at the hypothetical level (De Giacomo et al., 1997; L'Abate, 1997b, 2002a, 2002b).

Therefore, from a continuum going from inferred (i.e., internal) to observable (i.e., external) relationships (Table 12-1), attachment is the most inferred, followed by the circumplex. Selfhood is intermediate between the

Table 12-1
Theoretical Integration of Six Relational Models According to a Continuum of Internality-Externality

Internality <————————————————————————> Externality

MODELS					
Attachment	**Circumplex**	**Selfhood**	**EPM**	**Family Paradigms**	**Family Typology**
Secure	Friendly	Selful	Sharing	Environmental-balanced	Balanced
Dismissing	Dominant	Selfish	Maintaining	Achieving-distancing-limiting	Disconnected
Preoccupied	Submissive	Selfless	Accepting	Consensus-preoccupied	Traditional
Fearful	Hostile	No-self	Antifunction	Emotionally strained	

two other models, with the EPM being the most external and observable, extending into family types and paradigms. By the same token, while the attachment model has been evaluated extensively around the globe, with the circumplex and the two family models receiving some empirical support, the other two models (selfhood and EPM) are "new kids on the block." They are in need of extensive evaluation from those who are extraneous to their creation and validation. Both attachment and EPM represent the theory from which they originated, in the sense that theory and model are both isomorphic with each other and are indistinguishable from each other. The attachment model summarizes and sustains by itself the whole object relations theory. The same is the case in the EPM, as derived from systems theories. The model is the theory. The selfhood model, on the other hand, is but one of the models sustaining the theory, even though, admittedly, it is the major model on which a great deal of the theory stands or falls (L'Abate, 2002a, 2002b).

Consequently, one way of integrating the theory and the EPM with the models considered in Chapter 1 is to align them along a dimension of internality, that is, the so-called intrapsychic, inferred traits or states, to externality, that is, visible and relatively available interpersonal dimensions of relationships (Table 12-1). Once this framework is created, we can align each style inferred from internal working models from attachment with the two major dimensions of the circumplex model, power or dominance, and orthogonally to the dimension of warmth or nurturance. Thus far, going from left to right of Table 12-1, it is easy to see how relational styles of attachment should result in corresponding dimensions of the circumplex model and, even more, with selfhood personality propensities and the EPM coordinates. As presented in Chapter 5, both authors and their collaborators have demonstrated and are now in the process of replicating the same study. These studies, however, share a major shortcoming. They derive from individuals' responses to a self-report, paper-and-pencil questionnaire rather than direct observations of relationships.

A major conceptual and empirical jump is required in going from individuals to the two models of family paradigms and family typology. There is no doubt that individual variables become obscured once there are real interactions with multipersonal systems like the family. Yet there is also the possibility that individual factors may enter and influence family relationships. The more rigid and entrenched these individual factors are, whether positive or negative, the greater the possibility of their entering to influence intimate relationships. For instance, one would hypothesize that Secure, Friendly, Selful, Sharing individuals will very likely match and mate with similarly differentiated partners. Together they will develop balanced family relationships. By the same token, insecure individuals might mate, match, and mismatch with similarly undifferentiated individuals, producing any of the other dysfunctional family patterns.

Can we be more specific in our hypotheses? We shall try to consider more particularly the role of gender and personality as major determinants or independent variables that will affect individual and multi-relational patterns. A major issue lies in considering ethnic, socio-economic, and cultural influences. These three independent variables cannot be ignored, except to hypothesize that they might exacerbate or weaken any of the connections made here. For instance, in many cultures that support and even reward male dominance over female submission, it will be possible to predict that there will be a predominance of insecure and undifferentiated relationships. However, even here one needs to consider the role of personality factors as mediators of multi-relational patterns. For instance, in the Italian culture, as supported by the work of Cusinato and L'Abate (2002), socio-economic variables play a major role in producing differentiated personality propensities, as in the personal and professional experience of both these writers. By the same token, in cultures in transition from a male-dominant to more egalitarian gender roles, it is easy to see how personality factors enter into multi-relational contexts. For instance, when the first writer and his wife were invited into the home of a senior colleague in Japan for supper, the host's wife remained in the kitchen while the host and guests were eating. When the wife of the writer asked why the hostess was not joining us for supper, we were informed that that was the custom. When wonderment was expressed about this custom, the explanation was that the hostess could not speak English. She would be embarrassed to be present without being able to join in the conversation. Examples of this gender separation are present in many Middle Eastern cultures, where the role of the woman is relegated to the kitchen, while men enjoy the fruits of the woman's labors. Individual differences, however, exist in cultures as mediated by religious, socio-economic, educational, and ethnic factors. Hence, whatever we can hypothesize here at this time is strictly limited to the Western European and North American cultures.

Whether these hypothetical links are valid depends a great deal on future research oriented toward finding empirical correlations among various models, as illustrated by the study by L'Abate et al., (2000) summarized in Chapter 5. Hence, the future is open for comparative testing about the validity of theoretical models about intimate relationships.

A striking similarity among these models is the presence of one positive, functional characteristic (first line of Table 12-1) and of two or three dysfunctional ones. Thus far, the only evidence to link at least three of these six models is the study (Chapter 5) connecting the attachment, selfhood, and EPM models. This study included clinical and non-clinical respondents. A replication with medical students has been completed, and results are in the process of being analyzed. If this integration is in some ways valid, it would suggest the importance of comparative model-testing as the wave of the future, especially evaluating personality characteristics and functioning in intimate relationships. This integration may well serve as a blueprint for this type of comparison.

CONCLUSION

This work has attempted to integrate a theory and a model of intimate relationships that derive from diverse conceptual and theoretical backgrounds. Their theoretical assumptions, postulates, and models complement each other in many ways, not only theoretically but also including preventive, therapeutic, and rehabilitative practices. It will be the task of future investigations to evaluate the validity of both the theory and the model in comparison with similar theories and models.

Appendix A

Evaluation of Concerns

Name ____

ID ______________________ Age _______ Sex _______ Date _______

The purpose of this checklist is to find what kind of concerns are affecting you at the present time. Please read the statements below and rate them according to whether they apply to you most of the time, sometimes, or not at all

	This statement applies to me: Most of the time	Sometimes	Not at all
1. Helplessness (feeling completely unable to cope or to deal with a situation)	___	___	___
2. Feelings of worthlessness	___	___	___
3. Loss (feeling completely lost and alone)	___	___	___
4. Feelings of inferiority	___	___	___
5. Abandonment (feeling abandoned and left out)	___	___	___
6. Feeling guilty	___	___	___
7. Comfort (not having anyone to comfort and support you)	___	___	___
8. Feeling like a failure	___	___	___
9. Closeness (not having anyone to be close to and to confide your hurts with)	___	___	___
10. Fear of criticism	___	___	___
11. Love and loss of love (unable to be loved by someone important to you)	___	___	___
12. Perfectionism	___	___	___

	This statement applies to me: Most of the time	Sometimes	Not at all
13. Protection (feeling no one looks after you)	___	___	___
14. Afraid to make mistakes	___	___	___
15. Nurturance (feeling without sufficient nurturance or care from anyone)	___	___	___
16. Wanting acceptance and approval	___	___	___
17. Rejection (being rejected by someone you love)	___	___	___
18. Wanting to achieve well	___	___	___
19. Overdependency (relying too much on someone else)	___	___	___
20. Self-criticism (being very hard on yourself)	___	___	___

Instructions for Scoring:

Note: It is up to the professional whether respondents should score this test or not.

Add all of the odd-numbered statements (1, 3, 5, etc.) together, giving 2 points for check marks made under "Most of the time" and 1 point for check marks made under "Sometimes." Do the same, that is, add all of the even-numbered statements (2, 4, 6, etc.) together, giving 2 points for check marks made under "Most of the time" and 1 point for check marks made under "Sometimes."

Totals for odd-numbered statements ______
Totals for even-numbered statements ______

If your total for odd-numbered statements is a great deal (5 points or more)* higher than the total for even-numbered statements, then your concerns may stem from depending too much on others. If your total for even-numbered statements is a great deal (5 points or more) higher than the total for odd-numbered statements, then your concerns may stem from being too self-critical. If your two totals are within a few points (less than 5) of each other, then your concerns stem from depending too much on others and being too self-critical. Whatever the conclusion, regardless of your scores, rest assured that both kinds of concerns can be treated successfully.

*Note that this range is based on clinical rather than experimental evidence. Consequently, it should be interpreted conservatively and, ideally, with evidence from other sources.

Appendix B

What Applies to Me That I Agree With?

Name ______________________________ Sex ____________ Date ____________

The purpose of this questionnaire is to see which situations listed below apply to you that you agree or disagree with. Circle which situation applies to you or you agree with: (1) always, a great deal, or most of the time; (2) somewhat or sometimes; or (3) not at all or never. If an item does not apply to you at all, circle N/A. For instance, if you do not have a father or a partner or the item is something you have not experienced, circle N/A. References to mother or father may mean any caretaker, adoptive stepmother or father.

	Applies to me			
1. Strong men don't cry	1	2	3	N/A
2. I want to be rational and in control	1	2	3	N/A
3. Things have worked out pretty well for me	1	2	3	N/A
4. I am a non-conformist and proud of it	1	2	3	N/A
5. I do not care what my mother tells me; I do what I like	1	2	3	N/A
6. I do not care for others as much as I care for myself	1	2	3	N/A
7. My parent(s) were strict but gave me room to make up my mind	1	2	3	N/A
8. My father wanted me to do what he told me or else	1	2	3	N/A
9. I am different from my mother	1	2	3	N/A
10. I do not like to share myself with others	1	2	3	N/A
11. I do not need anyone to take care of myself	1	2	3	N/A
12. I really love my parent(s)	1	2	3	N/A
13. Solving problems with a loved one is very hard for me	1	2	3	N/A
14. My mother was the boss in my family	1	2	3	N/A
15. I am very conventional in everything I do	1	2	3	N/A
16. Clothes do not matter to me	1	2	3	N/A

		Applies to me			
17.	I am proud to be maladjusted	1	2	3	N/A
18.	I am very impulsive	1	2	3	N/A
19.	My parents got along pretty well	1	2	3	N/A
20.	I want to go beyond college in my education	1	2	3	N/A
21.	I like my life the way it is, without any changes	1	2	3	N/A
22.	I like to be close to someone	1	2	3	N/A
23.	I tend to explode at the slightest provocation	1	2	3	N/A
24.	I tend to be rather pessimistic (negative) about anything that happens to me	1	2	3	N/A
25.	If people do not agree with me, I write them off for good	1	2	3	N/A
26.	I am very much like my mother	1	2	3	N/A
27.	I tend to go from one extreme to another	1	2	3	N/A
28.	My parent(s) (caretakers) were very abusive of me	1	2	3	N/A
29.	I cannot live without my father	1	2	3	N/A
30.	My mother and I are like two peas in a pod	1	2	3	N/A
31.	I like to keep things inside of me	1	2	3	N/A
32.	I am a very dependent person	1	2	3	N/A
33.	I feel loved unconditionally	1	2	3	N/A
34.	My parent(s) did not know how to solve problems together	1	2	3	N/A
35.	Chaos would describe my family of origin	1	2	3	N/A
36.	I do not have a self of my own	1	2	3	N/A
37.	I do not really care how I look	1	2	3	N/A
38.	My social adjustment leaves much to be desired	1	2	3	N/A
39.	I am a very anxious person	1	2	3	N/A
40.	My parents were always fighting	1	2	3	N/A
41.	I did very well in school	1	2	3	N/A
42.	I like the way I am	1	2	3	N/A
43.	My mother and I are very close	1	2	3	N/A
44.	I keep my cool no matter what happens	1	2	3	N/A
45.	I tend to be rather optimistic (positive) about anything that happens to me	1	2	3	N/A
46.	I like for things to stay the same as they are	1	2	3	N/A
47.	I am very much like my father (adoptive or stepfather)	1	2	3	N/A
48.	I look after myself and let others take care of themselves	1	2	3	N/A
49.	My parents let me do whatever I liked	1	2	3	N/A
50.	I cannot live without my mother	1	2	3	N/A
51.	My father and I are like two peas in a pod	1	2	3	N/A
52.	Whenever I am tense or uncomfortable I tend to relieve the tension by doing something	1	2	3	N/A
53.	I do not like to be dependent on anyone	1	2	3	N/A
54.	I have never felt loved	1	2	3	N/A
55.	I really do not know how to solve problems with another person	1	2	3	N/A
56.	I like to please others	1	2	3	N/A
57.	I am very confused about who I am as a person	1	2	3	N/A

		Applies to me			
58.	Appearance is unimportant to me	1	2	3	N/A
59.	I do not care whether others see me as adjusted or maladjusted	1	2	3	N/A
60.	I am a very depressed person	1	2	3	N/A
61.	My partner and I fight quite a bit	1	2	3	N/A
62.	Education is not important to me	1	2	3	N/A
63.	I do not like change	1	2	3	N/A
64.	I am very satisfied with my partner	1	2	3	N/A
65.	My father and I are very close	1	2	3	N/A
66.	I try to behave appropriately regardless of the situation	1	2	3	N/A
67.	I do not like changes in my relationships	1	2	3	N/A
68.	I am very much like one of my brothers (sisters)	1	2	3	N/A
69.	I care for others more than I care for myself	1	2	3	N/A
70.	My parent(s) were not only very strict but let me know if I did not do what they wanted me to do	1	2	3	N/A
71.	My mother wanted me to be very much like her	1	2	3	N/A
72.	My mother and I are very much the same	1	2	3	N/A
73.	I want to be left completely alone	1	2	3	N/A
74.	I do not like to keep things inside myself	1	2	3	N/A
75.	Being dependent is for sissies	1	2	3	N/A
76.	Real love does not exist	1	2	3	N/A
77.	Solving problems with someone close is very hard for me	1	2	3	N/A
78.	I like to have someone tell me what to do	1	2	3	N/A
79.	I like tradition very much	1	2	3	N/A
80.	I like to look my best all the time	1	2	3	N/A
81.	Adjustment is a relative term	1	2	3	N/A
82.	I have a criminal record	1	2	3	N/A
83.	Fighting is a way of life in my family	1	2	3	N/A
84.	I have achieved well in school	1	2	3	N/A
85.	I am very flexible	1	2	3	N/A
86.	My partner and I fight all the time	1	2	3	N/A
87.	My siblings (brothers and sisters) and I are very close	1	2	3	N/A
88.	My temper is something to behold	1	2	3	N/A
89.	I want to grow, take risks, and make changes in my life	1	2	3	N/A
90.	My mother requires that I do everything she tells me	1	2	3	N/A
91.	I do not care for myself at all	1	2	3	N/A
92.	My parent(s) were very violent with me	1	2	3	N/A
93.	My father wanted me to be very much like him	1	2	3	N/A
94.	My father and I are very much the same	1	2	3	N/A
95.	I do not want to see my father at all	1	2	3	N/A
96.	I keep my feelings to myself	1	2	3	N/A
97.	I like to be independent from others	1	2	3	N/A
98.	My parent(s) showed me how to love	1	2	3	N/A
99.	I do not know how to negotiate	1	2	3	N/A
100.	I like to be on top of situations	1	2	3	N/A
101.	As a whole I am very passive	1	2	3	N/A

	Applies to me			
102. Who I really am is more important than how I look	1	2	3	N/A
103. Socially I am a misfit	1	2	3	N/A
104. In the past I have had trouble with the law	1	2	3	N/A
105. My family life was never harmonious	1	2	3	N/A
106. School achievement is my major goal	1	2	3	N/A
107. I welcome chances to change things in my life	1	2	3	N/A
108. Partners can be a pain in the neck	1	2	3	N/A
109. My family is a very close-knit one	1	2	3	N/A
110. I can keep myself under tight control	1	2	3	N/A
111. I hate to be told what to do	1	2	3	N/A
112. My father requires me to do everything he tells me without back talk	1	2	3	N/A
113. I care for myself a great deal	1	2	3	N/A
114. My parent(s) were very lenient with me	1	2	3	N/A
115. My mother pretty much allowed me to rely on my judgment	1	2	3	N/A
116. I am very much like my mother	1	2	3	N/A
117. I am very much like my father	1	2	3	N/A
118. I am somewhat like my mother	1	2	3	N/A
119. I am somewhat like my father	1	2	3	N/A
120. I am different from my father	1	2	3	N/A
121. If I get made, I do not care who I hurt	1	2	3	N/A
122. There is no such thing as independence	1	2	3	N/A
123. I do not know how to love	1	2	3	N/A
124. I wish I knew how to negotiate with someone I love	1	2	3	N/A
125. I do not like to have someone on top of me	1	2	3	N/A
126. I like to be creative in my relationship with others	1	2	3	N/A
127. You cannot judge a book from its cover	1	2	3	N/A
128. I like to feel accepted by those I love and who love me	1	2	3	N/A
129. I have been hospitalized for mental illness	1	2	3	N/A
130. In my family there was always an upset	1	2	3	N/A
131. I finished high school in the top 33% of my class	1	2	3	N/A
132. Our partnership is solid no matter how much we argue	1	2	3	N/A
133. In my family we hug and touch each other often	1	2	3	N/A
134. I have very little control of myself	1	2	3	N/A
135. Usually I do the opposite of what I am told to do	1	2	3	N/A
136. I do not care what my father tells me; I do what I like	1	2	3	N/A
137. I do not care for anyone, including myself	1	2	3	N/A
138. My parent(s) let me do whatever I pleased	1	2	3	N/A
139. My father pretty much allowed me to rely on my judgment	1	2	3	N/A
140. I am the opposite of my mother	1	2	3	N/A
141. I like to get even with whoever has slighted me	1	2	3	N/A
142. I wish I knew how to love	1	2	3	N/A
143. I like to negotiate and solve problems with someone I love	1	2	3	N/A
144. My family of origin was very democratic	1	2	3	N/A

		Applies to me			
145.	I hate social conventions	1	2	3	N/A
146.	I am mentally ill	1	2	3	N/A
147.	I hate fighting; I like to discuss what I disagree with	1	2	3	N/A
148.	I finished college in the top 33% of my class	1	2	3	N/A
149.	Partners come and go	1	2	3	N/A
150.	I have seen my parents cry together	1	2	3	N/A
151.	I do not like to be controlled by anyone	1	2	3	N/A
152.	I hate to conform to society's or anyone's standards	1	2	3	N/A
153.	I do not listen to my mother or any other authority figure	1	2	3	N/A
154.	I was never allowed to do anything on my own	1	2	3	N/A
155.	My mother wanted me to do what she told me or else	1	2	3	N/A
156.	I am the opposite of my father	1	2	3	N/A
157.	I am completely cut off from my mother	1	2	3	N/A
158.	I am completely cut off from my father	1	2	3	N/A
159.	I strike back if I am crossed	1	2	3	N/A
160.	I can take care of myself, and I do not need anyone's help	1	2	3	N/A
161.	I do not know how to love unconditionally	1	2	3	N/A
162.	There was no clear leadership in my family	1	2	3	N/A
163.	I take all the sexual opportunities I can get	1	2	3	N/A
164.	I like to dress differently than other people	1	2	3	N/A
165.	I have visited a mental health professional	1	2	3	N/A
166.	My siblings (brothers and sisters) got along pretty well	1	2	3	N/A
167.	I dropped out from high school	1	2	3	N/A
168.	My partner and I never argue	1	2	3	N/A
169.	Closeness with someone scares me	1	2	3	N/A
170.	I cannot stand people who lose their cool	1	2	3	N/A
171.	I think that life sucks	1	2	3	N/A
172.	I do not listen to my father or any other authority figure	1	2	3	N/A
173.	My mother was very lenient	1	2	3	N/A
174.	My mother punished me regardless of what I did	1	2	3	N/A
175.	I do not want to see my mother at all	1	2	3	N/A
176.	I like to share my hurts with someone I trust	1	2	3	N/A
177.	I do not know what unconditional love means	1	2	3	N/A
178.	My father was the boss in my family	1	2	3	N/A
179.	If I can, I like to take advantage of others	1	2	3	N/A
180.	At times I have needed psychiatric help	1	2	3	N/A
181.	Sibling rivalry was rewarded in my family	1	2	3	N/A
182.	In school I received many awards	1	2	3	N/A
183.	If I cry, I do not want anyone to see me	1	2	3	N/A
184.	My father was very strict	1	2	3	N/A
185.	My father punished me regardless of what I did	1	2	3	N/A
186.	I cannot love anyone, including myself	1	2	3	N/A
187.	My family taught me to do for others	1	2	3	N/A
188.	I am pretty rigid in how I think and how I behave	1	2	3	N/A
189.	At times I have felt suicidal	1	2	3	N/A

		Applies to me		
190. For me, athletics was always more important than grades	1	2	3	N/A
191. In my family we often tell each other "I love you"	1	2	3	N/A
192. In my family I was given space to make up my mind	1	2	3	N/A
193. I like to take charge of situations	1	2	3	N/A
194. For me things are either black or white with nothing in between	1	2	3	N/A
195. I am a very strong person	1	2	3	N/A
196. I tend to worry a lot	1	2	3	N/A
197. Religion is very important to me	1	2	3	N/A
198. People who study a lot are nerds	1	2	3	N/A
199. Sex is very important to me	1	2	3	N/A
200. I love to massage and be massaged	1	2	3	N/A

Scoring Instructions

Please note that this is still an experimental test and that criteria for its reliability and validity need to be established. Consequently, this test cannot and should not be used for clinical or other purposes except research.

Depending on whether the item's valence is positive (+) or positively worded (+) or negative (–) or negatively worded (–), add or subtract points. For instance, if answer #1 is circled for item 168 (negatively worded, –), subtract 1 point; if answer #2 is circled, add 0 points; if answer #3 is circled, add 1 point. For item 132 (positively worded, +), if #1 is circled, add 1 point; if #2 is circled, add 0 points; if #3 is circled, subtract 1 point. This rule applies to each item regardless of the number of asterisks an item receives.

Score 1 point (1 asterisk) for responses that fall into the Symbiosis-Alienation (Abusive-Apathetic) style, subtracting or adding points according to what answer is circled, as noted above.

Score 2 points (2 asterisks) for responses that fall into the Sameness-Oppositeness (Reactive-Repetitive) style plus either subtracting 1 point, adding 0 points, or adding 1 point depending on which number (1, 2, or 3) is circled, as noted above.

Score 3 points (3 asterisks) for responses that fall into the Similarity-Different (Creative-Conductive) style plus either 1, 2, or 3 points depending on how an item is answered, as noted above.

Scoring for Consistency

Some items are repetitious, even though they may be worded differently. Hence, one should look for contradictions, inconsistencies, and reversals. One point should be subtracted for any evident and obvious contradiction, defined as an answer that is different from an answer given to a similar item, as in the case, for instance, of items 11 and 160, 129 and 146, or 161 and 170, as well as items related to education. Of course, scoring for consistency is not as objective as it could be, since what is similar to one judge may be different to another. However, if not subjectively, the examiner could become aware qualitatively of possible contradictions in the answers throughout the process of scoring.

Interpretation

This process can proceed in different ways:

1. Total of points accumulated: the more points, the greater will be self-differentiation. N/A answers do not count and should be subtracted from the totals for each situation.
2. Qualitatively and ideographically: the examiner could compare the number of points accumulated in the Abusive-Apathetic style with points accumulated in the other two styles, Reactive-Repetitive and Creative-Conductive, divided by the number of items in each style. These ratios should give an idea of how differentiated the respondent is.
3. Quantitatively and nomothetically: as long as norms are still available, it will be difficult to reach any definite conclusion. Researchers who have accumulated norms will be able to render more objective interpretations than just qualitatively subjective conclusions about each individual. Items with one asterisk refer to the Abusive-Apathetic style; items with two asterisks refer to the Reactive-Repetitive style; items with three asterisks refer to the Conductive-Creative style.

Item Valence, Number, and Weight by Situation

A. Distance: –1*; +22***; +43***; +65***; +87***; +109***; +133**; +150**; –169*; –183**; +191**.

B. Control: +2**; –23*; +44**; +66***; –88*; +110**; –134*; –151*; –170*.

C. Positivity/Negativity: +3***; –24*; +45***; –171*.

D. Interaction Outcomes: –4**; –25*; –46*; –67*; +89***; –111**; –135**; –152**.

E. Characteristics: –5*; +26**; +47**; +68***; +90**; +112**; –136*; –153*; –172*.

F. Personality Propensities: –27*; –48**; –69**; –91*; +113**; –126*; –137*.

G. Parental Styles: +7***; –28*; –49**; +70***; –92*; +114**; –138*; –154*; –173**; –184**.

H. Parental Practices: +8**; –29*; –50*; –71**; –93**; +115***; +139**; +155**; –174*; –185*; +192***.

I. Identification: +9***; –30*; –51*; –72**; –73*; –94**; –95*; +116**; +117**; +118***; +119***; +120***; –140**; –156**; –157*; –158*; –175*.

J. Directionality: –10**; –31**; +52**; +74**; +96**; –121*; –141*; –159*; +176***.

K. Dependencies: –11**; –32*; –53**; –75*; +97**; +122***; –160*.

L. Ability to Love: +12***; +33***; –54*; –76*; +98***; –123**; +142**; –161**; –177**; –186*.

M. Ability to Negotiate: +13**; –34**; –55**; +77**; –99**; +124**; +143***.

N. Power Orientation: +14**; –35*; –56**; –78**; +100**; –125**; +144***; –162**; +178**; +187***; +193***.

O. Identity Formation and Sexual Orientation: +15**; –36*; –57*; +79**; –101*; +126***; –145**; –163**; –179**; –188**; –194*; +195**; +197**; +199***; +200***.

P. Appearance: –16**; –37*; –58**; +80***; +164**; +102***; +127***.

Q. Level of Adjustment: –17**; –38**; –59*; +81***; –103*; +128***.

R. Most Likely Psychiatric Diagnoses: –18*; –39*; –60*; –82*; –104*; –129***; –146*; +165**; +180**; –189*; –196*.

S. Family or Intimate Relationships: +19***; –40*; –61**; –83*; –105**; –130**; +147***; +166***; +181**.

T. Academic Achievement: +20***; +41***; –62*; +84**; +106***; +131***; +148***; –167*; +182***; +190**; +198*.

U. Resistance to Change: +21**; +42**; –63**; +85***; +107***.

V. Relationship Satisfaction: +64***; +86*; –108*; +132***; –149*; –168*.

Appendix C

The Self-View Questionnaire

This questionnaire will help you and us learn how you see yourself in relation to others in the present, in the past, and in the future. Put a check or cross in the columns that best indicate how you see yourself in relation to others.

Family Name and First Name ____________________________________
Gender ________________________ Age ________________________

Present

	With all people	With most people	With some people	With none	Most of the Time	Sometimes	Never
1. empty/absent	___	___	___	___	___	___	___
2. participant/sharer	___	___	___	___	___	___	___
3. solitary/reserved	___	___	___	___	___	___	___
4. tenacious/egocentric	___	___	___	___	___	___	___
5. docile/surrendering	___	___	___	___	___	___	___
6. altruist/involved	___	___	___	___	___	___	___
7. mysterious/ambiguous	___	___	___	___	___	___	___
8. collaborative/mediator	___	___	___	___	___	___	___
9. abstract/unpredictable	___	___	___	___	___	___	___
10. sharing/innovative	___	___	___	___	___	___	___
11. rebel/antagonist	___	___	___	___	___	___	___
12. dominant/dictatorial	___	___	___	___	___	___	___
13. two-faced/false altruist	___	___	___	___	___	___	___
14. unpredictable/altruist	___	___	___	___	___	___	___
15. inconclusive/disorganized	___	___	___	___	___	___	___
16. confused/chaotic	___	___	___	___	___	___	___

Past

	With all people	With most people	With some people	With none	Most of the Time	Some-times	Never
1. empty/absent	___	___	___	___	___	___	___
2. participant/sharer	___	___	___	___	___	___	___
3. solitary/reserved	___	___	___	___	___	___	___
4. tenacious/egocentric	___	___	___	___	___	___	___
5. docile/surrendering	___	___	___	___	___	___	___
6. altruist/involved	___	___	___	___	___	___	___
7. mysterious/ambiguous	___	___	___	___	___	___	___
8. collaborative/mediator	___	___	___	___	___	___	___
9. abstract/unpredictable	___	___	___	___	___	___	___
10. sharing/innovative	___	___	___	___	___	___	___
11. rebel/antagonist	___	___	___	___	___	___	___
12. dominant/dictatorial	___	___	___	___	___	___	___
13. two-faced/false altruist	___	___	___	___	___	___	___
14. unpredictable/altruist	___	___	___	___	___	___	___
15. inconclusive/disorganized	___	___	___	___	___	___	___
16. confused/chaotic	___	___	___	___	___	___	___

Future

	With all people	With most people	With some people	With none	Most of the Time	Some-times	Never
1. empty/absent	___	___	___	___	___	___	___
2. participant/sharer	___	___	___	___	___	___	___
3. solitary/reserved	___	___	___	___	___	___	___
4. tenacious/egocentric	___	___	___	___	___	___	___
5. docile/surrendering	___	___	___	___	___	___	___
6. altruist/involved	___	___	___	___	___	___	___
7. mysterious/ambiguous	___	___	___	___	___	___	___
8. collaborative/mediator	___	___	___	___	___	___	___
9. abstract/unpredictable	___	___	___	___	___	___	___
10. sharing/innovative	___	___	___	___	___	___	___
11. rebel/antagonist	___	___	___	___	___	___	___
12. dominant/dictatorial	___	___	___	___	___	___	___
13. two-faced/false altruist	___	___	___	___	___	___	___
14. unpredictable/altruist	___	___	___	___	___	___	___
15. inconclusive/disorganized	___	___	___	___	___	___	___
16. confused/chaotic	___	___	___	___	___	___	___

Appendix D

Additional References about the EPM

De Giacomo, P. (1988). *Psicoterapie brevi secondo un modello relazionale.* Bari: Ed. Fratelli Laterza.

De Giacomo, P. (1989). Brief interactive therapy in anorexia nervosa, phobic obsessive disorders, depression, and psychosis. *AFTA Newsletter*, *37*, 29–31.

De Giacomo, P. (1992). The Elementary Pragmatic Model: From theory to therapeutic practice. *Annuali dell'Istituto Superiore di Sanita'*, *28*, 169–176.

De Giacomo, P., Marconi, P. L., Storelli, M., De Giacomo, A., Giovannelli, M., Masellis, R., Anelli, F., Carrieri, G., Lattanzio, A., Tarquinio, C., & Lavorato, E. (2002). *Counseling on line col Modello Pragmatico Elementary Model.* Fasano (Brindisi), Italy: Schena.

De Giacomo, P., Margari, F., & Rutigliano, G. (1997). *Ottimizzazione della visita psichiatrica: ovvero dell'arte modulare dello psichiatra.* Milano, Italy: FrancoAngeli.

De Giacomo, P., Margari, F., & Santoni-Ruggiu, A. (1989a). Short-term interactional therapy of anorexia nervosa. *International Journal of Family Psychiatry, 10*, 111–122.

De Giacomo, P., Margari, F., & Santoni-Ruggiu, A. (1989b). Successful one-session treatments of anorexia nervosa: A report on fifteen cases. *International Journal of Family Psychiatry, 10*, 123–132.

De Giacomo, P., Margari, F., & Santoni-Ruggiu, A. (1992). *Psicoterapia interativa breve.* Rome: Edizioni NIS.

De Giacomo, P., Margari, F., Santoni-Ruggiu, A. (1993). Schizophrenia: Interactive perspectives. In G. Benedetti & P. M. Furlan (Eds.), *The psychotherapy of schizophrenia* (pp. 243–252). Seattle: Hogrefe & Huber.

De Giacomo, P., & Pereira, O. G. (1997). *Psicocoterapias pragmaticas breves.* Lisbon: Tupam Editores.

De Giacomo, P., Pierri G., Corfiati, L., Silvestri, A., Lefons, E., & Tangorra, F.

(1984). An elementary pragmatic approach in system-therapy. *International Journal of Family Psychiatry, 4*, 65–74.

De Giacomo, P., Pierri, G., Lefons, E., & Mich, L. (1990). A technique to simulate human interactions: Relational styles leading to a schizophrenic communication pattern and back to normal. *Acta Psychiatrica Scandinavica, 82*, 413–419.

De Giacomo, P. Pierri, G., Santoni-Ruggiu, A., Catucci, A., De Nigris, S., Zavoianni, L., & Blasi, G. (1999). New trends in family therapy of schizophrenia: Technique and results of a controlled study. *Dynamic Psychiatry, 45*, 312–322.

De Giacomo P., & Santoni-Ruggiu, A. (Eds.). (2000). The Elementary Pragmatic Model. In K. J. Miller & J. S. Mizes (Eds.), *Comparative treatments for eating disorders* (pp. 236–257). New York: Springer.

De Giacomo, P., & Silvestri, A. (1985). An Elementary Pragmatic Model in family therapy. *International Journal of Family Therapy, 6*, 245–263.

De Giacomo, P., Silvestri, A., Corfiati, L., Lefons, E., Pierri, G., Pazienza, M. T., & Tangorra, F. (1981). Einer interaktiven "logischen" therapie: Ein theorisches modell fuer therapie und bevertung der veraenderung. *Familiendynamik, 2*, 148–157.

De Giacomo, P., Silvestri, A., Pierri, G., Pazienza, M. T., Corfiati, L., Lefons E., & Tangorra, F. (1981). Un modale de base des relations humaines. *Therapie Familiale, 6*, 243–256.

De Giacomo, P., Silvestri, A., Pierri, G., Pazienza, M. T., Lefons, E., Corfiati, L., & Tangorra, F. (1981). Prescrinoes no casal segundo uma nova teoria sistemica. *Terapia Familiar e Comunitaria, 2*, 223–232.

References

Acitelli, L. K., Kenny, D. A., & Weiner, D. (2001). The importance of similarity and understanding of partners' marital ideals to relationship satisfaction. *Personal Relationships*, *8*, 167–185.

Acitelli, L. K., & Young, A. M. (1996). Gender and thought in relationships. In G. J. O. Fletcher & J. Fitness (Eds.), *Knowledge structures in close relationships: A social psychological approach* (pp. 147–168). New York: Guilford.

Albano, A., & Chorpita, B. F. (1995). Treatment of anxiety disorders of childhood. *Psychiatric Clinics of North America*, *18*, 767–784.

Alexander, J., & Barton, C. (1995). Family therapy research. In R. H. Mikesell, D. D. Lusterman, & S. H. McDaniel (Eds.), *Integrating family therapy: Handbook of family psychology and systems theory* (pp. 199–215). Washington, DC: American Psychological Association.

Ambrosini, M., Cusinato, M., & Scilletta, C. (2002). Structured intervention on "likeness modalities with important others" in teaching family psychology. Paper presented at a symposium on Relational Models for Comparisons of Family Variables at the 4th Congress of the International Academy of Family Psychology, Heidelberg, April 8.

Arnt, A., & Veen, G. (2001). Evaluation of others by borderline patients. *Journal of Nervous and Mental Disease*, *189*, 512–521.

Aron, A., & Aron, E. N. (1996). Self and self-expansion in relationships. In G.J.O. Fletcher & J. Fitness (Eds.), *Knowledge structures in close relationships: A social psychological approach* (pp. 325–344). New York: Guilford.

Atkinson, L., & Zucker, K. J. (Eds.). (1997). *Attachment and psychopathology.* New York: Guilford.

Averill, J. R. (1997). The emotions: An integrative approach. In R. Hogan, J. Johnson, & S. Briggs (Eds.), *Handbook of personality psychology* (pp. 513–541). San Diego: Academic Press.

Baer, D. M. (1982). The imposition of structure on behavior and the demolition of behavioral structures. In D. J. Bernstein (Ed.), *Response structure and organization* (pp. 217–254). Lincoln: University of Nebraska Press.

Bakan, D. (1968). *Disease, pain and sacrifice: Toward a psychology of suffering.* Boston: Beacon Press.

Barker, R. G. (1968). *Ecological psychology: Concepts and methods for studying the environment of human behavior.* Stanford, CA: Stanford University Press.

Barnett, R. C., & Hyde, J. S. (2001). Women, men, work, and family: An expansionist theory. *American Psychologist, 56*, 781–796.

Bar-On, R., & Parker, J.D.A. (Eds.). (2000). *The handbook of emotional intelligence: Theory, development, assessment, and applications at home, school, and in the workplace.* San Francisco: Jossey-Bass.

Barone, D. F., Hersen, M., & Van Hasselt, V. B. (Eds.). (1998). *Advanced personality.* New York: Plenum.

Barrett, P. M. (2000). Treatment of childhood anxiety developmental aspects. *Clinical Psychology Review, 20*, 479–494.

Bartholomew, K. (1990). Avoidance of intimacy: An attachment perspective. *Journal of Social and Personal Relationships, 7*, 147–178.

Bartholomew, K., & Horowitz, L. M. (1991). Attachment styles in young adults: A test of a four-category model. *Journal of Personality and Social Psychology, 61*, 226–244.

Bartholomew, K., & Perlman, D. (Eds.). (1994). *Attachment processes in adulthood.* London: Kingsley.

Bateson, G. (1972). *Steps to an ecology of mind.* New York: Ballantine Books.

Bateson, G. (1980). *Mind and nature.* Glasgow, UK: Fontana/Collins.

Baumeister, R. F., Smart, L., & Boden, J. M. (1996). Relation of threatened egotism to violence and aggression: The dark side of high self-esteem. *Psychological Review, 103*, 5–33.

Baumeister, R. F., & Tice, D. M. (1996). Rethinking and reclaiming the interdisciplinary role of personality psychology: The science of human nature should be the center of social sciences and humanities. *Journal of Personality Research, 30*, 363–373.

Baumeister, R. F., & Tice, D. M. (2001). *The social dimension of sex.* Boston: Allyn & Bacon.

Beck, A. T., & Young, J. E. (1985). Depression. In D. H. Harlow (Ed.), *Clinical handbook of psychological disorders* (pp. 206–244). New York: Guilford.

Becvar, D. S. (2001). *In the presence of grief: Helping family members resolve death, dying, and bereavement issues.* New York: Guilford.

Beidel, D. C., Turner, S. M., & Morris, T. L. (2000). Behavioral treatment of childhood social phobia. *Journal of Consulting and Clinical Psychology, 68*, 1072–1080.

Bennett, J. B. (2000). *Time and intimacy: A new science of personal relationships.* Mahwah, NJ: Erlbaum.

Berkowitz, L. (2000). *Causes and consequences of feelings.* New York: Cambridge University Press.

Bernstein, G. A., & Borchardt, C. M. (1991). Anxiety disorders of childhood and adolescence: A critical review. *Journal of the American Academy of Child and Adolescent Psychiatry, 30*, 519–532.

Bersheid, E., & Hatfield-Walster, E. (1969). *Interpersonal attraction.* Menlo Park, CA: Addison-Wesley.

Birmaher, B., Ryan, N. D., & Williamson, D. E. (1996). Depression in children and adolescents: Clinical features and pathogenesis. In K. I. Shulman, M. Tohen, & S. R. Kutcher (Eds.), *Mood disorders across the life span* (pp. 51–81). New York: Wiley.

Birtchnell, J. (1993). *How humans relate: A new interpersonal theory*. East Sussex, UK: Psychology Press.

Bison, I., Colazzo, L., Malinverni Silvestri, D., & Mich, L. (1989). The Elementary Pragmatic Model: A possible approach for setting up a user model. In S. Benford (Ed.), *Proceedings of the first European Conference on Computer Supported Cooperative Work 89* (pp. 389–401). Nottingham, UK: University of Nottingham.

Bissonnette, V. L., Rusbult, C. E., & Kilpatrick, S. D. (1997). Emphatic accuracy and marital conflict resolution. In W. Ickes (Ed.), *Emphatic accuracy* (pp. 251–281). New York: Guilford.

Blatt, S. J., & Homann, E. (1992). Parent–child interaction in the etiology of dependent and self-critical depression. *Clinical Psychology Review, 12*, 47–91.

Blatt, S. J., Quinlan, D. M., Chevron, E. S., McDonald, C., & Zuroff, D. (1982). Dependency and criticism: Psychological dimensions of depression. *Journal of Consulting and Clinical Psychology, 50*, 113–124.

Bohart, A. C., & Greenberg, L. S. (Eds.). (1997). *Empathy reconsidered: New directions in psychotherapy*. Washington, DC: American Psychological Association.

Bonanno, G. A., & Keltner, D. (1997). Facial expression of emotion and the course of conjugal bereavement. *Journal of Abnormal Psychology, 106*, 126–137.

Borman, W. C., & Penner, L. A. (2001). Citizenship performance: Its nature, antecedents, and motives. In B. W. Roberts & R. Hogan (Eds.), *Personality psychology in the workplace* (pp. 3–16). Washington, DC: American Psychological Association.

Boszormenyl-Nagy, I., & Spark, G. (1973). *Invisible loyalties*. New York: Harper & Row.

Bowen, M. (1978). *Family therapy in clinical practice*. New York: Aronson.

Bowen, R. C., Offord, D. R., & Doyle, M. H. (1990). The prevalence of overanxious disorder and separation anxiety disorder: Results from the Ontario Child Health Study. *Journal of the American Academy of Child and Adolescent Psychiatry, 29*, 753–758.

Bowlby, J. (1988). *A secure base: Parent–child attachment and healthy human development*. New York: Basic Books.

Bradley, S. J. (2000). *Affect regulation and the development of psychopathology*. New York: Guilford.

Bronfenbrenner, U. (1979). *The environmental ecology of human development*. Cambridge, MA: Harvard University Press.

Bullough, B., Bullough, V. L., Fithian, M. A., Hartman, W. E., & Klein, R. S. (1997). *How I got into sex: Personal stories of leading researchers, sex ther-*

apists, educators, prostitutes, sex toy designers, sex surrogates, transsexuals, criminologists, clergy and more . . . Amherst, NY: Prometheus Books.

Burgess, E. W. (1926/1972). The family as a unity of interacting personalities. In G. D. Erikson & T. P. Hogan (Eds.), *Family therapy: An introduction to theory and technique* (pp. 4–15). Monterey, CA: Brooks/Cole.

Burgess, R. L., & Huston, T. L. (Eds.). (1979). *Social exchange in developing relationships*. New York: Academic Press.

Byng-Hall, J. (1995). Creating a secure family base: Some implications of attachment theory for family therapy. *Family Process, 34*, 45–58.

Byrne, D. (1971). *The attraction paradigm*. New York: Academic Press.

Cacioppo, J. T., & Gardner, W. L. (1999). Emotion. *Annual Review of Psychology, 50*, 191–214.

Canary, D. J., Emmers-Sommer, T. M., & Faulkner, D. (1997). *Sex and gender differences in personal relationships*. New York: Guilford.

Carver, C. S., & Scheier, M. E. (1999). Stress, coping, and self-regulatory processes. In L. A. Pervin & O. P. John (Eds.), *Handbook of personality: Theory and research* (pp. 553–575). New York: Guilford.

Cassidy, J., & Shaver, P. R. (Eds.). (1999). *Handbook of attachment: Theory, research, and clinical applications*. New York: Guilford.

Chafetz, J. S. (Ed.). (1999). *Handbook of the sociology of gender*. New York: Kluwer Academic/Plenum.

Churchman, C. W. (1979). *The systems approach and its enemies*. New York: Basic Books.

Cipolli, C., & Silvestri, A. (Eds.). (1985). *Comunicazione e sistemi*. Milano: Angeli.

Clark, M. S. (1986). Evidence for the effectiveness of manipulations of communal and exchange relationships. *Personality and Social Psychology Bulletin, 12*, 414–425.

Clark, M. S., Pataki, S. P., & Carver, V. H. (1996). Some thoughts and findings on self-presentation of emotions in relationships. In G. J. O. Fletcher & J. Fitness (Eds.), *Knowledge structures in close relationships: A social psychological approach* (pp. 247–324). New York: Guilford.

Clark, M. S., & Reis, H. T. (1988). Interpersonal processes in close relationships. *Annual Review of Psychology*, 39, 609–672.

Cobb, C.L.H. (1996). Adolescent–parent attachments and family problem solving. *Family Process*, 35, 57–82.

Colazzo, L., Malinverni Silvestri, D., & Mich, L. (1982). An application of the Elementary Pragmatic Model to electronic communication. *Annali Istituto Superiore di Sanita', 28*, 245–252.

Colazzo, L., Mich, L., Malinverni Silvestri, D., & Schal, T. (1991). An experiment on computer-mediated communication supported by the coordinator using a pragmatic model. In K. Gorling & C. Sattler (Eds.), *Proceedings of the International Workshop on Computer Supported Cooperative Work* (pp. 34–58). Berlin: Institute for Information and Rechentechnik.

Colazzo, L., Mich, L., & Silvestri, L. (1999). User modeling in didactic applications: A pragmatic approach. In G. Cummings, T. Okamoto, & L. Gomez (Eds.), *Advanced research in computers and communications in education. Vol. 1.* Tokyo: IOS Press.

Coleman, D. (1986). Structured enrichment (SE) with low income black single parent families. M.A. thesis, Georgia State University, Atlanta.

Colombi, F. (2002). Relationship competence in teenagers, young adults, and adults (males and females). Poster presented at the 4th Congress of the International Academy of Family Psychology, Heidelberg, April 8.

Compton, S. N., Nelson, A. H., & March, J. S. (2000). Social phobia and separation anxiety symptoms in community and clinical samples of children and adolescents. *Journal of the Academy of Child & Adolescent Psychiatry, 39*, 1040–1046.

Constantine, L. L. (1993). The structure of family paradigms: An analytical model of family variation. *Journal of Marital and Family Therapy, 19*, 39–70.

Conville, R. L. (1991). *Relational transitions: The evolution of personal relationships*. Westport, CT: Praeger.

Cordova, J. V., Jacobson, N. S., & Christensen, A. (1998). Acceptance versus change interventions in behavioral and couple therapy: Impact on couples' in-session communication. *Journal of Marital and Family Therapy, 24*, 437–455.

Corsi, M., & Colombi, F. (2002). Relationship answer competence in teenagers and adult people. Paper presented at a symposium on Relational Models for Comparisons of Family Variables at the 4th Congress of the International Academy of Family Psychology, Heidelberg, April 8.

Corsi, M., & Scilletta, C. (2002). Relationship competence and self-importance in gender differences and in different ages. Paper presented at the 4th Congress of the International Academy of Family Psychology, Heidelberg, April 9.

Costa, P. T., Jr., & Widiger, T. A. (Eds.). (1994). *Personality disorders and the five-factor model of personality*. Washington, DC: American Psychological Association.

Cowan, P. A. (2002). Foreword. In J. P. McHale & W. S. Grolnick (Eds.), *Retrospect and prospect in the psychological study of families* (pp. xv–xvi). Mahwah, NJ: Erlbaum.

Crittenden, P. M., & Claussen, A. H. (Eds.). (2000). *The organization of attachment relationships: Maturation, culture, and context*. New York: Cambridge University Press.

Cusinato, M. (1996). L'ambito dell'intimata' coniugale. *Famiglia, Interdisciplinarita', Ricerca: Rivista di Studi Familiari, 1*, 3–37.

Cusinato, M. (1997). *TRD: Test di relazione diadica: Manuale di istruzione*. Treviso, Italy: Edizioni Centro della Famiglia.

Cusinato, M., Aceti, G., & L'Abate, L. (1997). Condivisione del dolore e intimita' di coppia. *Famiglia, Interdisciplinarita', Ricerca, 2*, 31–49.

Cusinato, M., & Ambrosini, M. (2002). A computer task connecting selfhood and similarity models. Paper presented at a Symposium on Relational Models for Comparisons of Family Variables at the 4th Congress of the International Academy of Family Psychology, Heidelberg, April 8.

Cusinato, M., Ambrosini, M., & Pastore, M. (2002). A computer task connecting selfhood and similarity models. Paper presented at a Symposium on Relational Models for Comparisons of Family Variables at the 4th Congress of the International Academy of Family Psychology, Heidelberg, April 8.

Cusinato, M., & L'Abate, L. (1988). A scale to measure various aspects of intimacy.

Unpublished manuscript, Department of Psychology, Georgia State University, Atlanta.

Cusinato, M., & L'Abate, L. (1995). A spiral model of intimacy. In S. M. Johnson & L. S. Greenberg (Eds.), *The heart of the matter: Perspectives on emotion in marital therapy* (pp. 108–123). New York: Brunner/Mazel.

Cusinato, M., & L'Abate, L. (2002). The Dyadic Relationships Test: Creation and validation of a model-derived, visual-verbal instrument to evaluate couple relationships. Manuscript submitted for publication.

Cusinato, M., & Pastore, M. (2001). Uno strumento di valutazione dell'importanza di se' e di altri: Analisi delle strutture tassonomicha in prospettiva evolutiva. *Eta' Evolutiva: Rivista di Scienze dello Sviluppo*, *69*, 5–18.

Dadds, M. R., Heard, P. M., & Rapee, R. M. (1992). The role of family intervention in the treatment of child anxiety disorders: Some preliminary findings. *Behavior Change*, 9, 171–177.

De Giacomo, P. (1993). *Finite systems and infinite interactions: The logic of human interaction and its application to psychotherapy*. Norfolk, CT: Bramble Books.

De Giacomo, P. (1995/1999). *Mente e creativita'*. Milano: FrancoAngeli.

De Giacomo, P., & De Giacomo, A. (1997). *Psicoterapia: Un metodo basato su un modello relazionale della mente*. Fasano (Brindisi), Italy: Schena.

De Giacomo, P., & De Nigris, S. (2001). Computer workbooks in psychotherapy with psychiatric patients. In L. L'Abate (Ed.), *Distance writing and computer-assisted interventions in psychiatry and mental health* (pp. 114–133). Westport, CT: Ablex.

De Giacomo, P., & Iadicicco, R. (2001). *Manuale di Zen occidentale: La logica della saggezza*. Rome: Hermes.

De Giacomo, P., L'Abate, L., & De Giacomo, A. (1997). Integrating models of human interaction: Three models, one reality? *Italian Journal of Psychiatry and Behavioral Science*, *7*, 18–23.

De Giacomo, P., Pierri, G., Lefons, E., Corfiati, L., & Renna, C. (1989). Evidenza sperimentale della difficolta' dello schizofrenico a mantenerre il proprio mondo nella relazione. In P. Pancheri & G. C. Reda (Eds.), *Progressi in Psichiatria Vol. III—parte prima* (pp. 375–393). Rome: CIC Edizioni internazionali.

De Giacomo, P., Pierri, G., Lefons, E., & Mich, L. (1990). A technique to simulate human interactions: Relational styles leading to a schizophrenic communication pattern and back to normal. *Acta Psyciatrica Scandinavica*, *82*, 413–419.

De Giacomo, P., Pierri, G., Santoni-Ruggiu, A., Buonsante, M., Vadruccio, F., & Zavoianni, L. (1997). Schizophrenia: A study comparing a family therapy group following a paradoxical model plus psychodrugs and a group treated by the conventional clinical approach. *Acta Psychiatrica Scandinavica*, *95*, 183–188.

De Giacomo, P., Silvestri, A., Pierri, G., Lefons, E., Corfiati, L., & Tangorra, F. (1986). Research on the effects of psychodrugs on human interaction. *Acta Psychiatrica Scandinavia*, *74*, 417–424.

DeLuca, J. W. (1989). Neuropsychology technicians in clinical practice: Precedents, rationale, and current deployment. *The Clinical Neuropsychologist*, *3*, 3–21.

DeLuca, J. W., & Putman, S. H. (1993). The professional/technician model in clinical neuropsychology: Deployment characteristics and practice issues. *Professional Psychology: Research and Practice*, *24*, 100–106.

Derlega, V. J., Metts, S., Petronio, S., & Margulis, S. T. (1993). *Self-disclosure*. Newbury Park, CA: Sage.

Dewey, J., & Bentley, A. F. (1949). *Knowing and the known*. Boston: Beacon Press.

Dinkmeyer, D., Pew, W. L., & Dinkmeyer, D. C., Jr. (1979). *Adlerian counseling and psychology*. Belmont, CA: Wadsworth.

Dobson, K. S., & Craig, K. D. (Eds.). (1998). *Empirically supported therapies: Best practice by professional psychology*. Thousand Oaks, CA: Sage.

Donovan, C. L., & Spence, S. H. (2000). Prevention of childhood anxiety disorders. *Clinical Psychology Review*, *20*, 509–531.

Doyle, K. O. (1999). *The social meanings of money and possessions: In search of a talisman*. Thousand Oaks, CA: Sage.

Duck, S. (Ed.). (1982). *Personal relationships 4: Dissolving personal relationships*. London: Academic Press.

Duck, S. (Ed.). (1988). *Handbook of personal relationships: Theory, research and interventions*. New York: Wiley.

Duck, S., & Gilmour, R. (Eds.). (1981a). *Personal relationships 1: Studying personal relationships*. London: Academic Press.

Duck, S., & Gilmour, R. (Eds.). (1981b). *Personal relationships 2: Developing personal relationships*. London: Academic Press.

Duck, S. W. (1973). *Personal relationships and personal constructs: A study of friendship formation*. Chichester, UK: Wiley.

Duck, S. W. (1993). *Individuals in relationships*. Newbury Park, CA: Sage.

Dunst, C., Trivette, C., & Deal, A. (1988). *Enabling and empowering families: Principles and guidelines for practice*. Cambridge, MA: Brookline Books.

Ekehammer, B. (1974). Interactionism in personality from an historical perspective. *Psychological Bulletin*, *81*, 1026–1048.

Elliot, A. L., & Church, M. A. (1997). A hierarchical model of approach and avoidance achievement motivation. *Journal of Personality and Social Psychology*, *72*, 218–232.

Elliot, A. L., & Covington, M. V. (2001). Approach and avoidance motivation. *Educational Psychology Review*, *12*, 73–92.

Emery, F. E. (Ed.). (1969). *Systems thinking: Selected readings*. Middlesex, UK: Penguin Books.

Endler, N. S., & Magnusson, D. (Eds.). (1976). *Interactional psychology and personality*. Washington, DC: Hemisphere.

Erber, R., & Gilmour, R. (Eds.). (1994). *Theoretical frameworks for personal relationships*. Hillsdale, NJ: Erlbaum.

Esterling, B. A., L'Abate, L., Murray, E. J., & Pennebaker, J. W. (1999). Empirical foundations for writing in prevention and psychotherapy: Mental and physical outomes. *Clinical Psychology Review*, *19*, 79–96.

Ewen, R. B. (1988). *An introduction to theories of personality*. Hillsdale, NJ: Erlbaum.

Fabrizio, C., & Franzoso, T. (2002). Relationship answer competence and self-importance level in teenagers, young adults, and adult people. Paper presented at a symposium on Relational Models for Comparisons of Family Variables at the 4th Congress of the International Academy of Family Psychology, Heidelberg, April 8.

Feeney, J., & Noller, P. (1996). *Adult attachment*. Thousand Oaks, CA: Sage.

Fehr, B., & Broughton, R. (2001). Gender and personality differences in conceptions of love: An interpersonal theory analysis. *Personal Relationships*, *8*, 115–136.

Ferrari, M., & Sternberg, R. J. (Eds.). (1998). *Self-awareness: Its nature and development*. New York: Guilford.

Firestone, R. W., & Catlett, J. (1999). *Fear of intimacy*. Washington, DC: American Psychological Association.

Fischer, G. T., McElwain, B., & DuBoise, J. T. (1995). Existential approaches to psychotherapy. In R. H. Mikesell, D. D. Lusterman, & S. H. McDaniel (Eds.), *Integrating family therapy: Handbook of family psychology and systems theory* (pp. 335–351). Washington, DC: American Psychological Association.

Fisher, L., & Ransom, D. C. (1995). An empirically derived typology of families: Relationships with adult health. *Family Process*, *34*, 161–182.

Fletcher, G. O., & Fincham, F. D. (Eds.). (1991). *Cognition in close relationships*. Hillsdale, NJ: Erlbaum.

Foa, U. G., Converse, J., Jr., Tornblom, K. J., & Foa, E. B. (Eds.). (1993). *Resource exchange theory: Explorations and applications*. San Diego: Academic Press.

Foa, U. G., & Foa, E. R. (1974). *Societal structures of the mind*. Springfield, IL: C. C. Thomas.

Ford, M. E. (1985). The concept of competence: Themes and variations. In H. A. Marlowe & R. B. Weinberg (Eds.), *Competence development: Theory and practice in special populations* (pp. 3–49). Springfield, IL: C. C. Thomas.

Forthofer, M. S., Markman, H. J., Cox, M., Stanley, S., & Kessler, R. C. (1996). Association between marital distress and work loss in a national sample. *Journal of Marriage and the Family*, *58*, 597–605.

Francis, G. (1990). Anxiety disorders. In A. S. Bellack, M. Hersen, & A. E. Kadzin (Eds.), *International handbook of behavior modification and therapy* (pp. 633–647). New York: Plenum.

Franzoso, T., & Corsi, M. (2002). Self-importance level and relationship answer competence in drug abused people compared with non-clinical individuals. Paper presented at a symposium on Relational Models for Comparisons of Family Variables at the 4th Congress of the International Academy of Family Psychology, Heidelberg, April 8.

Franzoso, T., & Modica, D. (2002). Self-importance and relationship competence in drug abusers and non-clinical controls. Paper presented at a symposium on Relational Models for Comparisons of Family Variables at the 4th Congress of the International Academy of Family Psychology, Heidelberg, April 8.

Furlani, P., Silvestri, A., Lefons, E., Tangorra, F., De Giacomo, P., Pierri, G., & Corfiati, L. (1984). A microcomputer network for human research and therapy. Paper presented at the 24th International Symposium: Mini and Microcomputers and Their Applications, Bari, June 5–8.

Ganahl, G. F. (1981). Effects of client, treatment, and therapist variables on the outcome of structured marital enrichment. Ph.D. dissertation, Georgia State University, Atlanta.

Garber, J., & Flynn, C. (1998). Origins of the depressive cognitive style. In D. K. Routh & R. J. DeRubeis (Eds.), *The science of clinical psychology: Accomplishments and future directions* (pp. 53–93). Washington, DC: American Psychological Association.

Gergen, K. J. (2001). Psychological science in postmodern context. *American Psychologist*, *56*, 803–813.

Gilbert, P., & Andrews, B. (1998). *Shame: Interpersonal behavior, psychopathology, and culture*. New York: Oxford University Press.

Gilmour, R., & Duck, S. (Eds.). (1986). *The emerging field of personal relationships*. Hillsdale, NJ: Erlbaum.

Goldberg, S., Muis, R., & Kerr, J. (Eds.). (1995). *Attachment theory: Social, developmental, and clinical perspectives*. Hillsdale, NJ: Analytic Press.

Gough, H. G., & Heilbrun, A. B., Jr. (1972). *The Adjective Check List Manual*. Palo Alto, CA: Consulting Psychologists Press.

Graae, F., Milner, J., Rizzotto, L., & Klein, R. G. (1994). Clonazepam in childhood anxiety disorders. *Journal of the American Academy of Child and Adolescent Psychiatry*, *33*, 372–376.

Gray, W., Duhl, F. J., & Rizzo, N. D. (Eds.). (1969). *General systems theory and psychiatry*. Boston: Little, Brown & Company.

Gray-Little, B., Baucom, D. H., & Hamby, S. L. (1996). Marital power, marital adjustment, and therapy outcome. *Journal of Family Psychology*, *10*, 292–303.

Greenberg, L. S., & Paivio, S. C. (1997). *Working with emotions in psychotherapy*. New York: Guilford.

Gross, J. J., John, O. P., & Richards, J. M. (2000). The dissociation of emotion expression from emotion experience: A personality perspective. *Personality and Social Psychology Bulletin*, *26*, 712–726.

Guidano, V. F., & Liotti G. (1985). A constructivistic foundation for cognitive therapy. In M. J. Mahoney & A. Freeman (Eds.), *Cognitions and psychotherapy* (pp. 101–142). New York: Plenum.

Gullone, E. (2000). The development of normal fear: A century of research. *Clinical Psychology Review*, *20*, 429–451.

Gurman, A. S., & Kniskern, D. P. (Eds.). (1991). *Handbook of family therapy: Volume II*. New York: Brunner/Mazel.

Gurman, A. S., Kniskern, D. P., & Pinsof, W. (1986). Research on the process and outcome of marital and family therapy. In A. S. Gurman & D. P. Kniskern (Eds.), *Handbook of family therapy: Volume II* (pp. 565–624). New York: Brunner/Mazel.

Haley, J. (1976). *Problem-solving therapy*. San Francisco: Jossey-Bass.

Hamilton, B. (1994). A systematic approach to a family and school problem: A case of separation anxiety disorder. *Family Therapy*, *21*, 149–152.

Hansen, J. C., & L'Abate, L. (1982). *Approaches to family therapy*. New York: Macmillan.

Harter, S. (1987). The determinants and mediational role of global self-worth in children. In N. Eisenberg (Ed.), *Contemporary topics in developmental psychology* (pp. 129–242). New York: Wiley.

Harter, S., Waters, P. I., Pettitt, L. M., Whitesell, J. K., Kofkin, J., & Jordan, J. (1997). Autonomy and connectedness as dimensions of relationship styles in men and women. *Journal of Social and Personal Relationships*, *14*, 147–164.

Hartup, W. W., & Rubin, Z. (Eds.). (1986). *Relationships and development.* Hillsdale, NJ: Erlbaum.

Harvey, J. H., & Weber, A. L. (2002). *Odyssey of the heart: Close relationships in the 21st century.* Mahwah, NJ: Erlbaum.

Hayes, S. C., Strosahl, K. D., & Wilson, K. G. (1999). *Acceptance and commitment therapy: An experiential approach to behavior change.* New York: Guilford.

Hendrick, S. S., & Hendrick, C. (1992). *Romantic love.* Newbury Park, CA: Sage.

Hinde, R. A. (1979). *Towards understanding relationships.* London: Academic Press.

Hinde, R. A. (1997). *Relationships: A dialectical perspective.* London: Psychology Press.

Hogan, R. T., & Roberts, B. W. (2001). Introduction: Personality and industrial and organizational psychology. In B. W. Roberts & R. Hogan (Eds.), *Personality psychology in the workplace* (pp. 3–16). Washington, DC: American Psychological Association.

Hogg, M. A. (2000). Identity and social comparison. In J. Suls & L. Wheeler (Eds.), *Handbook of social comparison: Theory and research* (pp. 401–421). New York: Kluwer Academic/Plenum.

Holtzman, W. H. (1961). *The Holtzman Inkblot Technique (form A and B).* New York: Psychological Corporation.

Holtzman, W. H., Thorpe, H. S., Swartz, J. D., & Herron, E. W. (1961). *Inkblot perception and personality.* Austin: University of Texas Press.

Hough, L. M. (2001). *I/Owes* its advances to personality. In B. W. Roberts & R. Hogan (Eds.), *Personality psychology in the workplace* (pp. 19–44). Washington, DC: American Psychological Association.

Howe, D., Brandon, M., Hinings, D., & Schofield, G. (1999). *Attachment theory, child maltreatment, and family support: A practice and assessment model.* Mahwah, NJ: Erlbaum.

Jacobs, M. K., Christensen, A., Snibbe, J. R., Dolezal-Wood, H. A., & Polterok, A. (2000). A comparison of computer-based versus traditional individual psychotherapy. *Professional Psychology: Research and Practice*, *32*, 92–96.

Jacobson, N. S., & Margolin, G. (1979). *Marital therapy: Strategies based on social learning and behavior exchange principles.* New York: Brunner/Mazel.

Jessee, E., & L'Abate, L. (1981). Enrichment role-playing as a step in training of family therapists. *Journal of Marriage and Family Therapy*, *7*, 507–514.

Johns, L. C., & van Os, J. (2001). The continuity of psychotic experiences in the general population. *Clinical Psychology Review*, *21*, 1125–1141.

Johnston, T. B., Levis, M. M., & L'Abate, L. (1987). Treatment of depression in a couple with systematic homework assignments. *Journal of Psychotherapy and the Family*, *2*, 117–128.

Jones, E. E., Farina, A., Hastorf, A. H., Markus, H., Miller, D. T., & Scott, B. A. (1984). *Social stigma: The psychology of marked relationships.* New York: Freeman.

Jordan, K. B., & L'Abate, L. (1995). Programmed writing and psychotherapy with symbiotically enmeshed patients. *American Journal of Psychotherapy, 49*, 225–236.

Jordan, K. B., & L'Abate, L. (1999). The tape of the mind workbook: A single case study. *Journal of Family Psychotherapy, 10*, 13–25.

Josselson, R. (1994). Identity and relatedness in the life cycle. In H. A. Bosma, T.L.G. Graafsma, H. D. Grotevant, & D. J. de Levita (Eds.), *Identity and development: An interdisciplinary approach* (pp. 81–102). Thousand Oaks, CA: Sage.

Juster, F. T., & Stafford, F. P. (Eds.). (1985). *Time, goods, and well-being*. Ann Arbor, MI: Institute for Social Research.

Kahneman, D., Diener, E., & Schwarz, N. (Eds.). (1999). *Well-being: The foundation of hedonic psychology*. New York: Russell Sage Foundation.

Kantor, J. R. (1959). *Interbehavioral psychology*. Chicago: Principia Press.

Kantor, J. R., & Smith, N. W. (1975). *The science of psychology: An interbehavioral survey*. Chicago: Principia Press.

Kashdan, T. B., & Herbert, J. D. (2001). Social anxiety in childhood and adolescence: Current status and future directions. *Clinical Child and Family Psychology Review, 4*, 37–61.

Karasu, T. R. (1996). The specificity versus nonspecificity dilemma: Toward identifying therapeutic change agents. *American Journal of Psychiatry, 143*, 687–695.

Kearney, C. A., & Silverman, W. K. (1990). A preliminary analysis of a functional model of assessment and treatment for school refusal behavior. *Behavior Modification, 14*, 340–366.

Kelley, H. H. (1979). *Personal relationships: Their structures and processes*. Hillsdale, NJ: Erlbaum.

Kelley, H. H., & Thibaut, J. W. (1978). *Interpersonal relationships: A theory of interdependence*. New York: Wiley.

Kelley, H. H. et al. (1983). *Close relationships*. New York: Freeman.

Kempler, W. (1981). *Experiential psychotherapy with families*. New York: Brunner/Mazel.

Kennedy-Moore, E., & Watson, J. C. (1999). *Expressing emotion: Myths, realities, and therapeutic strategies*. New York: Guilford.

Keppel, G. (1991). *Design and analysis: A researchers' handbook*. Englewood Cliffs, NJ: Prentice-Hall.

Kerr, M., & Bowen, M. (1988). *Family evaluation*. New York: Norton.

Kiesler, D. J. (1996). *Contemporary interpersonal theory and research: Personality, psychopathology, and psychotherapy*. New York: Wiley.

Kinderman, P., & Bentall, R. P. (1997). Causal attributions in paranoia and depression: Internal, personal, and situational attributions for negative events. *Journal of Abnormal Psychology, 106*, 341–345.

King, N., & Tonge, B. J. (2000). Trends in research on child anxiety and school refusal: An introduction. *Clinical Psychology Review, 20*, 427–428.

King, N., Tonge, B. J., Heyne, D., & Ollendick, T. H. (2000). Research on the cognitive-behavioral treatment of school refusal: A review and recommendations. *Clinical Psychology Review, 20*, 495–507.

Klein, R. G., Koplewicz, H. C., & Kanner, A. (1992). Imipramine treatment of children with separation anxiety disorder. *Journal of the American Academy of Child and Adolescent Psychiatry*, *31*, 21–28.

Koch, P. B., & Weis, D. L. (Eds.). (1998). *Sexuality in America: Understanding our sexual values and behavior*. New York: Continuum.

Kochalka, J., Buzas, H., L'Abate, L., McHenry, S., & Gibson, E. (1987). Structured enrichment training and implementation with paraprofessionals. In L. L'Abate, *Family psychology II: Theory, therapy, enrichment, and training* (pp. 278–287). Lanham, MD: University Press of America.

Kochalka, J., & L'Abate, L. (1997). Linking evaluation with structured enrichment: The Family Profile Form. *American Journal of Family Therapy, 25*, 361–370.

Korzybski, A. (1949). *Science and sanity: An introduction to non-Aristotelian systems and general semantics*. Lakewille, CT: International Non-Aristotelian Library Publishing House.

Kutcher, S. P., & Marton, P. (1996). Treatment of adolescent depression. In K. I. Shulman, M. Tohen, & S. R. Kutcher (Eds.), *Mood disorders across the life span* (pp. 101–126). New York: Wiley.

L'Abate, L. (1964). Specialized training and innovations in psychodiagnosis. In H. P. David & L. Blank (Eds.), *Sourcebook for training in clinical psychology* (pp. 157–174). New York: Springer.

L'Abate, L. (1968a). The laboratory method as an alternative to existing mental health models. *American Journal of Orthopsychiatry*, *38*, 296–297.

L'Abate, L. (1968b). The laboratory method in clinical psychology: An attempt at innovation. *The Clinical Psychologist*, *21*, 183–184.

L'Abate, L. (1968c). Screening children with cerebral dysfunctions through the laboratory method. In C. H. Haywood (Ed.), *The diagnosis of brain-damage in school-age children* (pp. 128–158). Washington, DC: Council for Exceptional Children.

L'Abate, L. (1969a). The continuum of rehabilitation and laboratory evaluation: Behavior modification and psychotherapy. In C. M. Franks (Ed.), *Behavior therapy: Appraisal and status* (pp. 476–494). New York: McGraw-Hill.

L'Abate, L. (1969b). An input-output approach to psychodiagnosis of children. *World Journal of Psychosynthesis*, *1*, 68–73.

L'Abate, L. (1971). Receptive-expressive functions in kindergarten children and adolescents. *Psychology in the Schools*, *8*, 253–259.

L'Abate, L. (1973). The laboratory method in clinical child psychology: Three applications. *Journal of Clinical Child Psychology*, 2, 8–10.

L'Abate, L. (1974). Family enrichment programs. *Journal of Family Counseling*, 2, 32–38.

L'Abate, L. (1976). *Understanding and helping the individual in the family*. New York: Grune & Stratton.

L'Abate, L. (1977). *Enrichment: Structured interventions with couples, families, and groups*. Washington, DC: University Press of America.

L'Abate, L. (1979). Aggression and construction in boys' monitored playtherapy. *Journal of Counseling and Psychotherapy*, 2, 137–158.

L'Abate, L. (1981). Skill training programs for couples and families. In A. S. Gurman & D. P. Kniskern (Eds.), *Handbook of family therapy* (pp. 631–661). New York: Brunner/Mazel.

L'Abate, L. (1982). Skill training and structured enrichment for marriage and family life. In P. A. Keller & L. G. Ritt (Eds.), *Innovations in clinical practice: A sourcebook* (pp. 299–308). Sarasota, FL: Professional Resource Exchange.

L'Abate, L. (1983). *Family psychology: Theory, therapy, and training.* Washington, DC: University Press of America.

L'Abate, L. (Ed.). (1985a). *Handbook of family psychology and therapy: Vols. I & II.* Homewood, Il: Dorsey.

L'Abate, L. (1985b). Structured enrichment (SE) with couples and families. *Family Relations, 34,* 169–175.

L'Abate, L. (1986). *Systematic family therapy.* New York: Brunner/Mazel.

L'Abate, L. (1990). *Building family competence: Primary and secondary prevention strategies.* Newbury Park, CA: Sage.

L'Abate, L. (1992). *Programmed writing: A self-administered approach for interventions with individuals, couples and families.* Pacific Grove, CA: Brooks/Cole.

L'Abate, L. (1994a). Book review. De Giacomo's finite systems and infinite interactions. *American Journal of Family Therapy,* 21, 89–94.

L'Abate, L. (1994b). *A theory of personality development.* New York: John Wiley & Sons.

L'Abate, L. (1994c). *Family evaluation: A psychological approach.* Newbury Park, CA: Sage.

L'Abate, L. (1996). Theory building, theory testing, and training in family psychology. In M. Cusinato (Ed.), *Research on family resources and needs across the world* (pp. 57–72). Milan, Italy: LED.

L'Abate, L. (1997a). The paradox of change: Better them than us! In R. S. Sauber (Ed.), *Managed mental health care: Major diagnostic and treatment approaches* (pp. 40–66). Bristol, PA: Brunner/Mazel.

L'Abate, L. (1997b). *The self in the family: A classification of personality, criminality, and psychopathology.* New York: Wiley.

L'Abate, L. (1998a). Discovery of the family: From the inside to the outside. *American Journal of Family Therapy,* 26, 265–280.

L'Abate, L. (1998b). How should a theory of personality socialization in the family be evaluated? Strategies of theory testing. *Famiglia. Interdisciplinarita' Ricerca, 3,* 5–32.

L'Abate, L. (1999a). Being human: Loving and hurting. In A. C. Richards & T. Schumrum (Eds.), *Invitations to dialogue: The legacy of Sidney Jourard* (pp. 81–90). Dubuque, IA: Kendall/Hunt.

L'Abate, L. (1999b). Taking the bull by the horns: Beyond talk in psychological interventions. *The Family Journal: Therapy and Counseling for Couples and Families, 7,* 206–220.

L'Abate, L. (2000). Psychoeducational strategies. In J. Carlson & L. Sperry (Eds.), *Brief therapy strategies with individuals and couples* (pp. 396–436). Phoenix, AZ: Zeig/Tucker.

L'Abate, L. (Ed.). (2001a). *Distance writing and computer-assisted interventions in psychiatry and mental health.* Westport, CT: Ablex.

L'Abate, L. (2001b). Hugging, holding, huddling and cuddling (3HC): A task prescription in couple and family therapy. *Journal of Activities in Psychotherapy Practice, 1,* 5–12.

L'Abate, L. (2002a). *Beyond psychotherapy: Programmed writing and structured computer-assisted interventions*. Westport, CT: Ablex.

L'Abate, L. (2002b). *Family psychology III: Theory building, theory testing, and psychological interventions*. Lanham, MD: University Press of America.

L'Abate, L. (2002c). *Personality in intimate relationships: Socialization in the family and other settings*. Manuscript submitted for publication.

L'Abate, L. (Ed.). (in press-a). *The role of workbooks in mental health: A practical resource for clinicians*. Binghamton, NY: Haworth.

L'Abate, L. (in press-b). Systematically written homework assignments: The case for homework based treatment. In L. L'Abate (Ed.), *The role of workbooks in mental health: A practical resource for clinicians*. Binghamton, NY: Haworth.

L'Abate, L., Boyce, J., Fraizer, L. M., & Russ, D. (1992). Programmed writing: Research in progress. *Comprehensive Mental Health Care*, *2*, 45–62.

L'Abate, L., & Brown, E. C. (1969). An appraisal of teaching machines and programmed instruction. In C. M. Franks (Ed.), *Behavior therapy: Appraisal and status* (pp. 396–414). New York: McGraw-Hill.

L'Abate, L., & Colondier, G. (1987). The emperor has no clothes! Long live the emperor! A critique of family systems thinking and a reductionistic proposal. *American Journal of Family Therapy*, *15*, 19–33.

L'Abate, L., De Giacomo, P., McCarty, F., De Giacomo, A., & Verrastro, G. (2000). Evaluating three models of intimate relationships. *Contemporary Family Therapy: An International Journal*, *22*, 103–122.

L'Abate, L., Farrar, J. E., & Serritella, D. A. (1992). Prevention of addictive behaviors. In L. L'Abate, J. E. Farrar, & D. A. Serritella (Eds.), *Handbook of differential treatments for addictions* (pp. 308–324). Boston: Allyn and Bacon.

L'Abate, L., Ganahl, G., & Hansen, J. C. (1986). *Methods of family therapy*. Englewood Cliffs, N.J.: Prentice-Hall.

L'Abate, L., & Harrison, M. G. (1992). Treating codependecy. In L. L'Abate, J. E. Farrar, & D. A. Serritella (Eds.), *Handbook of differential treatments for addictions* (pp. 286–306). Boston: Allyn & Bacon.

L'Abate, L., & Hewitt, D. (1988). Toward a classification of sex and sexual behavior. *Journal of Sex and Marital Therapy*, *14*, 29–39.

L'Abate, L., Johnston, T. B., & Levis, M. (1987). Treatment of depression in a couple with systematic homework assignments. *Journal of Psychotherapy and the Family*, *2*, 117–128.

L'Abate, L., & Jurkovic, G. (1987). Family systems as a cult: Boom or bankruptcy? In L. L'Abate, *Family psychology II: Theory, therapy, enrichment, and training* (pp. 19–27). Lanham, MD: University Press of America.

L'Abate, L., Kearns, D., Richardson, W., & Dow, W. (1985). Enrichment, structured enrichment, social skills training, and psychotherapy: Comparisons and contrasts. In L'Abate & M. Milan (Eds.), *Handbook of social skills training and research* (pp. 581–603). New York: Wiley.

L'Abate, L., & Lambert, R. G. (1996). Changing depression test scores through programmed writing: A test of a selfhood model of personality propensities. Paper presented at the annual meeting of the American Psychological Association, Toronto, Canada, August 9.

L'Abate, L., Lambert, R. G., & Schenk, P. (2001). Testing a relational model of psychopathology with the MMPI-2. *American Journal of Family Psychology, 29*, 23–39.

L'Abate, L., & McHenry, S. (1983). *Handbook of marital interventions.* New York: Grune & Stratton.

L'Abate, L., O'Callahan, J. B., Piat, J. D., Dunn, E. E., Margolis, R., Prigge, B., & Soper, P. (1976). Enlarging the scope of intervention with couples and families: Combination of therapy and enrichment. In L. Wolberg & M. L. Aronson (Eds.), *Group therapy 1976: An overview* (pp. 62–73). New York: Stratton Intercontinental Medical Books.

L'Abate, L., & Odell, M. (1995). Enlarging practices and roles of family clinicians. In M. Harway (Ed.), *Treating the changing family: Handling normative and unusual events* (pp. 321–339). New York: Wiley.

L'Abate, L., & Rupp, G. (1981). *Enrichment: Skill training for family life.* Washington, DC: University Press of America.

L'Abate, L., & Stevens, F. E. (1986). Structured enrichment (SE) of a couple. *Journal of Psychotherapy and the Family, 2*, 59–67.

L'Abate, L., & Thaxton, L. M. (1981). The differentiation of resources in mental health delivery systems: Implications for training. *Professional Psychology, 12*, 761–768.

L'Abate, L., Ulrici, P., & Wagner, V. (1981). The E-R-A model: A heuristic framework for classification of skill training programs for couples and families. *Family Relations, 30*, 307–315.

L'Abate, L., & Wagner, V. (1985). Theory-derived, family-oriented test batteries. In L. L'Abate (Ed.), *Handbook of family psychology and therapy* (pp. 1006–1032), Pacific Grove, CA: Brooks/Cole.

L'Abate, L., Wagner, V., & Weeks, G. (1980). Enrichment and written messages with couples. *American Journal of Family Therapy, 8*, 36–44.

L'Abate, L., & Weeks, G. (1976). Testing the limits of enrichment: When enrichment is not enough. *Journal of Family Counseling, 2*, 70–76.

L'Abate, L., & Weinstein, S. (1987). *Structured enrichment programs for couples and families.* New York: Brunner/Mazel.

L'Abate, L., & Wildman, R. W. (1979). The AVOM: A modality-derived, age-limited and modality-related test of intellectual functioning. *Psychology in the Schools, 16*, 408–413.

L'Abate, L., Wildman, R. W., O'Callaghan, J. B., Simon, S. J., Allison, M., Kahn, G., & Rainwater, N. (1975). The laboratory evaluation and enrichment of couples: Applications and some preliminary results. *Journal of Marriage and Family Counseling, 1*, 351–358.

L'Abate, L., & Young, L. (1987). *Casebook of structured enrichment programs for couples and families.* New York: Brunner/Mazel.

Last, C. G. (1992). Anxiety disorders in childhood and adolescence. In W. M. Reynolds (Ed.), *Internalizing disorders in children and adolescents* (pp. 61–105). New York: Wiley.

Leary, T. (1957). *Interpersonal diagnosis of personality.* New York: Ronald Press.

Lease, C. A., & Strauss, C. C. (1993). Separation anxiety disorder. In R. T. Ammerman & M. Hersen (Eds.), *Handbook of behavior therapy with children and adults: A developmental and longitudinal perspective* (pp. 93–107). Boston: Allyn & Bacon.

Leff, J. (1994). Working with the families of schizophrenic patients. *British Journal of Psychiatry, 164*, 71–76.

Lefons, E., Pazienza, M. T., Silvestri, A., Tangorra, F., Corfiati, L., De Giacomo, P., & Pierri, G. (1979). Possibilita' di riconoscimento di stati depressivi secondo il test SISCI-I. *Psychiatrica Messanensia, 1*, 25–30.

Levis, M. M. (1987). Short-term treatments for depression using systematic homework assignments. Ph.D. dissertation, Georgia State University, Atlanta.

Lilienfeld, R. (1988). *The rise of systems theory: An ideological analysis.* Malabar, FL: Krieger.

Lindaver, P. (1998). Le persone in relazione: Tre modelli teorici a confronto. *Famiglia, Interdisciplinarita', Ricerca, 3*, 101–114.

Loeber, R., Farrington, D. P., Stouthammer-Loeber, M., Moffitt, T. E., Caspi, A., & Lynam, D. (2001). Male mental health problems, psychopathy, and personality traits: Key findings from the first 14 years of the Pittsburgh Youth Study. *Child Clinical and Family Psychology Review, 4*, 273–297.

Loevinger, J. (1957). Objective tests as instruments of psychological theory. *Psychological Reports, 3*, 635–694.

Lutz, T. (1999). *Crying: The natural & cultural history of tears.* New York: Norton.

Macy, M. (1996). *Working sex: An odyssey into our cultural underworld.* New York: Carroll & Graf.

Magnana, A. B., Goldstein, M. J., Karno, M., Miklowitz, D. J., Jenkins, J., & Fallon, I.R.H. (1986). A brief method (FMSS) for assessing expressed emotion in relatives of psychiatric patients. *Psychiatric Research, 17*, 203–212.

Mansdorf, I. J., & Lukens, E. (1987). Cognitive-behavioral psychotherapy for separation anxious children exhibiting school phobia. *Journal of the American Academy of Child and Adolescent Psychiatry, 25*, 222–225.

Marks, I., Shaw, S., & Parkin, R. (1998). Computer-aided treatments of mental health problems. *Clinical Psychology: Science and Practice, 5*, 151–170.

Marlowe, H. A., & Weinberg, R. B. (Eds.). (1985). *Competence development: Theory and practice in special populations.* Springfield, IL: Thomas.

Maruna, S. (2001). *Making good: How ex-convicts reform and rebuild their lives.* Washington, DC: American Psychological Association.

Mascolo, M. F., & Griffin, S. (1998). *What develops in emotional development?* New York: Plenum.

Mayerfeld, J. (1999). *Suffering and moral responsibility.* New York: Oxford University Press.

McAdams, D. P. (1988). *Power, intimacy, and the life story: Personological inquiries into identity.* New York: Guilford.

McAdams, D. P. (1996). Alternative futures for the study of human individuals. *Journal of Personality Research, 30*, 374–388.

McCrae, R. R., & Costa, P. T., Jr. (1997a). Conceptions and correlates of openness to experience. In R. Hogan, J. A. Johnson, & S. R. Briggs (Eds.), *Handbook of personality psychology* (pp. 269–290). Orlando, FL: Academic Press.

McCrae, R. R., & Costa, P. T., Jr. (1997b). Personality trait structure as a human universal. *American Psychologist, 52*, 509–516.

McCubbin, H. L., Thompson, A. I., Pirner, P. A., & McCubbin, M. A. (1988). *Family types and strengths: A life cycle and ecological perspective.* Edina, MN: Burgess International Group.

McGuire, W. J. (1997). Creative hypotheses generating in psychology: Some useful heuristics. *Annual Review of Psychology, 48*, 1–30.

McMahan, O., & L'Abate, L. (2001). Marital adjustment and programmed distance writing with seminarian couples. In L. L'Abate (Ed.), *Distance writing and computer-assisted interventions in psychiatry and mental health* (pp. 135–156). Westport, CT: Ablex.

Miell, D., & Dallos, R. (Eds.). (1996). *Social interaction and personal relationships.* London: Sage.

Mikesell, R. H., Lusterman, D. D., & McDaniel, S. H. (Eds.). (1995). *Integrating family therapy: Handbook of family psychology and systems theory.* Washington, DC: American Psychological Association.

Miklowitz, D. J. (1995). The evolution of family-based psychopathology. In R. H. Mikesell, D. D. Lusterman, & S. H. McDaniel (Eds.), *Integrating family therapy: Handbook of family psychology and systems theory* (pp. 183–197). Washington, DC: American Psychological Association.

Miklowitz, D. J., & Goldstein, M. J. (1997). *Bipolar disorders.* New York: Guilford.

Minuchin, S. (1974). *Families and family therapy.* Cambridge, MA: Harvard University Press.

Mittelstaedt, H. (Ed.). (1960). The analysis of behavior in terms of control systems. In *Transactions of the Fifth Conference on Group Process.* New York: Josiah Macy, Jr. Foundation.

Montgomery, B. M., & Duck, S. (Eds.). (1991). *Studying interpersonal interaction.* New York: Guilford.

Moos, R. H. (1974). *Family Environment Scale (Form R).* Palo Alto, CA: Consulting Psychologists Press.

Moyer, A. J. (1994). Cybernetic theory does not explain family and couple process: Systems theory and dialectical meta-theory. *American Journal of Family Therapy, 22*, 273–281.

Muris, P., Merckelbach, H., Schmidt, J., Gadet, B., et al. (2001). Anxiety and depression as correlates of self-reported behavioral inhibition in normal adolescents. *Behavior Research and Therapy, 39*, 1051–1061.

Nardin, B., Gallo, F., Carubolo, R., Fabrizio, C., & Aquario, D. (2002). A structured program for parents to learn emotional coaching. Paper presented at the 4th Congress of the International Academy of Family Psychology. Heidelberg, April 9.

Nathan, P. E., & Gorman, J. M. (Eds.). (1998). *A guide to treatments that work.* New York: Oxford University Press.

Neill, J., & Kniskern, D. P. (1982). *From psyche to system.* New York: Brunner/Mazel.

Neimeyer, R. A., & Stewart, A. E. (1995). Constructivist and narrative psychotherapies. In R. H. Mikesell, D. D. Lusterman, & S. H. McDaniel (Eds.),

Integrating family therapy: Handbook of family psychology and systems theory (pp. 452–468). Washington, DC: American Psychological Association.

Nicholson, I. R. (1998). Schizophrenia and the family. In L. L'Abate (Ed.), *Handbook of family psychopathology* (pp. 280–310). New York: Guilford.

Noam, G. G., & Fischer, K. W. (1996). *Development and vulnerability in close relationships*. Mahwah, NJ: Erlbaum.

Nolen-Hoeksema, S. (1995). Epidemiology and theories of gender differences in unipolar depression. In M. V. Seeman (Ed.), *Gender and psychopathology* (pp. 63–87). Washington, DC: American Psychiatric Press.

Norcross, J. C., & Goldfried, M. R. (Eds.). (1992). *Psychotherapy integration*. New York: Basic Books.

Ollendick, T. H., & Huntzinger, R. M. (1990). Separation anxiety disorder in childhood. In M. Hersen & C. G. Last (Eds.), *Handbook of child and adult psychopathology: A longitudinal perspective* (pp. 133–149). New York: Pergamon.

Olson, D. H. (1993). Circumplex model of marital and family systems. In F. Walsh (Ed.), *Normal family processes* (pp. 104–137). New York: Guilford.

Osborn, A. (1992). *The art of creativeness: Principles and procedures of creative problem solving*. Milan, Italy: FrancoAngeli.

Owen-Smith, P. (1985). Family process and self-concept in early childhood. Ph.D. dissertation, Georgia State University, Atlanta.

Ozinga, J. R. (1999). *Altruism*. Westport, CT: Praeger.

Pastore, M., & Bertuola, L. (1999). Analisi delle strutture tassonomiche del Self-Other Profile Chart. *Famiglia, Interdisciplinarita', Ricerca, 4*, 89–106.

Patterson, G. R. (1985). Beyond technology: The next stage in developing an empirical base for parent training. In L. L'Abate (Ed.), *Handbook of family psychology and therapy* (pp. 1344–1379). Homewood, IL: Dorsey Press.

Peak, H., Muney, B., & Clay, M. (1960). Opposite structures, defenses, and attitudes. *Psychological Monographs: General and Applied, 74*, No. 8.

Pennebaker, J. M. (1997). *Opening up: The healing power of expressing emotions*. New York: Guilford.

Pennebaker, J. W. (2001). Explorations into the health benefits of disclosure: Inhibitory, cognitive, and social processes. In L. L'Abate (Ed.), *Distance writing and computer-assisted interventions and psychiatry and mental health* (pp. 33–44). Westport, CT: Ablex.

Pennebaker, J. W., & Francis, M. E. (1999). *Linguistic inquiry and word count (LIWC): A computer-based text analysis program*. Mahwah, NJ: Erlbaum.

Pereira, O. G., & Ferreira, C. P. (1985). Applicazioni del modello di De Giacomo e Silvestri in psicologia. In C. Cipolli & A. Silvestri (Eds.), *Communicazione e sistemi* (pp. 166–168). Milan, Italy: FrancoAngeli.

Perez, M., Pettit, J. W., David, C. F., Kistner, J. A., & Joiner, T. E., Jr. (2001). The interpersonal consequences of inflated self-esteem in an inpatient psychiatric youth sample. *Journal of Consulting and Clinical Psychology, 69*, 712–716.

Pervin, L. A. (1996). Personality: A view of the future based on a look at the past. *Journal of Personality Research, 30*, 309–318.

Phillips, L. N. (1968). *Human adaptation and its failures*. New York: Academic Press.

Pilkington, C. L., & Piersel, W. C. (1991). School phobia: A critical analysis of the separation anxiety theory and an alternative conceptualization. *Psychology in the Schools*, *28*, 290–303.

Plutchik, R., & Conte, H. R. (Eds.). (1997). *Circumplex models of personality and emotions*. Washington, DC: American Psychological Association.

Popper, C. W. (1993). Psychopharmacological treatment of anxiety disorders in adolescents and children. *Journal of Clinical Psychiatry*, *54*, 52–63.

Praeger, K. J. (1995). *The psychology of intimacy*. New York: Guilford.

Pronko, N. H. (1980). *Psychology from the viewpoint of an interbehaviorist*. Monterey, CA: Brooks/Cole.

Ravich, R. A. (1992). Recent advances towards a meta-typology of human relationships. In C. Loriedo, G. Pierri, & G. Vella (Eds.), *Typology of human relations and change* (pp. 161–167). Rome: Istituto Superiore fi Sanita'.

Reid, R., McMahan, O., & L'Abate, L. (2001). Workbooks and psychotherapy with incarcerated felons: Research in progress. In L. L'Abate (Ed.), *Distance writing and computer-assisted interventions in psychiatry and mental health* (pp. 257–267). Westport, CT: Ablex.

Reis, H. T., & Knew, C. R. (1996). What we know, what we don't know, and what we need to know about relationship knowledge structure. In G.J.O. Fletcher & J. Fitness (Eds.), *Knowledge structures in close relationships: A social psychological approach* (pp. 169–191). Mahwah, NJ: Erlbaum.

Reiss, D. (1981). *The family's construction of reality*. Cambridge, MA: Harvard University Press.

Reiss, D., & Klein, D. (1987). A family-centered approach to problems of etiology and treatment of psychiatric disorders. In T. Jacob (Ed.), *Family interaction and psychopathology: Theories, methods, and findings* (pp. 203–255). New York: Plenum.

Riordan, R. J. (1990). Scriptotherapy: Therapeutic writing as a counseling adjunct. *Journal of Counseling and Development*, *74*, 263–269.

Riva, G. (2001). The mind over the Web: The quest for the definition of a method for Internet research. *Cyberpsychology & Behavior*, *4*, 7–16.

Roberts, B. W., & Hogan, R. (Eds.). (2001). *Personality psychology in the workplace*. Washington, DC: American Psychological Association.

Routh, D. K., & DeRubeis, R. J. (Eds.). (1998). *The science of clinical psychology: Accomplishments and future directions*. Washington, DC: American Psychological Association.

Ruben, B. D., & Kim, J. Y. (Eds.). (1975). *General systems theory & human communication*. Rochelle Park, NJ: Hayden.

Russell, G., Jr. (1997). A book review and three extracts on single bit information exchange (SBIE) & the Elementary Pragmatic Model (EPM). *ASCAP Newsletter*, *10*, 7–13.

Saarni, C. (1999). *The development of emotional competence*. New York: Guilford.

Saarni, C. (2000). Emotional competence: A developmental perspective. In R. Bar-On & J.D.A. Parker (Eds.), *The handbook of emotional intelligence: Theory, development, assessment, and applications at home, school, and in the workplace* (pp. 68–91). San Francisco: Jossey-Bass.

Salvo, P., Fabrizio, C., & Cristante, F. (2002). Self-importance level and relationship answer competence in individuals with eating disorders. Paper presented at a symposium on Relational Models for Comparisons of Family

Variables at the 4th Congress of the International Academy of Family Psychology, Heidelberg, April 8.

Salvo, P., & Radoni, C. (2002). Self-importance level and relationship answer competence in individuals with eating disorders. Paper presented at the 4th Congress of the International Academy of Family Psychology, Heidelberg, April 9.

Salvo, R. (in press). The adult attachment questionnaire: A construction and a contribution towards its statistical validity. *Testing, Psicometrica, Metodologia.*

Salvo, R., Cusinato, M., & Rossetti, N. (1996). Attaccamento e relazione di coppia. *Famiglia, Interdisciplinarieta', Ricerca 1*, 5–16.

Salvo, R., & Minervini, P. (n.d.). A model of attachment in adult relationships and a model of self-importance: A theoretical and methodological comparison (unpublished manuscript). Dipartimento di Psicologia Generale, University of Padova, Italy.

Salzen, E. A. (1995). Why are there eight primary emotions? *ASCAP Newsletter*, *8*, 8–11.

Sanford, K. (1997). Two dimensions of adult attachment: Further validation. *Journal of Social and Personal Relationships*, *14*, 133–143.

Scherer, K. R., & Davidson, R. J. (2001). Editors' note on debate concerning emotional intelligence. *Emotion*, *1*, 195.

Schniering, C. A., Hudson, J. L., & Rapee, R. M. (2000). Issues in the diagnosis and assessment of anxiety disorders in children and adolescents. *Clinical Psychology Review*, *20*, 453–478.

Schwartz, R. M., & Garamoni, G. L. (1989). A structural model of positive and negative states of mind: Asymmetry in the internal dialogue. *Advances in Cognitive Behavioral Research and Therapy*, *5*, 1–62.

Schwebel, A. I. (1993). Family defense mechanisms: The concept and its utility to family scientists, practitioners, and educators. *The Family Journal: Counseling and Therapy for Couples and Families*, *1*, 31–41.

Scilletta, C., Ambrosini, M., & Cusinato, M. (2002). Structured intervention on "likeness modalities with important others" in teaching family psychology. Paper read at the 4th Congress of the International Academy of Family Psychology, Heidelberg, April 8.

Scott, J., Cully, M., & Weissberg, E. (1995). Helping the separation anxious school refuser. *Elementary School Guidance and Counseling*, *29*, 289–296.

Seeman, M. V. (Ed.). (1995). *Gender and psychopathology*. Washington, DC: American Psychiatric Association.

Shannon, C. E., & Weaver, W. (1964). *The mathematical theory of communication.* Milano, Italy: Etas Compass.

Shaver, P. R., Collins, N., & Clark, C. L. (1996). Attachment styles and internal working models of self and relationship partners. In G.J.O. Fletcher & J. Fitness (Eds.), *Knowledge structures in close relationships: A social psychological approach* (pp. 25–61). Mahwah, NJ: Erlbaum.

Shaw, J., Kennedy, S. H., & Joffe, R. T. (1995). Gender differences in mood disorders: A clinical focus. In M. V. Seeman (Ed.), *Gender and psychopathology* (pp. 89–111). Washington, DC: American Psychiatric Press.

Shirk, S. R., & Russell, R. L. (1996). *Change processes in child psychotherapy*. New York: Guilford.

Silvestri, A., De Giacomo, P., Pierri, G., Lefons, E., Pazienza, M. T., & Tangorra, F. (1980). A basic model of interacting subjects. *Cybernetics and Systems: An International Journal, 11*, 113–127.

Silvestri, A., Lefons, E., Corfiati, L., & De Giacomo, P. (1988). Evolution of interactional human behavior with age: A theoretical/experimental approach. *Cybernetics and Systems: An International Journal, 19*, 15–39.

Silvestri, A., Pereira, O. G., & Ferreira, C. P. (1987). Simulation of development of individual interactional patterns. *Cybernetics and Systems: An International Journal, 18*, 489–515.

Simpson, J. A., & Rholes, W. S. (Eds.). (1998). *Attachment theory and close relationships*. New York: Guilford.

Skinner, A.C.R. (1976). *One flesh, separate persons: Principles of family and marital psychotherapy*. London: Constable.

Sloan, S. Z. (1983). Assessing the differential effectiveness of two enrichment formats in facilitating marital intimacy and interaction. Ph.D. dissertation, Georgia State University, Atlanta.

Smith, N. W., Mountjoy, P. T., & Ruben, D. H. (Eds.). (1983). *Reassessment in psychology: The interbehavioral alternative*. Washington, DC: University Press of America.

Smith, R. (1992). *Inhibition: History and meaning in the sciences of mind and brain*. Berkeley: University of California Press.

Solomon, J., & George, C. (Eds.). (1999). *Attachment disorganization*. New York: Guilford.

Sperling, M. B., & Berman, W. H. (Eds.). (1994). *Attachment in adults: Clinical and developmental prospectives*. New York: Guilford.

Sperry, L., & Carlson, J. C. (Eds.). (1996). *Psychopathology and psychotherapy: From DSMI-IV to diagnosis and treatment*. Philadelphia: Taylor & Francis.

Spiegel, J. (1971). *Transactions: The interplay between individual, family, and society*. New York: Science House.

Sternberg, R. J. (1986). A triangular theory of love. *Psychological Review, 93*, 119–135.

Sternberg, R. J., & Barnes, M. I. (Eds.). (1988). *The psychology of love*. New Haven, CT: Yale University Press.

Stevens, F. E., & L'Abate, L. (1986). Structured enrichment (SE) with a couple. *Psychotherapy and the Family, 2*, 59–67.

Stevens, F. E., & L'Abate, L. (1989). Validity and reliability of a theory-derived measure of intimacy. *American Journal of Family Therapy, 17*, 359–368.

Stierlin, H. (1977). *Psychoanalysis and family therapy*. New York: Aronson.

Strauss, J. S., & Carpenter, W. T. (1972). The prediction of outcome in schizophrenia. I. Characteristics of outcome. *Archives of General Psychiatry, 27*, 739–746.

Stuart, R. B. (1980). *Helping families change: A social learning approach to marital therapy*. New York: Guilford.

Suls, J., & Wheeler, L. (Eds.). (2000). *Handbook of social comparison: Theory and research*. New York: Kluwer Academic/Plenum.

Surgeon General. (1999). *Mental health: A report of the Surgeon General.* Rockville, MD: U.S. Department of Health and Human Services, National Institutes of Mental Health.

Sutton, S. K. (2002). Incentive and threat reactivity: Relations with anterior cortical activity. In D. Cervone & W. Mischel (Eds.), *Advances in personality science* (pp. 127–150). New York: Guilford.

Swensen, C. H., Jr. (1973). *Introduction to interpersonal relations.* Glenview, IL: Scott, Foresman, & Co.

Swensen, C. H., Jr. (1985). Love in the family. In L. L'Abate (Ed.), *The handbook of family psychology and therapy: Vol. 1* (pp. 357–377). Homewood, IL: Dorsey.

Taylor, G. J., & Bagby, R. M. (2000). An overview of the alexithymia concept. In R. Bar-On & J.D.A. Parker (Eds.), *The handbook of emotional intelligence: Theory, development, assessment, and applications at home, school, and in the workplace* (pp. 40–67). San Francisco: Jossey-Bass.

Tesser, A., Felson, R. B., & Suls, J. M. (Eds.). (2000). *Psychological perspectives on self and identity.* Washington, DC: American Psychological Association.

Thayer, R. E. (1996). *The origin of everyday moods: Managing energy, tension, and stress.* New York: Oxford University Press.

Thibaut, J. W., & Kelley, H. H. (1959). *The social psychology of groups.* New York: Wiley.

Thyer, B. A., Himle, J., & Fischer, D. J. (1993). Separation anxiety disorder. In R. T. Ammerman, C. G. Last, & M. Hersen (Eds.), *Handbook of prescriptive treatments for children and adolescents* (pp. 144–158). Boston: Allyn & Bacon.

Tonge, B. (1994). Separation anxiety disorder. In T. H. Ollendick, N. J. King, & W. Yule (Eds.), *International handbook of phobic and anxiety disorders in children and adolescents: Issues in clinical child psychology* (pp. 145–167). New York: Plenum.

Topping, K., Bremer, W., & Holmes, E. A. (2000). Social competence: The social construction of the concept. In R. Bar-On & J.D.A. Parker (Eds.), *The handbook of emotional intelligence: Theory, development, assessment, and applications at home, school, and in the workplace* (pp. 28–39). San Francisco: Jossey-Bass.

Vakoch, D. A., & Strupp, H. H. (1995). Psychodynamic approaches to psychotherapy: Philosophical and theoretical foundations of effective practice. In R. H. Mikesell, D. D. Lusterman, & S. H. McDaniel. (Eds.), *Integrating family therapy: Handbook of family psychology and systems theory* (pp. 200–216). Washington, DC: American Psychological Association.

Verzolato, N., Cristante, F., & Salvo, P. (2002). Self-importance level and relationship answer competence in females suffering from affective disorders. Paper presented at a symposium on Relational Models for Comparisons of Family Variables at the 4th Congress of the International Academy of Family Psychology, Heidelberg, April 8.

von Bertalanffy, L. (1968). *General systems theory: Foundations, development, applications.* New York: George Braziller.

Vorauer, J. D., & Ross, M. (1996). The pursuit of knowledge in close relationships: An informational goals analysis. In G.J.O. Fletcher & J. Fitness (Eds.),

Knowledge structures in close relationships: A social psychological approach (pp. 369–396). New York: Guilford.

Vuchinich, S. (1999). *Problem solving in families: Research and practice.* Thousand Oaks, CA: Sage.

Watson, D. (2000). *Mood and temperament.* New York: Guilford.

Weeks, G., & L'Abate, L. (1982). *Paradoxical psychotherapy: Theory and practice with individuals, couples, and families.* New York: Brunner/Mazel.

Weintraub, M. D. (1981). *Verbal behavior: Adaptations in psychopathology.* New York: Springer.

West, M. L., & Sheldon-Keller, A. E. (1994). *Patterns of relating: An adult attachment perspective.* New York: Guilford.

Westen, D. (1995). Integrative psychotherapy: Integrating psychodynamic and cognitive-behavioral theory and the technique. In R. H. Mikesell, D. D. Lusterman, & S. H. McDaniel (Eds.), *Integrating family therapy: Handbook of family psychology and systems theory* (pp. 217–242). Washington, DC: American Psychological Association.

Westen, D., Muderrisoglu, S., Fowler, C., Shedler, J., & Koren, D. (1997). Affect regulation and affective experience: Individual differences, group differences, and measurement using a Q-sort methodology. *Journal of Consulting and Clinical Psychology, 65,* 429–439.

White, R. W. (1959). Motivation reconsidered: The concept of competence. *Psychological Review, 66,* 297–333.

Wildman, R. W. (1976). Structured versus unstructured marital interventions. Ph.D. dissertation, Georgia State University, Atlanta.

Wile, D. B. (1979). An insight approach to marital therapy. *Journal of Marriage and Family Therapy, 5,* 43–52.

Wine, J. D., & Smye, M. S. (Eds.). (1980). *Social competence.* New York: Guilford.

Winnicott, D. W. (1965). *The maturational processes and the facilitating environment.* New York: International Universities Press.

Yarbrough, D. M. (1983). Effects of structured negotiation training on dyadic adjustment, satisfaction, and intimacy. Ph.D. dissertation, University of Georgia, Athens.

Yonkers, K. A., & Gurguis, G. (1995). Gender differences in the prevalence and expression of anxiety disorders. In M. V. Seeman (Ed.), *Gender and psychopathology* (pp. 113–130). Washington, DC: American Psychiatric Press.

Yzang, O.C.S. (Ed.). (1992). *Theories of love development, maintenance, and dissolution: Octagonal cycle and differential perspectives.* New York: Praeger.

Zirkel, S. (2000). Social intelligence: The development and maintenance of purposive behavior. In R. Bar-On & J.D.A. Parker (Eds.), *The handbook of emotional intelligence: Theory, development, assessment, and applications at home, school, and in the workplace* (pp. 3–27). San Francisco: Jossey-Bass.

Author Index

Subject Index

About the Authors

LUCIANO L'ABATE is Professor Emeritus of Psychology at Georgia State University.

PIERO DE GIACOMO is a Professor of Psychiatry and Director of the Institute of Psychiatry at the Medical School of Bari University, Italy.